Children of Deh Koh

Children of Deh Koh

YOUNG LIFE IN AN IRANIAN VILLAGE

• • •

Erika Friedl

Syracuse University Press

The paper used in this publication meets the minimum requirements
of American National Standard for Information Sciences—Permanence
of Paper for Printed Library Materials, ANSI Z39.48-1984. ∞

Library of Congress Cataloging-in-Publication Data
Friedl, Erika.
Children of Deh Koh : young life in an Iranian village / Erika
Friedl. — 1st ed.
p.   cm.
Based on research carried out between 1965 and 1994.
ISBN 0-8156-2756-4 (alk. paper). — ISBN 0-8156-2757-2 (pbk. :
alk. paper)
1. Children—Iran—Social conditions.   2. Children—Iran—Social
life and customs.   3. Iran—Social life and customs.   4. Iran—Rural
conditions. I. Title.
HQ792.I7F75   1997
305.23'0955—dc21   97-25579

For
Fateme, Ramin, Elahe, Ashkan,
Zahra, Amin and Nastaran,
who were at it not so long ago,
sunny, stormy, sweet, and strong.

Erika Friedl is professor of anthropology at Western Michigan University. She is the author of *Women of Deh Koh* and coeditor of *In the Eye of the Storm: Women in Post-revolutionary Iran.*

Contents

Acknowledgments

This book is based on ethnographic research I carried out between 1965 and 1994, during eight visits to a tribal region in Southwest Iran. In all, my husband and I were there for more than six years, often accompanied by our two daughters. We spent most of the time in a village I call Deh Koh, which I will describe a little later.

As always, I am grateful beyond words to our friends in Deh Koh, especially Mr. Aziz Azizi and Mrs. Golrokh Pakbas, our unwaveringly gracious, kind, and supportive hosts of many years, and their children, who make every visit unforgettable and each departure harder than the previous one. For invaluable help while learning Luri in Deh Koh many years ago, I thank Mrs. Gordaferin Boir Ahmedi Fard and her late husband, Mr. Heydar Rokhforus, and for clarifications of terms and idioms that were new to me since I concentrated on working with children, I again thank Mrs. Golrokh Pakbas. Several friends in Shiraz, Isfahan, and Tehran have made our short stays in the big cities thoroughly enjoyable over the years. Their hospitality is much appreciated. I further wish to thank the many anonymous government officials in Iran who treated us with consideration and politeness and helped us surmount bureaucratic difficulties. We are much indebted to their goodwill. Reinhold Loeffler, my teammate for more than thirty years, has contributed inspiration and intellectual energy to our enterprises in Iran and at home. In Europe, Dipl.Ing. Helmut and Sylvia Friedl, Hertha Schaffer, Albert and Dorle Götzelmann, Bernhard and Dipl.Ing. Hedwig Lütke Entrup, Walter and Inge Kanzler, Dr. Josef and Gertrud Tomasch, and the late Drs. Werner Dutz and Alfred Janata, together with their wives, have given us support on many levels, and were indefatigably cheerful about it, too, while our daughters Kati and Agnes, when not in Deh Koh with us, have kept things together for us at home in the United States. Dr. Christof Schaafhausen most generously talked over issues relating to children with me, and Patricia Pawlicki kindly let me stay with her in Michigan's Upper Peninsula for a winter so I could write without disturbances during a sabbatical year, which Western Michigan University optimistically granted me for 1994–95. I owe special thanks to Agnes Loeffler for her valuable editorial suggestions and for her encouragement, and to Dr. Dan Bradburd for his critical reading of the manuscript.

For funding various stages of research in Deh Koh, I gratefully acknowledge support from the Wenner Gren Foundation for Anthropological Research, the National Endowment for the Humanities, the Social Science Research Council, the Joint Committee on Near and Middle East of the Social Science Research Council, Western Michigan University, and the American Council of Learned Societies with funds provided by the National Endowment for the Humanities and the Ford Foundation.

A Note on Transliteration

Luri is an unwritten southwest Iranian language. My rough trans-
literations of Luri terms are based on transliteration rules used for the
International Journal of Middle East Studies. I do not attempt pho-
netic accuracy.

Introduction

Initially, the research for this book was motivated in good part by frustration. After I had spent—wasted, I thought many times—countless hours trying to talk to, or simply to understand, one or the other woman in Deh Koh over the din and racket, the incessant tucking, hitting, poking of her whining, screaming, nagging youngsters, or to keep her attention on what she had set out to talk about, I decided I was a fool to continue to get annoyed at what I couldn't change, the more so as I had only vague notions about what was going on between these cross and dissatisfied children and their seemingly helpless mothers, whose threats and curses, yells and blows, promises and sweet-talk seemingly all were for naught. I started to pay close attention, first, to get anything at all out of the miserable situation of being surrounded by crying children who drove their mothers to distraction, but soon out of genuine fascination. Monotonously dreary as they seemed to be, these behaviors were pieces, colored by bright affects, of the large puzzle of the children's ethos. As tests of limits of a mother's patience, they revealed codes for expectations, for expressing frustrations, for strategies for the negotiation of power that were not easily observable otherwise. In addition, other lengthy interactions between an adult and young children are rare; children mostly keep to the company of other children, they tend to clam up in the presence of strangers, and they play in hard-to-observe places and rarely with adults, let alone a relative stranger like me.

As soon as I started to look more closely at children, I realized how little I knew about the emotional and cognitive world they inhabit, despite the fact that my own two daughters had been part of that world for several years throughout their childhood. Professionally, the concerns of adults had been more important to me than those of children; most information on children was mediated through adults. I had neglected over half the population I claimed to study.

What applies to me and the children of Deh Koh holds true for social scientists and children in Iran generally: although more than half the population of Iran is under the age of fifteen, few psychologists, educators, and social scientists actually focus on the development, not to speak of the culture, of children. Adults seem very devoted to their children and concerned about their welfare but can say little about them when asked. Literature on children is scarce. One can start research anywhere, in a city, a village, a tent camp, on any topic concerning children, and be a pioneer.

The place where I have been a pioneer of this sort, Deh Koh and the tribal area to which it belongs, I selected because it seemed the wisest thing for me to do at the time, and not because this village is typical in a statistical sense of the people of Iran. Until we have more ethnographies from other villages and tribal areas, nobody, I think, will know how typical childhood in Deh Koh may be of other parts of Iran. But during my travels around the country since 1965 I have formed the opinion that similarities to other places, villages, and towns, and to other social classes, are far greater than are differences, especially on the level of the philosophical parameters within which children are taught to move. Furthermore, the skills and attitudes children learn in Deh Koh, their strategies for dealing with the world, are suitable for life in the wider world of Iran, as scores of successful workers, traders, students, and professionals testify who have emigrated from Deh Koh over the years.

"Child" is an essentialist category for a developmental stage of humans and animals that people in Iran share with us. It is a self-evident and commonsensical category, juxtaposed to "adult," even if the boundary between the two is not well demarcated. However, no sooner was my attention firmly focused on children than the category itself became fuzzy. Instead of "children," I saw very different individuals, boys and girls, young, not so young, quiet, bold, noisy, shy, whiny, funny, bright, cheeky, sad, full of vigor, small, tall, anywhere in between, on scales that are fluid. Attempting to generalize and compare, I was stumped by the recognition that each child is constituted as such not only by factors like age, sex, unique looks, character, and affiliation with a certain family, but also by the stories in which it figures and in which others talk about it. The experiences of childhood vary greatly.

All individual differences notwithstanding, however, "child" (*bacce*) and "children" (*baccyal*), in the abstract, exist in the minds and language of the people and prompt adults and children to behave and to relate to each other in certain ways, to expect others to behave in certain ways, and to be disappointed, if not necessarily surprised, if the expectations are not met. This normative aspect we might call the folklore of childhood—the customs and their rationalizations surrounding child-stages. I try to mind both: the folklore of childhood with its normative categories and assumptions, and what children and adults make of it in the course of everyday life. Indeed, what children learn from encounters with this lore through interaction with others is the focus of this book. For this kind of learning, I assume that the enculturation process works on a level where behavior, speech, emotions, concepts, and explanatory logic are acquired holistically. I assume that, early in a child's life, habituation establishes concepts as well as patterns for the expression of feelings, even for feelings themselves; for expectations of reactions from others to one's own bodily or verbal utterances; for the courses of interactional encounters; for the logic of common sense. These assumptions are my guide. I consciously try to avoid jargon.

The organizing principle for the book is that of development in the loose sense in which it is used in Deh Koh: children start to grow in their mother's womb and continue for some fifteen years to grow and change after they are born. Experience and tradition have established that children's survival and the course of their intellectual and moral development depend on the care that different stages of growth require. Assumptions and rationalizations guide the care. Developmental stages in the first few years of life are more clearly defined than are later stages: baby and toddler are separated by walking, while our teenager stage, for example, does not exist: a girl in her midteens likely is married, a woman, wife, and mother; a boy of that age is just a boy (*kurr*), a lad (*caqlei*), a little more likely to disappoint expectations of reason and services created by his increasing size than is a younger boy, but not granted a teenager ideology that would excuse his dissatisfactory behavior. Boys' reason develops more slowly than that of girls. This gender assumption is behind different expectations for males and females of the same age, making chronological age a poor organizing principle. Likewise, children of the same sex grow in body and reason at different rates, people say; some mature earlier, some later, regardless of age in years. Even in schools, children's ages in each class may vary several years. Accordingly, I abandon the developmental scheme in the book after the toddler stage, and instead describe the children's world from different thematic angles, mostly play and other children's activities, until at the end I return to the developmental scheme and present some of the notions that concern young, unmarried people today.

The themes I selected are popular in Deh Koh. I do not dwell much on toilet training, for example, and not at all on menarche, because they are not dwelt on in Deh Koh: all children learn to use the toilet eventually—there is no reason for concern or effort. Menstruation is not a topic of discussion unless it is in the context of pregnancy or sickness. By contrast, naming relatives is a concern; anecdotes and stories are topics of discussions; play is the "salt and sugar of the day," as a youngster declared. I decided to stick with these topics and to subordinate others to them.

As an anthropologist who is trained to look for signs of "culture," I avoid psychological questions and psychological interpretations of what I see and hear, no matter how tempting they might sometimes be. I am not qualified to present childhood experiences in terms of their influences on the formation of adult personalities, or to draw attention to psychoanalytic or developmental aspects of childhood beyond what people in Deh Koh themselves say. For this reason, projective data, like drawings by children, for example, of which I collected hundreds, will not be discussed in this volume. Rather, I try to furnish insights and data on models and choices Deh Koh offers for children's behaviors and on their rationalizations. I look for local criteria for the evaluation of thoughts about children and actions by them and toward them in moral, or any other, terms, for the social and philosophical context in which children grow up. Thus, I limit myself quite consciously to tracing shared cognitions and practices. Frequently, my accounts are descriptive and detailed; in a few cases, my awareness of power differences and their habituation and reproduction is guiding the presentation; in all cases, the main question behind my text is: what do children learn from it all?

.   .   .

Like other social scientists, I am well aware of the limitations inherent in the traditional, reductionist, and overly cerebral tenor of traditional anthropological writing in which the experiential side of human existence easily gets lost and real people with real feelings disappear. But I am also disappointed with many of the new ego-centered attempts to situate the anthropologist in the construction of ethnographic reality self-consciously and self-reflexively. No matter how well intended these attempts might be, they nevertheless carry the danger of producing travelographies filled with trivialities and revelations about the researcher's personal life that add yet another layer of "text" without necessarily furthering insights into what moves the people with whom the researcher interacts in seemingly continuous soul-search mode. Ethnography no longer is driven just by the theoretical mode in which the writer is trained and by the ethnographer's skills as researcher and writer—and this is just as well—but by the quest for new insights on the postmodern plane on which everybody ought to have a "voice" and from where essentialist statements and categories ought to be banished. There is no consensus as to how this tall order is to be filled. Consequently, ethnographers today are experimenting with various forms of thinking and writing about "the other." This book constitutes one such experiment: children, who have the fewest rights in any society, get center stage, a "voice," even; what others say about them and do to them is seen as it affects them practically and is presented in a format that, intermittently at least, invites the reader to be where they are and to feel what they might feel.

The experiment includes the reader. Although I present concepts and categories, and the logic that binds them into choices for thoughts and actions, as I deem relevant—as the editor of Deh Koh's culture I am, after all, providing my own reading—I intentionally refrain from presenting cut-and-dried conclusions and from spinning analyses. Key concepts come up again and again in stories, examples, and scenes, as well as in the more conventional frames of customs and beliefs in which anthropologists cast "culture." I find these concepts indispensable in talking about the different stages in a child's life. Pointing at them with emphasis, however, seems superfluous. Instead, I try to provide as much context as possible to let the reader develop a feeling for how the key concepts are played out, as it were, for individual children, for boys and girls, for younger and older ones. The stories and anecdotes I selected from literally hundreds are meant not only to highlight different qualities of children's lives, as stories usually do, but to demonstrate how one or the other concept or cognition or assumption about children is phrased in words and actions.

Different readers will pick up on different cues and will form different opinions of life in Deh Koh. None, I think, will get the impression that life is all that easy for anybody there, including children. This view agrees with that of the villagers. Those readers who might come to the conclusion that life for children in Deh Koh is especially bleak and rough, that children are dealt with harshly, unfairly, as we say, ought to consider that with very few exceptions children, as a category, nowhere in the world are treated very well; that they are entirely at the mercy of adults, with few rights and even fewer advocates of their rights; and that romantic notions of "happy childhood" mystify this reality. In Deh Koh, a long history of poverty and exploitation in all likelihood has left its mark on how people see the world and act in it, but there is no indication that it caused childrearing to be the way it is, and children to be the way they are. Some factors even favor children: children are seen as assets by their elders; there is no alcohol in the village, no gambling, few guns, few cigarettes; there are no drunk fathers or mothers and few activities that would divert scarce money and resources from the families and, thus, indirectly, from children; elaborate etiquette and decorum drive up the threshold for violence within the village; there are no pubs and no pub brawls; public fights are very rare and regarded as scandalous. The children themselves, despite the lack of much that makes life easy, by and large accept their limitations without much concern and make use of their few choices to their advantage. Rules and restrictions are considerable and follow the patterns of authoritarian structures: within a hierarchy bounded by God at the top and by "nature" at the bottom, responsibility and obedience work together to keep everybody in line and the whole system functioning. Responsibility reaches from top downward, in care and control formulated in rules backed by power and force, if necessary. Obedience, the flip side of responsibility, extends upward. The hierarchy has two main parallel branches: age and sex; with these two criteria women are located lower than males over, roughly, the age of ten; children as a category are located lower than adult men unconditionally, save for great differences in the respective family's status; and girls are lower than anybody else. Practically, this means that girls ought to obey the commands of their mothers, elder sisters, their brothers, and their fathers, while being responsible for their younger siblings. Boys of around ten can expect that their wishes and commands will be heeded by their younger siblings, elder sisters, and mothers, although not always without contestation. Boys experience and internalize early on that their wishes have precedence over those of their sisters; most girls learn to surrender a toy, a goody, space, to a brother without fuss. Male heads of households can be absolute rulers in their families, if they so wish. Few are, but the demands of full responsibiliy for the welfare and the behavior of their wards is so heavy a burden that many men see force as necessary to elicit the obedience and cooperation needed to keep everybody in line. The authoritarian social relations and all their rationalizations and moral underpinnings in Deh Koh, and in Iran generally, levy considerable stress and restrictions on children. Together with minding rules and living with the restrictions of their subordinate position, however, they also learn how to manipulate authorities, subvert expectations, and create their own sources of "power of the weak." Life could be much better, but it is good, an eight-year-old girl told me about herself.

Since about 1970, when the state started to integrate the tribal area into its administrative and political stuctures after many decades of political oppression, warfare, and dearth, the people of Deh Koh even developed hopes of continuing improvement of conditions of life in the future for their children. What is locally understood as a "modern" way of life also includes slight modifications in the structures of authority: children of illiterate peasants come back from the city as doctors or engineers; some women have jobs and incomes that change their husbands' position of power; children no longer simply are taken as their fathers' economic assets (if a son) or liability (if weak or a daughter) but as individuals with an acknowledged right to healthy food, to education, opinions, and a life of their own in the future.

.   .   .

One difficulty of ethnographic writing, posed by the factor of time, of the forever outdated "ethnographic present," proved surprisingly easy to handle. Although I have concentrated on the observation of children only during my most recent visits to Deh Koh in 1989, 1992, and 1994, I have been collecting data concerning children since 1965 on topics such as schools, health, projective tests, games, folktales, and other folkloric material. Some activities, customs, and ideas have changed over the thirty years, and the politico-ideological and economic situation has changed dramatically, but on the level at which I am talking about children, little has become obsolete. New ideas are added without necessarily profoundly changing the way in which children are conceptualized and dealt with or understand themselves. All the information gathered over the span of thirty years proved relevant for tracing, "constructing," the children's world and the experience of childhood in Deh Koh, despite often seemingly contradictory features. Occasionally, I find it necessary to situate an observation in a specific time; otherwise, the emphasis is on features or processes that transcend a specific time horizon.

The perpetually delicate political situation in Iran imposes limitations on the choice of topics and on the format. For obvious reasons I refrain from making observations that might remotely embarrass people politically, even if they concern as important a feature for children as schools. No amount of clever pseudonyms could shield completely a particular teacher or student discussing school politics, for example. Thus, the government's ideological influence on children during the Pahlavi regime, as well as in the Islamic Republic, is not addressed directly. However, in my opinion, this information is not absolutely necessary for an understanding of childhood in the village beyond the few references I do provide; Deh Koh itself is a powerful molder of it's children's world.

Pseudonyms and modifications in individual children's and adults' circumstances provide a modicum of anonymity. A few women from my earlier book, *Women of Deh Koh*, appear in this book under the names given to them then, but not consistently so. Unfortunately, the demand for discretion makes it impossible to follow individual children over the years, or to paint particular children's personalities, or to locate one or the other child precisely in its relationships and in its stories. Some of the most telling anecdotes or circumstances had to be omitted altogether because they would have identified particular people too clearly. Although most people in Deh Koh don't mind "being in a book," such a position might easily take on a life of its own to the detriment of the person.

As a woman, I gain access to women in Deh Koh and to female children after the age of eight more easily and naturally than to men and older male children. This is a methodological limitation I have to accept. But my many years of living in Deh Koh have made me familiar in enough houses to facilitate watching interactions between brothers and sisters and fathers and children in informal settings. Over the years, I have learned enough of the local language, a dialect of Luri, to be able to follow conversations easily. My deficiencies in fluency of speech are rarely a problem because my style of fieldwork does not include speech-making, and the people around me have adjusted most generously to my accent and other shortcomings. My only real communication problem is with some educated young men who insist on speaking formal (in contrast to vernacular) Farsi laced with Arabic, which I, having learned both Luri and vernacular Farsi from the villagers, do not command well.

Comparison with children in the United States or elsewhere, present or past, is strictly avoided as beside the point. No matter how inspiring one or the other feature might be for contrast with what "we" do or think, or to draw similarities and differences, this book is about contexts surrounding growing up in a particular village in Iran, last visited in 1994, and ought to be read as such. Comparisons and thoughts about what light they might throw on theories of childhood, cognitive growth, moral development, specialization of affect, formation of identity, learning, creativity, understanding of the world, may come later. Here, I wish to stick to basics, to make a beginning.

Children of Deh Koh

1 · Places

Deh Koh, which means Mountainville, is my pseudonym for a large village in the high mountains of southwest Iran, where my husband, our two daughters, and I have lived off and on since 1965. The people of Deh Koh are Lurs, speak Luri, and are Shi'a Muslims* like all native inhabitants of the tribal province to which their village belongs. The population of Deh Koh has grown steadily from a few dozen people in a small huddle of stone-and-adobe houses at the turn of the century to close to four thousand on last count, mostly by a combination of high birth rate and falling infant mortality rates. About half the people in Deh Koh are younger than fifteen years of age. This growth leaves its marks on the shape of the village.

From afar—from the new highway through the mountains, for example, which passes the village less than a mile away—Deh Koh looks like a sprawl of gray buildings covering a hill, the dale between this hill and another one, and the wide, long slope beyond these hills, with runners of new streets into fields and gardens to the east, south, and west. Were it not for the craggy, snow-covered peaks of Snow Mountain towering above it, the place would look like a great many other villages in Iran, bursting at its seams, half under destruction, half under construction, as people say, with the ambience of a settlement whose appearance is dictated by bulldozers, cement blocks, and wide, straight, bare streets without shade. At the outskirts, big elementary schools and high schools for boys and for girls, and a sports complex for boys and men, sit in former fields, heavy, chunky signs of growth. Stores and shops in concrete-and-steel, boxlike buildings

*Adherents of the second-largest Muslim sect, which is dominant in Iran. Shi'ites acknowledge Ali, the Prophet Muhammad's cousin and son-in-law, and Ali's descendants as leaders.

1

line the main road through the settlement. In the old part of the village, three stately mosques have been raised to replace the old one, which was a large adobe house with a flat dirt-covered roof of the common traditional sort, and also an old shrine, built when the village was new, about a hundred years ago. The old cemetery behind the shrine was planed recently, its gravestones buried with cement, to become the courtyard of a new, big mosque-complex eventually. Until then, the level space is a convenient playing field for boys and young men. "Tae kwon to" is painted in large, white, English letters on a wall left over from one of the houses razed for the new religious center, speaking to the young men who frequent the place. Old buildings, old ideas, old people will have to make way, people say; the times belong to our children.

Several crooked irrigation channels still run downhill through the village along the alleys, but the alleys are slated to become streets as houses are destroyed to make way for a new grid of roads. People start new compounds in their fields or new brick houses on the sites of their old adobe houses in the old neighborhoods of the village, trying to enclose as much privacy as possible within cement-block walls. Fancy, two-story, urban-inspired houses stand next to old mud-brick courtyards that include several one- or two-room houses and barns for a cow or two, some goats or sheep, an occasional donkey. Chickens have the run of the village. A water pipeline and electricity have been in the village since before the revolution of 1979, changing standards of cleanliness and habits of study for students. Now the village also has telephone lines but still no sewers for waste water of any kind. The villagers see garbage as a big, smelly problem; streets as dusty and dirty; irrigation channels as filthy. Children are admonished not to play in the muck and dust, to leave garbage alone, to stay out of the channels. Deh Koh, says a local teacher, right now does not know whether it is a village or a town, poor or prosperous, old-fashioned or modern.

Despite noise and dust, it still is a good place to live, people say. Winters are cold and snowy, summers hot but less stifling than in the lowlands. A short walk uphill brings one into clear air, into green gardens strung along irrigation channels with quick, cool water. But Deh Koh is growing, growing way beyond its agricultural base and local resources, and people increasingly are looking elsewhere when thinking about the future of their children.

There is no industry to speak of in Deh Koh; not yet, anyway. Plans are drawn in offices in Tehran and in the provincial capital for turning the picturesque area into a tourist place: the new mayor, a contractor, has already bulldozed the top of a boulder-strewn, brush-covered hill above the village to make the site attractive for a hotel. For the time being, this space and the wide path leading up to it are used as play spaces by boys. Bulldozing the landscape "is called progress," people say; they do not quite know what to think of it. For children, especially for boys, trucks and bulldozers are signs of might and progress for sure, spectacles to be watched with fascination.

Deh Koh started out as a largely self-sufficient agricultural village several days' journey from the next city. Over the past twenty-five years, most families in Deh Koh have come to rely on income from sources other than traditional agriculture and transhumant animal husbandry. They rely on salaries from teaching, from administrative and other jobs in government agencies and a bank or two; on wages for labor in construction locally and elsewhere; on income from investments in trucks or shops; on income from trading—several food stores, dry-good merchants, and sellers of books and school supplies are competing for patronage—or from small businesses like car-repair, welding, television-repair, and carpentry. For a few years, two urban-style bakeries have been offering an alternative to women baking bread at home. About half their customers are children, often waiting in line for hours for their families' daily stack of bread, or for their own staple sustenance in the case of boys from the tribal area who live in Deh Koh to attend school. Two butchers have been selling meat from cows, goats, and sheep they slaughter outside their shops, for many years. A confectioner bakes cookies and other sweets to sell by the pound to adults but also by the piece to boys who drop in after school if they have money for a bottle of pop and a treat. Girls do not ever do this, for propriety's sake. Two wheat mills have been operating in Deh Koh for decades, as have a gunsmith and a carpenter, a tinner, a farber. Over the years, one or the other man has tried to keep a teashop-restaurant; several taxis and truckers have established themselves, as has a photographer and recorder of weddings on video. In the fall, the apple harvest gives an income to several dozen men and boys for a few weeks. Over the years, three or four establishments for teaching girls and young women to weave urban, oriental rugs have had little success; working conditions are generally poor, hours long, wages too small to make a difference. None of the women weavers of nomadic-style tribal rugs and flatweaves used locally has young apprentices; their skills and products are considered old-fashioned. A couple of young women have learned to be seamstresses and practice their craft with varying success. Banks and co-ops give loans. The very poor get alms as always and some financial assistance from the government or from religious organizations. For now they get by, people say, but what will happen to the children in the future is a big, worrisome question.

Orchards, fields, and local businesses may afford a livelihood for one or the other son of a farmer or craftsman in the future but not for three or four sons, not to speak of daughters. Not hard work in agriculture and small business but education that leads to a profession, preferably in medicine and engineering, and capital for business ventures are seen as the key to future success for Deh Koh's children, especially boys. The schools are full, but money for investment is scarce.

Most businesses are located along the new, wide road cutting through the village from east to west. All shopkeepers and craftsmen and most of the shoppers are men. Young men stroll up and down the street, hang around shops in droves, talking, looking; some work there. Boys run in and out between cars, trucks, tractors, motorbikes. Rarely are women or girls on the main streets. One gets the impression that the streets belong to men and boys, to cars and trucks. In side alleys too narrow for cars to negotiate, boys play "truck" by turning short sticks between their hands in front of them, a little to the left, a little to the right, as their steering wheels. They make "brrrr" noises as they hurtle themselves downhill, four or five together, scaring all life in the small space just as cars and trucks do on the wider streets. A wheelbarrow may become a motor vehicle as easily: the driver in the barrow steers with an imaginary steering wheel, the runner is the motor-energy behind, and both make fearsome noises as they crash downhill if they are not laughing too hard. The fastest, most ruthless and, for boys, most glamorous of all vehicles are the four-wheel station wagons driven by Revolutionary Guards. Little boys playing car therefore are likely either "trucks" or "Nissan Patrol." Imaginary cars have not driven imaginary horses out of business completely, though; riding on a stick-horse is still popular, mainly because one can beat the horse's imaginary rump incessantly with a long switch.

Children in the area frequently are victims of car accidents, especially on major roads through crowded villages. "The street" now connotes an axis of public life accessible to boys any time, but physically dangerous and potentially corrupting, too. A boy or young man who is said to "grow up in the street" is thereby labeled as maybe smart but certainly without proper supervision, a combination that is seen as a poor prospect for manners and responsible behavior later. A girl, especially above around the age of nine, who is seen in the streets frequently, will be talked about critically, her parents accused of negligence. Rarely is a girl seen lingering in the streets by herself. Girls stick to their neighborhoods.

Deh Koh is, unofficially and invisibly, divided into several quarters, *mal*. This term is used also for a camp of tents or branch huts. *Men mal* means in the camp, village, or quarter, depending on context. Together with *men tu*, in the house, it is contrasted with *ve sahra*, outside, in the open. The open porch, *eivan*, the courtyard, *hayat*, the alleys, *kuce*, the streets, *khiabun, rah*, all the open places where children are likely to congregate and to play are *ve sahra*. Garden, vineyard or orchard, *bagh*, field, *zamin*, hill, *tape* or *tell*, mountain, *koh*, and at the river, *tei rud*, qualify as *biabun*, a term connoting deserted places from simply uninhabited space to lonesome, dangerous wilderness. Children ought not to play *biabun* because they might get lost or meet discomfort and danger. Literally, *biabun* means a place without water.

The village quarters and various places around the village have names that children learn to associate with certain qualities. *Sheruni*, a stretch of wooded land along a stream to the south of Deh Koh, is taken to be inhabited by potentially dangerous djenn, and to be avoided. "The Hill" is a preferred, if steep, rocky playground, surrounded by the spreading village like an island in the sea. "Bloodrock" is an outcropping of gray rocks above the orchards where, reportedly, several people have fallen to their death over the years. "Flower-mountain" is a green valley high above the village that has become a popular place for weekend outings for city-people and government employees. Children no longer associate it with "summer herding camp," as their parents still do, but with romantic notions of leisure. The "New Cemetery" is a weedy place where, on Thursday afternoons, one can see groups of women wailing at graves and where one can expect to get lemonade or a goody, the customary offerings for the dead given away at this occasion. "Going to *bandun*," or to *ser kalanje*, two slopes covered with vineyards and orchards, likely means one is drafted to work in one's father's vineyard for the day. "I walked all the way to *ser kalanje* and back," said four-year-old Lale proudly, knowing that her playmates would recognize a heroic performance when they heard the name.

Children find their way inside and outside the village with the help of traditional place names and with special markers such as the house of somebody they know, a big boulder, an old tree, a peculiar courtyard door, a ruin, the mosque, a water channel. Above and below, this side and that side, left and right, in front and behind, mark directions in contexts that may shift as the speaker, in his or her mind, progresses along the way. "Below grandfather's courtyard, and this side of the butcher's shop" sounds like one direction but is not; the speaker, an eight-year-old boy, had made a left turn in his mind somewhere below his grandfather's place. Rather than trying to tell me how to get to a certain person's house, my neighbor instructed her eight-year-old to lead me there: "First you go to Fateme's father's house; before you get there you take the alley that leads toward the old graveyard; the house Khanom wants is right opposite the new house with the big door, hear me, behind it, on the other side, to the left." This instruction she accompanied by wiggling her right hand and then slapping her left forearm with her right hand. The girl found the place, which I had thought most unlikely; she had made two turns her mother had failed to spell out, avoiding what both knew to be a dead-end alley into which I would have marched for sure, and the deserted path to a courtyard ruined in the big earthquake in 1991. She made those adjustments because she was familiar with the neighborhood, and not because she had picked up on further nonverbal cues from her mother. I, with a rigid, linear, north-south orientation of the map I had constructed based on geometry and spotty local knowledge, found myself increasingly at a disadvantage in the rural sprawl with no street names or house numbers to help my writing-based sense of location. Often, children were my guides, but often, they were confused too.

It used to be that the village and the expanse of fields, gardens, and pastureland beyond were utterly familiar to children, especially boys, as soon as they could run along with their siblings and cousins. One could not get lost in the village. Well-defined compounds consisted of houses and other buildings of close patrilineal relatives. They were separated by walls or by narrow, winding alleys that divided the village into the different neighborhoods. Courtyards and alleys were playland for all. Shortcuts over roofs, under staircases, through narrow tunnels between houses, across courtyards, and up and down ladders made travel fast and easy across one's own tightly clustered neighborhood and across the whole village. The shortest way from the house of one of our neighbors to an abandoned garden beyond still is up a ladder to the low roof of a barn and from there into, and down, a walnut tree: all the children in the neighbor's house and their playmates use this route, to startling effects of sudden appearances and disappearances, instead of going out into the street and around what amounts to a whole block, and then through somebody's yard, as I would have to do. The map children construct for moving around in the village includes not just alleys, footbridges, staircases, and narrow channel-crossings, but any natural or manmade feature that can be climbed over, jumped across, squeezed by, or transversed fast enough to make pursuit by an angered adult unlikely, such as running across a roof or the length of a neighbor's verandah, which is considered rude. For children, the village spreads on a grid on three levels, the ground, second-floor verandahs, and roofs and trees. Just as children-on-the-move know of physical impediments and how to circumvent them, they also know of sharp dogs, of friendly or unfriendly neighbors, of work patterns of adults that make the use of a certain route more or less advisable at certain times. Often, as I was walking through the village in the alleys, a bunch of children appeared in front of me, disappeared, and met me again, seemingly out of nowhere, a little farther along my way. As a dignified adult woman I was confined to the street and a sedate pace, while they moved alongside and ahead of me over the roofs and porches above my head. In the course of a few hours of running loose in the village, children may visit, however briefly, many a courtyard, peer over many a wall, see much. The more mobile, cheeky children—and not all are like this, of course; there are shy and meek homebodies, too—are well informed of goings-on in Deh Koh, a source of intelligence for their relatively house-bound elder women relatives at home. Girls are considered much better at such intelligence gathering than are their brothers, but their movements never reach as far as do those of their brothers. Their radius of movement shrinks rapidly, for propriety's sake, just at the age when they become really good at observing and reporting.

The spatial expansion of Deh Koh, which started when the village was founded about a hundred years ago and has accelerated very quickly since about 1975, and the relative isolation of new houses with their solid walls around as yet empty courtyards make the village less accessible and manageable for children as well as for adults. Traffic on the newer, wide streets limits and separates hither from yon much more strictly than did the narrow old alleys and paths. Girls especially often do not even know where farther-away relatives live— their customary circle of movements is not big enough. Children stick to their own small neighborhoods more than did previous generations, to their own compounds, the space outside their own front doors. Their cognitive maps of the place have white, unmapped territories. The pacification of the area after 1965, however, and the subsequent integration of Deh Koh into a web of roads throughout the province has widened everybody's horizon considerably and has increased the area one can easily travel and know about for all, including children. Little Nastaran, at three, has been to the city, by car; in her father's orchard, a one-and-one-half-hour march away, on foot, in midsummer heat; in the next town visiting her mother's relatives, by bus; in the next village, a good mile away, to see the doctor, both on foot and by car. But she has never been in the house of relatives who live at the other end of the village, and she plays mostly in a small area around her father's house, in her grandfather's courtyard next door, and occasionally in one of her mother's paternal cousins' places, to be reached via two alleys between other relatives' courtyard walls. She knows a few more places because either a parent or a sibling has taken her there once in a while. Occasionally, she will be allowed to accompany her father or an elder brother to a store on main street. Her map does not include the courtyard of the immediate neighbor below her father's house, although it belongs to a paternal uncle, mostly because there is no girl of compatible age there; visiting this house, if only to use the superior swing in this uncle's big tree, would be embarrassing, says Nastaran. In all, the territory familiar to her is considerably smaller than was her elder brother's when he was her age. The rapidly expanding size of Deh Koh, the increase of traffic in the throughfares, and her status as a girl limit the mastery of locale for her. Seven-year-old Masume's sphere of action centers around her father's and her two paternal uncles' adjacent courtyards, both accessible to her without having to go out into the street, with a spatial extension beyond the farther of the two uncles' houses, into her family's orchard, and into a temporarily vacant piece of land. About a half-mile of alleys connect this area for her with the school and an uncle's house next to the school. Her favorite sister's marriage to a relative in another neighborhood opened this large and populous courtyard for her socially, too, hanging, as it were, at the end of a long string of alleys, which she prefers to use to avoid the wide, busy street. Twenty-year-old Sara, a student in the city, knows her way around the city "by taxi and on foot, day and night," as she says, but has not visited the house of a girl cousin in Deh Koh since she was thirteen, and had to ask directions to the house of another relative, whose sick wife she wanted to visit. "This is not right," she says, "but it is Deh Koh custom to keep girls at home."

Boys of all ages have the run of the village and its surrounds without many restrictions, just as they have always had. Their games dominate life in the alleys after school; they may congregate in the gardens, go on outings in the mountains, play soccer or volleyball on the makeshift playing field near the boys' school, ride the bus to town, hang around main street, help out in a relative's store, shoot at sparrows in trees from a flat roof, chase cats, steal apples or walnuts in an unwatched orchard, sit on the strip of grass dividing a stretch of Main Street, talking, watching traffic and passers-by, studying. At examination times, they slowly ambulate in deserted places, book in hand, mumbling lessons to be committed to memory. One meets them working, playing, fighting, reading, talking to each other everywhere. They place restrictions on their movements and associations voluntarily for reasons of their own or may have restrictions placed on them by their elders because of animosity between a parent and other people, for example; or an acute shortage of money might make movement requiring expenses difficult, but very few limits are set for them by gendered attributes of village spaces. One such space off-limits to boys is the girls' school.

All children in Deh Koh attend elementary school, girls as well as boys; most attend the next level, sixth through ninth grade, too, but fewer girls than boys finish it. All schools are segregated by sex. The girls' schools and the schoolyards are preferred, enclosed study- and play-spaces "safe" for girls. Hoda, age twelve, leaves for school in the morning almost an hour early and cuts short her lunch hour to play hopscotch in her school's yard and to talk with her schoolmates whom she is not likely to see elsewhere because they live in different neighborhoods. No boys and no men other than an occasional male teacher are allowed on her school's premises. She feels she can play there without reproach, even without the veil-wrap she is required to wear on the way to school. For a girl, summer vacation is a somewhat lonely time—unless she has sisters or girl cousins living close by, she will not have many playmates when school is not in session. A few years after the revolution, girls in high school were not allowed to gather in the school yard for a time, officially on grounds that their idle talking interfered with their studies; rumor had it, however, that the prohibition was enforced to prevent political assembly.

From the age of about nine or ten, girls' uses of spaces in the village increasingly are patterned after those of the women. Young girls may be sent on errands to a store, to deliver a message, or to fetch and carry things to or from somewhere if a brother is not available or denies a request for such services. But the older a girl gets the more likely she will resist such requests and the less likely she will be asked to render services that take her out and into other people's houses, for propriety's sake. Exceptions are exactly this, exceptions, noticed as such, and rationalized duly, just as adult women who go shopping frequently or are in other people's houses often avoid being talked about only if special circumstances such as widowhood, old age, or an emergency puts their out-of-placeness into the context of extraordinary requirements. After the age of fourteen or fifteen, however, girls are much more careful about appearances in places "among people," as they say, than are married women. When a woman whose husband and eldest son were absent from the village for a few weeks asked her fifteen-year-old daughter—asked her halfheartedly, for sure—to take the big garbage pail across the village to one of the dump containers, the girl flatly and resolutely refused on grounds of "being ashamed" to be out in the street, doing the work of a man. The woman finally took the heavy pail herself, "in the middle of the night," she said, to avoid meeting anybody. Two older, unmarried girls of around eighteen who, at different times in the last decade, have paid little attention to such spatial restrictions, were from two relatively small, poor families and strong religious regime supporters. Both criticized the local customs of so-called bashful behavior in girls that keep them anchored to their father's houses, and saw adherence to "proper" Islam as a way to liberate girls from overprotected and unproductive confinement in movement. Both moved relatively freely, albeit meticulously well-covered, in the village and the next town; they went shopping, haggled over prices with shopkeepers, went out to their father's gardens and orchards, visited relatives, and attended weddings alone, without tarnishing their reputation beyond the ambiguous assessment of being brash and forthright, and an occasional shake of the head when their names were mentioned. Neither, however, found a "good" husband in Deh Koh. Whether this is a function of their families' relatively low standing, of their own behavior, or just bad luck nobody is willing to decide.

Girls tend to play in small groups, games that require little space: a few yards around a swing in the courtyard; a corner of the open verandah in front of the house; the space around the water basin in the yard; a big log or a low wall to sit on, squeezed next to each other; the rungs of a ladder; any space big enough to sit opposite each other for playing jacks or cat's cradle; a tiny space next to a woman with a baby; a pole to climb, a spot to watch others from. Even their dancing and merrymaking at weddings is largely stationary: they hop up and down in place or sit in a circle chanting and clapping their hands. None of the traditional girls' amusements require fast movement over a territory beyond a few square yards. The new ball games introduced in school are played only in dedicated school spaces. Excursions into gardens and the wilderness beyond for collecting grass or wild vegetables, or walks to a herding outpost in a remote mountain valley, are related to the work women do. Girls play there, of course, even while they ought to be working—children are children, people say—but this kind of play is the same as in the village; it does not incorporate the expanded space girls find themselves in. "Don't go too far, you might get lost," they admonish each other, or one may say, "I'm afraid a wolf will get me if I walk too far away." Most recently, a few women teachers who have come to Deh Koh from cities try to get girls "out more," as one phrased it, by occasionally organizing chaperoned outings for their students with the express purpose of "having fun." These mostly take the form of picnics in the mountains, where the girls' main use of the wide open space is to collect firewood in a circle around the camp for a fire for tea. Rare as these outings are, the girls love them.

One's own family's house and courtyard are spaces one can use

with the least restrictions. Children of both sexes are free to socialize
at home with a minimum of decorum, although accessibility of available spaces is not entirely equal. As a rule of thumb, any space at
home is open to children unless or until men, boys, or, to a lesser
degree, women, demand it for their purposes. A sister may study in a
quiet spare room but will vacate it if her brother wants to study there;
girls will disappear from the verandah where they have been playing
when an elder brother arrives to entertain his friend there; a sixteen-
year-old girl who was an able and gracious hostess to me in the absence of her mother retired to the kitchen the moment her father and
elder brother entered the room. Even the kitchen, the quintessentially
female space in any Deh Koh house, is subject to this rule: should
father or a brother, especially an older one, sit down there he likely
will sit in the preferred place, back against a wall, goings-on in his
line of vision. Children may use any space in the house that is not
locked and not claimed by an adult. However, the more children congregate in a particular place, the less likely will they be shooed: when
an elder brother, coming home from high school, found his two sisters and three little girl cousins playing on the verandah, he went into
the kitchen/utility room without a word to drink tea and rest a while
there. Had he found only his sisters on the rug on the porch he would
have sat with them and they likely would have left soon.

Houses and courtyards do not afford many exclusive special-pur-
pose spaces. This lack of structure opens up most house space for a
variety of uses for children. A rug on the verandah becomes a sitting
area, a place to visit and drink tea, a space to take a nap. The flat
surface of the gritty cement walk serves as a place to spread note-
books to do homework one minute and to run a wheelbarrow-truck
on the next, to have a talk with grandmother, to wash a rug, to fight
with a sibling, to throw a tantrum everybody in the neighborhood can
watch, to play hopscotch, to chase chickens. Steps become desks; any
place where one takes a bowl with food becomes a dining area; a
small radio-cassette player in a quiet corner makes for a pleasant
hour idled with tapes; an old rag rug, a cushion, and books turn the
pantry into a study for a while; the roof, a wide, level expanse of
space, is good for just about any game until one is chased off it. None
of these spaces provide much of what we call privacy. Until one is
very secretive and circumspect, where one is in the house and what
one does there is known to others.

Except on snowy, wet, cold winter days children are encouraged to be outside during the day. Indeed, in the sparse, traditional houses in Deh Koh, children find so little entertainment and are likely to meet such disapproval when bringing in dirt, playmates, turmoil, that a father's house is not much more than the place to eat, to find one's mother and other relatives should one need them, and to sleep. With television, the attitude toward house spaces, in particular the room where the television set stands, has changed for children. "Children's hour" likely finds the younger ones around the television set in their own house or a grandfather's or other relative's in late afternoon, and at night the little children are likely to fall asleep while watching whatever program the government-run broadcast agency has scheduled. "How strange that I cry over the children in the movie while my own lie here cold on the floor!" my hostess once commented after an especially teary film from India.

Young children may fall asleep anywhere. They slowly get quiet, drowsy, and droopy until they lie somewhere on a rug, on a veil-wrap, dead to the world, oblivious to any amount of noise or commotion around them. A mother, an elder sibling, somebody eventually will drag them into a corner and cover them with a blanket, a quilt, a veil, until it is time to take them home slung over a shoulder or until the room is ready to be turned into a bedroom for all by the spreading of foam mattresses and bedding on the rugs on the floor. Toddlers often demand to be put to bed crankily and with perseverance; older children may get down a mattress and cover from the stack of bedding themselves and go to sleep earlier than the others. Everybody sleeps in the same room, old and young, boys and girls, unless the house is spacious enough to provide separate sleeping quarters for older sons and daughters. Rarely does anybody want to sleep alone, though, especially not girls and young women, who say they are afraid of staying alone—simply afraid, not afraid of any particular danger. Listening to them, one gets the impression that their world has many fear-inspiring places, even though this does not necessarily keep them from using them. "The water will take you!" puts fear into the hearts of young children playing at the irrigation channels, but will not keep them from playing there. Older girls are "afraid" to wash clothes by themselves at the channels too far upstream from the village, are "afraid" to go to town alone, to ride a bus. Sixteen-year-old Soheila remembers how she, a rather fearless and sure-footed kid, would help her scaredy-cat girl-cousin climb the walls behind their house when she was mad at her. "When we were at the top I would climb down again very fast and tell her to jump down if she wanted to see her mother again—just to make her cry with fear to be left alone up there." A few potentially scary places at home are avoided by children: windowless barns and outhouses in the old courtyards, and the bath and storage rooms in newer houses. These are likely to be dark and deserted and are said to be frequented by djenn. Children say they are afraid to go there alone even if they do not know about the djenn-lore. Seven-year-old Mahmud prefers to relieve himself behind the woodshed rather than to use the indoor toilet in his father's house because to get there he has to pass doors to the bath and to a storage room, the two places in the house of which he is truly scared. But he and his playmates find his grandfather's well-lit new outhouse with its modern plumbing a very convenient place to lock themselves into when pursued and to get water from to fill syringes and other weapons. And no matter how scary or dangerous a place is, safety is in numbers always. "Mother, go with me," I heard a six-year-old boy urge her, "I have to beat up Mahmud on the Hill, but I am scared to go there alone."

2 · The Children and I

My name in Deh Koh is *khanom*, which is a generic term of address for a woman, much like "ma'am" is for us, and also a rare first name. Only a few people, young or old, know my full name, and nobody says it. Unlike my own name, Khanom is easy to say, even for very young children, and puts me in a neat category: it marks me as belonging to the national, urban culture rather than to the realm of relatives in the village, yet as less formal and specific a person of respect than is one whose last name is added to *khanom* such as a teacher or other official. I fit the vague term: unostentatious in dress and manner, I try to prevent drawing attention to myself. This is a persona that suits me and has helped me to gain acceptance in Deh Koh as a familiar stranger but, in interacting with children, my quiet introversion leaves me with few natural entertainment skills for breaking the ice of unfamiliarity and for keeping children's attention easily. In addition, I consciously refrain from introducing gadgets foreign to local children, such as toys, books, or stories. For attracting them I largely rely on the children's curiosity. But in Deh Koh, young children are taught to be respectful in the presence of adult guests and strangers, to show *tars*, fear and respect born of fear, and older children are expected to be reserved, attentive, seen but not heard, if they want to avoid reprimands for shaming their parents with ill manners. Their curiosity, therefore, rarely takes them beyond scrutinizing me, silently following my moves, and listening to me talking. Addressed by me directly, especially in the presence of other adults, they likely will go into a patterned, well-practiced shyness-mode: averting, even covering, eyes and face, dropping the head or tucking it in with raised shoulders, wringing hands, half hiding behind somebody else, squirming, giggling, and, if talking at all, muttering monosyllabic answers. Even at the height of a noisy, violent altercation with its mother, a young child will act shy toward a stranger like me, signaling opposite messages of submission and aggression, propriety and ill manners simultaneously. Any direct, verbal engagement by an adult outside a narrow circle of family thus likely is kept as short as possible by a child; questions are answered in the speediest way, whether the answer makes sense or not; requests may fall on deaf ears. When children, especially little girls, find themselves observed at play by an adult, they likely will stop playing and leave. Older boys in such a situation may do the same or else exaggerate whatever they are doing: shout louder, run faster, jump higher, for the sake of their audience. If I point a camera at them, they will abandon their activity altogether to pose or to jostle for the center position in the photograph. The inability or unwillingness of children to interact "reasonably," as people say, with nonfamiliar adults is ascribed to the child-stage of development; although criticized, evasive behavior is expected until children are "old enough to know better," as one seventeen-year-old young man explained. Especially in girls, the shyness routine is taken as a sign of propriety. Under these circumstances, trying to get an understanding of how children construct and see their world and themselves in it entails very hard work, unlike any other I have undertaken in Deh Koh.

As additional hardship, children in Deh Koh rarely are alone by themselves, and I rarely am allowed to be alone with children. As an outsider and guest in every house in Deh Koh, no matter how familiar I am there, my contacts with children are mediated through my adult hosts, who very likely want to keep attention focused on themselves. In the presence of adults, I cannot expect to interact with children of any age free of interference. Adults or elder siblings will speak for them, correct them, prompt them, order them, explain to me what they think they mean, and to them what they think I want. By local definition, children are people who know little and have not much of importance or of interest to say in the company of adults. Their elders—adults as well as elder siblings—are afraid that the little ones might annoy me, might misinform me out of ignorance, might tire me, might be disrespectful, might say things or might use language that would disgrace their parents. They need to be shielded and controlled; I have to be shielded from them.

As I am a figure of outside authority in the authoritarian family structure of Deh Koh, mothers invest me with certain qualities that they use when they try to discipline and train their young children. "Stop crying, Khanom is watching," they will say, menace in their voice, or "Be quiet or Khanom will cut off your ear," or "Look at her bag, she has needles and scissors in there . . .!" Unless they are very new to this game, children treat this strategy with the disbelief it deserves and under loud protest, knowing very well that they can expect a piece of chewing gum from me rather than pain. But the aspect of potential power or danger my strange and curious looks and talk suggest is enforced by their mother's gestures and increases the likelihood of shyness responses to my advances.

It is just as well that my personal style of fieldwork in Deh Koh generally centers around listening and watching rather than talking, questioning, and doing. It proved the least invasive, least disturbing, and most successful methodology for dealing with children. Rather than insisting on engaging them, I try to be as inconspicuous as possible, to observe rather than to direct, to be silent rather than to ask questions, to wait for requests rather than to make them. When I do ask, I mostly try to get children to project, to talk about themselves by drawing something, by telling me a story, by explaining something. I cannot be choosy but have to seize the smallest opportunities. "I'm angry at my brother, I'll beat him up!" a four-year-old girl shouted, enraged, fists high, storming onto the porch where I was sitting with her mother. "But he isn't here," I said. "I'll find him and then beat him up," she yelled and ran off, leaving me with her pattern of conflict resolution and of discharging anger. Working with children who are extraordinarily reserved in company has taught me to register minute clues to their inner lives, to relationships, to cognitions, by watching their behavior, from body language to traces their games leave behind, from repertoires for expressing emotions to anything, anything they might say or sing or chant to themselves or to others. I have become an expert eavesdropper in Deh Koh.

In groups, boys between the ages of three and twelve are expected never to be far from *sholuq*, noisy pandemonium, from being wild and without manners, *fuzul*. Girls are said to have a lot more sense than boys when they are amongst themselves; they play much more quietly, they whisper and giggle. The dynamics in neither group invites participation by adults. My observations of group behavior therefore are based on watching happenings in the alley near our house—a spot favored by neighborhood children because of its relative spaciousness—from vantage points like a corner of a verandah and a window, and by watching children play in three courtyards I could overlook from our first home in Deh Koh and three others from our second home. However, over the years I have spent in Deh Koh, a great many chance encounters with children playing around various people's houses where I was visiting, and goings-on in the alleys and gardens while I happened to be there, have furnished countless hours of additional observations. I jump at every chance I get to talk to children without other figures of authority present, as long as the child is willing to interact in some way. By far most of these encounters are very informal and unstructured. Masume, a little girl of seven I have known since she was born, and whose house I visited almost daily, once came into a room where I was sitting, temporarily alone, with a tray of food for herself. My presence caught her by surprise; she did not want to give in to the first impulse, which was to run away—she knew me well, after all—but she could not bring herself to simply sit down and eat in front of me, either. After an obvious internal struggle, which made her screw up her face, giggle, dance and turn with her tray, she decided to sit down in a corner and eat facing the wall while talking to me. Talking to a back was a novel and somewhat unsettling experience for me but the whole scene had been full of Masume's messages about herself, about solving a problem of propriety, about concepts that structure relationships. It was a wind-fall opportunity.

Just about all children over the age of five in Deh Koh know me by sight or at least know about me, "khanom." There are about eight hundred of them. Of these, I know about two hundred by sight, fewer by name. It is a source of endless frustration for me, trying in vain to keep up with new children and with young people I have known since birth who now have children themselves. They all expect me to know them, and I often fall short of expectations. The children in my neighborhood and I have a greeting game, though, that circumvents the problem of recognition: when they see me they shout "*salam*," the official, urban-style greeting, and I stop to greet them back likewise, which other adults would not do. The children get a kick out of it and so do I, especially when one or the other of the bolder ones tries to mispronounce the greeting the way I do. With most of the children I am thus on good terms.

One issue, however, involving mostly boys of between six and twelve years of age, causes friction between them and me, year after year: the boys' relentless hunting of sparrows and kittens, stoning of dogs, chasing of anything that moves. Young birds and kittens are played with to death; chickens and cats are stoned and shot with slings for the fun of it; dogs are stoned and beaten partly because of fear, but mostly as a pastime, rationalized by the dogs' inherent, reli-giously unlawful, "dirty" status. These games of cruelty—identified as such and as sinful in Deh Koh, yet also as to be expected from ignorant and as yet ill-mannered children—are the only activities I interfere with. Adults approve of my interventions but the boys are disgusted. Not much is lost for me, however, because boys of that age are all but inaccessible to women anyway: too old to be around women, too young to have learned how to deal with women and girls properly and politely.

For information on this age group, I rely on observations of games, on interactions I observe without participating, and on conversations with individual boys as a visitor in their homes. In one way or an-other, I clarified most of my observations in talks with a son of our host of many years, whom I have known and been close to since he was born, and in countless discussions of children with mothers, aunts, and siblings.

There is no reason for me to be concerned about those of my interventions that express values the children hear from their own elders, too. More problematic are my few interferences into family affairs, and, equally unsettling, a few cases where I failed to interfere with how adults dealt with children. I have come to deeply regret my lack of medical interference when a little girl in my neighborhood was suffering with recurrent bouts of untreated giardiasis. But when, two years later, my remorseful insistence on testing and treatment of acute giardiasis* in a three-year-old boy precipitated a drop in the authority of a local woman healer, my conscience troubled me again. Similarly, my and my husband's prevention of the imminent severe beating of a twelve-year old boy by his temporarily berserk father challenged the father's authority position in his family, a realization that does not sit lightly; but choosing not to intervene in the beating of a screaming girl by her father, which I heard while passing by their house a little later, did not make me feel any better. Quite generally, the level of what we would call domestic violence against women and children, no matter how readily and matter-of-factly local people justify it or see it as part of life, is not easy for me to live with. These feelings, too, are less ethnocentric than they look at first glance, however; being kind to one's wife and children instead of beating them up, people say in Deh Koh, is much better, much more befitting a good Muslim, than what most men do in Deh Koh. It is a sign of superior morality. Yet, they add, it might also be that elsewhere children and women are better behaved, more reasonable, and therefore they need less punishment.

There are other, simpler regrets, such as for never having bought anything from Rahmat, the tireless, always cheerful little street vendor whom I have passed a hundred times during his endless summers behind a box with pencils and sweets. Although I had good reasons for resisting his smile, I am sorry for his disappointment. Fortunately, I know he harbors no ill feelings. Indeed I hope that all children have forgotten or forgiven me the disappointments or discomforts I might have caused them from time to time, trying to learn what it means to be a child in Deh Koh.

*Protozoan infection causing periodic diarrhea, which, untreated, can lead to severe health problems.

3 · Three Children and a Man with a Flute

Outside, hot, heavy July air weighed down the flat dirt roofs, silently parched land, and village. Hazy dust hung in the trees along the irrigation channels, over fields and orchards. From down the hill the rhythmic clang-bang of a pestle pounding in a brass mortar rang through the gray leaves of the walnut tree in Huri's yard. A few drowsy flies buzzed around. In the blazing sunlight, the climb up the garbage-strewn, steep, rocky hill to Huri's house had seemed very long. I was glad of the cool darkness inside the thick adobe walls. Propped against a green, velvet-covered cushion in her good room, and surrounded by the smell of stale rose water and sheep emanating from the thick wool rugs on the floor, I had time to catch my breath while the daughter of my hostess served me: a plate with cucumbers and a glass of lemonade stood on a stainless steel tray in front of me on the red rug. Thirteen-year-old Marzia was filling in for her mother, who was "on her way," as Marzia had put it earnestly. Only her younger brother and a little girl-cousin were around. All three children were now outside somewhere.

I sat alone for quite a while, comfortable in the dim stillness, moving around the room with my eyes: orange-patterned plastic sheeting covered the poplar beams on the ceiling. On the cracked wall, painted green a long time ago, hung a triangle sewn of strings of wild rue-pods,* against the evil eye; a ball of dried hedgerose buds; a color print of the Prophet Muhammad (faceless, for to render his likeness would be blasphemy), with his bearded son-in-law Ali; a color drawing of a stiff Lur rifleman in ancient costume; a large poster of a green alpine landscape with fat cows; and a watercolor painting of two partridges facing each other over a nest with eggs. A very colorful curtain with rows of boats covered the half-open doorway, and a white one embroidered with a spindly flower in a purple vase was pulled away from the only small window. It hurt my eyes to look into the shimmering light of the empty, baking

---

*Small, pea-like fruits said to guard against the evil eye.

courtyard outside. On the window sill, a picture of a man playing a flute leaned against a golden vase holding red plastic flowers. A large kilim* covering the household goods stacked along a short wall faced the fireplace in the opposite wall. The clear, bright red and blue lines in the repetitive patterns on the kilim and in the tribal rugs on the floor brought color and life into the dim room. I watched little puffs of dust rise where my finger traced a white chevron on the rug on which I was sitting.

Bored and drowsy, I decided to wait just a few more minutes before I would get up to look for the children outside. My leaving the room would confuse Marzia; a guest ought to sit and rest quietly. Before I had to force the issue, however, the three children pushed each other inside in a bunch, almost pulling the boat curtain down. They squatted between the door and the bright square of the window, pressed against the wall, trying to use as little space as possible. Marzia, Huri's only daughter, and Marzia's younger brother, Hasan, age twelve, together with their visiting cousin, Leila, who was nine, were ready to entertain and be entertained. They watched me with blank faces, still, unsmiling, sitting properly, feet tucked under. Leila was hidden altogether in her veil-wrap. She kept moving her eyes between me and Hasan. My customary polite questions after health and school predictably and promptly were disposed of by short "yes" and "no" and "thank you": well-mannered children like these three wanted to keep their mouths shut and reduce unavoidable answers to monosyllables. Silence was descending. I looked around the room for something I could use as a focus for a conversation. I got up—alarm spread on their faces—and took the picture of the flute player from the window. "With your permission," I said, and the three politely mumbled, "Of course," following my movements with their eyes. The six-by-ten-inch wooden frame held a painting on glass of what to me looked like an asthenic, narrow-shouldered young man with a pale face, downcast eyes and a big black moustache under a large nose. A high, light-brown hat sat firmly on curly black hair. Clad in a long, robelike brown coat, nothing but one booted foot showed as he squatted under the leafy, drooping branches of a willowy tree. With short, pale fingers he was playing a long wind instrument, a recorder, maybe, or an oboe. A dark bird was suspended in the foliage. A few

*A rug in a particular flat-weave technique with geometric designs.

tufts of greenish-brown fluff around the man and the tree suggested that he was sitting on a grassy knoll.

I sat down under the window, next to Marzia.

"Very nice," I said, "*mashallah*, praise be to God," rubbing dust and fly-specks off the glass with my shirt sleeve. "What is this?"

"A picture . . ."

"A drawing . . ."

"Nothing . . . glass . . . ," they said. I waited. "My uncle painted it," said Marzia. "He also painted the partridges on the wall over there."

"Really? Very beautiful, *mashallah!*" I said, and looked back at the flute player.

"He painted it on glass," mumbled Leila, hand over her mouth, from half behind Marzia's back, and shooting a quick glance at Hasan. "Out of a book," said Marzia. "He copied it out of a book. He likes to paint." Hasan moved across from me to get a better look. I held the picture so that all three could see it well. They studied it, saying nothing.

I tried again. "Very well," I said, kindly and encouragingly, I thought. "Now tell me what your uncle painted here—it is not a partridge—"

"No."

"No."

"No."

"—not a house—"

"No."

"No."

"No."

Silence.

"Leila will tell us something," I suggested, looking at her. This was a mistake. Leila pulled her veil-wrap over her face with a swift, practiced gesture and dived behind Marzia's back, giggling. Hasan and Marzia ignored her. Marzia was waving a persistent fly away from her face.

More silence. Patience, patience. I switched my tactics. "Who is this in the picture?" I asked, pointing to the young man.

"I don't know," a three-voiced chorus, without hesitation. Time for the cardinal sin of a suggestion or I would not get anywhere. "It might be a man or a woman," I said.

"A man," in unison again. Hasan looked at me, relief and curiosity in his eyes. At last they got an answer right; what else might I want? "How can you tell this person is a man?" More close inspection of the picture. Leila peeked over Marzia's shoulder. More silence. Hasan moved a finger across his upper lip, absentmindedly, then looked at Marzia. Her eyes went over the figure, up and down, left and right. "He is playing a flute," she said at last. Her brother and her cousin were relieved. "Yes, yes." She was stating the obvious. "Women don't play the flute," said Hasan.

"Right," said Marzia, straightening and retying her scarf.

By now I had become somewhat disheartened. The only man I could think of playing something like a flute in Deh Koh was Ahmad the Blind, who sometimes sat outside the bus station playing for money. This might be a direction. "For whom do you think he is playing?" I asked. They reflected. "For himself," said Marzia.

"Yes," said Hasan, playing with his toes, getting fidgety. "No one else is there." This was plausible for Leila too. "Yes," she said, looking at Hasan and me, "only one man is there."

"He is a shepherd," Hasan said to his toe. Right, the others agreed, he is a shepherd. Shepherds play the flute by themselves. It was a safe deduction. "All right," I said. "So this shepherd who is sitting in the grass, maybe—?"

They nodded: "Yes, a meadow," Leila whispered.

"—This shepherd is playing a flute. Who might hear him play? What do you think?" I started to feel stubborn and unreasonable. Blasted flute-player, blasted flies, blasted heat. Little rivulets of sweat were trickling down under my loose shirt.

"This is not known. There is no one else in the picture." Marzia was eyeing me suspiciously. What was I after? I decided to leave the poor man, who to me was looking more melancholy and forlorn by the minute.

"Here is something else," I said, pointing to the bird.

"Bird," said Leila.

"Tak, tak," said Hasan, squinting down an imaginary rifle pointed at the window.

"Sinful," Marzia hissed, nudging him with her elbow. "No manners, no sense!" Hasan grinned. Leila's eyes darted between Hasan and Marzia, then rested on the picture again. Pause. No more was coming.

"And here—" I pointed to the tree.

"Flower," said Marzia but quickly corrected herself when Hasan made a doubtful noise that sounded like "stupid—wrong—lie." "No, a tree, I mean," she cried.

"I wonder what kind of tree this might be."

"It is a date-palm," said Leila, scrutinizing the tiny, brownish leaves. "Wrong, wrong," Hasan cried, "it is a willow tree. There is a picture in my school book—" But Marzia was impatient now: "It is a tree, just a tree, no particular tree. This shepherd plays a flute under a tree."

I tried to explain. "Look," I said, reasonably, "I want you to tell me something about this picture, about the man, the tree, the bird, anything you think might be going on here . . . about why he is sitting here, or what the bird is doing. Tell me a story about it." Hasan puckered his face. Obviously I was not satisfied with their answers. Wanting to be helpful, they bent over the picture again.

"There is a man," Hasan started, slowly.

"He is playing the recorder," said his sister.

"Sitting under a tree," said Hasan.

"In the shade!" said Marzia. "It is hot!" She looked at me. "Right?" she asked. I nodded. "And there is a bird," whispered Leila, "sitting in the tree. There is nothing else."

Here the interview ended. Even an obtuse anthropologist has to take a hint as massive as this one. The flute player went back up to the red flowers. Marzia left to fetch tea, taking Leila with her. I moved back to the cushion, swatting at flies and watching Hasan rummage for his catapult under the kilim. The sparrows were chirping invitingly in the walnut tree.

·   ·   ·

Measured by our expectations of projective interviews, this one was a near-failure. But given the circumstances of working with children in Deh Koh, it was nothing short of several strokes of luck.

The first lucky circumstance in this slow and dry interview was that I had come to Huri's house at a time when Huri was in the bath, downstairs next to the woodshed. Bathing takes hours. But Huri, notified by Marzia of my approach while I had been dragging myself up the hill, had instructed her to tell me that she was "almost finished," to put me in the good room (the key to which was handed Marzia out the bath door), to make me comfortable, and to get me to wait. Marzia had strict orders to keep me there at all costs and to make sure Hasan and Leila behaved themselves. Hasan was dispatched to get cucumbers, Marzia to make lemonade and tea.

For me it meant I had three children to myself, probably for more than an uninterrupted hour, without the presence of an adult who could claim my attention by virtue of etiquette that required well-mannered children to be quiet in the presence of guests, and by preference: Huri, alone in the house on the hill for many hours on end, welcomed my visits and did not want to waste precious time listening to her children talk with me. Had Huri not been engaged so compellingly with soap and suds, she would have structured and dominated the conversation as she had done many times before; she would have spoken for the children, even if I had addressed them specifically. As in her opinion children knew nothing she did not know better, I could not have persuaded her to leave me alone with them for longer than a few perfunctory, simple sentences.

Encounters with children are hampered further by expressions of bashful reluctance (*kejalat*) that are part of children's, especially girls', proper conduct in dealing with strange adults. The shyness game—little girls' practicing of *kejalat* is often called play, *bazi*, by their elders—ranges from avoiding eye contact, tucking the face into the chest, hiding one's face behind a hand or a veil, giggling into one's veil with head squeezed between shoulders, refusing an answer or barely audibly whispering one, to instant flight and hiding outside the door in a good listening position. Boys show less shyness but are more likely to run away. I think Marzia sat and talked with me without playing the shyness game because she knew me well; because her mother had put her into the role of a hostess, that is, an adult woman, which Marzia, at thirteen, had learned to play by apprenticeship and observation; and because no other adult was around, especially no man in front of whom she would have felt compelled to display shyness. Her younger cousin, however, whom I did not know well, and who did not have any responsibilities toward me, fell into the hide-and-giggle-mode when I addressed her personally, but was emboldened enough by Marzia's frankness to participate in the discussion, such as it was, from her safe place behind her cousins' backs. Repeatedly, however, Leila looked for guidance, approval, and recognition, especially from Hasan. To her, Hasan not only was the man in the house at the time, but, as a cousin, also was in the category of highly eligible potential future marriage partner for her. She used this occasion to check him out.

Another lucky feature was the three children's lack of distraction by other children. Usually, if I start an interaction with one or two children, in no time there will be four or five others joining us. Any question or remark from me, even if emphatically addressed to a particular child, is treated as public property: all children try to answer. Too often this results in—for me—unintelligible noise or in arguments over opposing views, or else a spokesperson emerges in the group who speaks for all until challenged or shouted down. It was my luck in Huri's house that the group remained small, stable, and peaceful. Marzia, though, clearly dominated the group as a spokesperson. She merged her host-adult role with that of the elder sister and cousin into a position of relative power vis-à-vis the others. Hasan accepted his sister's gender marker for the man in the picture, the not-so-obvious recorder, despite the more obvious hair, hat, moustache, and male clothes, which he noticed. Leila seconded Hasan's shepherd interpretation after Marzia had accepted it, despite the man's unsuitable attire and a glaring absence of sheep. Marzia stopped Hasan in his tracks when he showed signs of wandering into idiosyncratic interpretation with the shooting pantomime.

Except for this small incident, no child dared to step outside the frame they tacitly had set themselves from the beginning: that of statements of the picture's literal content. They constantly reinforced each others' literal approach and defenses, not out of hostility or stupidity or lack of interest but out of a defensive habit born of fear of "getting it wrong." Rather than using fantasy to infuse the picture with meaning and action when expressly asked to do so, they claimed lack of knowledge to hang on to the safely obvious. In this, they were motivated by the experience that the less one volunteers and the more obvious is the observation, the less likely one is to get into trouble.

This anxiety about getting it wrong has its roots, I think, in early childhood experiences and is fostered in school; from first grade on, most learning is by rote. A well-identified and clearly presented body of knowledge, of "right" facts, has to be learned out of books, verbatim. Upon questioning by an authority, one either knows the right answer, the exact words, or one does not. Competition among children inside and outside of class is fierce: children do not give each other time to think a problem through, to formulate an answer, to correct a mistake. At the slightest hesitation, the first error in the recitation of an answer by a student, others will take over immediately. Thus Marzia responded hastily and loudly to Hasan's doubt about her flower interpretation of the tree so as not to let him steal her thunder. And she grew suspicious of my intentions and insecure of her abilities to "see" the picture "correctly" when I insisted on further talk about it. This suggested to her that there was something she ought to see but did not—that she was failing. Like a bad teacher, I wanted information from her that I had not identified beforehand as something to be known. It would have required considerably more confidence than they had in themselves and in the others' tolerance toward "mistakes" for any one of the three to talk about something that obviously was not there.

I was lucky in a third way. Marzia's father had died a few years earlier. Her elder brother exhibited the uneasy, controlling attitude toward women, especially toward unmarried sisters, common of most young men in Deh Koh. Indeed, brothers are said to set much stricter, narrower limits for conduct and movement for their sisters than do the young girls' fathers. Had her elder brother been present, Marzia would have served cucumbers, lemonade, and tea without saying a word. Hasan, still the younger sibling rather than the protective, supervising brother he would be in a few years, accepted Marzia's leadership in the discussion of the picture. Had he been just a little older, or maybe simply bigger and bolder than Marzia, he hardly would have let her identify the figure in the picture as male by the flute. Hasan came very close to identifying him by his moustache. What Marzia would have said without Hasan present, however, we will never know.

The flute theme was yet another piece of good luck in this austere interview. Instead of talking about moustache, hat, or black curls, Marzia, after much hesitation, chose the flute as masculine marker. Leaving aside the tempting Freudian interpretion of the symbolism of the flute itself, we may ask what cognitive process this preference suggests.

At the age of thirteen, despite thin arms and legs, Marzia was reaching marriageable age. She had learned housekeeping skills. She was going to school, but her elder brother was urging her to quit because crossing the village on her way to and from school several times a day was becoming morally risky despite her black veil-wrap. As a "mature" (*dorosht*) girl, Marzia's and thereby her brothers' honor was endangered in a very physical sense by every lustful glance a man cast on her—and there are no other glances, brothers say. The boy had all but convinced Huri. Accordingly, during summer vacation Marzia was kept at home most of the time in an isolated house that did not see many visitors. Marzia had learned to accept the view that men were dangerous for her—"A girl ought to be afraid of men," she said on another occasion—and thus male attributes, even only in a picture, were hard for her to acknowledge. Talking about the picture she even pretended not to see them at all; she ignored moustache, coat, hair, hat, foot—which a woman never would have shown—as danger signs. She deemed only the recorder neutral enough, after long hesitation, to be identified as male.

For a time, I had known about Marzia's lonely life in the repressed atmosphere created by her elder brother, a fundamentalist for whom the conduct of his only sister was an important measure of his family's piety and dedication to the Islamic Republic. Under these circumstances, I had suspected that men probably would be an even more fascinating threat to her than to other girls who lived in less isolated and more sex-integrated families. But Marzia would not say so—not to others, not to me. By not acknowledging the obvious markers of maleness in the picture, by her hesitation and evasions, Marzia was telling me that the repression I had felt in her house and deduced from her brothers' zealous attitude was also felt by her.

The final good fortune was my ability to observe a brother-sister pair at an identical task. Hasan was the most lively of the three. He moved the most, gesticulated with his arms, shook out his legs. He used more space than his sister, looked at her less than she looked at him, did not fiddle with his hair or a head-covering. Twice, with the shepherd suggestion and the shotgun, he dared to transcend the very obvious. He voiced distrust easily ("lie, lie," and "wrong," he said twice in the short scene) and judged information by its verity: the tree was not a flower, not a date-palm but a willow tree. He knew more and better than his elder sister even if, for the time being, he was deferring to her leadership in questions of proper behavior and dealing with the foreign woman. In sharp contrast to Marzia and Leila, who projected no aggression, Hasan "shot" the bird. While Marzia was struggling with ambivalent feelings toward the male figure and with her responsibility to give "right" answers, Hasan was playing his way through the interview, a great emotional distance away from his sister. And when the interview was over, he and the girls immediately moved into affectively and cognitively different gender-coded spaces and activities: shooting sparrows in the courtyard for him, brewing and serving tea in the house for Marzia and Leila—slightly disapproved-of, childish play-aggression for him, and work, food handling, and family face-keeping for the girls.

4 · Big Belly

Pregnancy Theory

It is very unlikely that any one child in Deh Koh has heard the local theory of conception in the compact form that follows here. But it is equally unlikely that there is a child who has not heard it in bits and pieces. Although young children who ask where babies come from may be told that God gives them, pregnancies and pregnancy talk are so common that knowledge about children growing in a mother's belly (*kom, del, zir del*) is ubiquitous. Even the half-hearted attempts of some adults to make very young children believe they sprang from their mother's belly button does not convince children for long, nor are they meant to convince them. In earlier days, observations of lambing provided children with analogies, but with the decline in animal husbandry this source of knowledge has become less accessible. However, pregnancies are discussed freely among women in the presence of children, with terms that are combinations of words used in everyday speech and thus are easily understood by children. The theory about procreation guides discussions and practices. Casual exclamations such as "Her womb is burned," curses such as "Seed of a dog!" or "If only I had miscarried you!" which children hear frequently, express theories obliquely but consistently enough to make intuitive sense to children. Accordingly, even young children know without question that a child grows in a mother's belly and suspect that a father had put it there during hidden activities at night, under the covers. They also realize that these activities are somehow *zesht* (obscene), provoking *kejalat* (shame). "After we had the first two children, my husband and I always slept separate—I here, he over there. We would have been ashamed if our children noticed us do it," a very pious woman told me in the presence of her two youngest daughters. I did not have the nerve to ask her how she got the rest of her eight children.

This is what children may learn about the nature of pregnancy from watching and listening:

• God willed that men have seeds and that women have a womb, the child-bag. Upon ejaculation of seed-fluid, a man's seed falls into the woman's womb, which contains blood. If the blood "eats" the seed, no pregnancy occurs. If the seed is stronger than the blood, a child will grow. If the mother's humoral disposition is warm, the child, referred to as such from the moment of conception, will be a "child" in the narrow sense, that is, a boy. If the mother's humoral nature is cold, it will be a girl. If the womb is clean, the child will be beautiful, with light, clear skin, but if it is not clean, the seed might not mix properly with the blood, or else the womb might not be able to take care of the child. If a child nevertheless grows in a "dirty" womb, it will be dark-skinned and ugly.

• Various unhealthy conditions can prevent or complicate a pregnancy. Insufficient monthly flow of blood will leave the womb "dirty," as will pus. A "dry" or "crooked" womb will make conception difficult, as will a "weak back." Specifically, the small of the back is said to be connected to the womb by nerves and blood vessels, as evidenced by back aches during pregnancy and delivery. "Preventive" pills prevent the proper mixing of seed and blood or else spoil the seed as well as the blood; obviously, they are unhealthy.

• The newborn's first, dark excrement is taken as proof and result of the blood-eating in the womb. A strong mother with rich, clean blood is likely to produce a strong child. A weak mother with little or weak blood likely will have a weak child. Unconsumed blood is expelled as afterbirth.

• The dramatic expulsion of blood at birth means that birth has a cleansing effect on the womb. For this reason, doctors in Deh Koh may suggest another pregnancy for a woman with a persistent womb ailment caused by "dirt," such as an infection.

• If one could look into the womb one could recognize a boy as such already twenty days after conception: he has tiny testicles, shaped like lentils. A girl is a formless lump of meat for sixty days.

• A child comes to life in three stages; from seed-in-the-womb to the first fetal movement felt by the mother, the child grows and differentiates in body but has no individuality, no character, no soul. A child's first movement in utero, around four months, is the sign that God is giving it a soul (*jun*) at that moment. The child will take on some of the character qualities and the looks of the person at whom its mother happens to look at the time it gets its soul. From then on, it will move and will grow quickly into a person but cannot yet hear, see, talk, or think. The gradual acquisition of senses, beginning after birth, is the third stage in its coming-to-life.

• This system is created, willed, by God, as is every single pregnancy. Different women's different fates (*qesmat*) and different fortunes (*shans*) account for the variations, for the chance happenings and unforseeable circumstances that result in different experiences and outcomes of pregnancy.

Western biomedicine, as mediated through the Iranian, Pakistani, Indian, and Bangladeshi physicians accessible to people in Deh Koh, and through local health care workers such as midwives, is easily integrated into this system because the medical professionals share, or at least do not dispute, many of the local ideas. But even where health professionals' ministrations differ from the local model, they are interpreted in Deh Koh as providing one more choice for intervention should something go wrong in a pregnancy. These procedures, such as tests, medication, cesarean section, do not necessarily challenge the local assumptions, if for no other reason than that nobody takes the time to explain the biomedical theory of conception and gestation to the villagers.

Until very recently, pregnancies were presented to children as an expected, and expectable, product of marriage. Married women were pregnant and/or nursing most of their lives. No longer getting pregnant was a sign of old age. Never getting pregnant was a serious anomaly worth discussing and getting upset about like any other severe anomaly. The recent strong revival of birth control in the Islamic Republic brought condoms to some homes (which little boys, if they can get their hands on them, use as balloons) and the possibility of preventing pregnancies by various other means, but the trend to smaller families is too new to have had a discernible effect on the theories of pregnancy.

The theory of procreation has a moral dimension: a husband has a right to demand sex (*jakhousi*, literally sleeping in one place, or *nazdiki*, closeness) and children from his wife. Refusing sex, as older women are said to do, or limiting children against the husband's wish, which is sinful and legal grounds for divorce, may prompt a man to take a second wife. Women talk about this. A co-wife is worse than sex and more children. "We have no choice," women say, shrugging their shoulders, setting sexual urges and activities in very gendered ethical contexts for the children who hear them.

Pregnancies and whatever activities precede them are firmly situated within the framework of marriage. Outside of marriage, they are presented as illegitimate, obscene, scandalous. The story of a young woman who got pregnant out of wedlock and was burned, together with her lover, on orders of the then-chief of Deh Koh some fifty years ago is still told in Deh Koh with horror-tinted approval. Homosexuality either is unknown, said to be impossible, or else relegated to the moral aberrations and depravities of some corrupt individuals and to city life. Unspecified hints of children "playing" with each other occasionally when they are sure of privacy are linked to children's innate lack of understanding, propriety, and moral strength, as well as childish, and therefore often inappropriate, curiosity. The separation of boys and girls partly is reasoned on the likelihood of such bad behavior if they are left alone together. No precautions are taken for boys alone or girls alone.

Pregnancy Terms

Tokhm means semen as well as seed in botanical contexts. In Farsi, a hen's egg is also called *tokhm*, "seed of a hen." This strikes people in Deh Koh as odd. They use a special term, *khag*, for any bird's egg, including a hen's. By implication, this makes seed a clearly male thing in Deh Koh, and egg a female thing, and "seeding" a child a male task or achievement. Although children might not know what their father's seeds look like or consist of, the concept of growth-out-of-a-seed is familiar even to the very young. Seeds provide the link between father and children, just as they do between last year's wheat and this year's.

Just as a plant seed carries the program (*barname*) for the future plant, a father's seed contains the plan for the child and for many of the child's qualities. The seed of a morally depraved father, a thief, for example, will produce a morally depraved child. *Tokhm haram,* religiously unlawful, polluted, seed, and *tokhm sag*, seed of a dog—the dog is treated as a highly polluting animal—are frequently used curses.

The seed is sown when the semen fluid (*shevet*) falls into the child-bag, the *baccedun* (*dun* is a woven container such as a salt bag or a straw bag). A metaphor for the womb is storage vessel (*zarf ambar*). This vessel can be clean (*pak*), healthy (*salem*), strong (*qott*), or else dirty (*kassif*), burned (*sokht*), crooked (*picide*), weak (*zaif*), full of pus (*cerk*), torn (*deres*), damaged (*kharab*) and thus unable to take care of the child. To take care (*safd kardan*) is used for taking care of children before and after birth: the mother functions as a replacement of her womb. *Bacceme* means "I am pregnant."

Bacce is used for children ("*baccyal sholuq nakonin,*" i.e., "children, don't make a ruckus") but more often connotes boys, from infants to unmarried young adults. A boy talking about his male classmates will say "*baccyal*"; a girl talking about her female classmates likely will say "*duaral,*" "girls." The question of how many *bacce* a person with five children, for example, has, likely will be answered with: "Three, and two girls." A *baccedun*, then, is a vessel for a boy, and for a girl too.

A young girl's womb is clean inside; no cleansing is necessary and the blood stays there, ready to receive seed. Women suspect that men's seed fluid may dirty their wombs, and cite the Qoranic proscription of a ritual bath after intercourse in support. An old woman no longer needs blood to nourish a fetus; eventually, blood and the womb-bag dry up, depriving her of monthly cleansing: old women feel sick, complaining about symptoms that are taken to point to pollution of the womb.

Less specifically, the place where a child grows in the mother is referred to as *kom,* stomach. This term connotes the stomach proper, the place where food goes, but also the whole abdominal area. "He can't fill her belly," said about a man and his wife, may mean the man cannot fill her stomach with food or else with a child. Either meaning, but especially the latter, is a strong insult for a man. "A child fell into the stomach" means to be pregnant, as do *kom boland* or *kom gyepu*, big belly, while a *kom kucek*, a small, flat stomach, means to be not pregnant.

"A child cleanses the belly" refers to the alleged cleansing properties of a pregnancy, which ends with the expulsion of a lot of "black, dirty" blood, the *joft-e bacce*, that which is "paired up with the (newborn) child" through the *naf*, which is both navel and umbilical cord.

The womb contains mostly *khin*, blood. In all forms outside the body, blood is a pollutant. The monthly flowing-out of dirty, dark blood renders a woman ritually unclean: she is not to pray until she has performed the prescribed ablutions and washed her blood-soiled skirt. Menstruation is referred to as *binamaz*, without prayer. Missing the blood flow for a couple of months, not having "to wash one's skirt," is a sign of likely pregnancy. In the womb, the child eats or drinks (*khordan* covers both) the blood with its mouth; after birth it excretes the end product of this food as tar, *khil*. Until recently, it was said that a newborn was polluted by the blood it ate and with which it was covered.

Inside the womb, the child gets food and also its *jun*, the soul. God gives the soul directly. Before this moment, the child is alive in the sense that it is eating and growing, but it has no personality, no specific vitality, no soul. When pressed to explain the difference between *jun* and *ruh*, the Arabic word for the concept of soul in a religious context, people equate them, but *ruh* is not used spontaneously in the context of pregnancy. In the local philosophy of life, *jun* is more than *ruh*; it is linked to being alive physically, as a person. Before a child *ve jun uma*, has come to life, in utero, many people see no ethical reason why it cannot be aborted, in contrast to governmental law and theology.

Jun is a term of endearment children hear often. It may replace the child's personal name or else be tagged on to it: "*Jun, jun*, come here," or "*Zahra-jun*." Misbehaving children "pull the soul out by the nose" of their exasperated father or mother. Children and adults swear by the *jun* of fathers and brothers: an orphan girl's plight in a folktale is captured by the words "she had nobody to swear by." A person too sick to talk or eat "doesn't have a soul": the personal, individual vitality has all but left, the person is more or less unconscious, only the breath, *nafas*, is present still. "His/her soul returned," means that the person has come back to life, is participating again in his/her surroundings. A misbehaving child may hear, "In the presence of what [despicable, ill-mannered] person did you get your life-soul?!" A pregnant woman ought to be treated with consideration because she "has to bear the burden of two lives." This burden may intentionally or spontaneously "fall": *ve bar raftan* means to miscarry.

Some women get pregnant again soon after giving birth; *polu kardan* is a term used specifically for this condition. A woman who "makes *polu*" will be weak soon and bear weak children. She is pitied. A little girl, asked the whereabouts of her very old great-grandmother, said, "At the doctor's; the poor woman makes *polu*." Other women do not get pregnant for two or more years after each birth, they are *shetorza*, spacing children like a camel. This is just the way it is, a function of a woman's disposition. Breastfeeding is known to retard conception, but not infallibly so; even at times when all women nursed, some conceived often, some rarely.

Listening to women, children get the impression that getting pregnant is not a problem, that it is natural and happens all the time, and that people count on it, but that avoiding pregnancy is a problem, a task that needs a lot of effort.

Pregnancy Practices

A woman ought to get pregnant as soon as she starts receiving seeds, right after marriage. "She got pregnant in the bridal chamber" is said with a mixture of satisfaction and pity—with more satisfaction (over the bride and groom's demonstrated fertility) by the groom's family, more pity by the bride's, especially if the bride is very young. Enough young brides got pregnant before menarche to substantiate in Deh Koh the belief that the monthly flow of blood is independent of sexual maturity. A girl is deemed mature (*dorosht*) when her breasts start to grow and her cheeks and arms start to fill out, and when household chores can be delegated to her with some confidence. The Qoranic lower limit for a girl's marriage age, nine years, is more or less compatible with this notion, although lately people have started to challenge it.

Falak was about twelve years old, she thinks, when she got married, and pregnant five months later without having had a period. Four months later, she miscarried. The physician explained that her

"place for the child" was too narrow, and that the premature pregnancy had injured her womb. Three years later she still had not conceived again. After the unsuccessful wooing of a very desirable
young woman, peeved Fazel quickly married the easiest available relative, a barely thirteen-year-old, very small cousin. She became pregnant within two months, carried the child to term, but almost died
delivering, said her mother-in-law. Fearful of another near disaster
Fazel opted for birth control: he ordered his wife to take contraceptive
pills for the next two years.

For a young woman who is under close observation for the first
signs of good news, the first pregnancy is something to be bashful
about. Mamanir giggled and squirmed and cried, "No, no, she is
lying!" when her mother-in-law pointedly told me that Mamanir had
not had to wash her skirts for two months and had lost her appetite.
A woman at the end of her childbearing years may be bashful again
and might want to hide her pregnancy. Both the young bride and the
older woman are ashamed not so much of being with child than of
the implied acknowledgment of sexual activity to which the young
woman is not accustomed, and about which the old one feels that it is
no longer appropriate for her.

Pregnant women are said to be unreasonable, quarrelsome, and
teary. These behaviors are ascribed to a female weakness in reason
that is heightened during pregnancy because the womb is taking care
of an increasingly big and heavy load. "My mother is so weak, she
cries about everything, whether she is pregnant or not," said a four-
teen-year old boy. Pregnant women are said likely to be sick to their
stomachs and to have food aversions or food cravings such as for
sweets, meat, sour food, or dirt. However, although explained by the
pregnancy, odd behaviors of pregnant women are rarely tolerated
well by others. The mother-to-be is not allotted better or more food or
spared work unless she has helpers—an unusually compassionate
mother-in-law or husband's sister, or grown daughters of her own.
During her last pregnancy, at around age forty-three, Gordi cried for
meat, which her three grown and well-off daughters took turns providing for her at great cost. Rarely is a pregnant woman that lucky.

Getting or being pregnant is declared good (khub); being pregnant
often is difficult (moshkel, sakht). It makes women weak, especially if
the pregnancies follow one another closely. Women say they feel har-

rassed, troubled (*ajes, badbakht*). "Only husbands and old women want us to have many children," said a mother of eight; "men because they don't know what a trouble it is, and old women because they have forgotten." Although children seem to be unmoved by their mothers' laments, older children often are resentful of more siblings whom they have to help raise. Hajar concealed her eighth pregnancy from her eldest son, who was away on studies, until he visited when the baby was two months old, "Because he would be furious," she said. "Don't you get pregnant again, you old woman, you ought to be ashamed!" was Ashraf's final admonition to her mother before she left for the next term at the teacher training college.

Since about 1992, when the government started to promote birth control, women of all ages talk about the disadvantages of large families. "I wish I only had had the first two or three children—the others are only troubles," women say, in front of their children. "I am glad you didn't!" cried five-year-old Masume, her mother's eighth child, at such an occasion. Because large families, "too many children," are in large part blamed officially for the nation's economic problems, and birth control has become a national issue, pregnancy is more ambiguous than before, when only the mother's comfort was at stake. Children hear that they are a problem for the nation, their families, and their mothers, but this does not seem to bother them. As members of a large family, however, children have many occasions to resent being crowded and being inconvenienced by many siblings and forced to compete with them for scarce resources. For older children, their mother's repeated pregnancies pose a threat to their own comfort, imply a future potential burden of work and responsibilities, and, recently, imply a sign of rural backwardness. A childless, unmarried professional urban woman, visiting a big wedding in Deh Koh, declared in front of a room full of local women and girls that she had chosen to remain single because none of her suitors consented to the childless marriage she wanted. Two female high school students in the audience were impressed. Discussing the topic, they settled on wanting two children at the most, they said, and wondered how to write such a limit into a marriage contract.

Pregnancy has become a debatable issue; "fate" has taken on a different meaning for women and men now that pregnancies can be controlled.

Contraception

According to the midwife's records, of 525 children delivered by her between 1971 and 1976, twenty-four (4.5 percent) were the tenth to eighteenth child of the mother. One Deh Koh woman claims to have had twenty-four pregnancies; three children survived. Nazi, for example, had been pregnant six times in six years; by the time she was twenty, four of her children were alive, one had died at nine months, and one miscarried. Nazi "makes *polu.*" A neighbor of ours said he only had to look at his wife to get her pregnant. She "makes *polu.*" Despite her claims to have used pills, condoms, and coitus interruptus, she, so far, has had nine pregnancies in twenty-three years. Three of these she tried to abort herself, two successfully so. Now, she says, she sleeps with her husband "with fear and trembling," afraid to get pregnant yet again.

In the summer of 1994 the local physician said that pregnant women in Deh Koh are in very poor health. With few exceptions they are anemic and malnourished. They have too many pregnancies, too closely spaced, and many miscarriages. Newborns look like premature babies, birthweight is low, and mothers have insufficient milk. It was worse in the past, though. Women claim negative side effects for every birth control device. They use contraceptives unreliably; men reject condoms. Only after five or more children do women start to consider having their tubes tied. For these reasons, the doctor said, abortion will become the important birth control device it had been under the previous regime if it is again legalized by the government. Women will use abortions to space children.

Over the years, all physicians in Deh Koh have had similar complaints: women do not use the devices as prescribed. The result is many accidental pregnancies. The doctors claim that women are not serious about birth control because they are afraid that their husbands will take another wife if they do not have a child every year. Women are afraid to ask about birth control; they are very bashful.

Amene, a teacher who takes all laws and regulations seriously, in 1980 wrote to an office for questions regarding the faith, for guidance on birth control. The office replied that abortion was forbidden on the death penalty for the abortionist; prevention of pregnancy through drugs, condoms, IUDs, was allowed. Amene has this information in writing. In 1992, a mullah told us that preventive measures are allowed, provided the husband gives his wife permission to use them. The children are, after all, his property. Abortion is forbidden. In 1994, a mother of seven, when I asked her how the clergy might justify legalization of therapeutic abortion, said, "They'll say, 'Before the child gets it's soul it is only a lump of meat and therefore can be aborted.'"

Contraceptive devices have been known in Deh Koh since the late 1960s, when the government started to push birth control and thereby implicitly introduced choice in having children. For several years, the Islamic Republican government discouraged birth control measures, although only abortion, which had been freely available under the shah, was outlawed. Pills and other devices were hard to come by for the villagers, however. Women were swept into a pro-birth mood by propaganda and by each others' examples. Since 1992, aggressive birth control propaganda and aspirations for a middle-class lifestyle in a rapidly worsening economy are reversing this mood. By 1994, Deh Koh women were quite sophisticated in their knowledge about contraceptive methods. The contraceptive devices distributed or administered to women in Deh Koh, according to records kept at the government health clinic and by the midwife, are illustrated in table 1.

Condoms (*kondom*) are unpopular with men and women. Condoms are called bad, repulsive, uncomfortable. They require organization: they have to be handy when needed on very short notice, yet hidden well enough so that the children cannot appropriate them as toys. In the crowded, bare living quarters in Deh Koh, this is hard to accomplish.

The insertion of an intrauterine device (*dastegah*) requires the effort of regular trips to the district clinic in town, and entails considerable emotional discomfort for a woman, especially if the physician is a man. IUDs do not work reliably either, women say; quite a few mothers can point to an "IUD child." A physician will not place an IUD in a woman who suffers from a "womb-wound," that is, infections or ulcerations. Such ailments are endemic in Deh Koh, say the health care workers. Despite these shortcomings, the use of IUDs has increased.

Contraceptive drugs (*qors jelougiri*) are thought by everybody to be very "warm" and thus to cause rashes, headaches, and swelling of limbs. They are said to have *zeft*, an unhealthy quality that accounts for abdominal pains, backaches, general malaise, and dry breasts.

Table 1
Contraceptive Devices Used in Deh Koh

	1988–89	Percent	1991–92	Percent	1993–94	Percent
Condom	48	6.3	28	3.8	17	2.0
IUD	35[1]	4.6	48	6.5	111	13.1
Drugs	375	49.3	339	46.0	264	31.2
Tubal ligation	2[2]	0.3	80	10.8	114	13.5
Norplant[3]	0		0		3	0.3
Total	460	60.5	495	67.3	505	59.7
No contraception[4]	300	39.5	240[5]	32.7	341	40.3
All fertile women	650	100.0	735[5]	100.0	846	100.0

[1]By year's end the number had dwindled to 18.

[2]In 1989 no records were kept on this; the actual number likely is a little higher.

[3]No official records are available because implants are not done at the local clinic. The actual number might be higher.

[4]This category also includes pregnant and lactating women.

[5]These numbers are inexplicably and unrealistically low.

Suspicions, even "proof" of deleterious effects, and gruesome anecdotes abound. A young mother of three reported that during a stomach operation for ulcers the doctor found that all the contraceptive pills she had ever swallowed had been compressed into a ball of white, hard stuff in her stomach. This story did not surprise anybody. The pills dry up the monthly flow of cleansing blood, leaving the womb dirtier by the month, people argue. Only postmenopausal women seem to profit from the contraceptive pills' alleged warm humoral qualities, which soothe their cold bones.

Having to swallow a pill every day whether one had sex or not does not make sense to the women and is a bother in any case. "I always take two when I remember to eat them," said Leila, "to make up for the days I forget about them." The doctor rolls his eyes at such stupidity, as he calls it.

Since about 1991, tubal ligation (*lule bastan*) has become the preventive measure of choice for those who are determined not to have any more children. The first woman to opt for this procedure in 1991 had had seven difficult pregnancies, of which four children survived, was deadly afraid of another pregnancy, and succeeded in convincing her husband of the danger. As this procedure cannot be used for spacing children, it is out of the question for younger women. It is not fool-proof either. Tamane's sixth child (eighth pregancy) was delivered by cesarean section in the county hospital. During the operation, the surgeon, with her husband's consent, performed a tubal ligation as well. Tamane, who was about twenty-eight years old at the time and had complained bitterly about the burden of many children, nevertheless was very angry and depressed when she was told. Then she got pregnant again anyway, much to everybody's chagrin.

There also circulates the rumor, allegedly spread by personnel at the clinic, that tied tubes may cause cancer. Despite these problems, tubal ligation had been chosen by close to 24 percent of all fertile women (some 200 of about 850 fertile women) by the end of 1994.

Vasectomy is talked about in negative terms. I know of no case in Deh Koh.

Implants (*nurplant*) have become available recently, but as of 1994 only at the county hospital or in the city.

Coitus interruptus is considered unreliable for prevention of pregnancies and bad for a man's health, but is practiced nevertheless.

Abstinence is taken to have no spiritual, religious, or health merits. It is practiced by necessity only. Even if a man could be abstinent easily, which people claim is doubtful, the dammed-up seed fluid likely would make him ill, even cause his flow to dry up, or make him blind. It is therefore a sin for a wife to refuse her husband. Abstinence is not considered a healthy way of birth control.

Too liberal an expenditure of seed fluid, however, makes a man age prematurely. He has to be firmly in command of his sexual output to stay well; a wife has no right to demand sex, and an overly alluring or experienced wife will ruin her husband. It is just as well that women, after the bridal-chamber nights are over (or else after the forty days of passion and infatuation, *ashoqi,* that are said to start in the bridal chamber are up, or, at most, after the first child is born) lose interest in sex so predictably that it is all but expected that women "don't like sex." "Once is like a hundred times!" said Goli, about age twenty-five, and the mother of four children. Those who continue to like to be "close to their husbands," as is said euphemistically, are taken as exceptions.

For women, abstinence has no direct negative effects other than the discomfort of repressed sexual urges, people say. Indirectly, abstinence prevents the cleansing benefits of timely pregnancies: has child-less Maryam not died of a strange illness in her prime middle-age while her fertile sisters are alive, ailing and wailing, but alive? In any case, young women's sexual desires, although acknowledged to exist, are said to wane quickly after marriage, unlike men's; even a woman's forced abstinence during a prolonged absence of her husband is not discussed as a hardship.

Girls and boys learn from listening to adults' discussions of these matters that men need sex to be well, but that a man is in danger of being deprived of it by poor or unfeeling parents who refuse to pro-cure a wife for him early, or by a fiance's family who takes any excuse to make him wait, or by his own circumstances as a student, soldier, or jobless pauper that make it financially impossible to get married; and, later, by a reluctant wife. Girls learn that men are after sex al-ways, which for an unmarried girl poses an ever-present, socially grave danger, and for a wife means many children, which in itself is a harrassment. A husband accused of *asiat kardan*, troubling his wife, may be one who abuses her verbally or physically, and also one who forces her to have sex and to become pregnant.

Sherife took her seventh baby off the cradle after only two months and bedded him next to her at night. "I know why," said her neigh-bor. "So that her husband cannot get to her." All laughed. For the children who listened, even if they did not quite get the joke, it nev-ertheless entailed a commentary on husband-wife relations, a pro-gram for wifely behavior, and a stereotype about women's attitudes toward sharing a bed with a husband at night.

There are some people, few and mostly men, who deem all contra-ceptive measures as arrogant interference with the will of God, as sinful. Discussing such cases, women usually and swiftly cut through the seeming piety and reduce the philosophy to a self-serving motif. A middle-aged man in the village forbids his tired, sickly wife any birth control with the will of God argument. The woman has borne six daughters in eight years. One died. She is exhausted. "He wants sons, that's all," she says.

In its simplest form, the will of God argument can be applied to justify any status quo: barrenness and high fertility, the birth of a child and the death of a child. But protective measures are equally God's will, people argue, and ought to be used.

Barrenness, Miscarriage, Abortion

Only dumb, lazy, or desperate people blame all troubles on the will of God. Most people in Deh Koh argue that the laziness or lack of knowledge that result in pregnancy problems cannot be excused with the alleged will of God; only after all choices for curing barrenness have been exhausted, all doctors seen, the most powerful amulets written, the last penny spent, can one conclude that a calamity is the will of God. One of our neighbors was childless after many years of marriage but refused to see a doctor or to as much as try local medicines or amulets, citing the will of God. Unanimously, she was criticized as foolish, even sinful because she rejected God's provisions of potential help. Tala, childless still after years of treatments for her barrenness, now may say, "It's the will of God," absolving herself from further trying. Our steadfast neighbor cannot, except that her very inactivity and stubbornness itself are, of course, lastly the will of God too, her fate (*qesmat*), written on her forehead (*pishunish neveshte*). If He had wanted her to see a doctor, He would have made her go. He had not.

People know about infertility in men, but rarely does a man explore this possibility if his wife does not conceive. Pregnancy is a woman's affair. Others might whisper that one or another woman's barrenness "is really because of *him*," that "his brother didn't have any children either," or "after he died his childless wife remarried and had children," but I do not know of a single man who sought treatment for infertility.

Some dramatic circumstances such as accidents, illnesses, or outrageous behaviors may cause barrenness or miscarriages, women say; a Deh Koh woman's decade-long barrenness commonly was ascribed to her earlier alleged liberties with several men. This line of argument is not validated by other examples, though; none of the few other women of questionable repute around Deh Koh are barren. Only sometimes does God punish sins in this life, people say, by barrenness or in other ways.

After five daughters, Effat had a son who died when he was two. She was so inconsolably sad about his death that her "womb burned" (*baccedun sokht*) with sorrow and she no longer could conceive.

Pus in the womb may prevent conception. It may accumulate because of a cold or for other, unspecified, reasons. This condition is most successfully treated with medicine from a physician.

The recent cases of two women who had gotten married in their late twenties and were childless still after several years make some think that their idle wombs may have "dried up" prematurely. The two women are used as a case in point by those who argue for early marriage of girls.

Finally, one woman claims that the touch of a djenn left her womb "soft" (sos) so that it cannot hold a child anymore.

Miscarriages (ve bar raftan, to miscarry) are frequent in Deh Koh. Few women report they never had one. Various models are available to explain miscarriages and suggest preventive measures.

Undue physical exertion (whereby "undue" is a post-hoc judgment: an undue strain is one followed by a miscarriage) may lead to miscarriage. Qeta had been warned by the physician not even to lift the milk pail; she did not heed his advice and died, miscarrying. Qobra lost a boy in her fourth month after pushing a heavy suitcase across the floor.

A young woman miscarried twice, each time after a fight. A loud and violent one she witnessed between neighbors one night made her miscarry within an hour; during the other, between herself and her husband, her husband threw her down, which started intermittent bleeding that ended when a physician in the hospital in town performed a kuretash (dilation and curettage).

Three of Periza's four miscarriages were due to her womb "recognizing the smell" of the first miscarriage and promptly miscarrying again; her womb had gotten used to miscarrying, she said. She was advised to carry a written, Qoran text–based amulet and to cleanse her womb of the lingering "smell," the memory of miscarriage, with an oral dose of sandalwood powder mixed with dry gall of a mountaingoat. I asked Periza a leading question: might her very young marriage age have had something to do with the miscarriages? Yes, she said, of course: "I was very small (kucik, small and undeveloped in body) when my parents gave me away in marriage. I didn't have breasts yet, and my womb was small too, for sure." Being small at the time of one's first pregnancy does not necessarily explain a miscarriage, though, when Periza was young, all girls were more or less "small" at the time of their marriage, yet many did carry their children to term, people argue.

Vaginal bleeding in a pregnant woman is a sure sign of trouble: it means that the child will be deprived of food or will be flushed out along with the blood. Perijan, who has cut a great many umbilical cords in her days, knows how to handle it; if the bleeding is painless, a woman must try to make her blood coagulate by eating something cool (in the humoral sense), and a medicine made of starch, roasted lentils, and bone marrow of a sheep, pounded together to a powder. In addition, the woman should have an amulet made for her with coagulative effects, a lock-tie (*qolf band*), done by an experienced and efficacious person who speaks a certain Qoranic verse over a lock while locking it, or a string-tie (*deshk band*), a piece of string over which an appropriate text was spoken while it was tied. A woman is also well advised to rest a lot. "And you show me one who can afford this!" Perijan added. If the bleeding does not stop, the woman should see a doctor.

A sickly woman, who was unhappy about her eighth pregnancy, saw hope in a slight vaginal bleeding and the small size of her stomach. "Maybe the child will go away," she said. "I can't sit at another cradle, I don't have the strength."

No explanations are forwarded for slight, painless bleeding. But if the bleeding is accompanied by pain, it is to be taken as a sign that the child has a defect (*eib*), and the woman ought to eat foods that make the womb "soft" so that the child will "fall out" of it. There are several herbal medicines known to have abortive properties, such as teas made of parsley and of dandelion leaves. Jumping up and down, kneading the abdomen, or being beaten "dig" the child out of the womb so that it "leaves."

A widower with five children made his second wife abort a child by pummeling her abdomen. He said he could not provide for any more children.

A woman who wants to abort a fetus is likely to swallow a handfull of pills from her drug cache of unconsumed medicines that various physicians had prescribed over the years: analgesics, antibiotics, vitamins, laxatives, antidepressants, antiparasitic drugs, "pills of all colors." People know of a severely handicapped child in another village, the result of the mother's failed attempt to abort it with pills. The doctor calls the women names for not taking precautions against pregnancies to begin with and then endangering their own health.

Children, especially boys, are not likely to hear about these dangers and procedures in detail. However, at the very least, they learn to identify married women with pregnancies; they learn that women are in charge of pregnancies, that they control knowledge about them and wield considerable resources for handling them. Without mothers' big bellies under their long, loose tunics, there would be no children. Pregnancies are common, a fact of life, yet obviously burdensome and the reason for women's complaints and ill health. "Other women are pregnant for a while," explained the four-year-old son of an overweight, ailing woman, "but my mother is pregnant always. She has a big belly and keeps saying, 'Oh me, oh my!'"

Pregnancy Stories

All the following stories were told in the presence of several children. I have edited them for clarity.

Mamalus, a mother of six grown children, said, "When I was pregnant with my first child—little, tiny, a child myself—I was after sweets wherever I could find them. Nothing else tasted good. This was years and years ago, before every child had cookies and candies glued to its grimy hands. The only sweets then were dates, brought on donkeys all the way from Kazerun—the dust! The dirt! The flies! One day I got hold of a few pennies, which in a hurry I took to the store, a mile away, to buy a bowl of dates. By the time I passed the old cemetery on my way back, I had eaten every single one and licked the bowl and my fingers too. All those warm dates! I fainted. A neighbor found me lying among the dead in the thistles and the thorns, and brought me home, somehow. Somebody told my husband to slaughter a young rooster—cool, cool meat!—and to roast it for me, and I ate it, too. It landed right on top of the date-hill in my stomach, and then I felt well again."

. . .

Huri, an outspoken and ambitious mother of five children, said, "The mullahs and the scriptures say this rhyme: 'A child is the work of the father, the mother only comes after.' This is supposed to mean that the father is most important in the making of a child, and the mother is only a servant. But this is not true. Just the opposite: God has given each mother the warm heart [del suz] that makes her get up in the middle of the night to give the child water, to take it outside, to be troubled when it is ill, and to fluff its pillow and feed it and take it to the doctor. But a father?! A father isn't home, he doesn't hear his children cry; he doesn't care who eats the food he brings home . . . This proverb is the work of the mullahs and the Prophet to make women seem unimportant. It cannot be God's word because it is obviously wrong—everybody can see plainly how wrong it is. Once I argued about it with our mullah. He said, I, an illiterate woman, shouldn't doubt what is written. But I doubt anyway—just because it is written doesn't mean it is right!"

.   .   .

Alia, a young and rather bashful mother, talked about what young children might think about their parents' sexual activities: "Children know something is going on, something they are not supposed to see. Girls are more modest about this. They are more likely not to know or not to let on that they know than are boys. When my second son was about three, he developed a bad habit. Sometimes at night he would lie awake until he noticed that we were moving around under the blanket. Then he sat up and started to either whine or giggle. I put him down, and after a while my husband started his business again, and the boy sat up and giggled. I said, 'Sleep, dear, hush, hush,' and he pretended to fall asleep, and when he saw the blankets move, he sat up and clapped his hands . . . So it went until we gave up. The boy knew exactly that he annoyed us, that something was going on we did not want him to know about. Children know that what their parents do in bed is embarrassing long before they know what they do."

.   .   .

According to Tahera's husband's brother's wife, "Last summer Tahera was pregnant. Her two little sons are very rude and unruly [fuzul]. My mother-in-law heard them curse somebody with very foul language. When she said, 'Dear, dear, such language is very impolite,' they cursed her, too, sitting on the roof safely. The old woman complained about it to Tahera. Tahera said she should mind her own business, and then some—she has a long, quick tongue. The old woman was hurt. In the evening, when her son, Tahera's husband, asked her why she was a sourpuss, she told him. Quick-tempered as he is, he tongue-lashed Tahera, who tongue-lashed right back, and so he got more furious and beat her up, and dragged her near her father's house, fetched him and her mother to watch him, and beat her more. It was a big fight. Tahera had a broken arm, two knocked-out teeth, a black eye, and a bump on her head. 'She always is mean when she is pregnant,' her husband said. He is right. And with every pregnancy she gets meaner still.'"

.   .   .

Nurensa's old mother-in-law said, "Nurensa is pleasant, a good wife, a little slow-witted. She doesn't pay attention. Some years ago, before we had the water pipeline, we had to do our wash at the irrigation channels. Although she was pregnant, she took her wash to the brook down the hill where 'they' [djenn] hang out. She was all alone, too. When she got back home she was shivering, rolling her eyes, and laughing without any reason. Wild rue fumigations did not help, nor did warm food or anything else we tried. We took her to the doctor but his medicines didn't work either. We took her to the Jewish amulet writers in Shiraz, who wrote several prayer amulets [da'a] for a lot of money. She got better, but the child died soon after birth. The djenn, the devil, had hit her at the brook. There is no cure for this."

.   .   .

Various people remember the cause of Golgol's miscarriage a few months after she had gotten married in 1985.

Golgol, in 1992, recalled, "I had a fright when I saw how my neighbor's six-year-old daughter was killed by a truck. The driver had delivered a load of sand at the neighbor's house. As he was backing out, he asked if the road was clear, but just then the little girl ran forward . . ."

Said Golgol's mother, in 1989, "Golgol was alone too much in her husband's house. One day a crazy old man who roams the area, all of a sudden, without politely coughing or shouting or knocking to announce his coming, jumped into the house, a big stick in his hand. She was scared, all alone, who wouldn't be . . ."

Maryam, Golgol's aunt, said in 1985, "Golgol was sitting at the water channel when a woman joined her, a woman with beads around her neck—she had a "child-stone" for sure. Right away, Golgol felt a pain in her abdomen . . ."

Golgol's husband's sister remembered in 1985, "An earthquake came . . . Mid-morning several women miscarried because the earth-quake frightened them."

A neighbor woman, who had been with her shortly before it happened, said in 1985, "A cat kept slinking around the house, crying like a woman in labor pains . . . It was one of "them," for sure, envious of Golgol's baby."

And Golgol's brother, in 1989: "Golgol probably lifted something heavy or carried something. For sure it was her fault. Women miscarry a lot in Deh Koh. Deh Koh women are weak."

.　　.　　.

The only truly scandalous pregnancy within the last twenty years happened in a neighboring village. It agitated people in Deh Koh as well. An unmarried girl of about sixteen got pregnant by a young man who, supported by his family, denied what to most people was obvious. Had he married her, the affair, although still grievously scandalous, would have been settled. But he refused to marry her. A highly regarded man in Deh Koh, distantly related to both families, summed up choices and efforts then: "We made the girl try everything: she drank medicine, jumped up and down, kneaded her stomach—nothing. It is as if God himself wanted this child. If it were not for the gendarmes, somebody would kill her for sure—a brother, a cousin. They have threatened to do so. One of the very pious people here, a rich man, a Haji,* offered the girl's father money to take her to Shiraz and abandon her there, to be rid of the problem. She would have become a prostitute! Such a heathen, a devil! This is not what our religion says. No, no. The young fellow has to marry her, he absolutely has to!" (He did, eventually.)

.　　.　　.

Leila, a very spirited mother of four children, spoke about why she is yawning in mid-morning: "It is the condoms. I keep them under lock and key with the medicines. Two nights ago—well—we needed one. He said, get one. But I couldn't find the key in the dark—it's such a tiny key! I looked everywhere. He was pretty mad. Yesterday I found the key, and he called me a scatterbrain and took it so as not to

---

*The honorific title for a person who has made the pilgrimage to Mecca (the *hajj*).

run into this problem again. And last night, well, we needed the key, but now he couldn't find it. He turned all his pockets inside out and trampled around the house. I split my side laughing. He stepped on one kid, then another. They all woke up, one needed to pee, the other wanted water, the third wanted to play . . . We didn't get our business done and didn't get enough sleep either. And he is looking for the key still!"

5 · Dreaming a Horseman

People say:

If a pregnant woman dreams of a horse or a rider, her child will be a boy. "I have seen enough riders for a cavalry regiment," said Mamalus, "yet I only have three sons!"

.   .   .

If a pregnant woman's belly stays small she is carrying a boy. Whereupon Peri made a pledge to make a pilgrimage to the shrine of Bibi Hakime for a healthy boy, but then her small belly released a healthy girl, confusing Peri as to whether she had to fulfill her pledge.

.   .   .

If the pregnant woman's "inside" felt cool and moist for the penis at the time of conception, the child will be a girl; if it feels dry and warm it will be a boy. But it is not easy to get a husband to report on this, women say.

.   .   .

A sickly, weak pregnant woman is likely to carry a girl, a strong and healthy one, a boy. "Lies, lies," said Afi, "because my sister . . ."

.   .   .

In any given time period, such as a few weeks, a few months, or a year, either more boys or more girls are born. Boys and girls come in bunches, women say, and sing this: "Just my bad luck: when it's a boys' year my belly is empty. When it's a girls' year my belly is big."

. . .

If a woman gives birth to a daughter during a month when many boys are born people say, "Too bad—she has bad fortune [*kamshans*]."

. . .

After the birth of a girl and after every menstrual period until the mother is pregnant again, the mother ought to eat *garmi*, food that is especially "warm" in the humoral sense, so that the next child will be a boy. "Ei, true enough," said Mehri, "but it doesn't always work."

. . .

Nosrat, asked by the doctor at the clinic why she had so many children, said: "One for the sheep, one for the cows, one for the wheat, one for firewood, one for the school to get a salary later, one for work in Kuwait to earn money so that his brother can go to school—and daughters are born in between anyway!"

. . .

When our neighbor's first child, a daughter, was born twenty years ago, nobody went to his place of work to let him know. He was very angry about it, reprimanded his mother, and remembers it to this day. A year later, his young wife bore a son; the old woman sent a grand-daughter to the new father right away, and he gave the messenger the customary gift for bringing such good news. "I am as happy about a daughter as I am about a son. But the old women are incorrigible," he said.

. . .

Of Asiye's son's ten children, the last five are boys. Said Asiye at the birth of her son's tenth child: "If my daughter-in-law had had girls, I would have called her names for having so many children— but boys, well, the more the better."

. . .

A woman said: "My cousin had a daughter, then a son who died within days. The third child was a girl again. Even before the umbilical cord was cut the attending women started to wail—*lak, lik*—as if somebody had died. The mother lost her voice. Since then, she is sitting around dumb, without life, cannot work either. The doctors cannot do anything for her. Now her husband wants to take another wife . . ."

·   ·   ·

Mariam fainted and had a very heavy blood flow that almost killed her after the midwife told her that her third child was yet another girl, said her sister.

·   ·   ·

A man's first child, a son, born prematurely, died. His second child, again born too early, was a daughter. But he took her to the hospital in the city right away; the baby was in the incubator for three months, and survived. Said a neighbor woman: "This is a good Muslim! All the expense for a daughter!"

·   ·   ·

Some people think the new mother of a daughter needs consoling. They may say, "It does not matter—a baby girl is better than a young dog"; or, "It doesn't matter, a daughter is good, too"; or, "A good daughter is better than a bad son"; or, "Cheer up, daughters are sweeter than sons."

·   ·   ·

I was asking why nobody was visiting a neighbor woman who had given birth a few days earlier. A twelve-year-old girl promptly said, "Because she had only a daughter!" Her mother then gave her a little speech about how the sex of a child should not make a difference for a good Muslim. The girl looked bewildered.

·   ·   ·

"My son learned to walk, my bread is secure," goes a proverb. Yet there are so many sons who don't take care of their old parents . . . and so many sons fight with each other over their father's land, people say.

. . .

A neighbor's third child was his third daughter. Everybody—his mother, father, brother, father's sister—sighed and looked sad. Nobody thanked the midwife, nobody volunteered to take her home in the middle of the night. "Scandalous!" said Leila. "And all of them educated people, too!"

. . .

A teacher had a new son, his second. He was so happy he slaughtered a ram, "Like the heathens do," said one of his colleagues.

. . .

Since 1992, following governmental propaganda for two-children families, rumors circulate that for any child after the third the government will not issue identification papers or rationing cards, will not allow it to attend school, will charge high tuition for school, will bar it from attending college, and will levy a special tax. By the end of 1994, I had found only one case in Deh Koh of such punishment (a higher than expected hospital bill for a delivery) but talk about these threats had intensified.

. . .

Said a policeman in his late twenties, "The government says after the third child it is over. But we say, 'What if these three are daughters? What then?!' There has to be a son or two, absolutely."

. . .

A grandmother, after she learned that her daughter-in-law had received a Norplant implant: "Too bad she is barring her road, with only two children." She used the term *bacce,* which usually is translated as "child"; the young woman had two sons but also two daughters.

. . .

Says one of the oldest women in Deh Koh: "We all say, 'Sons! Sons! The more sons the better!' I said it too and I say it still. Yet, where would I be without my daughters? Who would feed me, bathe me, visit me? Daughters have a warm heart for their parents, sons don't."

. . .

If a woman has had several sons in a row, she or her husband likely will make a pledge to a saint or will make a blood-sacrifice of a chicken or a lamb to ward off the potential ill effects of the evil eye and people's envious and admiring talk. If a woman has had several daughters in a row, Jahanperi said, "She'll make a hundred pledges for the next child to be a son!"

. . .

Of nine newborns in thirty-one folktales told in Deh Koh, four are girls; five, a pair of twins among them, are boys. Of the four girl-infants, one, with the help of fairies, grows into a prince-charming beauty; one, a sister to seven brothers, is a werewolf who kills her family; one, a sister to four brothers, is ordered killed by her father, who knows she is a werewolf; one is left to die by her father because she is a girl.

Of the five boy-infants, two, a pair of twins, later help to find their father's murderer; one, a pea-boy, the only survivor of a great many peas-turned-into-children whom the overwhelmed mother kills in despair, competently aids his father; one, born of a virgin, later exposes a promiscuous woman who then is executed; one, an illegitimate child, becomes a trickster-hero who kills his unchaste mother and brings death and disaster to many questionable people in his successful attempts to help his good uncle.

. . .

"The first two of my infant daughters died. Both were weak. I looked at them and thought, 'There is nothing but troubles ahead of girls; you are much better off dead.' I didn't nurse them. Now I have four sons and a daughter."

. . .

Asked if there are more boys or more girls in Deh Koh, most women say, "More girls." Then they quickly add that it does not matter.

. . .

Table 2

Male: Female Ratio of Young
Children in Deh Koh

Year	Age	Males	Females	Males : Females
1991	0–1	61	76	44.5 : 55.5
1994	1–4	320	303	51.4 : 48.6

Yet it probably does matter. Table 2 shows data gathered by local midwives and government census-takers. These figures must be approached with caution because they may contain errors owing to underreporting of boys or girls, for different reasons, and owing to a shift in the administrative boundaries of Deh Koh. However, the sex ratio figures fall within those reported for the whole tribal area in the official census published by the government. At best, they suggest the connection between gender schema as expressed in folk wisdom and anecdotes, and different survival chances for male and female children.

6 · Into the World

Birth

Women expect that forty days before birth a child in the womb turns around into the head-down position. Until a decade or so ago, if the child did not turn, the woman was made to lie on her back, feet propped up high against the wall, or else was swung back and forth in a blanket. If this failed, mother and child were said to be in danger of dying. Today, in such a case, the mother has the choice of a cesarean section at the county hospital. This is not an appealing choice, though; the maternity ward there is said to be literally and metaphorically dirty. As an alternative, the local midwife says she has turned "several" children manually over the past twenty years in mothers who did not respond to the swinging and leg-lifting.

A little hero (*pahlevan*) is born (*avord*, brought, or else *ve dunya iya*, comes into the world) nine months, nine days, nine hours, etc., after conception. A girl's birth is less predictable; roses (*gol*) stay fickle all their lives.

A woman in labor decides when it is time for somebody to fetch a midwife (*mama*). She likely will wait until her labor pains (*bad*) have become regular, and might not even let on earlier that she is in labor so as not to cause unnecessary commotion. Women helpers from the husband's and wife's close relatives congregate around the delivering woman under the leadership of the husband's mother, if possible. Men and children are kept out of the delivery room; men and older boys because "it is none of their business," younger children and girls because they are "underfoot." Except in emergencies, a delivery is the only occasion off-limits to all but adult women. Children learn about birth from listening to the commotion surrounding it, to comments, to birth stories. Because girls are more likely to be interested in these stories and to be around women more than are their brothers, they will learn more about birth than will the boys. Boys, however, are likely to hear more curses that involve their birth, usually from an infuriated mother: "If only you had died at my feet!" "If only Yal (a djenn) had taken you away!" "Woe to the midwife who cut your umbilical cord!" As it is with most other curses and scoldings, boys are unimpressed, but they learn from them the vocabulary of birth, the categories that structure birth.

People believe that labor pains are unavoidable in Deh Koh, in Iran, and in the Third World, but not in the West; they believe wealth and access to knowledge can reduce pain or prevent it altogether. Things being what they are in Deh Koh, however, birthing is a woman's inescapable pain. A woman in labor paces up and down the room clutching her sides, moaning and groaning, bending over double, screwing up her face, shrieking, snapping scissors, biting into her arm or a piece of wood, all to make her pain bearable. For children hovering nearby in the house, these noises mark a birth. "When they get a child women carry on like you would not believe," an eight-year-old boy informed me. "They show off." During the night before the last day of a wedding party, women in high spirits sometimes enact each others' birth performances. A woman will stuff a blanket into her skirt, clutch her sides, and start a gyrating, jumpy solo dance with shrieks and groans that bring down the house, until she "delivers" the blanket, "just as, by my soul, my sister did last year," or "my aunt always does." Another woman may feel challenged to better the mockery with her own pantomime of pain in an even raunchier performance of the first dancer's style of giving birth. In the past, such parties often got very noisy, with jokes about sex and some women cross-dressing and imitating men. In the more modest and very much quieter postrevolutionary times, the merrymaking at these occasions is subdued. Young, unmarried girls are not encouraged to attend these parties. They might have fallen asleep long before the performances start, but those who stay awake get two very strong messages along with the fun: they get a script for behavior during delivery, and they learn that the carryings-on of a delivering woman are exaggerated and laughable.

Saintly intervention elicited through invocations may lessen labor pains, women believe. Saint Mary is said to be especially sympathetic to delivering women because she gave birth to Jesus all alone in the wilderness. An unproblematic birth is proof of her efficacious intercession: one never knows how bad delivery might have been without her help. A woman may also try to lessen her labor pains by forgiving the divorce-settlement stipulated in the marriage contract. This is not regarded as a big comfort, though, if for no other reason than that it can only be done once.

Even if not much can be done to lessen labor pains effectively, by bearing them a delivering woman is forgiven all her sins. This popular notion is challenged by school children now who quote what they learn in religion class: only if a mother dies in childbirth are her sins forgiven, will she go straight to heaven like a soldier dying in Holy War. "Ha!" said a mother of four children, a skeptic, to this, "and how do mullahs know?"

Until 1975 in Deh Koh, and in many places in the area still, a woman delivered while squatting over a bed of fine sand in which a black and white bead on a blue-and-white string may have been buried to ward off djenn and the evil eye, and to make the child beautiful. The midwife and another woman helped to push or supported the delivering woman's back from behind. The child fell, literally, into the midwife's hand. Blood and afterbirth later were swept up with the sand and buried outside. The government midwives attending in Deh Koh since the early 1970s insist that a woman deliver the child onto a sheet of plastic over an old blanket or mattress on the floor while lying on her back, or else the doctor will scold them. "It is a mess now," says a former midwife. "Blood everywhere!"

The very moment the baby is born, two angels (*maleka*) are said to alight on its shoulders to keep a record of the new person's good and bad deeds throughout life, and to protect the child from harm. Many a child is rescued from injury and death when falling off a verandah, for example, by an angel who catches it in time, people say. The religiously founded notion of the score-keeping of sins starting at birth is at variance with another notion, though, which holds that young children are innocent, their misdeeds without sin until the children's intellect, and thereby ability for moral judgement, has developed. For the first few years of a child's life, people in Deh Koh feel that the angels are too busy watching over the child's physical welfare to keep track of childish pranks.

A newborn has to cry right away if it is to stay alive. The louder it cries the stronger and healthier it is taken to be. Newborns cry because they do not like to come into this world, women say; children like it much better inside their mother's belly than outside. A man who once offered the opinion that the child cries because it is sorry for not having come out earlier was snickered into silence by the women. A newborn's first utterance, thus, is taken to be a sign of vitality and dissatisfaction simultaneously.

As the midwife rubs down the newborn with a rag, she inspects it carefully for the workings of its limbs, the color of its skin, any unusual markings. If a child is born with teeth, somebody in the family will die soon. If a newborn has a birthmark, somebody will recite this rhyme: "A spot on the hand, you will go to Meshhed; a spot on the foot, you will go to Kerbela; a spot on the thigh, you will have honors and wealth; a spot on the solar plexus, you will die soon." If a newborn's lips, nails, or skin are discolored, or if the child has a big, black spot on the small of its back, people will take this as a sign that the child-stone (*mohre bacce*) had hit it in the womb, and that it will most likely die. Had there been a lunar eclipse while the mother was pregnant, a dark spot would be expected at the place on the baby's body that was closest to where the mother had touched her belly during the eclipse. Very good news, such as the birth of a healthy boy, is announced loudly to the outside and spread further to all the interested. Less good news, such as the birth of a healthy girl, is spread more slowly and quietly. Problems such as obvious birth defects leak out of the delivery room slowly; nobody wants to be the bearer of bad news. Older children usually are messengers of birth news.

A very weak newborn might be introduced to the mother with the wish, "Now that you have seen its face, may you not see its death." Otherwise, many *bismillah*s (in the name of God) and *mashallah*s (what God wills) will accompany the baby's first moments, especially if it is a boy, together with explicit wishes, such as, "May its parents' shadow never leave its head," or "May you have a good life."

The midwife ties and cuts the umbilical cord. This is regarded as so important that "to cut the cord" (*naf boridan*) is synonymous with "to deliver," and it bestows some authority on the midwife over the children she has delivered; years later she can remind them of her service to lend weight to an opinion or to a request.

If the afterbirth does not come, the government midwife will give injections, but the traditional massage of the abdomen reportedly was just as effective.

The care newborns ought to receive is the same for boys and girls. In the past in Deh Koh and in other places still, the grandmother or another woman immediately dipped a finger in cow dung and stuck it deep into the newborn's mouth. This was meant as an aid against the dangers of the child-stone, but also as a gesture of subjugation: years later, a misbehaving child might hear from an angry adult, "Has nobody put a finger in your throat when you were born?!" The dung was followed by a few drops of melted butter mixed with a particular herb (*ourishom*), and by sugar-water. Soot mixed with fat (*sirmei*) was put under the baby's eyes to "strengthen" them. In order to purge the child's blood from the impurities that eating the mother's blood in the womb had produced, incisions were made with a knife or a razor blade (*tikh, tikh zadan*) on various parts of the body. A baby was said to need such purging again whenever it cried a lot. Such bloodletting could be repeated every ten days until the child was three months and ten days old. Hurijan, who is about sixty years old, can show scars on her neck and shoulders she claims are from her baby days. She is convinced that a lot of babies' ailments today could be avoided or relieved by timely blood letting. Another old woman, however, has several scars on her calves, and feels sorry for her sufferings as a baby. "Damn all these superstitions [*khorafat*]!" she said. "Nobody knows how many babies they killed!"

Bloodletting no longer is done in Deh Koh, but the butter medicine and sugar still are a baby's "first taste of the world," women say.

The midwife or another woman swaddles the child and puts a cap on its head (*kolapit kardan*). Even opponents to the claim that a baby needs to be wrapped firmly to prevent crooked limbs insist that babies prefer to be swaddled; tightly wrapped babies are quieter and sleep better than babies who spend so much time moving their arms and legs in the air that they get cold, tired, and cranky.

The baby bundle is put on some rags or a blanket on the floor between the mother and the wall, or into a wall niche or some other convenient, marginal place in the delivery room; it is covered completely with a veil or a skirt or some piece of cloth, and seemingly ignored to fool the djenn into believing that no birth has happened. When I, visiting a new mother, asked the woman's little daughter where her new sister was, she looked around the room, puzzled, and then shrugged her shoulder. "My mother just had her in her lap. I don't know where she put her." As further precaution somebody may put a piece of iron—an iron tripod from the fireplace, for example— into the irrigation channel outside, because iron frightens away djenn who might happen to fetch water there, who otherwise might enter the house and steal the new mother's liver. A chicken liver may be nailed to the door for the djenn to take instead of the mother's.

The baby's face ("nose") should not be exposed at all until the umbilical cord has fallen off. After this has happened the infant is ready to be strapped onto the cradle (*takhte*) on an auspicious day— never on a Saturday, or else the child will be *vasveru*, a crybaby.

For the first child, the mother's mother or elder sister will prepare the necessary baby clothes and diaper-rags, or else the mother has to beg them from neighbors. For all following children, the mother is responsible for the clothes herself. Quite generally, the more children a woman has had the less fuss is made about her new birth, and the fewer women will be in attendance. A few women claim to have given birth by themselves, without any help. The traditional local midwives stayed with a new mother to do chores for her such as washing baby clothes, but the government midwife stays only for the birth itself. Some women are up and about the day after birth, others take weeks to get back on their feet, depending on their strength (*quve*, or *hal*, health, well-being). There is widespread belief that in earlier times women gave birth more easily than today, and that women of old were stronger, except, of course, those who died delivering. In contrast to earlier times, the government midwife in Deh Koh claims not to have lost a single mother under her care during twenty years of working in Deh Koh.

The more women attend a birth and keep a delivering woman company, the better protected the new mother is considered to be. The number of visitors over the first few days, the expenses the new mother's husband incurs for hosting the visitors, the amount of "noise," as people say, that is made around the event, stand in direct relationship to the sex of the newborn (more noise for boys, less or none for girls) and the social and financial standing of the new father and his people, but also reflect the birth order: the birth of a son after several daughters likely will be celebrated more lavishly than will the birth of the third daughter in a row, or even a third son in a row. About the party after the birth of his only brother, a five-year-old boy said, puzzled, and shaking his head, "They are making a big noise at home for a very, very, small baby. I don't know what has gotten into them."

With the government's aggressive antibirth propaganda since 1992, older, "enlightened" siblings of a new baby are likely to disapprove of the new birth loudly, especially in families aspiring to middle-class status and to *pishraft*, the getting-ahead attitude of development proclaimed necessary to catch up with the Western world economically. The government now blames, among other things, the high birth rate for Iran's Third World problems. "Our family will never amount to anything if mother keeps bringing new children," said a fourteen-year-old girl about her fifth sibling. The relative prosperity of one local family frequently is ascribed to its small size: "Only three children! No wonder they can afford to build a big house!" Behind his uncle's back, a sixteen-year-old boy commented on the birth of this uncle's second son, his sixth child, "Maybe now that he has two sons he will stop making more children—he is an embarrassment for the whole family." A young man, the eldest of seven children, looking at his new brother, gloomily commented, "I'll be a doddering old bachelor fellow by the time my father will get around to buying me a wife with all these to feed!" And a three-year-old boy had his own reason to protest his new sibling: "What, a girl?!" he yelled at his mother. "I said I want a brother—throw this one away and bring a boy!"

Birth Stories

The audience for all the following encounters and stories included several children.

Perijan, a mother and grandmother, talks about what her mother told her about her birth. "When I was born, most Deh Koh people took their herds to the valleys and hills around the village. In early spring they took them down toward the river. My mother was pregnant with me then. I was her eighth child, her last one. She went into labor on the migration. It was raining. She just stepped aside when she knew I was about to come, stayed behind with a couple of other women—a herd of sheep and goats cannot be stopped because of a birth! She delivered me in the rain—her sister held a veil over her like a roof—and cut the cord, and wrapped me up. An hour or so later she was on the road again. It was very cold and wet, but she kept me under her velvet jacket, warm and dry. In the evening the people pitched the tents. There was so much rain, water everywhere. My mother put me in a hammock-cradle to keep me off the wet ground. At night a puppy climbed in with me because it was freezing! Such a dirty, polluting animal—it probably kept me alive, though."

.   .   .

Mahin has just returned from the county hospital with her three-day-old son. It was her fourth birth; two daughters are alive, one son had died. The midwife had sent her to the hospital because the child was overdue and Mahin had a "weak back" and "pains in the side." This baby is the first clean, healthy, seemingly happy, well-sized infant I have seen in Deh Koh. His birth weight was a sensational 3700 grams (about eight pounds). Everybody is immensely pleased. There is a big party with a stream of visitors. Only Mahin's husband has a complaint: the hospital charged him 6000 Toman, the equivalent of his worker's wages for twelve days of work. The billing office informed him that as of October 1994 the hospital had to charge 500 Toman for the first, second, and third child, and 6000 Toman for the fourth, and more still for further children. He had been able to bargain them down to 1500 Toman.

The baby gets a bath every day, says Ziba, Mahin's mother-in-law, torn between bragging and disapproval. He lies next to his mother on her mattress on the floor, loosely wrapped in a clean blanket, arms and face free. "Three times a day Mahin changes all his clothes!" Ziba says, proud and yet scandalized. "We wash them, the two grand-mothers—that's what we are here for, aren't we?!" Mahin is taking stock in cleanliness alone: the baby has no beads, no black line under the eyes (*sirmei*), no amulets. Beads and amulets had not kept her first baby boy alive, Ziba explains. "Mahin thinks it is all superstition." She winks at me. "Mahin doesn't want to use the cradle either" (an-other wink; "We'll see about THAT," her eyes say). The women dis-cuss the advantages of cradles: no flies, no fleas, no dirt, much warmer . . . Mahin knows better than to argue. She keeps a huge, happy smile on her face.

Ziba's younger sister, a visitor, remembers: "Years ago I had to stay with Ziba after this new father here was born—day and night, a tiny little child myself. Nobody else was around—Ziba's husband was working in Kuwait, her mother-in-law was dead, our mother was with the animals in the mountains. Ziba didn't have enough milk. In the middle of the night she poked me: get up, warm some milk. I was so tired, I fell asleep holding the pot over the fire, until my hand burned and I dropped the pot. My big sister bawled me out and threw a log at me! And now look at Mahin sitting here for three days, clean, warm, a nice mother-in-law—*mashallah*, times have changed."

·   ·   ·

Ahmad, a middle-aged man, asked about news of a difficult birth in the next village where he had just visited, said: "The woman is all right now. The afterbirth did not come. The midwife sent for the doc-tor, but these young doctors—ei, they never had a baby, what do they know? He gave her an injection and serum, and he scolded every-body for the ax that they had tied around the umbilical cord, and the dirty floor, and the flies . . . He said she would bleed to death if he tried to take out the afterbirth by hand. She would have to go to the hospital. This was yesterday. But instead her people brought a wise old midwife from the village down by the river. She rubbed the woman's belly with a warm tea glass, round and round, from noon to sundown, they said. Then the afterbirth came, all is well. It was noth-ing, really."

.   .   .

Huri, a mother of five children, is talking with me about methods
to reduce labor pains: "What a big lie it is to say that labor pains will
be less if a woman forgives her divorce-money! God made the pain,
and He will know why, even if we don't, and only He and the saints
can help, saints like Saint Mary, like Saint Zeynab.* But even if it were
true, for a little less pain I am to give away my money? Never! They
may cheat other poor women with their talk, but not me."

.   .   .

Hurijan, an old local herbalist, is telling a room full of visitors
about djenn: "Many years ago I was helping out when my father's
sister delivered. The child was born, but the aunt, all of a sudden,
died; her soul [*jun*] had left, and her breath [*nafas*] was about to leave
her. Everybody was wailing. I went outside, crying. There I saw a
strange woman sitting at the irrigation channel, washing a liver. I
called her: 'Hei, you, what are you doing here?' She got up, quickly
turned around, ran toward the house, disappeared in the door, I after
her. At that moment my aunt came back to life . . . That's what they
do, those whose names are better not spoken . . ."

.   .   .

Hejab, a young mother, talks about her encounter with a djenn: "A
few days after my daughter here was born, I was all alone in the
house in the afternoon. However often I asked my sons to stay with
me, they didn't—ei, children! What can one expect! It was hot, I fell
asleep. I saw our old neighbor, who had died years ago, come in the
door with a log of firewood in his hand. He hit me over the head with
it. It hurt so much that I woke up with a start. Nobody was in the
room, but my head was aching on the right side for a long time. It
had been one of 'them,' surely; who else?"

.   .   .

Maryam, a young mother, her husband, and I are discussing *nasr*,
pledges other women have made for their newborn children. A
neighbor woman had promised a visit to the shrine of Bibi Hakime if

*Daughter of Ali and Fateme, granddaughter of Muhammad.

her son was born healthy. Had my hostess made any pledges for her children, I ask. "No," she says. "Pledges are of no use. If a child is born with only one leg, all the pledges in the world won't make another one grow. Pledges and amulets are all lies, swindles. My son told me that an amulet writer's son in his class, first year in high school, told the other boys he would write amulets for them—for money, of course—so that they would pass the tests. And then he himself flunked three subjects! And his name means 'True-word!' What a joke! All a swindle; well, almost all . . ."

. · ·

Sakine, a former midwife, is visiting a woman who had given birth the day before. The room is full of women and children. We are talking about the gold ring on the baby's cap and the blue bead on a safety pin on the swaddling clothes. Sakine explains: "Gold and the blue bead are very important, even today in the age of the doctors. Many women wear a gold bracelet, a ring—dangerous for babies! The evil eye is around, too—it is God's will. Only gold and the blue bead work against their power. Better safe than sorry!" Did the new mother worry about the child-stone, somebody asks. No, she says, her mother-in-law had told her that she had never used one, that none of her children were ever harmed by it, that therefore it was not in her "milk," that is, her children and the children's children, the new baby included, were not affected by it. Sakine disagrees: "You were just lucky," she says. "In Deh Koh people are considerate, nobody uses one; that's why you are safe. But the child-stone is a killer. It killed one of my own daughters. She was four, five days old, big, healthy, fat, nothing wrong with her. A neighbor woman came to cut her, to let the dirty blood out. The baby cried, *jig, jig, jig*. It was very bad. In the afternoon it turned black all over. The woman came back, took one look at her, and said that the child-stone had hit her, that she was as good as gone. By dusk she was dead. The stone on which the woman had sharpened the knife with which she had cut the baby happened to be a child-stone, for sure."

. · ·

After Behrokh's fourth birth, her second son, five women with eleven young children are visiting. Everybody is happy except Behrokh: "Four children in five years! It is so bad . . . I can't take care of them . . . I don't know what to do . . . Even my five-year-old says she is ashamed of me! I didn't want another child, not so soon after the third."

"Don't talk like this, girl!" says a visitor. "Be grateful that your daughter has a sister, every one of your children has a brother and a sister, thanks be to God." Behrokh smiles. "But now it is enough, I swear," she says. (But fifteen months later she had another baby.)

. . .

Sari was living in the city of Kerman for a year while her husband was working there. She is telling this story and similar ones to a large audience including about a dozen children who are all ears: "A woman in Kerman delivered a child. When the midwife wanted to dress and wrap it, it jumped away. Somebody caught it, but it jumped away again. It had four legs now and a dog's head! The mother for sure must have had committed a terrible sin for this to have happened.

"Another woman went to the garbage dump to empty her garbage pail. There she saw a wrapped-up bundle—it was a newborn baby. The woman thought, 'Dear me, this must be an unwanted girl which the father and mother threw away.' She pitied the baby, took it home, offered her breast. The child bit into the breast and did not let go of it. Somebody unwrapped the child—it was a dragon with the head of a baby! A doctor cut away the breast but the woman died."

A listener commented, "Goodness—in Deh Koh girl-babies at least are only this and not anything worse!" And a five-year-old girl pestered her mother to unwrap her baby to make sure it was not a snake or a dragon.

7 · Big Belly Dangers

The Cultural Context

However common and mundane pregnancy and birth are in Deh Koh, they are considered to be uncommonly fraught with dangers (*khatar*) for the mother and the child. Women scrutinize themselves, newborns, and each other for signs of problems and use a rich body of lore to interpret them. One cannot say what effects these feelings, prescriptions, and rituals have on a fetus, except that low birth weight, high infant mortality, and a high number of self-reported miscarriages suggest a low level of the kind of health and circumstances that favor uncomplicated pregnancies and good vital signs in newborns. Older children observing women and listening to their worries and counsels come to link the inevitability of pregnancies and babies with complaining mothers, with fuss and danger. Although pregnancy and babies rank unequivocally "good" on a good-bad scale, the goodness is tempered by expressions of worry, pain, and fatigue by the mother, which cloud life for her other children as well as provide the models for thinking about pregnancy and birth and for handling them.

Common sense attention is given foremost to the requirements and effects of a pregnant or nursing woman's humoral disposition, *mejaz*.

A woman with an especially cold (*sard*) disposition is likely not to conceive at all or to conceive a girl, people claim. A woman is well advised to spare no effort to prevent this, or at least to increase the likelihood of conceiving a boy, and to improve her health, which in turn makes conceiving a boy more likely. Certain foods, herbs, and potions are said to render her disposition warm (*garm*) and to strengthen her womb. The ingredients of these mixtures contribute their warm qualities cumulatively. Perijan's recipe for one such medicinal food, *majime*, includes walnuts, almonds, sesame seeds, dillseed, honey, and some herbs I cannot identify. For ten days after each period, a woman ought to eat a few tablespoons of it daily.

More powerful even is *celdava*, "fortymedicines," but I did not find anybody who could remember all forty ingredients. Forty is a portentous number. Women store various herbs and seeds and spices in bottles and bags and bundles hanging from nails or stuffed in a storage space. "My grandmother is a pharmacist," a fifteen-year-old boy mocked the old woman's big bundle of herbs.

Abijan, after bearing six daughters (two of whom died in their first year), was implored by her mother and mother-in-law to use a dietary preventive, at least to eat halva, which is very "warm." She did not, and her seventh child again was a girl, proving the old women right. If a woman pregnant with a girl eats humorally cold food such as pomegranates or oranges, she will cool her already cold humoral state, and her body might swell, her bones ache; she might even become strange in the head. Troubled, quiet Parvane, who lives with her old parents because she cannot take care of herself, is this way because she got cold-sick after she ate a whole bag of pomegranates when she was pregnant the first time, her mother sometimes says. The cold went to her head.

Not much harm is done if a woman who is pregnant with a boy eats "warm" food, making her own disposition warmer yet. She might get an itchy rash, for example, or a swollen face, which she can cure easily by drinking a glass of lemonade or eating a cucumber.

In line with local dietary theory and in line with the orders of local physicians, most of whom subscribe to the same humoral model, a delivering woman or new mother must not eat or drink food that is cold and damp in the humoral sense, such as rice or tea, because she might get ill from it, and her baby might get crampy and achy and develop a cough. The ideal food for pregnant and lactating women is said to be lamb kebab and chicken kebab, and "warm" foods made of walnuts, butterfat, eggs, and other expensive ingredients. No woman in Deh Koh can count on getting such a costly diet.

Pregnancy and birth put a woman in a heightened state of vulnerability to harmful, extra-human powers innate in several kinds of djenn, the evil eye, certain rocks, minerals, plants, odors, and more. Uncontrolled contact with these powers may lead to miscarriage, ill health, or death of a mother and her child. Although today people do not seem to be overly anxious about these dangers, they are discussed, and children see women take precautions. They learn that it is a mother's responsibility to beware of them.

The most potent of these powers are djenn. In different contexts, djenn are equated with *peri* (fairy) and *sheitun* (devil). Regarding pregnant women and infants, they mostly are referred to simply as "they" (*ingelo*); it is considered dangerous to talk or even think of djenn by name because they might take it as a summons. The unbelievers (*kafir*) among them are malevolent. "They" inhabit an invisible world created by God, which is parallel to our human world. Usually invisible, they may on occasion appear in the form of people or animals such as cats or mountain goats. If angered, but sometimes without obvious reason, they may hit (*zadan*) a pregnant woman, causing her to miscarry, to become sick, to be in pain, or to become deranged. Especially from dusk to dawn, they are said to linger around certain places: the building where the dead are washed; near flowing water, especially near a certain brook south of Deh Koh; in trees, near grave-yards, in abandoned buildings, bathhouses, outhouses, barns, and at the traditional fireplaces. Any woman, but especially a pregnant one and a new mother, obviously ought to avoid these places. But what, women say, is one to do with loads of wash, with children to be bathed, a cow to be fed and milked? Thus, a pregnant woman is in a bind: she ought to avoid djenn-places but also ought to do her duties, which take her to such places. Rich women have it easier; djenn are said to avoid modern fixtures like indoor toilets and modern kitchens. A rich woman who has a washing machine, indoor plumbing, and no barn duties does not need to worry much about djenn. For this reason and others, rich city people are safer and healthier than are poor vil-lagers, adults and children say in Deh Koh.

In the delivery room, djenn are said to be after the mother's liver (*jigar*). They are also jealous of the baby, especially during the first ten, or better, forty, days; they might steal the baby or exchange it for their own, sickly one. A baby indicates that it might be a changeling by fussiness, weakness, or lack of growth. In earlier days, to probe this possibility, the baby's weight might have been balanced with salt. This was said to kill a changeling. Now, people say, it is enough to give the baby's weight in salt away to the poor to prompt the djenn to return the real child. Leaving a baby who is suspected of being a djenn's child alone in the outhouse or the bath for a while is another option; people expect that the djenn-mother will have pity with her exposed infant and exchange it back for the human child. Actual changeling stories are rare. But such deliberations are discussed in front of children and thus become part of the world in which they place themselves, the infants around them, and, later, their own chil-dren. At the very least, children translate the djenn message into feel-ing uneasy or even fearful alone around bathhouses and outhouses.

A new mother and her infant should not be left alone at all; the mother should avoid the fireplace, the barns; she should not pour ashes and water outside, especially not hot ashes and hot water, be-cause these unintentionally may hurt a djenn or, worse, a djenn's child, which will prompt the djenn to retaliate. All discarding of wa-ter and ash is to be preceded by murmuring a precautionary *"bis-

millah," which drives away the djenn. This is done routinely, even by young children. Likewise, wearing an iron bracelet or a salt crystal will drive away djenn and is accomplished easily. A hair of a wolf, the teeth of a mountain tiger, a piece of iron, a Qoran placed close to the baby, will protect it from curious djenn. None of these measures are entirely safe, though. Pregnant women and new mothers have to be on guard because djenn may take advantage of any little breach in precautions. During a visit, I found my hostess worriedly rummaging through bundles to find a spare iron bangle to replace the small piece of iron one of her older children had ripped off the new baby's pillow and promptly lost. A neighbor finally lent her an amulet of several anti-djenn items to tide her over the lapse in protection.

Of all djenn, the one who keeps closest to a person is his/her *homza*, a person's djenn-twin, born at the same time. The djenn-twin might trouble a pregnant woman out of jealousy. A mother of six children in our neighborhood said that her djenn-twin was angered by her marriage and made her miscarry twice. A woman cannot do much to keep a djenn-twin at bay, though.

As modern appliances replace old technologies, many traditional djenn danger spots are disappearing from consciousness. Zahra, age ten, like most girls her age has never heard that sitting next to a fire-place may be dangerous for a woman. For her, the fireplace in an old house still is a place of relative honor and therefore appropriate for men, but the lore that rationalizes and mystifies women's exclusion from that high-status space has disappeared.

Deadly but rare is the child-stone or child-bead (*mohre bacce*), a smooth, reddish to black pebble with a hole through it for a string. A sickly infant who dies despite all efforts is taken to have been killed by some woman's hidden child-stone. This danger can only be avoided if the mother carries one on herself, but thereby she is endangering others. It therefore is considered "heathen" in Deh Koh, very sinful, not to warn others if one is carrying a child-stone. One woman entered the public bathhouse in the next village, saw her pregnant cousin sitting there, said, "Oh dear, had I known you are here I would have left 'the bead' at home." The cousin miscarried "right then and there," she said.

Deh Koh women pride themselves on not using the child-stone anymore, although the belief in its efficacy is very much alive, as is the belief in another substance with similar properties, a weed (*alaf beoui).* Because of these dangers, pregnant women and new mothers are wise to stay at home, to avoid places where many women gather, such as wedding parties or doctors' offices.

The evil eye (*tië shur, nazar*) too is best prevented by avoiding exposure to anybody's admiring looks, and by carrying an amulet, a salt crystal, or a blue bead,* all of which are said to deflect or absorb a dangerous gaze. Danger from the evil eye is not confined to women around childbirth, though, but may strike anybody and anything. As an admiring glance or remark by a person who has the evil eye will make an infant seriously ill, no considerate person will comment positively on an infant or a child without precaution, just to be on the safe side, and no mother in her right mind will show off her infant unless it is heavily protected against the evil eye.

The danger from "forty days" (*celle*) is easier to avoid. A pregnant woman is not to visit a new mother until forty days after birth, or else the new mother's "forty days might fall" on her, causing her to miscarry. Likewise, somebody's forty days after a birth or a death may "fall" on a newborn and make it sick. Two new mothers of infants younger than forty days ought to avoid meeting each other for that reason. If a corpse is carried by a new mother's house, somebody has to lift up the baby to prevent the dead's *celle* from harming it.

Anything with a strong odor (*bu*), from perfume to food, from the smell of a baby to the reek of an outhouse, but also the lingering figurative odor of an illness or a medication, may hurt an unborn and a newborn child. Guarding against it is sheer impossibility—the world is full of smells. It is wise not to take an infant out among people and their various odors. A pregnant woman who smells somebody else's cooking ought to eat some of the food so as to prevent her child from being born with light eyes (*souz*, green, green-blue) that might carry the evil eye. Occasionally, pregnant women of low esteem are said to walk around their neighbors' houses on purpose so as to get fed without having to lift a finger.

Fright (*houl, tars*) is not easily controlled by a pregnant or lactating woman either. Any sudden, unexpected happening can cause a woman "to make fright" (*houl kardan* is an active verb: she is doing the fright). It is an ever-present danger; a loud noise, a child falling off a verandah, the sudden wailing of women lamenting a death, bad news, all

---

*Turquoise-colored ceramic beads of various shapes, said to ward off the evil eye.

can cause a woman to shiver, faint, get a severe headache, lose her tongue, get heart palpitations, and miscarry or lose her milk. The stronger and healthier a woman, people say, the less severely will she be bothered by a fright. Few pregnant women and new mothers are strong and healthy, though. Formerly, a particular bead (*mohre tars*) was used to prevent fright, but beads have all but gone out of style and use in Deh Koh. Eating some humorally very warm food such as halva made with walnuts and clarified butter, or eggs fried in butter, or at least dates, will offset some of the ill effects of a fright, as will a drink of water in which a piece of gold, such as a ring, has been put. But such procedures have to be administered immediately after the fright—a spooked woman is not likely to muster the wit and energy for it herself.

Gold (*tala*) and amber beads (*mohre zardiun*) are said to carry the danger of jaundice for an infant for up to three months after birth unless a piece of gold or an amber bead is kept near the cradle. The yellow color provides the analogy to jaundice.

Wheat flour, meat, or a gun, all high-status male items, may "strike" an unprotected infant; their innate power will make the child ill. To prevent this, somebody ought to lift the child up when such items are brought into the house, murmuring the charm-verse, "Don't you strike so that I won't strike you."

Fatigue (*khastegi*) makes infants yawn excessively and give signs of being unwell. To prevent this, a tired person, such as a man coming home from work or a traveler, ought to rest outside the house a little before entering to prevent the transfer of his/her exhaustion onto the infant. A date-pit near the baby is said to further protect against this danger.

Infants and their mothers are said to catch cold (*sarma, ceimun*) easily. Even warm water and warm air may make a child "eat cold" (*sarma khordan*), which quickly can lead to more serious health problems. The mother's womb is very vulnerable to a special kind of cold (*sim keshidan*), especially if she has to do the family wash. Women with many children are likely to complain about womb ailments because they cannot avoid washing clothes in cold water every day.

Older children are drawn into the common-sense system of danger and of caring for newborns by explanations adults give for their actions, and by scores of commands ("Leave baby's bangles alone!"); prohibitions ("Make sure your pregnant mother doesn't eat these oranges"); precautions (amulets pinned to a baby's clothes); rituals (burning wild rue after a birth); exclamations (*"mashallah," "bismillah"*); curses ("If only a djenn had taken you when you were born!"); terms of endearment (*"junom, rudom,* my soul"); lamentations ("I am so tired, my bones ache, nobody is here to help me"); expectations ("I'll get my little sister to stay with me so I won't be alone at night while my husband is gone"); requests ("Take this bowl with halva to your pregnant mother"); admonitions ("Stay outside—you are hot and tired; this isn't good for the new baby"); teases ("We have too many children—should we give the new baby away or you?"); comments ("Another baby girl, poor mother"); whispers ("She miscarried again, last night); and the hundreds of little remarks and actions in which the reproduction of children is framed and which are the vehicle for the reproduction of the birth culture in the next generation.

The Affective Context of Danger

According to my own observations and to various health clinic physicians I have met over the years since the first health clinic was established near Deh Koh in 1965, women in Deh Koh suffer from anemia, avitaminoses (especially of vitamin B-complex), nutritional deficiencies (protein, calcium, zinc, iron), and infections (intestinal parasites including giardiasis; sinusitis; vaginal infections; and severe colds and respiratory infections). Domestic physical violence is common, including against pregnant or nursing women. Given their ill health and few resources, women have too many pregnancies, spaced too closely together. Marriage age, and with it age at first pregnancy, is in the midteens (rising slowly) with all the medical problems it entails for mother and child. The rate of miscarriages is high, birth weight is low, newborns are weak. "Women and their babies in Deh Koh are very unhealthy," said a woman physician who practiced in the area in 1994. "From a medical point of view, pregnancies in the whole area ought to be treated as health crises."

These factors and the experiences they structure determine the affective frame of pregnancies and birth in Deh Koh. Women present themselves as "sick," and their babies as tentative, as to be pitied. Individual women who are strong and healthy and who have uncomplicated pregnancies and healthy, vital children are the exception as far as women's cognition is concerned.

In addition, women tend to be anxious and depressed. In 1992, the local physician said there was "hardly a woman" in the village who had not been at one time or another on pain medication, tranquilizers, or antidepressants for nonfunctional aches and pains, fatigue, excessive worrying. Frequently, women causally link the onset of their own particular "nervous weakness," as they say, including a case of epilepsy and at least two cases of severe depressive psychosis, to an early or a traumatic pregnancy or birth.

Even women who are relatively healthy—and there are more healthy women now than twenty years ago—and live in relatively peaceful households still complain. At best, pregnancy is a burden with a temporal limit. Most pregnant women and especially those who already have children, have to keep performing their routine duties with little help from others and no special dietary or other allowances for their condition. For some, these duties are light, much lighter than they were for their own mothers; women's work in animal husbandry ceased for most women when husbands got out of this increasingly unprofitable enterprise. Modern household technologies reduce the heavy labor previously required for cooking, washing, and heating. Most women nevertheless have to spend long hours bending, hauling, lifting, climbing, carrying as always, and they resent it; they point out readily that their pains and their efforts in bearing children are not for their own benefit but are a service rendered to their husbands, who do not give them the recognition they deserve for their toils and troubles.

Judging by their complaints, pregnant women rarely are comfortable and contented. Complaints are voiced not just to me or a physician, but are the background noise to small talk among the women themselves. The world, they say in ever so many words, directly and in metaphors, is a hard place for most everybody, and certainly so for them.

Philosophically, pregnancy and birth are intrinsic to God's order in *this* world. In heaven, men still have sex but nobody gets pregnant, women point out, but here pregnancy and birth are a norm, expectable and expected, a desirable confirmation of God's plan, needing no further explanation. Pregnancy is *khub*, good, it is said, it is what ought to be. Barrenness needs to be explained, not fertility. Pregnancy is unavoidable, unless one makes special, sustained efforts. Yet, for all its normalcy and essential goodness, bearing children extolls a heavy price from the mother, and from her alone: discomfort and pain at best, death a distant, but real, worst possibility. Suicide and death related to the reproductive process are the leading causes of death of young women in Deh Koh. The long-range benefits of reproduction, however, are claimed by the father or, in case of a daughter, by another family altogether. This conflict easily produces resentment—a resentment of what is presented as God's order, a forbidden resentment.

No other time in a woman's life is taken to be so fraught with dangers as the time of pregnancy and birth. Dealing with dangers is a mother's responsibility; the wiser, more circumspect, more knowledgable, stronger, and industrious a woman is, the more likely will she conceive a boy and the better off her children will be. Any potential harm to a new child may be attributed to a mother's negligence, lack of knowledge, laziness, or stubborn disregard of the counsel of older women. Although it would be a vast exaggeration to say that women lose much sleep over these responsibilities or see themselves as inadequate to the task of being mothers, they are well aware, and resentful, of this line of demands.

A woman who has borne several daughters but no or only one son is anxious about the next pregnancy, especially so as the sex of the child may be seen as the result of her own humoral disposition by others. Mothers of several daughters ascribe the sex of a child to the will of God rather than to humoral disposition or similar factors. They claim that the sex of the child makes no difference to them personally, that they even prefer daughters over sons because daughters are "sweeter" and are a mother's closest companions, but that husbands and husbands' parents want boys to enlarge their own families, thereby inconveniencing, "killing" their wives and daughters-in-law.

The emotional baggage women carry in relationship to their husbands and his natal family thus is projected onto pregnancy and birth: women provide children and labor primarily to further the husband's family's interests; children are his children, legally and customarily. Not surprisingly, older pregnant women with sons, who are well established vis-à-vis their husbands and in-laws, whose parents-in-law are feeble or dead, who have substantial help from growing daughters, may express embarrassment over a new pregnancy and the sexual activity it implies, but complain much less about ill health and the woes of life than they did during pregnancies when they were younger. Yet they watch their own sons' wives' bellies and babies with as much proprietary interest as their own mothers-in-law did—and were cursed for—twenty years earlier. A mother indentifies with her sons' interests; she will judge her sons' wives by their ability and willingness to supply him with adequate services, including children.

Pregnancy, birth, and children thus are located in the field of emotions and behaviors that are functions of interfamily politics and power negotiations shifting in the course of the life cycle of parents and relatives.

Relief and satisfaction over a newborn's sex, health, beauty; quiet joy over a "sweet" daughter; loud joy and pride over a son are mixed with anxiety over yet another daughter, one too many children, resentment of demands, criticism, pain, increase in workload and responsibility. Both sides of this ambiguity are communicated to children verbally and through the care and attention they receive not just from the mother but from everybody in the community.

8 · Named Lion, Named Rose

The pool of personal names in Deh Koh includes about 190 male and slightly fewer female ones. Among them are old-fashioned ones no longer used for naming new children, as well as trendy, urban names a father or elder sibling brings home from the city or reads in a book. The names cover a large semantic field, with many political and emotional connotations that point boys and girls cognitively in very different directions. Some of the names are so loaded that parents or older children change them as political or cultural circumstances change.

The traditional farming-pastoral lifestyle of Deh Koh is reflected in a long list of male names such as Ghucali (Ram-Ali), Gorgali (Wolf-Ali), Keshavars (Farmer), Shirkhan (Lion-Khan), Baruni (Rain-born), Kohzad (Mountain-born). A name of this sort alludes to a little boy's future economic duties and the desirable qualities of strength and agility necessary to fulfill them. To make it in the mountains, they suggest, one better have the powers of a ram, wolf, or lion. In folksongs these animals metaphorically stand for men.

Traditional names for women do not refer to women's labor, strength, or societal input, although women had to work hard and skillfully at a young age. Instead they allude to beauty and nobility of bearing: Siminrokh (Silverface), Javaher (Jewel), Golbibi, Bigol, Golbanu (Roselady—I counted some twenty-five names that are "rose" or "blossom" compounds), Perijan (Fairy-soul), Houri, Parvane (Butterfly), Hejab (Modesty).

Such traditional names are considered old-fashioned now and no longer are popular for naming new children. Recently, a young man who did not like his fiancée's old-fashioned name wanted to change Mahrokh (Moonface) to the modern urban name Ladan (Nasturtium), but the registrar refused this non-Muslim name. Now some people call the young woman Ladan, some Mahrokh. She does not voice a preference.

Similarly old-fashioned is another group of names, reflecting a remarkable circumstance of the baby's birth or the father's attitude toward the newborn he is naming: Bemunali (Stay-Ali), for example, was given to a boy born after several siblings who had died; Shukrallah (Thanks-be-to-God) may mean, "Thanks, but we have enough children now!"; Rastegu (Truth-Speaker); Khodanazar (God-behold). In the tribal camps and in the small hamlets around Deh Koh, such names are common still. Several names of this kind, like Lazy-one, Beggar-schlemiehl, occur also in popular folktales. In Deh Koh, few such names were created for girls.

The most unusual name in the area around Deh Koh is Fereshtebordebi, "Angel-who-had-been-stolen." About fifteen years ago, people say, a woman was walking to another village. Her little daughter, Fereshte, "Angel," ran after her but arrived neither there nor back at home. All the villagers turned out to look for her, beating canisters with sticks and shouting, all night long. At that time, two men happened to be searching for a lost donkey in the mountains. In a high pasture they came upon a strange wedding party. They heard a little girl cry. When they said, "*Bismillah*," the party took off into the air, taking the little girl, who was Fereshte, with them. The djenn—for this is what they were—dropped her. She was unharmed but cried for her "father and mother," the djenn. At home she ate nothing but milk-rice without getting full, and otherwise acted strangely, too. It took several prayer-amulets and many months of care before she was herself again. The name, though, stuck.

A third group of names reflects Muslim piety. "Ali," the name of the Prophet's cousin and son-in-law, whom Shiite Muslims recognize as Muhammad's legitimate political successor, and "Allah," God, are often combined with local terms: Wolf-Ali, God-wanted. Other pious names are purely Arabic: Ruh-Allah, Habib-Allah. No such names were constructed for women. Names of Qoranic and other religious notables such as Hosein, Hasan, Loqman, Reza, and Muhammad are popular for men, as are their female counterparts such as Zeynab, Maryam, Fateme,* and Hava (Eve) for women. This is one category of names equally accessible to men and women. Their popularity has risen in the Islamic Republic to the point where little Amins and Zahras jokingly are numbered by teachers to tell them apart in classrooms. One little Zahra, playing with another one, declared, "I am our own Zahra, and this Zahra belongs to somebody else." For four-year-old Amin, all boys are "Amin" until proven otherwise; announcing the birth of a cousin, he said, "Aunt Maryam just got an Amin."

The Persian heroic past recounted in the epic, Shahname, provides a slate of names for both boys and girls, such as Khosrow, Farhad, Eskandar, and Bahram for men, and Rudabe, Shirin, Simdokht, and Behjad for women. Toward the end of the Pahlavi years, these names, together with names of the Shah's family, took on the additional meaning of regime support. People who had named their children after the legendary heroes Kavus or Shahrokh, for example, or Farah or Ashraf after the Shah's wife and sister, found the names a political embarrassment a few years later, and even changed them. In the Islamic Republic such names, if given to a newborn, are likely to express veiled protest against the government. They are political statements and, as such, often rejected by officials in charge of furnishing birth certificates and identification documents.

Today, Arabic-Qoranic names are most popular for newborns in Deh Koh. They project the safe image of a family dedicated to Islam and the regime. They cause no raised eyebrows with government officials. "'Maryam' is much easier to carry than is 'Rose-Rose,'" a new mother who counted four new Maryams among close relatives said in 1994. The only competition for popularity these names have in Deh Koh today comes from the urban culture. There, 17 years into the

---

*The Prophet Muhammad's only daughter, wife of Ali, and mother of Hasan, Hosein, and Zeynab.

revolution, a wider choice of names has become acceptable: "chic" names of Iranian and Arabic origin such as Behzad, Fardin, Eshaq, Hadi, and Mohsen for men; Nasrin, Parvin, Soheila, and Forugh for women; and, for women, names of specific flowers that are unnamed in Deh Koh or do not even grow locally, such as Lale (Tulip) or Nastaran (Sweetbriar). These are seen as neutral, neither Pahlavi-regime oriented nor embarrassingly backwoodsy, and not obviously *hezbollahi* (Party of God, i.e., fervently pro–Islamic Republic) either. Our newborn future teacher, parents say, better be called Mahmud or Keyvan rather than Worker, Shah-Lover, Sun, or Ruhallah, the politically trendy name of Ayatollah Khomeini, to save him embarrassment later. Children thus are tied by their names to their parents' political fields and to the fashion of the day in the popular national culture.

One man called his third son, born before the revolution, by a name he had heard in town. When the young people in his family told him it was a girl's name, he changed it to Farokh, the name of a legendary king. After the revolution, concerned with cultivating a pro-revolutionary image, he wanted to change it to Mahmud, one of Ayatollah Khomeini's names. But Farokh, fourteen then, made rude fun of the idea, and his mother even got angry. "We'd have a lot to do if we wanted to change names with the regimes!" she said. Farokh is Farokh still. When Flower-face applied for the university, her father changed her rural, old fashioned name to Zahra, which would fit better her new, urban, modern status. Her cousin Soheila is happy that her own parents had had the good sense to give her a "chic, beautiful" name sixteen years ago.

Rules of Naming

Customarily, a father selects the name for his child. Rarely does a mother as much as voice a preference for a name, especially for a first- or second-born. The lower a child is in the birth order, the more likely the mother or an elder sibling will suggest names.

Five days after she was born, one baby still didn't have a name because her father had not gotten around to looking one up in the Qoran. Her mother called her "Teeny-bits" because she was so tiny and weak. A young teacher named her children, who were born during their father's long absences, Ali and Fariba. Ali is the name of the Prophet's beloved and loyal cousin and son-in-law; Fariba has no religious connotation. The mother explained, in front of the children:

"Fariba first has to grow up and demonstrate by her behavior that she is worthy of a good name such as Maryam or Fateme." Ali, she said, got his "good" name so he would be as good as Ali was.

A name may be chosen from a religious book or may reflect the day or circumstances of the child's birth or the personal preference of the father or name-giver. Sahir was born at the time of *sahir*, the breaking of the fast in the evenings in Ramadan, the month of fasting. She is the only person with this name in Deh Koh. A month before Fateme was born in 1972, long before the revolution, her father saw her in a dream and knew that people were calling her Fateme. He took it as an omen and a suggestion that this name would be "good" for her. At that time there were only two other Fatemes in the village. A young bride from Deh Koh was taken to Imam Reza's shrine in Meshhed by her husband. There a woman predicted that her first child would be a girl, and recommended that she be named Najame after Imam Reza's mother. When the first child indeed was a girl, the mother insisted on this—in Deh Koh unusual—name. Another little girl's modern flower-name was chosen by her seventeen-year-old brother "in protest of bigotry," he said.

The name a child gets should be "free," that is, no close living relative should have it. In modern Deh Koh, this rule is almost impossible to follow because too many people are interrelated. A grandmother counted three Zahras among her thirty-two grandchildren in 1994. Naming a child after a dead relative not only is permitted but is said to honor the dead person. Lionkhan was named after a dead grandfather. He loathed the name. When his father wanted to open a bank account in his name in town the banker said that Lionkhan was not a proper name. The boy was very happy about it and chose Mansur, a name of Arabic origin and not dated.

A name has to "stick" with a child to be permanent; it has to agree with the child as shown by the baby's good development, by everybody using the name, by the baby's proper response to the name. Names that do not "fit" can, should, even, be changed. The name a man gave his first son turned out to be used already by a distant relative. The father changed it when the child was about one month old. The name he had given the second child he changed after two months when he read a "better" one in a math problem in a schoolbook. The third child's name was not permitted by the old regime's registrar because it "cheapened" the shah. Thus, a different name was entered on the birth certificate, but the old name "stuck" to the child and remained the name by which it was addressed. When the fourth child was born, after the revolution, the rejected name was permitted. It became the new baby's official name on the birth certificate, while he is called by his elder brother's registered name. The fifth child's name "stuck" although it is not religious and although a close relative used it at the same time. "I am tired of worrying about names," said the father.

When little Hematallah, born before the revolution, was not doing well and had many health problems, his father changed his old-fashioned name to the heroic Farhad, that is, changed a religious one to a royalist-nationalist one. The boy "did well from then on," says his mother.

A father gave his little daughter the very chic, urban name Mozhgan. But the baby was sickly, small, weak. When she was a year old she could hardly sit. Everybody expected her to die—her father even suggested that her mother let Mozhgan die; they would make another, better child, he said. From several signs the mother came to suspect that the baby was a changeling, a djenn's child substituted for her own when she had been left alone for a moment sometime soon after birth. An amulet-writer in Deh Koh wrote three prayer-amulets. (One to burn under the cradle; one to cover with beeswax, put in water, and then wash the child with the water; the third to be sewn into a piece of fabric and hung around the baby's neck until the string broke.) He also suggested changing her name to Masume Zahra, a religious one. Since then, as Masume Zahra, she has been doing well, and her parents like her very much; obviously, they say, the djenn had exchanged the sickly child for their real, well child again.

The name of a dead sibling may be given to the next-born, together with the dead child's birth certificate. Some children thus are younger than their documents show them to be.

If a government official issuing an identification document disagrees with the name, for example on grounds that it is not "Muslim," a child may end up with two names: one in the document, another used for address. Similarly, if an older child is dissatisfied with his or her name, the name can be changed easily.

In the teacher training college in Isfahan, Mehrvafa's classmates and teachers teased her. "Mehr-what?" they said. She got tired of her unusual, old-fashioned name and called herself "Zahra." Ashraf, a devout young *hezbollahi* high school student named, embarrassingly, she thinks, after the former Shah's sister, would much rather be called Fateme like the Prophet's daughter but her father will not permit the name change.

Says another young woman, "So many children dislike their names that I will call mine 'First Son' and 'Second Daughter' and so on, and let them decide on their names themselves later."

Most of the more popular names have two or three syllables. Longer names may be shortened in address (e.g., Aziz for Azizallah), but rarely is a name reduced to a diminutive, except for very young children: Mitra was Mimi for three years; Fateme was Fati as a toddler. Terms of endearment are *"rud," "jun,"* or the name suffixed with -*jun*, such as "Fatemejun" or "Alijun." Mothers often address their very young infant simply as *duar* (girl, daughter) or *kurr* (boy, son) or *aghlu* (baby).

9 · A Little One on My Cradle

The cradle, *takhte* (which also means board, platform, bed), is made ready after the baby is born. To prepare one ahead of time vaguely is seen as unhealthy for the child, an unintended invitation for djenn to linger. The traditional wooden cradle is made locally by carpenters. A shallow rectangular box rests on four legs, which are paired on two runners at the head and foot of the cradle box. Two strips of wood are bent across the top of the box from one side to the other, like bows, and are connected lengthwise at the highest point, some forty centimeters above the box, by a wooden rod. This serves as a handle to carry the cradle with, and together with the two bows provides support for a veil-wrap or a blanket to keep out flies and cold. Another thin bow with a small radius may be placed just over the infant's head to allow the covering to be brought closer to the body. If nothing else, infants learn in the cradle to exist long hours with little oxygen; as older children and adults they will be able to sleep, face covered by heavy blankets, through the night without any signs of discomfort.

A mattress, a sack filled with straw, chicken feathers, or a piece of foam rubber, fills the box. It is covered with a sheet of plastic and with diaper-rags. The baby, dressed in shirt and cap, is put on it on its back, rags are folded over it, and then it is tied to the cradle firmly with wide bands from the neck to the feet. This is the baby's sleeping position. The cradle can be carried from one place to another, as need be. It never leaves the house, though, unless the mother takes it to the summer pasture. In former times, on migrations, women carried the heavy cradles on their backs with the babies strapped onto them, or else cradle and baby were fastened atop a donkey's or mule's load. Very few women in Deh Koh still migrate to summer and winter pastures.

A baby may be strapped onto the cradle for many hours even while it is awake. Its field of vision is free of bed boards or other boundaries unless it is covered by a blanket, but movement is limited to the head. Expressions of feelings are thwarted, except through voice, movement of the head, and straining at the bindings. Yet, despite these confinements, or maybe because of them, children like the cradle as a place of security and comfort. One of a cranky toddler's options to deal with discontent is to crawl to the cradle and hug it or to demand to be strapped onto it.

Amulet-charms and beads hanging from the top rod serve as a focus for infants' eyes, as protection against dangerous extrahuman forces, and as play-objects for older babies whose arms may be left unbound. It is taken as a good sign of health and proper development if a baby plays with these things.

Infants are taken off the cradle for nursing and cleaning. If they are not on a cradle, they are carried on somebody's arm or lie in somebody's lap, most likely a mother's. A boy infant needs less cleaning and changing of diaper-rags than a girl because his penis can be stuck into a wooden or metal pipe that drains into a can hung outside the cradle footboard. Baby girls are wet pretty much all the time—wet and uncomfortable because they do not have a penis, women explain.

Over the past thirty years, a few ambitious, city-oriented young parents have brought urban-style swing cradles—deep wireboxes suspended between two connected metal stands—to Deh Koh. Not one of these has survived even one baby; people claim that babies are cold and cranky in them, and that the big, unwieldy contraptions are in the way and not sturdy enough to withstand older children's destructive habits such as climbing on them or swinging them very hard. The old wooden cradles are sturdier, more convenient, and much cheaper.

In houses that have little or no furniture—most of the houses in Deh Koh—the cradle is the most conspicuous and space-consuming fixture in the living area. A house without a cradle is an "old" house—its women are past childbearing. For most of a woman's life, the cradle will be a center around which she organizes her physical and emotional existence. While she is a young girl, the cradle in her father's house will hold a sibling or a brother's child who has to be rocked and taken care off. By the time she is about sixteen she likely will have a cradle of her own. Girls define themselves as cradle/baby people at a very early age, while boys, once they have left the cradle, do not return to it. The cradle is a quintessentially female tool, a gender marker, made by a man, just as a baby is made by a man, women say, and then turned over to a mother completely.

The Infant

Until recently, high infant mortality in Deh Koh led people to consider a newborn's stay tentative. "So far, so good—now we'll see whether it will roost or fly away," somebody is likely to mumble after a birth. Parents, especially a mother, ought not to get too attached to the infant too soon so as not to be saddened should it die. People say that men's stronger intellect and reason, *aql*, prevent a father from undue and unhealthy mourning, while women's weaker intellect render a mother susceptible to uncontrolled sadness in her heart (*del*). A dead young infant is washed quickly at home, wrapped, and buried unceremoniously in a shallow, unmarked grave. Infant mortality has much declined over the past generation, but the traditional ambiguity of joy and satisfaction over a newborn and simultaneous distancing from it during its first days of life is still strong.

An infant's earliest experiences are structured by the circumstances of care, and thus are largely a function of the parents' notions about infants. Above all, for the first forty days, the primary task of a mother is to keep the baby alive. The baby's survival depends on how well its essential needs, especially for food, are met, and how well a whole array of external dangers are kept at bay. Ultimately God and secondarily the father are responsible for the child, but as neither "has a breast with milk," as a mother explained, the day-to-day work of care falls first and foremost to the mother. The father has the indirect task of providing the mother with the food, shelter, and security she needs to raise his child.

In order to survive and to grow (*rosht kardan*) babies are said to need mother's milk, protection from cold, heat, and danger, and the kind of pity and empathy (*suzmun, delsuz*) that prompts a mother to forego sleep and comforts to provide for the child. Mothers are said to have these motherly qualities naturally, but some mothers have more than others. A beautiful, healthy, "good" baby is said to be easier to like and thus to take care of; it is "wanted" more than a weak, ugly, dark-skinned or in any way deformed or very troublesome one. Such preference is considered natural, too, and is discussed freely in front of children. My assertions that I liked my children equally well were politely not believed.

A mother's first milk is said to be "very strong." A weak newborn therefore might be fed sugar-water from a spoon or a bottle until its mother can provide regular milk. Many of the low-weight newborns have problems drinking from their mother's big, flat nipples on large breasts, and do not get enough milk. They cry much and "live at the breast," as a mother put it, trying to suckle. Not much attention is paid to burping. Vomiting milk after nursing is seen as quite usual and normal; "You spit out my good milk as if it was wolf-meat!" a mother will joke. If the child does not grow well, the vomiting likely will be interpreted as a sign that the milk has something wrong with it: it may be "too strong" or may carry "wind" from some food mother has eaten, or it may be spoiled from staying in her breast too long. The mother of a suckling son should not eat game, goat meat, and certain vegetables because the "wind" they contain will hurt the boy's testicles and make him cranky. If a mother has heartburn her baby, too, will get a stomachache and will be weak.

Some mothers are known as good milk providers—their children do well. "Strong milk makes a healthy child," people say. Others have little or no milk—naturally so or as the result of disease or a shock. A woman lost two children to "neglect, no milk" because of her deep sadness over her husband's physical and verbal abuse. Another woman "dried up" with fright after she saw a child fall off her porch. Her niece, who had a lot of milk, offered to nurse the baby, but when the baby vomited much and cried a lot the mother decided that her niece's milk was "bad" and fed the infant sugar-water instead with "a little" powdered dry milk. A very young mother had "no milk" for her thirty-five-day-old infant after she ate a piece of cheese that "curdled and dried" her milk just as cow milk curdles into cheese.

Certain drugs such as penicillin are said to dry up a mother's milk just as they dry pus in a wound; contraceptive drugs are said to have the same effect. In such cases, sugar-water, water in which rice had been cooked, or diluted cow's milk may be given to the baby in a bottle or with a spoon, with occasional wet nursing or some baby formula. Being nursed by several women, however, increases the likelihood that the infant will pick up bad character qualities through the milk. Later, such a child proverbially is unruly and a troublemaker, a "sixty-milk," (shashragi), one who was nursed by sixty different women. "He drank every woman's milk," may be given as explanation for somebody's rude behavior. A mother with insufficient milk thus poses the additional danger of harming her child's character if she goes to the great social length of asking other mothers to wet-nurse her infant to keep it alive. Baby formula is prohibitively expensive, and its use is officially discouraged. Only in rare exceptions will a parent get some at the clinic, free of charge. Traditionally, a baby whose mother had "no milk" was all but doomed.

A mother's milk is taken to convey more than nourishment and well-being. A sinful mother's milk is haram, religiously unlawful in a moral sense, corrupting the suckling infant. Some women's milk is said to produce "good" children. Years ago, Amene asked her then neighbor Setare to nurse her fifth baby a few times so that he might become as good-natured as Setare's own children. A few years later, Setare took credit for the boy's quiet, pleasant disposition and good looks. A few years later yet, after the boy had gotten into various troubles, she denied ever having nursed him.

The milk of a mother of a baby girl is considered very beneficial for the development of a boy, while no benefit is expected from feeding a girl milk from the mother of a boy. No explanations are given for this belief—it just is so, established through observation, people say. A weak male infant, troubled by "wind in the stomach" (our gassy baby), or a baby boy whose mother is willing to take extraordinary troubles, may be taken around to various women relatives and neighbors who are nursing baby girls, to be nursed a little. The nourishment the little boys get this way is minimal, but in extreme cases the occasional wet-nursing may well make the difference between life and death for the infant. Huri, who had "no milk" for any of her children and lost three to subnutrition, credits the "girl-milk" (*shir dovaru*) she begged for one of her sons for his survival. Regardless of the rarity of such nursing, however, the mere existence of the category "girl-milk" and the talk about the benefits of girl-milk for boys teaches children that females even as infants are good for men and boys, and that this goodness runs one way.

Halal and *haram*, religiously lawful and unlawful, enter the politics of nursing in yet another way: essentially, mother's milk is neither, but a mother can make her milk *halal* by declaring it as such for a specific child, anytime, retroactively. This is considered the strongest blessing a mother can bestow on a child. A mourning song for a dead young man goes: "Tell my mother to make her milk *halal* for me / because from this journey I will not return." Likewise, a mother may curse a child by declaring her milk *haram*. Sons are more likely recipients of such curses—daughters rarely will rile or agitate a mother to the point of provoking this strong a curse, women say.

In cases of a woman's serious resentment of her husband, not nursing a child is a way of getting back at him, no matter how great the emotional costs may be to the mother. Nursing thus becomes a political activity within a husband-wife power dispute in which a child is hurt by the mother as surrogate for the father. A mother's milk may also be withheld on orders or with the consent of the father. Reports of such cases for the past twenty-five years are few and involve female infants only. In either case, the message that belonging to father and being dependent on mother simultaneously can be a hurtful, life-threatening situation for infants is not lost on children.

The dangers that are expected to threaten an infant's life are the same as those a mother had to deal with during her pregnancy: djenn, evil eye, people's talk, compliments. The first ten days of life require the most circumspection, but the infant stays very vulnerable for the first forty days of life (*cellei bacce*). After forty days, a marked change in the infant's behavior—less crying, regular sleep, and developing senses—coincides with the waning of extrahuman dangers.

Written amulets, a hair or tooth of a wolf, the head of a rooster, something made of iron such as miniature replicas of tools or a bangle, a Qoran, all kept near the cradle or pinned to the infant's clothing, and fumigations with the burning seeds of wild rue are said to ward off djenn. Beads may be put under the cradle, hung on the cradle-handle, pinned onto baby's wrappings: blue ceramic beads and salt crystals are used against the evil eye, amber beads and pieces of gold against jaundice, date pits and certain beads against exhaustion, others against foaming at the mouth, against fright, against fever. Beads have become rare, however, and a mother who wants to use one has a hard time finding the right one.

On the tenth day, a newborn is supposed to get a bath in the bathhouse together with the mother, who has to perform a cleansing ritual on that day. As more and more people build bathrooms in their own houses, and because the public bath always was seen as a potentially dangerous place for infants because of the many women with their beads, fragrances, and admiring eyes, infants now get washed less ceremoniously and more often, at home. In 1994, Mahnaz even insisted that her newborn be washed in a plastic pail the same day he was born, much to her elders' consternation, but the baby survived despite dire grandmotherly prognosis. From then on, he got a pail-bath at least twice a week—the first baby in Deh Koh to be washed that often, said the grandmother.

Cleanliness as such, however, is ambiguous; a clean baby is beautiful (*tamiz*, clean, is a metaphor for beauty), yet this very beauty may attract fatal attention from a djenn or the evil eye of an admirer. A dirty, smelly, "ugly" (*zesht*) baby is, in this sense, much safer than a clean, nice one. "Look how dirty he is!" a mother will exclaim happily—in this form she safely expresses her pride and joy. From early infancy on, children hear mothers and siblings talk about them in negative terms that are emotionally balanced by positive messages through tone of voice and body language. Rarely does a child seem troubled by being called "ugly, dirty, in rags."

A young infant's social field is confined to immediate household members, especially members of its own, that is, its father's, family. A newborn ought not to be taken out among people recklessly, as a precaution against potential harm from the evil eye, smells, and cold. Thus, although every new child validates its father's and mother's status as a successful adult in public, the public is perceived as potentially dangerous for the new child, especially if women fondle, kiss, or touch infants as friendly village women are supposed to do. Only close relatives and trusted, tried outsiders who are known not to carry the evil eye (as I, luckily, was known to be), are considered safe around infants. But even those likely will refrain from loud praise and politely will accompany admiring attention with exclamations of "*mashallah.*" The double message to infants is obvious: people in the community are comfort, attention, fun, yet also potentially threatening.

Although an infant can be seen through this precarious stage almost exclusively by the mother, it is not integrated into her work patterns. Rather, it is a handicap for most of a mother's daily work routines. For example, when not strapped onto the cradle, a baby is carried on its mother's right arm, making any manual work next to impossible for the mother. Mothers usually sit while nursing or cleaning a baby. From the child's point of view, a mother who cares for it is a stationary mother; if she is working she is not caring for the child. As infants should never be left alone, not even while asleep, they compromise the mother's obligations to run errands, fetch water, milk the cow, wash clothes in the courtyard. The baby's elder siblings, especially sisters, are pressed into babysitting services as soon as marginally possible: "Rock the cradle," a mother told her two-year-old toddler. "This is a good girl, such an understanding girl, a big girl," she said to the little girl who, while rocking as best she could, was whining in protest and for attention. Jerky cradle-rocking on the short runners sometimes irritates the baby more than it soothes, as the little cradle-rocker vents anger and frustration on the cradle, the source of her own discontent.

As a new mother is not released from her customary obligations, the interaction between mother and infant is a compromise between two conflicting demands on her: optimal care of the infant to ensure survival and growth and the reliance of all other household members on her services. She is likely to fall short on both obligations. "A woman with many children has muddy water and bad firewood," a proverb goes. Even if an understanding husband might be content with an occasional bread-and-yogurt dinner, the other children, especially elder sons, will not be. "Why do you keep having new children if you can't take care of those you already have?" a fifteen-year-old, hungry son shouted at his mother on such an occasion. And a seventeen-year-old girl said, "Mother brings children like a donkey does— and I have to take care of them!"

The more children a woman has to take care of, the younger they are and the less help the woman has, the less attention the new infant will get. Infant care thus often is confined to what is seen as absolutely necessary. The baby is fed on demand but not necessarily before lengthy crying—"Unless a baby cries it won't get a breast" is another proverb—and without being taken off the cradle: mother offers her breast bending over the baby's mouth. She changes diapers once a day, wiping baby's bottom cursorily; she takes baby to the bath every one to three weeks, where, however, she also will have to wash her other young children.

The immediate, practical goals of care of a young infant are to make the baby sleep much and cry little. A wise mother will not put the infant into the cradle for the first time on a Saturday because otherwise it will be a crybaby (*vasveru, girvaru*). Sleep and silence in turn are taken as signs of the well-being of the baby, which in turn is a sign that baby needs no attention. Yet, even if the baby is quiet, "good," a conflict arises; a demanding, vigorous, loud infant is considered very burdensome, but the vigor is also a favorable indicator of the baby's vitality. Loud, strong infants grow up to be healthy, robust children, people say. Such children are scolded for being demanding, for being a nuisance, yet are approved of at the same time.

The Parents

The complementarity of paternal and maternal responsibilities toward the infant who is, however, the father's property, makes a child potentially vulnerable to being used as a bargaining chip in parents' disputes. A wife's strongest protest of ill treatment by her husband is to absent herself by suicide or by returning to her father, leaving "his" children, including an infant, behind. Mothers recognize their children as theirs and address their children as "my son," "my daughter," "my dear," but this tie has little legal validity. Legally and in terms of descent and local understanding, children belong to the father, who is fully responsible for their upbringing should the issue be raised. In most families, the issue never is raised. But some infants learn by their mother's desertion, in a very painful way, that they are their father's children, and older children learn from discussions of such events that parental discord may lead to abandonment by their mother. Absent fathers are not a cognitive problem for children— "Mothers always cope," people say—but absent mothers are.

A motherless (*bidei*) infant is the most pitiful and pitied child. Its prospect for survival is poor. Motherless children are said to be *sarraskho*, a kind of trouble: they are in everybody's way, dirty, unkempt, without manners; they are vulnerable, hungry, easy prey. A mourning song for a dead young mother expresses the fate of motherless children in two short lines: "The partridge mother had two chicks. She climbed a rock. / She hasn't returned, and the hawk has eaten the chicks."

In a tale of a girl who was stolen by a djenn, had two children with him, and later was found and taken away by her people, the djenn ends the story by killing his two crying children matter-of-factly. "What else could he have done?" commented the storyteller. "Without a mother the children were doomed anyway." The proverb "To break a hand is better than to break a leg, to lose a father is better than to lose a mother," is said to a child who has hurt a finger, for example. When a baby laughs, somebody may recite this verse: "Don't laugh, your mother died." Whereupon the mother counters, "That's a lie—I've just nursed you." And when a baby cries it might be told, "Don't cry, your father died," answered by mother, "Never mind, I've just nursed you." Although the infant may not understand, older children who hear these and similar sayings repeat them and thereby learn the women's point of view on the issue of father's versus mother's relative importance in bringing up children; even if children are their father's property in every sense of the word, without their mother life would be miserable at the very least.

A neglectful mother commits a sin—there is total agreement on this in Deh Koh—but in judging such mothers women make generous allowances. A woman lost two infants due to neglect, but this was seen as her husband's wrongdoing—it was his fault that she was depressed and dysfunctional. The poor children were to be pitied, of course, but it served him right to lose them. As for the mother—only God knows her sins, and He will pardon them because she is a simpleton.

Shahla left babies behind several times when she fled her abusive husband's house. About one such occasion a neighbor and relative said, "It was very bad of her to leave; the baby cried and cried. I said to her: 'You think your husband's son should die, and you have a point, but I pity the baby, I won't let him die, it is a sin.' And I washed him and I rocked the cradle, and I helped his father's mother to take care of him, and I scolded the father, and I personally took the baby to Shahla's father's house and made Shahla nurse him. But who am I to say she committed a sin? A baby is the father's child—if a man wants his children to be taken care of well he must take care of the mother well too."

When Golgol was three months old, her mother killed herself. Her father's mother, depressed over her daughter-in-law's suicide, killed herself too. The baby's father's sister, by her own account an over-worked woman then with five young children of her own, took pity on her brother's infant, a child belonging to her own father's group, after all, whose mother and natural substitute mother, her grand-mother, had deserted her, so to speak, thinking only of their own misery. She took care of her. Never did this aunt blame the two women for what she thought of as their neglect, though. In her view, they had been "poor, miserable, unfortunate" rather than sinful. Golgol now is one of the most sunny, positive women in Deh Koh— in her estimation, with which I agree—and a well-loved mother of ten very competent children. "I know from experience how hard life is for a motherless child. I was determined to be a good mother, to let nothing come between me and my children—not poverty, not hard work, not troubles from my husband, from his mother. And I have done it, may God be my witness," she says.

Of the dozen or so infants who were identified to me as having died of neglect (*narasidan-e bacce*), nine were girls. Although not a sample in any statistically sound sense, this finding corresponds to expectations based on my observations of how male and female in-fants are treated by their parents. Individual cases of great joy over a girl infant notwithstanding, baby girls receive a muted welcome, es-pecially from their father's relatives. Zeynab's father was beside him-self with joy over his firstborn, a daughter, cooing over her, playing with her, watching over her welfare with concern and pride. But, he said, he and a few other such fathers are exceptions; he even was ridiculed for "carrying on like this over a daughter" by his own mother. Baby girls are less likely fussed over; they receive less care that requires great expenses and receive less attention in the form of eye-contact and handling than do their brothers.

The customary preference for sons is not expressed in gender-coded terms or objects in a baby's early days. Luri does not have gender markers in pronouns or possessives: all terms for baby, *aghlu*, *kucelu*, *khordelu*, are gender-neutral. An infant's colors, clothes, cradle, blankets, and toys are not gender coded. Differences come into play subtly in people's cognitions and in small gestures toward the child.

Just as women are seen as weaker than men, baby girls are considered weaker than boys—weaker yet sturdier; the theory of female weakness contradicts the experience of actual infant vitality, but this contradiction is not addressed. In the medical-philosophical system of Deh Koh, weakness is aggravated by "strong" medicine just as a starved person's health will deteriorate if the person gorges him- or herself with rich food. For infant care, this cognitive model provides the rationalization for feeding "naturally weak" girls less, or less rich, food than boys. This does not mean that all girls actually are fed less well than boys—only that a rationalization exists for the practice, that it makes sense to everybody should it occur. Despite their postulated inborn weakness, however, female babies are known to suffer less from stomach disorders and other health problems than their brothers, and thus require less care. Thus, both inferior feeding and inferior care look reasonable, if need be. Furthermore, all children are said to be gifts from God and ought to be appreciated equally; girl children even are sweeter, more compassionate, and more supportive of parents from an early age on than are boy children, ever. Nevertheless, people, including women, support the preference for sons for structural and political reasons based on patrilineality. Such conclusions, of which there will be more as the child grows, make sense only within a logic of gender discrimination, a logic that is so well integrated into the verbal and affective contexts in which children grow up that it is rarely perceived as such or challenged.

Parents who treat yet another daughter well are lauded as "good Muslims," as people with charitable, generous hearts. They are wholeheartedly approved of—and openly or ever so slightly pitied. Parents who get yet another son are not commented upon at all lest their good fortune (shans-e khub) be jeopardized. Infant girls motivate far fewer nasr, pledges and promises of sacrifices and pilgrimages to saints, than do their brothers. Extra care they do receive might be accompanied by explanations such as "My heart burns for her"; "I pity her, I have a soft heart"; "it is sinful to let her suffer," explanations and justifications that extra service for a son does not require.

The differences are subtle. But every mother, without exception, even if denying differential treatment of her own sons and daughters, readily will tell a story of somebody else's differential care of different-sex babies. Neglect and preference are not condoned by religion. Mistreating or neglecting anybody in a person's care is a sin, but a sin others commit, not oneself. It "just so happened" that the baby the father dropped in a fit of rage was a girl infant; that the only treatably blind child in Deh Koh is a motherless girl who had never been taken to an eye doctor while she was little; that the two infants one woman lost because of her depression were girls. It just so happened that when Mehri left the village to take care of a social emergency for three days, it was an infant daughter who was left behind, crying with hunger. Every single dead male infant but three I could trace had died not by chance but despite considerable efforts and expenses. Until 1994, the female infant mortality rate was higher than the male one in Deh Koh as well as in Iran generally. For ever so many girl infants this translates into a smaller chance for survival, into less care, more frustrations and stress, traumas, longer periods of crying between nursing. But to what extent statistics or anecdotes "prove" this issue of so-called benign neglect is beside the point. For children, their elders' treatment of infant boys and girls and their talk about them in anecdotes, explanatory comments, proverbs, and lullabies, suggest to them that boys and girls not only are different but are of different value to people, that they ought to be treated differently. In the beginning this is confusing. The different treatment young children see their siblings get seems arbitrary; infant girls and boys in the cradle or, wrapped in a blanket, in somebody's lap, are undistinguishable from each other. "How do you know it's a girl?" asked Jamal, who is five, about his new sister. "This baby looks just like aunt Maryam's new boy!" Yet, by the time sex markers become obvious to children in clothes and hairstyles, gender differences in behavior and the child's identity and philosophy, together with supportive values, will have jelled into a powerful ideology.

10 · Lullabies and Jouncing Songs

Until a few years ago, a baby strapped on the cradle was sung to sleep while the cradle was rocked. The singer, always a woman, introduced and ornamented each verse with a sound made by rapidly flicking her tongue against the back of her upper front teeth while resonating air in her mouth: a string of rapid *l*s, petering out into "loi, loi." "To make *laloi*" means to go to sleep for a baby and young child. "To say a *laloi*" means to sing a lullaby. For reasons nobody in Deh Koh can quite explain, singing lullabies has become rare. Babies are rocked still but without being addressed orally.

Lullabies and rhymes chanted while a baby is jounced playfully are the first coherently patterned, longer speech events directed specifically at the child. They are the first verbal messages about life out there beyond the cradle and mother's lap and arms.

· · ·

Llll-laloi, loi, loi, a new cradle, my dear's cradle, with coral beads and silver balls. I'll count the beads into my dear's hands.

Llaloi, my dear, my pretty daughter, I'll put my dear in between velvet.

Both lullabies allude to the preciousness of a child and to the purported wealth of the father: coral, silver and velvet are expensive, beautiful items.

· · ·

Lllloi, laloi, flowerbud. May you stay in my heart forever.

Fear of loss through a baby's death or, later, potential emotional loss at the child's marriage frequently are expressed by women directly and in songs.

· · ·

Laloi, lloi, loi, welcome, dear, I have seen your happiness, I have seen you play with the children. Now that I have seen what a healthy, happy child you are I hope you won't die on me.

Laloi, dear, you are a good child, you do my bidding.

A mother's ever-optimistic expectation of obedience, help, and loyalty from children is expressed here. "Good" early on is introduced to the child as a gloss for these qualities.

· · ·

Lllloi, loi, how pretty are my baby's teeth—like the eyes of a rooster.

Baby's teeth and rooster's eyes are similarly small and shiny, thus pretty. Praise of a baby's beauty or strength is rare for fear it might attract the evil eye. Here, the analogy with the rooster makes it some-what safer because a rooster's head is said to ward off dangerous forces.

.   .   .

Laloi, lloi, nobody likes [wants] you. I'll make a charm against the evil eye to pin on your right shoulder.

Declaring the child as not wanted, as unattractive by implication, the mother tries to ward off the evil eye and to tell the djenn that the child is not worth bothering about.

.   .   .

Lllaloi, loi, flowerbud. The tiger roars in the mountains. No cow is left to eat, no calf, nothing but my dear one-year-old.

Threats of throwing a child to the wolves or abandoning it in the wilderness are popular with irate mothers to make children obey and to discourage them from straying far afield.

.   .   .

Llaloi, you old wolf with only one tooth, don't you dare eat my little dear!

Mother may threaten with the wolf or a tiger as in the previous song but also portray herself as the protector against the wolf, against all dangers.

Lloi, laloi, loi, a wolf came, a wolf came from Turkestan. The wolf was old and didn't eat my child. Sleep, baby, sleep.

.   .   .

Lloi, flowerbud. Your father went away to get a [second] wife, but now that I have you he won't take one after all.

One of the first messages a child gets from its mother about the family is that a childless woman is in danger of getting saddled with a co-wife, and that therefore children, especially sons, are important status-builders for the mother vis-à-vis her husband and his people. The very young baby is placed as a security shield for the mother between the mother and the father.

.   .   .

Llloi, You have a chic motherbrother with a rogue hat, you have a learned fatherbrother. Your father is a fearless fighter, your fathersister is a little crooked. Your mother is a bunch of flowers.

Mother gives an introduction to how close relatives are to be regarded.

.　　.　　.

Lllaloi, your father left for the men's council, your father left for the men's camp.

Your father is a great, important man—so are you.

.　　.　　.

Lllaloi, loi, my child [here the name is said], you threw me out and locked the door, with the dough-roller you hit my hand. I fell asleep at the spring. Two horsemen came from Turkestan and brought me here to Lurestan.

When I objected that this did not make much sense I was told not to mind, it was "just a lullaby." The mother is the one who hit the child and locked it out, or else a son is throwing out his mother. In either case, the rejected person is abducted and carried far away to the cradle in Deh Koh. Either interpretation is possible, the singers said, but could not explain how a son would get hold of a dough-roller. No matter who the actors are, however, intrafamily conflict is clearly expressed, as are fear of strangers and the dangers of the wilderness.

.　　.　　.

Lllaloi, I rock the cradle but the baby doesn't fall asleep. I raise it but it won't remember me later. Sleep, my dear, sleep . . .

Both are frequent complaints of mothers.

.　　.　　.

A baby is also addressed directly with rhymes chanted while it is held vertically under the armpits, thrown up a few inches and caught again to the beat of the chant. This jouncing is supposed to amuse children, but as far as I could see, it rather made them cry before long.

> The little boy, the little one
> took his lambs and kids behind the hill.
> The wolf came and took one.
> The boar came and frightened him.
> His motherbrother came and skinned the boar
> as ointment for his back.

Traditionally, "little boy" was tantamount to shepherd of young animals. Wolves, boars, snakes, bears, mountain tigers are all in a day's dangerous work, but a mother's brother will help out. Boar grease and boar hide are traditional remedies against rheumatism and joint-pains. As in other contexts, mother's brother is presented as a hero by the mother.

> My son, my son, my big pearl,
> your father threw a rock at my back.
> I have left him and haven't gone back for you.

The threat of a mother to leave her children behind while she is *ve qar*, living elsewhere because of ill treatment by her husband, here is expressed to babies in the playful, yet not very comfortable, context of jouncing.

> Until you have a fiancée you are my son.
> Once you are engaged you are my neighbor.
> When you have a wife you are a stranger to me.

A mother expresses to her son the fear of competition between her and her future daughter-in-law over access to him. She thereby teaches him that this rivalry is to be expected. Although a son is addressed, such songs are also sung to girls, who get the message indirectly.

> My daughter won't get married, she'll stay with me.
> Her motherbrother is a crown on my head.
> Her father is the shirt on my body.
> Her husband is my donkey's fart.

Privately, mothers often complain about their daughters' ill treatment by the daughters' husbands and commiserate with their married daughters' hard life in poor or unfriendly households. A woman's ill treatment in her husband's house thus becomes a stereotype from babyhood on. A woman's brother is presented as her "king," her potential protector, the link to her own people. The song provides a hierarchy of esteem for a girls' closest adult males—the brother or maternal uncle on top, the father upon whom she is dependent next, followed by daughter's husband and, by implication, one's own husband, seen from a different point of view.

> My daughter is better than a son.
> I won't give her to a Lur-khan.
> He'll take her behind a hill
> and kill her with a blunt knife.

This is a comment on the traditional political structure, on life under potentially abusive and oppressive tribal chiefs and landlords. It is also a comment on the dangers of marriage for a girl: a powerful husband may do with her whatever he wants.

> My son [or: the boy] is herding the lambs, is herding the kids,
> but his eyes are on the girls.
> Tell his mother to take him bread.
> Don't take him buttermilk, it is sour.
> Don't take him yogurt, it makes him sleepy.
> Take him butter, it cures fever.

Butter is the most expensive food; bread and buttermilk are a staple at home and for shepherds. The speaker is the boy's father or paternal grandmother, sketching the boy's future life, for which he ought to be well nourished by his mother. "It also says what is on boys' minds," said a mother who chanted this, with a wink.

> A crow came from afar with bloody wings.
> Its mother said, "Oh, dear me!"
> Its father said, "Nothing wrong with it!"

"That shows who has more compassion with a child!" said the mother who sang this verse.

A mother stops singing lullabies gradually as a child starts to sleep in bedding on the floor like everybody else. However, not long after, she likely will sing them to her next baby or her son's baby, or else the toddler will hear the familiar songs sung by other women to other babies. A mother's poetic messages will be augmented with observations in other contexts, but their emotional impact will stay with the child. A sixteen-month-old baby, suckling at his mother's breast while she was singing a rhyme about abandonment, started to whine, bit into the nipple, hit her in protest, and then snuggled closer still. "No, no," said the three-year-old sibling sitting next to them, "She is lying."

11 · A Little One on My Back

The Older Infant

According to local conventional wisdom, a baby does not have its senses until it is three months and ten days old. This belief neatly rationalizes the lack of attention paid to a baby's early utterances and body language. For example, a young infant, jounced repeatedly as a gesture of affectionate entertainment, inevitably will start to cry, to throw up even, which very likely will prompt laughter and kisses by the jouncer; babies like this game, I was assured. A baby who, to my understanding, is happily moving arms and legs lying in its mother's lap may be said to be tired and strapped back onto the cradle—a happy (*rahat*, at ease) baby is quiet in voice and body. An infant is handled with care, to be sure, but as a delicate thing without much perception. Even in cold wind it may be taken outside wrapped in nothing more substantial than a rag, and even this will be wet soon. Loud noises around a baby, children stumbling over the cradle, a toddler poking a baby hard, are treated by adults as if they did not matter much to an infant. After it is three months old, perception is expected to develop, including recognition of the difference between day and night. It is expected not to demand to be fed as frequently at night, to smile, to coordinate eye movements, to recognize mother, and to hear noises. Slowly, the generic baby becomes a person with a name that fits, character peculiarities such as crying easily or rarely, smiling readily or not, moving much or little, expressing likes and dislikes, and with social ties: it is somebody's sister or brother, may be introduced to another child as, "Look, a sister!" It is identified as belonging to certain people through possessive suffixes: "my son" (*kurrom*), "my dear" (*junom*), "his/her brother" (*kakash*).

The longer the baby stays alive the more its people, especially its mother, will get attached to it. This is taken to be according to God's natural order as revealed through observation. A very young infant who dies will not be missed much; it is likened to a bird that flies off a branch on which it had just alighted. But an older infant who dies is missed "like a bird whose song we have heard." The bird simile extends further: sparrow and baby both cry "jig, jig, jig"; a baby flailing its arms is said to spread its wings.

Grief over the death of a baby is said not only to distress the child's soul but to "burn" a grieving mother's womb, making it unfit for further pregnancies. "The death of a child burns either the mother's soul or her womb," goes a saying. No such dire consequence is postulated for a grieving father. Although detachment is relatively easy to achieve in the case of a dead newborn, it gets harder the older a dead child is. As children grow they settle into their parents', especially mother's, heart (*del*), people say.

There is no special term for "love" in any context in the language of Deh Koh. People and things are either "wanted" (*khast*), or "not wanted" (*nakhast*). "We want the baby very much," is the strongest expression of affection in the vocabulary of Deh Koh. The Farsi term *dust dashtan*, to like, be friendly with, to prefer, is used rarely in Deh Koh for relations between people. Playing the throw-baby-in-the-air game, for example, the jouncer may accentuate the rhythmic movements by chanting ad hoc rhymes such as: "I want you, I don't want you, baby, baby, beautiful boy/girl, ugly boy/girl, I want you, I don't want you." In this context, "I don't want you" is as much a rhythm/rhyme device and expression of ambivalence as it is a precaution against djenn and the evil eye, a connection also expressed in a lullaby: "Nobody wants you. I'll make an amulet against the evil eye to pin on your right shoulder." At any age, a misbehaving child may hear the threat: "If you do such-and-such I won't want you!" but rarely the positive opposite. Babies learn to read signs of affection like smiles, cooing, fondles, tickles, and kisses on the face, hands, feet, although not all these signs are entirely pleasurable. (Mothers and female relatives do not kiss baby boys' genitals in Deh Koh, as they are reported to do in other parts of Iran and the Middle East.)

Babies learn to respond to their elders' high-pitched baby talk or sing-song. They hear that the playmate gladly will sacrifice her/himself for the child (*qorbunet berram*), is willing to take the baby's future calamities on his own head, (*qassata men serrom*), and that a djenn ought to hit it (*yal bezanet*) because it is naughty, ugly, or bad, all uttered in one cheerful breath. This might not have an immediate effect on an incomprehending infant, but older children who hear babies addressed in this way get an ambivalent message. "Mother wants the son-of-a-dog," a three-year-old boy chanted about his mother and her new baby while playing at the water faucet. A playmate may "eat" a baby affectionately: the playmate "plucks" a piece from the baby's cheek, arms, belly, and "eats" it; this particular game, though, annoys older infants more than it amuses them. Babies experience that attention in the form of handling may be rather uncomfortable, rough, and scary, especially by siblings, and that their own reactions to the discomfort likely will be ignored. People will try to elicit a smile from baby by tickling or by rapidly touching its upper and lower lips, chin, both corners of the mouth with a finger while chanting, "Smile, smile—don't smile, don't smile—smile," etc. If it starts to cry during such entertainments, which happens frequently, it is told, "Don't cry, don't cry" (*magir*), and swung or tickled some more, or else turned on its stomach and patted on the back. In the end, mother likely will offer a breast, the most effective calming device.

A playmate likely will encourage even a very young baby to smile (*bekhand*) and to hit (*bezan*) somebody, child or adult, at the same time— "Laugh, laugh, this is a sister, hit her, hit her, ah, ah"—by guiding its hand into a hitting movement. Until about a decade ago, babies produced the hitting gesture and sound as some of their first voluntary gestures and utterances, right along with stretching arms to be picked up, for example. Recently, the hitting game seems to be losing some popularity, but a "hitting" baby still can expect to hear that it is strong (*zereng*), cute. It also can expect that the hit playmate will respond with mock I-am-hurt noises such as mock-crying or saying "ouch" and gestures that express pain, but that it will not hit back. Older babies may hit hard, pull at hair, really hurt a young playmate, but will hear no reprimand and get no retaliation. A three-year-old boy who was scratched across the cheek by the hitting baby laughed aloud along with the others but then hid behind his mother's back, whining and demanding consolation from her by drumming against her back.

A baby very frequently hears commands: come (*bia*), sleep (*bekhous*), eat (*bekhar*), let go (*vellesh kon*), hit (*bezan*), look (*seiko*), smile, (*bexand*), don't cry (*nagir*). It hears that it ought to be ashamed (*kejalat bekesh*) for soiling bed or pants, for throwing up, for showing naked legs or body if a girl, for crying, for being dirty. It learns early to expect that people will try to hinder and order nearly all its activities, and that the most effective way of refusing unwanted demands and of making one's needs and wishes known is by whining, crying, and howling.

Attention and care remain functions of the compromise between what a mother takes to be her baby's reasonable demands, given its sex, state of health, character, humoral disposition, and what the mother conveniently can afford to give. The last factor varies the widest, not only with a woman's character, abilities, workload, and age but also with household composition, the birth order of the baby, and the gender of elder siblings: elder sisters are pressed into service as surrogate mothers for siblings much more frequently than are brothers. The more adolescents and female adults are in the household, the more attention will the baby get. Children may compare the care they get or remember having gotten with what they think their mother ought to have done for them and with the care their mother is giving their younger siblings. Just as a mother and father ought to love all their children equally, they also ought to treat them equally. Realistically, however, children expect neither, even if they resent being short-shrifted. They learn early on that the care they get is partly dependent on how much, from whom, and how they demand it, and that caregivers can be manipulated, especially with outbursts of loud anger. "The more noise the more food," said a woman with eighteen grandchildren. "Even young birds in the nest know this."

Two examples will illustrate the range the different variables may produce. Fourteen-year-old Fariba had a seven-month-old baby, a small child with thin arms and legs, who could not sit well without support. She lived in her husband's father's house together with her husband, his parents, his two unmarried brothers, both in their late teens, and his ten-year-old sister. One late afternoon, her husband's parents, two visiting male relatives, and I were sitting on the porch on rugs around a tray with fruits and tea. Grandmother was holding Hekmat in her lap. The girl was dressed in pajama pants, a green sweater, and a knit cap. She had an amulet in red velvet hanging around her neck; her eyes were lined with *sirmei*. She was cranky. Her grandmother tried to keep her quiet by patting her thighs, clapping her hands, feeding her sugar and tea, offering a pacifier. She restrained her when she wanted to grab the tea glass, a spoon, or a cucumber; wiped her hands after she had squished a piece of sugar; wrestled a saucer away from her. The mother, a small, thin youngster, was running around in the background with water cans, teapot, glasses; she washed fruits and dishes, flitted in and out of the kitchen, all hectic movement without much direction, in the "I-am-very-busy" stance typical of as yet insecure, well-mannered, shy, young daughters-in-law. She declined several invitations to sit down. The baby was addressed by name, tickled, and spoken to briefly a few times by the visitors; her grandfather tried to entice her to face him, arms open, fingers wiggling: "*Bio, bio,* come, come," but just then, she wet her pants and her grandmother's shirt. The Grandmother handed her to Fariba, who yanked a dry pair of pants from the wash line, dressed her in the house, and then sat down behind her mother-in-law, holding the baby in front of her like a shield. She was hiding behind her mother-in-law and her child, observing not the child but the guests, their needs, ready to jump up for more tea, for a box with paper tissues, for an extra plate. The baby was fingering her earrings and her necklaces, which elicited automatic "Don't"s from Fariba. She was straining to crawl off the lap, reaching, in vain, for a tea glass, pulling at her grandmother's veil in front of her, whining. She got very restless, started to cry, and when she did not calm down after being turned on her stomach and patted on the back, Fariba offered her breast. This did not calm her much, though. A few minutes later, she started to scream, and her grandmother turned around and took her again. The young mother was off instantly, sloshing water in the background; unbidden, she had started preparation for dinner. The grandfather was playing with Hekmat now, talking to her, holding eye contact, lifting her, and swinging her lightly for a few minutes. Eventually, the grandmother proclaimed the baby "tired" and left with her for more nursing and to put her on the cradle, where her ten-year-old aunt would rock her to sleep.

Although Hekmat's mother, a youngster herself, was very busy, had little milk, and was rather weak, according to her mother-in-law and herself, the fact that the baby was the only young child in a hospitable house that included several older children, adults, and frequent visitors allowed for good care in the eyes of this family. The grandparents said that the baby got a lot of attention and diversion, that she did not have to spend much time on the cradle for lack of caretakers, that she "never cried for long." However, the mother complained to me that she was not allowed to feed Hekmat much else than her milk, which was insufficient, and that she had to argue to be allowed to take the baby to the well-child clinic for inoculations. She called her in-laws "uneducated and old-fashioned"; they were to be blamed for the baby's obviously weak condition. Hekmat herself looked to me like a rather grouchy baby who often did not feel well enough to smile and who was rarely left alone to play with anything. Frequently, she suffered from colds and diarrhea; not encouraged or even allowed to crawl or move much, her subnutrition-based weakness was compounded by lack of exercise. Yet the many people around her, who liked her in a somewhat distant way, provided a constant source of friendly human contact and diversion, which she seemed to count on and be comfortable with.

·   ·   ·

Mahperi is around forty years old and has an eight-month-old child, her sixth. Her only daughter and a son are at home only during school vacation. Her husband leaves early and comes home late, every day. Mahperi is alone at home with the baby while her three older sons are in school. Like most cradle-children at this age, the baby can sit but neither crawl nor stand, not even when supported. He looks well-nourished, though; Mahperi had enough milk for all her children, but she also feeds the new baby deliberately from all she cooks, she says. By her own estimates, with which her neighbors and I agree, she is a competent mother despite poor living conditions. Although nobody helps her in the house and with the care of a cow and chickens, she gets to all her obligations, but without a moment to spare. These obligations also include baby care more elaborate than for any of her other children: she gives him the juice of an apple every day, gives his behind a sponge bath every day, washes his hands and face at least once a day, changes his clothes daily, takes him to the public bathhouse weekly. He has a urine-pipe in the cradle and sleeps in the good room of her husband's two-room house during the day, away from noise, commotion, wind, smoke, and flies. A pair of plastic shorts prevent him from soiling the rug and his mother's clothes. Conscientiously, she takes him to the well-child clinic in the next village for inoculations and feeds him the vitamin drops handed out there. His habit of sucking and gnawing the lower lip for her is a sign that he has ear aches frequently—he wears a heavy knit cap day and night, summer and winter, to prevent them.

Mahperi says that this baby is a lot more work than the other children had been. In earlier times, she says, "We had no soap, no hot water, no clothes for babies, only rags, and no time. I had two cows and fifteen sheep and goats to milk, a sick father-in-law, and three children born one right after the other." (She spaced the next three children five years apart with contraceptive drugs.) "But in those times all children were alike: dirty, naked, flea-bitten. A clean, nice baby, people said, will be hit by the evil eye. And where is the evil eye now?! Ha! Now people talk about a dirty baby, not a clean one: 'Doesn't your mother take care of you?' they say." Mahperi thinks times have changed for the better. Her daughter brings home baby clothes from the city, and "always is washing him, even if he is not dirty." In other villages around Deh Koh, though, children are "dirty and naked" still, she says. "My husband's relatives, for example, and the women who come to the health clinic from all over the area . . ."

Mahperi describes her day: the baby wakes up "at six," which stands for early in the morning. She takes him off the cradle before he starts to cry loudly, nurses him, walks around with him on her arm or on her back as she makes tea for the other children. He gets some tea and sugar too, but she does not allow him to waste sugar cubes. After the children have left for school, he goes back on the cradle and is rocked to sleep. She "quickly, quickly" cleans her two small rooms, the kitchen/hall, the porch, the courtyard. Midmorning, she takes him off the cradle again—by then he likely will have been crying for a while—for more nursing. He will be on her arm or back, or nursing, while she prepares lunch for the other children. His brothers will take care of him while she clears away lunch—they have to keep him from crying and from putting things into his mouth and falling off the stairs. Sometimes she catches a wink of sleep in the early afternoon with him next to her on the floor within easy reach of her breast, but she also has to do her wash and all other household chores, with him either on the cradle or "in the way," and run errands. She takes him with her everywhere, on her arm or on her back, awake or asleep. When the children come home from school he has to go onto the cradle again while she prepares dinner. His brothers or a cousin might be persuaded to take him out for a little while or to rock the cradle to put him to sleep, to keep him from crying. At dinner, which is served on the floor, he sits on her or his father's lap, if he is awake yet, and is on the cradle again at around eight unless his father or siblings keep him entertained while Mahperi takes care of the animals and the dishes. Had she a school-age daughter at home or a young daughter-in-law, her life would be much easier, she says. "Sons are good, very good, but for a mother, daughters are better: they help, they work, they have pity, a soft heart."

One day the baby almost suffocated on a piece of apple his six-year-old brother had given him. "Mother, Saed is dead!" he yelled, and she yanked him off the cradle in the nick of time, turned the gasping child on his stomach over her knee and hit his back until the piece of apple fell out. In the evening, his seventeen-year-old brother beat the daylights out of the six-year-old for having been so stupidly bad (bi-aql, fuzul) as to make his baby brother suffocate, no matter how much the mother pleaded that it was a sin to beat the little boy, as he had not done it on purpose. With all the screaming in the house the baby could not sleep either.

Saed is handled little by his mother but handled disproportionately much—and roughly often—by his elder brothers and babysitters. His mother is responsive, especially to his nutritional needs, but not overly indulgent, because she does not have the time nor the help other women in her situation have from their adolescent daughters—this is what she communicates to me and to the baby. By and large she trained him to be a "good" baby, who sleeps much and well, eats without fuss, and, being well-fed and well-rested, is not cranky or sick much either. His big sister, although not around much, has a very great influence on his care. She, an educated young woman who knows about modern, enlightened ways of living, insists on much higher standards of cleanliness for her little brother, brings him baby clothes, a few toys, and, most important, insists on supplementary feeding at an age when most babies in Deh Koh still mostly get only mother's milk. In this case—a mother/daughter relationship rather than a mother-in-law/daughter-in-law one as in the previous case—it is much easier for the young woman to exert leadership and motivate the baby's mother to comply with "modern" ways of baby care, although they entail much more work and more expense. Her authority vis-à-vis her mother is based on superior knowledge, on school education. Mahperi proudly says that her daughter told her to care for the baby in certain ways because she had read it in her books. Were the daughter a little younger or would the household include a grandmother, little Saed most probably would be taken care of quite differently. Saed himself to me looks a little slow and doughy. He does not smile much but does not cry much either, and stares at things and people with wide-open eyes long before he responds to a challenge. He is "a good baby" now, but will be "a devil" soon, says Mahperi.

Milk, Food, and Health

Older babies still are nursed on demand, even if they are fed other food, too. The frequent nursing has taught the infant to demand the breast not only when hungry or thirsty but also when sleepy, cranky, stressed, or in pain. A mother's breast is a hiding place, warm, dark, and safe.

Playing "catch me" with an elder sibling, ten-month-old Abbas's home base was his mother's breast: he headed there on all fours whenever the pursuer came too close. He bumped against it, grabbed it, suckled, then turned to check on the pursuer with the nipple in his mouth pulled to astonishing length. His mother, who was deep in conversation with me, did not even seem to notice. Her movements of receiving the screeching baby and offering her breast time and again were automatic responses to his squealing approach—rarely did she, or any other mother, devote all her attention or her gaze to the nursing infant.

Girls are to be weaned between nine and eighteen months. They are said to need mother's milk less long than baby boys, either because they are weaker and ought to be weaned from strong mother's milk in order not to get sick, or to prevent them from getting "too strong"; girls ought to be weaker than boys because they *are* weaker than boys. Either explanation has roots in experience, people say. The explanations reveal the gender ideology boys and girls learn while listening to weaning rules. How long boys and girls actually are nursed differs widely with circumstances. Worst off are baby girls who are followed closely by the next sibling: Nurijan lost her milk when she got pregnant again two months after her daughter was born, she said. Behrokh weaned her eleven-month-old daughter only two weeks before her next child, a son, was born. She had nursed her so long against the advice from her mother-in-law, who saw this heroic nursing as superfluous, considering that the baby was only a daughter. Behrokh nursed her son until he was over two years old, as boys ought to be nursed, until she was pregnant again. Her last child, a daughter, she nursed for over three years, mainly because the little girl "didn't like to eat anything else." Behrokh also liked to nurse, she said, had a lot of milk, was infatuated with her very pretty and sweet daughter, and did not believe that the milk harmed the child. She did not nurse the toddler in front of other people, though, to escape criticism.

Long nursing rots a baby's teeth, causes diarrhea, makes children weak, and is especially bad for girls, people say. When an eighteen-month-old girl got diarrhea (*eshal*) and an eczema (*souda*) on her inner thigh, her mother diagnosed it as coming from her milk and promptly weaned her, whereupon the little girl "almost died," her mother said. The worst milk for a baby is considered to be the milk of a pregnant woman, but ever so many women who make *polu* know differently or have no choice but "to nurse with milk and nurse with blood" at the same time, as one such mother said. The alternative to nursing, baby formula, was popular for about ten years, between 1975 and 1985, with the usual problems of hygiene and improper dosage, but no longer is readily available and not affordable either. Now nursing is advocated as the healthy, natural, God-ordained nourishment for babies by health-care providers, in schools, newspapers, sermons, and posters.

Weaning is a traumatic affair for most children and their families. The intention of mother's weaning strategies are to make her breasts so distasteful that the child gives up nursing on its own, without fuss—a strategy that never seems to work smoothly. Behrokh colored her breasts bright red with ink to frighten little Leila: Leila would lift her mother's shirt, look in horror at the red blotches, start to scream, drop the shirt, lift it again, throw a tantrum, and start all over again. Amene said, "Pheew, yecch, ugly, dirty, hit it!" whenever her two-year-old son was nursing, to make an "enemy" of her breast. He played along by hitting the breast and saying "pheew," but then laughed and continued to nurse, occasionally, for another six months. Shahrbanu put pepper on her nipples to hurt her weanling's mouth; he screamed and pummelled her for almost a week. Zari daubed her breasts with the bitter juice of an herb to make her weanling spit, as did Afi with lime juice: the children licked, spat, howled, then nursed anyway. Banu hid her breasts under buttoned garments to make them "unaccessible like a buried treasure." Her son poked a hole in the cardigan, ripped her shirt, and found the pot of gold, she said.

The weanling is offered alternative food but rarely special food, except maybe cookies, and not on demand either. The baby likely will sate itself on tea and sugar; it likely will have cried itself to sleep more or less hungry long before dinner is ready; tough food such as meat, rare as it is for everybody, or bread, cannot be chewed easily by the weanling—by the time the baby has swallowed a few half-chewed bites dinner will be over. Not only is the inadequate food supply traumatic for the child but so is the sudden withdrawal of the maternal pacifier, which had helped the younger baby to cope with frustrations. So many weanlings are "weak, thin, cranky," that this condition just about describes a weaned child in Deh Koh; a postulated norm ascribed to a developmental stage perpetuates parental behavior that brings about this norm.

The various weaning efforts produce similar effects: the miserable weanling cries, screams, and does not sleep or eat for several long days and nights if the mother is consistent, off and on for much longer, if she is not. Behrokh ruefully washed her red breasts four times to placate inconsolably crying Leila, stretching the misery over six weeks. Setara, after she had weaned her nearly three-year-old son by refusal and diversion with sugar and candy, had so much milk still that her breasts swelled and hardened painfully. During the fifth night, she dreamt that the pain drained away, her heavy breast became light, and she rested easily. She felt so good that she woke up—and indeed, her breasts were empty: her son had sneaked up in the middle of the night and suckled them dry. But because old milk is very unhealthy, he started his weaned life with a terrible bout of vomiting and diarrhea, his mother said.

Even before weaning, most children get some food besides milk, at least casually. By about twelve months of age children likely are addicted to tea and sugar, the first foodstuff elders offer a child. While everybody is eating, the baby on mother's or father's lap will get a taste of rice, a piece of bread to chew on, some soup, all displayed within easy reach on the baby's level on the floor. Until recently, people ate with their hands, the easiest and most natural eating technique available for a baby. However, rarely is a special effort made to feed the baby food other than milk consistently, for various reasons. Fruits, yogurt, and other foods, for example, are said to be bad for an infant's health at times and withheld on purpose. "It is not becoming for her," said a seven-year-old girl, literally taking a raisin and a piece of walnut out of her loudly protesting eleven-month-old sister's mouth. Mahperi's little son got the thrashing of his young life for having given a piece of apple to his baby brother on the cradle, who had begged for it and then almost choked on it. Hejab had not given any of her older children fruits and other food as early as she did her seventh child. "Then we didn't have anything and we didn't know that such food is good for a baby. Now we know—the doctor, the midwife, the children in school tell us." By using this new knowledge, Hejab presents herself as a competent, modern mother. Her baby boy thus is linked to the urban national culture by the food he gets, by his modern name, the fancy clothes his siblings give him occasionally, and by his health checkups.

The health clinic in the next village runs a well-child clinic. Mothers bring their infants and young children there to be weighed and measured, and to receive vitamin syrup for the child as well as birth-control devices for themselves, if so desired. Every child in Deh Koh is on file there. In 1994, the staff said that all mothers participated. Those who do not show up on time are visited and reprimanded by the midwife-nurse, a young local woman who is highly respected for her skills. Infant mortality has declined, the midwife says, as have avitaminoses, anemia, and other malnutrition ailments that afflicted older babies in the past, but the majority of infants still are undernourished and weak (zaif). Subnutrition is so common and considered so "normal" that if a baby starts to sit up very early, at four months, or to stand up at seven or eight months, it is taken as a sign that somebody in the family probably will die. A thin (lish) baby is said to be strong later, while a strong, fat (qott, cakh) one is said to get weak later. The infant son of a woman teacher, although even taken to school occasionally to be nursed, was brought up mostly on expensive baby formula stretched with sugar-water, and on cookies. At twelve months, he could not stand on his spindly legs, not even when supported. I hardly ever saw him smile. "He is just like the other boys at his age," said one of his caretakers. Weakness, bouts of illness, and crankiness are hallmarks of the older infant-weanling stage. From all appearances, children at that age are not feeling very well much of the time.

As the baby gets older, it is said to become less vulnerable to dangers from extra-human forces, although some precautions ought to be taken still. Just as a baby is dependent on its mother for nourishment and comfort, it is dependent on her for health. The totality of care is subsumed under *safd kardan*, to take care of, to manage, to watch over. An ill baby is "a mother's concern day and night." An attentive, knowledgeable mother is aware of many medical resources, from herbs and home remedies she might have herself or know where to get to efficacious amulet writers, from local wise women health counselors to various health clinics, from physicians in town to alms, vows, and pilgrimages. The resources exist side by side; very few mothers set stock in just one course of treatment, especially if the health problem is not cured fast. An ill baby will ride on its mother's arm from one such source to another, associating her with all social contacts and treatments. A father is not engaged in health care unless extraordinary financial and organizational demands are warranted, such as a journey to a hospital in town or a pilgrimage to a distant shrine.

Most of Hurijan the Healer's patients are infants; most amulets are written for infants and young children; most of the patients at the health clinic in the next village are infants—the same infants in many cases, with the same ailments. A seven-month-old boy had a bad cough—"his chest was clogged," his mother diagnosed. When cough medicine left over from an earlier prescription for an elder sibling had no immediate effect, his mother took him to the physician at the clinic, who said he had whooping cough. The doctor's medicine made the baby "well," and medication was discontinued after a day or two. The cough started again. Back at the clinic, a group of women from the interior of the tribal area with their "sick, unwashed, wretched" children, said the mother, were waiting with them in the same room.

This time, the doctor's medicine did not help at all. The boy screamed, refused all food and drink, and "bent over backwards so that his head touched his feet," a sign of deep distress. His mother took him to Hurijan, Deh Koh's most sought-after local healer of children's ailments. She diagnosed an intestinal clogging, and pushed a little bit of a paste made of gunpowder and water into his mouth while his mother was holding him down. This medicine proved too strong for him. At night he got worse, "tossed his head back, had high fever, his nose and face looked small and pinched, his eyes were huge, and the inner corner of his eyes opened up." In this condition the frightened mother took him to her own mother, a wise woman and health counselor herself. The grandmother decided that the child must have been sickened by the smells from the sick, dirty, strange children at the clinic. She made a tea-medicine of chamomille, mint leaves, mint root, and other herbs, roasted together in hot ashes and then boiled in water. The boy's grandmother could see an improvement right away, but the mother, to cover all possibilities, asked the amulet writer to write an amulet for the boy. The man, who is said to have seen all the babies in Deh Koh at one crisis or another, diagnosed the boy as having caught a bad cold, which his mother should not make worse by feeding him cold-sour food. The baby got well. A less dedicated and resourceful mother might not have been able to save the child, said the boy's grandmother.

.   .   .

After Perijan's naughty ten-year-old son had spilled strong-smelling perfume on the rug at home, his five-month-old sister was throwing up what she drank. Her mother said she was sick from the smell of the perfume, that the smell had turned her humoral disposition from a healthy balance to warm. The diagnosis suggested certain remedies, which, however, did not help much. After about ten days of watching her retch and wane, Perijan took her to the clinic, where the physician gave her four different medicines, tetracycline nasal spray among them, which baffled Perijan and me. But from the forty-minute walk home in the hot afternoon, mother and baby got so hot that Perijan decided not to risk the drugs because should one of them be humorally warm, the baby's already warm and overheated condition might get worse. She decided to start medication slowly the next day with tetracycline, which she knew from other occasions to "work."

The baby, an exceptionally well cared-for and well nourished child, eventually recovered, more or less despite the medication she received. Her mother credited herself and her cleanliness, healthy milk, and special efforts for the recovery. As special efforts she counted constant monitoring of her daughter's condition and heightened attention to her signs of discomfort: the baby was carried around more, fed immediately on demand, kept especially clean and dry, and allowed to sleep without disturbances. "Now that we have her, I have to take care of her well," the mother said proudly.

.   .   .

A four-month-old boy had "milk hives" (*shirdun*), said his mother, yellow, greasy excrements that stain diaper-rags. He had a bellyache, identified as such by his squirmy motions. This condition is said to be brought about by holding an infant upside down while playing, for example. Easy as the diagnosis was for the mother, the physician said this was not a proper disease, that he could not cure it. He sent her to an amulet writer, but she decided to see Hurijan first. Before she got around to it, however, the baby got well again "by the grace of God."

.   .   .

Mahtab's four-month-old baby girl died.

Mahtab said, "Nothing was wrong with her. Suddenly, she started to cry and wouldn't stop. The next day we took her to the doctor. He gave her an injection and a syrup, but that evening she died."

Mahtab's mother said, "She had a little fever, nothing much. All of a sudden she died, for no reason."

Neighbors said, "Mahtab had too many children too close together, therefore the child was weak. Mahtab isn't a very competent mother, either. She didn't take any precautions against djenn and beads. In addition, the whole family has a lot of false pride (*taqabor*); they are too proud to consult local healers or use home remedies."

The physician said, "The child had bronchopneumonia in both lungs; by the time they brought her to the clinic it was too late."

When a few weeks later Mahtab's sister's baby had a cold, the baby's mother and both grandmothers took it not just to the clinic but to the hospital in the next city—a demonstration of dedication meant to erase all previous allegations of neglect.

Baby and the World

As the older infant is stronger now and outside dangers are said to be diminishing, it is taken out more often, sitting in its mother's arms or sleeping propped against her shoulder, under her veil-wrap, which protects it against cold, flies, wind, sun, and the evil eye. If a mother has to go out on a social call, the baby will be with her even if somebody at home could babysit. A baby-in-arms or, occasionally, on the back, validates a fertile, that is, normal, woman's identity. It is a woman's main claim to God-ordained womanhood, and its prime sign. In this sense, a woman needs a baby—not for survival, not as the baby needs her, but for indicating her place as a woman among the people. A woman without a young child is an unfortunate woman: infertile, old, or in other deplorable states precluding a steady flow of new children. A childless woman might even borrow a sister's or sister-in-law's baby to take on a visit, not to pretend it is hers, but because an empty lap and empty arms make a woman feel incomplete, "as if she had forgotten to put a veil-wrap around her," as a mother of eight children explained. When I took my neighbor's little daughter with me on visits a few times, women would get a soft look in their eyes and tell me that they understood my longing for another baby, with only two daughters to my credit. For a normal woman of childbearing age, being with a young child is the normal, the natural order of things. However, an older woman with a new baby also is uncomfortable; Perijan regularly left her latecomer baby with her sister if she had to be out in public because she was embarrassed by her old-woman motherhood, as she called it. The very recent trend to fewer children in Deh Koh is too new to be assessed in terms of changing attitudes and self-understanding of women.

A baby of either sex likely is surrounded by women of all ages during the day, by women's and children's noises, their smells, their movements, their rhythms. Men rarely handle infants; they rarely provide services like feeding, washing, rocking; they rarely take infants outside. Male and female infants learn the women's patterns of living but neither learn much about the men's. Male older infants, however, are talked to more often by men and boys than are female infants, and in more matter-of-fact ways, and will be taken into male company more frequently by their fathers.

The common, subnutrition-based weakness of older infants is compounded by lack of occasion and encouragement to move and to exercise muscles. Babies are kept out of harm's way: on the cradle, on somebody's arm or back, in a mother's lap. When on the floor they are forever prevented from crawling out of their mother's reach, from lifting themselves up, from reaching out, in order to keep them from hurting themselves. Stairs or porches have no railings. Freestanding kerosene stoves, open fires, boiling water kettles, hot teapots, knives, electrical outlets, all are within easy and dangerous reach of a crawling infant in houses where most activities take place on the infant's own level, the floor. Just like young babies, older ones, too, are discouraged from moving; they are encouraged to "sit properly," to stop running, not to make noise (*sholuq*), to stay next to mother, to wait, to drop what they hold onto. When sleepy or simply discouraged or whiny, a baby may crawl to the cradle, demanding to be strapped onto it. Only after it has mastered walking (between twelve and twenty months) will the ground-level horizon widen. Until then, the range of activity and mobility is a narrow circle around mother or caretaker; the outside world is seen from the height of mother's arm or somebody's back. Without toys or special, safe baby-spaces, anything the baby may find on the floor and may be able to grasp to play with likely is either potentially dangerous or breakable, and will be taken away. Babies are frustrated often and cry frequently—so frequently that crying and crankiness are considered normal attributes of babyhood. Prolonged crying and whining usually brings them attention. Already when only a few months old, some babies are *girvaru*, crybabies, who spend much of their waking time somewhere between whining and screaming.

Infant boys and girls wear the same kind of clothes, pants and tops, although girls may wear a skirt or dress over the pants, but there the similarity ends. Boys' hair is kept shorn, girls' is more-or-less long. Little boys frequently are half-naked, especially in summer, while a caretaker is looking for a dry pair of pants, while the cradle is readied, or after his bottom had been rinsed. A little boy's exposed genitals do not provoke affective reactions, although a mother may comment on the little penis (*kirr*) jokingly and touch it playfully. By contrast, a girl infant is not likely to be exposed, not even for a short time. While a mother is changing her diaper-rags on the cradle in the presence of others, she will shield the cradle, especially from boys.

Wet pants are replaced with dry ones quickly and under the protective cover of mother's skirt folds or veil-wrap in the presence of males. If a little brother and sister are in the bath together, the sister will wear shorts or pants; her brother likely will be naked. Girls learn at an early age what a little boy looks like, and may be changing baby brothers' diapers soon, while boys are not supposed to know what a girl's genitals look like—in theory of propriety, that is—until they get married. Five-year-old Gholam, who had two elder sisters and a baby sister and was recovering from circumcision, pointed to his four-year-old sister and said, "And when will *she* get it done?" The reaction he got from the women and girls around him at the time, giggling and laughter, left him frustrated, bewildered, and angry; as a boy, he found himself outside the women's world, kept from knowing what they knew. "A girl's things are a secret," a father summed it up for his three-year-old son.

While little boys' genitals do not receive any special attention except later at circumcision, little girls' do: they are hidden, a secret that, if revealed, brings embarrassment (*kejalat*). Girls' "things" are a source of concern, of potential shame from the time of birth; boys' are not. Therefore, as soon as little girls can sit, they are told time and again to sit properly (*dorost*), feet tucked under, skirt or pants covering all from the waist down to the feet as well as possible. When a baby girl is sitting next to her mother, the mother will watch her legs and feet, bending them back into the tucked-under position whenever the baby stretches them. Outstretched legs, a naked bottom, even torn and tattered pants are *zesht*, obscene in many ways for a girl, but they are of no social, moral, or aesthetic consequence for a little boy.

12 · *Tatalu and Beyond*

Pee and Such

Almost from the beginning a child's excrements are labeled mildly, amusingly disgusting: *ai* (poop), *lulu-e, bubu-e, kassif, gand* (dirty); a soiled baby or toddler is told to be ashamed (*kejalat bekesh*), with mock disapproval and smiles. A young child might not get cleaned promptly as long as it is on the cradle, and likely will be cleaned in discomfort—rinsed with cold water under a faucet or from a long-spouted toilet can, outside, in any weather—but it is not scolded seriously for being dirty and smelly or for soiling anything else. As in other situations, older siblings are less likely to be tolerant and more likely to voice disgust ("You stink! Mother, take her away!"); or to complain ("He never cleans himself; it is a shame; Mother, why don't you teach him . . ."). From about six months on, a mother or grandmother will take the child outside when it appears ready to defecate, to a corner of the veranda or the courtyard. Only the rare child will have diapers if it is off the cradle, and likely will wet any place or any lap it is sitting on. By about two years of age, most children are toilet trained and demand to be taken outside by saying "*ai*" to defecate, "*maza*" to urinate. Bed-wetting, however, especially by boys, is quite common until children are five or six years old. "Thank goodness for plastic sheets for the beds!" said a mother of three children under the age of five.

All elimination is done in a squatting position, which is comfortable for toddlers. Until about twenty years ago, people relieved themselves in the barns or outside somewhere, in places easy to use even for very young children. But the newer outhouses and toilets, with their relatively wide holes and wide, flat ceramic bowls, are unsuited for short legs. In houses with young children, the toilets therefore are "always dirty," people complain, further proof of the stereotype that a house full of children is untidy, dirty, and in ill-repair. Likewise, the long-spouted toilet cans used for cleaning oneself are far too unwieldy for little hands. Unless a caretaker accompanies a child to the toilet and helps with the ablutions, little bottoms are likely to be dirty too. Young children further are afraid to use an outhouse or even an indoor toilet alone. "A djenn will grab me," said a four-year-old girl after I had pressed for an explanation for her loud refusal to go there without her mother. "How do you know?" I asked, knowing that in this house no adult would say anything about djenn. "The children say so," she said.

For these reasons, and especially when frequent diarrhea makes elimination urgent, young children usually do their business outside in a quiet corner, behind a boulder, in the fields. Excrements, *gi*, in a courtyard or on the packed-dirt floor of a porch are not made much of: somebody will cover them with a little soil, scoop them up with a handy piece of wood or an iron ash-pan, and take them away. Urine on the floor or on rugs is almost totally ignored, inside and outside the house. Children acquire proper toilet habits easily, mothers say. There is nothing to worry about.

Farhad, three, two elder sisters, and a three-year-old boy-cousin and his four-year-old sister were playing "Fort" (*qale*) on the hard, bare earth in a corner of the courtyard. I watched them from the edge of a verandah above them. They were scratching the outlines of a cluster of rooms in the dirt with sticks and rocks. Farhad's sister fetched water in a leaky leather bucket. Dirt mixed with water made a mortar for the hand-wide high walls of stones and for tiny fire-places in the rooms. Farhad stacked broken twigs and sticks he had picked up around the yard in a space he declared to be a barn— stacks of firewood. One sister left, returning with a flat stone to use as a bread board. The other sister placed little stones of different sizes in the "tower" (*borj*) at the edge of the fort: the "lady," her "groom," and the "lady's child." A larger rock outside the fort was the "lady's horse." The boy cousin wondered aloud where to build a proper place for a horse. "No horse, a car, a car!" Farhad corrected him. "We cannot sit on a horse, we are too little!" Next, the boy cousin made a "field" outside the fort by spreading grass from the cowshed around it. "Don't!" cried his elder cousin. She said this whenever she looked at him, no matter what he did. He ignored her every time. The children talked incessantly, mostly to themselves, it seemed. Farhad's voice rose above the din: "I have to poop," he declared. He looked around the grid of the fort. "Poop, poop," he chanted.

"Go over there," his sister said, pointing at his barn. "No," he cried, "Nobody poops in the barn, do you hear me?! The barn is full of firewood! We need an outhouse." He took a long step across barn, tower, and car-horse. A few yards away, he scratched some pebbles and loose dirt into a rough circle about a foot in diameter. "Out-house," he yelled, "Look, here it is." He pulled down his pants, squat-ted, and aimed his load into the circle. The others ignored him, except his eldest sister, who casually told him to cover the stink with dirt. Without any further ado, he pulled his pants back up. A handful of dirt on the heap made a little mound on which flies gathered in-stantly. "Here is the outhouse, if any of you needs one," he cried. Nobody took him up on his offer.

Much later, after the deserted fort was just an odd little jumble of rubble, Farhad's grandmother, sweeping the yard, took the content of his outhouse to the barn on a small board.

Smiles and Whines

By the time a child is weaned it has mastered a Deh Koh toddler's most effective survival strategy: *bune gereftan*, whining with perseverance. The concomitant cognition is that of a small world where things and services can be obtained or kept by engaging the vocal chords from whining to screaming without giving up, without letting oneself be diverted. More than any other behavior, *bune gereftan* defines a toddler for the people in Deh Koh. By the time a child is around two years old, it also has learned to use smiles and coyness to get approval: children are said to be at their sweetest (*shirintarin*) at this age; they are appealing, especially if they are roly-poly (*haplehapo, cakh, qott*) and of pleasant disposition (*khoshakhlaq*), good (*khub*), and their blabbering (*gholghol, tatalas*) is turning to toddler-talk: a *tatalu* is a youngster just learning to talk. Children may play up to their elders' appreciation of their sweetness. When his little sister cries "Lamin, Lamin," seventeen-year-old Ramin melts with affection: "I'll be your saclifice, I'm at your selvice," he mimics her baby substitution of *l* for *r*, and showers her with hugs and kisses until she starts to squirm and yell, and then gives in to her demand: a piece of chewing gum, for example, which she chews fast and swallows.

Amin, who is three, was staggering home up the hill, crying. When nobody ran down to meet him he cried louder, then yelled at his mother, who was washing clothes at the courtyard basin: "Mother, don't you hear me cry?! Don't you know you have to say, 'Dear, *jun*, my life, what is wrong?'" His mother was so charmed by his sweet cleverness that she was ready to grant him any wish at that moment, she said.

A young child's smile is sweet, laughter innocent yet. A few years later, a blank, unsmiling face will be a sign of a well-mannered child, especially a girl, and laughter a sign of potentially loose morals. Occasionally, elder siblings, visitors, and parents will entertain a toddler specifically to elicit a smile: Zahra, age eleven, extends a hand, palm up, toward two-and-one-half-year-old Susan, who is tired and grumpy. "Play 'Crow,'" Zahra says. Susan does not move, or smile, or even look. Zahra takes Susan's hand and, slightly tapping her finger on Susan's palm, chants: "A crow sat over here, a crow sat over there, and said, '*Pellepellepelle*,'" tickling Susan's hand. No reaction from Susan. "Now you do it," says Zahra, but Susan keeps her hand stretched out. Zahra lets the crow flutter in Susan's palm again, and again, until Susan finally smiles.

Roughhousing such as riding horseback on big brother's back or flying airplane on father's foot soles while father is lying on his back, and guessing games like "Which (fist) is full, which one is empty?" produce smiles, laughter even. A smiling young child is rare, a special delight. Young children do not seem to find much to smile about, said Hurijan, healer of children's ailments. "And this is better so," she added. "Life isn't funny anyway." Besides, a very sweet young child is in danger of becoming spoiled (*nazeli*). Giving in to a child's demands too readily, hugging and kissing it "too much," picking it up too frequently, easily may make it get used (*amukhte vabi*) to indulgences so much that it will grow up to be ill-mannered and lazy, foulmouthed and, because its demands will increase with age, a pain to have around and to take care of responsibly.

Last-borns are said to be spoiled more likely than are children who have to share attention with younger siblings. Says Hoda, who is five and a sister of two younger siblings, comparing herself to same-age but last-born cousin Sari: "Her mother always says, 'Sari-*ruud, juun*'" (in a sweet sing-song) "while my mother only calls me: 'Hoda!' And if she does say '*Jun*' to me, she says, '*Junn*'" (shortly, in a no-nonsense voice). As the youngest in the family, Sari is very spoiled, says Hoda's mother.

However, all the smiles and sunny talk are less likely to produce wished-for objects, food, or attention than do patient whining, nagging ("I want gum, I want gum"), and aggression, such as hitting mother on the back, scratching her face, biting her hand, pulling her headscarf and braids, pinching her mouth. At an earlier age, as weanlings, children's well-being depended to a large measure on how successfully they could demand, beg, pilfer, wheedle food out of caretakers. By age three, they are well-practiced in these skills.

Successful children will learn soon when to use what strategy to greatest advantage. At age four Ali was a master of the quick sunny/cloudy/stormy play of voice, facial expression, and body language. He could, for example, almost simultaneously smile at his father (to get money from him) and whine-plus-hit his mother (to get money from her). He could moan pitifully, then turn around and flash his grandmother a brilliant smile that did not touch his eyes, then turn back and continue to whine. For him and other children, intimate adults thus are within their powers of manipulation through an exaggerated display of a few standardized emotions and at the price of trying perseverance.

Before regular weaning, most children will have tried all the food eaten in the family but will not have been fed regularly or, from the children's point of view, dependably, and not with easily manageable or preferred food. After having been weaned, a child is expected to eat adults' food at adults' schedules. As toddlers' sleeping patterns are not the same as those of adults, the youngsters miss meals often. A child who wakes up after breakfast has been cleared away, for example, readily will be given water, the only food children get simply for the asking, day or night, and tea and sugar, but even for bread, which is hard to chew, the child may have to whine until mother is ready to interrupt her work to provide it, often grouchily so. Of any other breakfast food that might have been available that morning, such as walnuts, scrambled eggs, leftovers from the previous evening's dinner, nothing likely will be left for the two-year-old. At lunch, the toddler will have to compete with elder siblings for the best food. About this situation, a woman remembers: "Our grade school teacher told us to eat slowly, to chew every bite carefully, to drink water with every bite. We looked at each other, pulling faces, and then Leila spoke for us all: 'If I do this, I won't get any food—I have three elder brothers who stuff their mouths with both hands!'" This is not to say that elder children will not look after their little siblings at all. They do, often touchingly so, but unreliably. And an elder brother or sister may display authority over a little sibling any time by giving, but also by withholding or by taking away, food: seven-year-old Forugh literally took a walnut out of her two-year-old sister's mouth, saying, "Walnuts are bad for her." Over loud protests of a toddler, his six-year-old sister took a piece of apple out of his hand "to see if it is any good." Another little one dropped the bread she had been chewing on; her eight-year-old brother threw it to the chickens "because it is dirty." She picked it out of the dirt again later and continued to eat.

Dinner is eaten after dark. By then, a toddler likely will be asleep after having whined and begged ("I am hungry, mother, I am hungry") some half-cooked rice in rice-water, half-cooked vegetables or legumes, some yogurt. Young children like to eat *kol*, half-cooked food, people say, turning a habit born of necessity into a purported preference. Most likely, the toddler will go to bed on bread eaten in the late afternoon, bread soaked in buttermilk, or some other ready (*hazeri*) food. Such food—milk, yogurt, butter, walnuts, dates, eggs— usually is in short supply, but there is always tea and sugar.

By age two, children likely are addicted to tea and sugar. Tea is available at breakfast, lunch, dinner, and in between; it is served to visitors always. At such an occasion, a two-year-old boy drank three small glasses of strong tea with nine lumps of sugar within minutes. Three-year-old Nilufar burned herself when she tried to pour tea for herself. Toddlers grab pieces of sugar whenever they can get their hands on an unwatched sugar bowl. Tea is given to young children with admonitions and disapproval—"Don't drink so much tea, it isn't good for you; drink less, it is *lulu-e*, bad, dirty; it'll make you sick, no wonder you are so weak"—but a child does not have to whine long for it. The same is true for sweets served at parties. "My little one here is so weak and sickly because he doesn't eat anything but candy," is a standard complaint in mothers' discussions of their toddlers. "Too much" candy is said to be unhealthy; it "burns" the liver, weakens the abdomen, makes children thin. But candy is known to be preferred toddler-food. "I have to give it to him to have some peace," a mother said.

A proverb sums up young children's subnutrition in sociological-critical terms: "Now that it depends on its father's bread it has become thin." This implies not only that weakness is normal, to be expected, but also that as long as the child was fed from mother's resources it was fat and healthy—fathers do not take care of their children well; they only want them as credit to their name, a mother said, explaining the proverb. Fathers, however, claim that young children simply are disobedient and unreasonable in regard to food preferences as they are in other regards as well, by nature, and that their mothers are lax and lazy in child care. Good care is shown by satisfied children. "Make your child agreeable" is a standard request to a mother from a man who is tired of listening to a whining or crying young child. This usually leads to more candy, more tea, and fosters exactly the kind of motherly response that perpetuates the toddler's bad habits—bad by local judgment—of demanding unhealthy food and of whining.

Between two and four years of age a child is said to be weak and pesky. Its main method for getting nonroutine care, for getting its special needs for food, sleep, and attention met, however minimally, is so commonplace for children of this age that adults ignore it as an expression of young children's innate naughtiness (*fuzuli*), which children will outgrow as the mind (*aql, hush*) develops along with the body. Toddlers are expected to be annoying whiners so routinely that time and again I observed how one was made to cry because it was expected to cry; how crying or whining were shushed, however unsuccessfully and with however little hope for success, because they were not taken so much as an expression of a need or a frustration than as a sign of childishness. For all its normalcy, though, a *girvaru* or *vasveru*, a habitually dissatisified child who whines and throws tantrums excessively and "for no reason" other than being disposed toward such behavior, is seen as a sore test of parents', especially a mother's, patience, which may give out any time, releasing an angry outburst of violence.

A mother said about her three-year-old *girvaru:* "Three times she got whacked today already, twice by me, once by her sister, but she doesn't give up—only when her brother beats her does she stop her whining."

Most *girvaru* are girls. Little girls' resources for dealing with frustrations are more limited, both spatially and behaviorally, than are those of their toddler brothers. Although boys may whine, cry, scream, and throw tantrums, they also may fight, throw rocks, attack their mother (not father) and siblings, run away, break things, and threaten to "kill," which their sisters are much less likely to do.

Whining develops as a reasonable strategy for wearing down the resistance young children meet everywhere. Adults and elder siblings likely will deny any request, interfere in any activity, foil any intention a toddler may initiate or express. But with insistence, perseverance, whining, and stealth, the children may in the long run, and with many accompanying signs of displeasure and disapproval from their elders, get what they want. At times the perseverance is truly heroic. Once I was sitting with twenty-month-old Zahra in her aunt's house with a box of sweets in front of us. Zahra had gotten a generous share but wanted more, mostly to unwrap each candy and play with it. Her aunt, after having said, "Dear, you'll get sick," and given other friendly admonitions and explanations, patiently would take the piece Zahra had managed to grab out of her hand, and prevent her from reaching the box by pushing it farther away from her. Zahra tried to get to the sweets over fifty times—successfully only once—and was not discouraged yet when her aunt finally put the box away. In this case, away from her mother, Zahra did not whine or throw a fit. She only ignored the "no" and pursued her goal undaunted by failure. Had her mother or her teenaged sister been with us, she would have whined to get them to give her candy, as I had seen her do on other occasions.

Without an appropriate audience, children can control emotional outbursts so well that the tantrum or crying seems to be mostly performance. Ali's whining-plus-smile ability is a case in point, as is a four-year-old boy's wild tantrum at the departure of his father without him, a tantrum that included rolling around in the dirt, threats to throw himself in front of the car, throwing rocks, and scratching his own face, but stopped instantly when the boy realized that his father, mother, and two sisters had left the scene. He picked himself up and ran away with a playmate without as much as a shrug. Three-year-old Susan followed a conspiratorial "I'll pretend that my leg hurts" to her sister and myself with a perfectly convincing limp accompanied by little moans and whining as long as she deemed necessary to get out of an errand her grandmother wanted to send her on.

Similarly left to her own devices without an adult around (I remained unseen), Nilufar, age two-and-one-half, was dealing with her four-year-old brother's teasing with admirable patience. She was sitting on the floor, a square, foam-stuffed cushion between her back and the wall and a tray with bread and yogurt in front of her. She was ladling yogurt into her mouth with pieces of flatbread. With her left hand she tried, again and again, and without success, to push her tangled hair out of her face. Her brother was shoving his plastic wristwatch into her hair. She tilted her head, pushed him away with her elbow, shouting, "Don't! Go away!" Elbows sticking out, she tried to claim more space while continuing to eat, awkwardly so. With the boy wriggling behind her, the cushion fell on her. She moved aside. Her brother grabbed it, threw it on her; she ducked, pushed it away; he threw it again, she kicked it aside, continuing to feed herself all the while and to push hair out of her eyes. After the sixth time, she calmly got up, carried the cushion to the far end of the room, and turned back to the tray and the food without looking at her brother at all. He fetched the cushion, dropped it on her again. She ignored it, stayed bent over the tray under the cushion, ate, fought her hair. The bowl was almost empty. The boy crawled toward her and pinched her in the ribs. She did not flinch. He pinched her behind from the other side; she ignored him again. Now she was finished eating. She rubbed her yogurt-covered fingers on her pants, pushed cushion and tray away, jumped up, and ran after him out the door, yelling, "Now I'll kill you!"

Shahpur, three, had been whining and poking his mother for money for about twenty minutes. He was not to be diverted, not with a cookie, not with tea. His sister got money to buy a notebook, whereupon he wanted money for a pencil, he said. "He lies," said his mother. "He has a pencil. He wants money for candy." He gave her a quick look with a slightly embarrassed, crooked grin, and turned his whining into a howl, his poking into hitting. After five more minutes, his mother threw him a bill together with a curse, and he left, smugness all over his little face.

Already at eighteen months, children in Deh Koh obviously go on the cognition that adults who say "no" are only playing hard to get, that most "nos" eventually can be challenged successfully. The *girvaru* I know, the young children who whine and cry almost incessantly, differ from non-*girvaru* children by a low tolerance of denials of requests and of mother's assertions of authority, and impaired judgment when choosing issues worth whining for. Hakime, for example, a prototypical *girvaru* at age three, once linked into one long whine three consecutive issues Nilufar would not even have opened her mouth for: nagging and whining gratingly, Hakime wanted her mother to catch a rooster for her (request denied with ridicule), then demanded a box of scarce detergent to pour on the wash her sister was washing (demand denied by scolding), and then wanted a piece of chewing gum, which her mother said she did not have but in the end produced anyway, saying, "Now go away, you have severed my head with your whining!"

Lures ("Come here—look, the candy in my hand—oh, the cat got it!"); empty promises ("I'll go to the store with you if you do this for me . . ."); stringing a child along ("Right away, dinner will be ready," said for two hours); teasing (dangling something just out of reach:

"Catch it, catch it!"); fear ("If you won't come, a wolf will get you"); and threats ("Don't, or I'll prick you with a needle!") are voiced liberally in the management of children of any age. After *da* (mother), Siahmaq's first word was *"dulu,"* (*durugh*, lie). Children learn from almost the beginning to distrust what they hear, including a "yes" or a "no" to a request. Any "yes" might have been a temporary whim, any "no" potentially stands only until it is changed to a "yes." It is up to the child—and frequently in its power—to bring about the change. The world is at once unreliable, aggravating, hostile even, and amenable to manipulation. A child learns to distrust the very people it is most dependent on—mother, siblings—and to get from them what it needs or wants by behaving in a disapproved-of manner. Any cursing, chewing-out, yelling, or even physical violence is a price the child sometimes has to pay, and learning to dodge punishment, to brush off verbal tirades, and to calculate risks are part of Deh Koh toddlers' routine survival skills.

During a visit, I was sitting at a big tray with candy, shelled walnuts, and apples. My hostess's daughter came in with her two-year-old son. As soon as he was on the floor he made a beeline to the tray and started to throw candy around. "Saman, Saman," his mother and grandmother cried, "Don't! Let the candy alone, it is dirty . . ." His mother draged him away by an arm. He screamed, then played for a little while with the candy he had in his fist. He unwrapped each piece, put it in his mouth, took it out again, rubbed it into the rug, contemplated his sticky fingers, licked, then headed back to the tray. "Saman, don't do this! This woman here" (pointing to me) "has scissors in her bag, she'll cut off your ears! Saman!" He was dragged back again, started to whimper, shook off his mother's hand, and escaped back to the tray. His mother picked him up and turned to walk out, but he screamed and kicked, and she was more interested in our conversation than in keeping her son from the tray anyway, so she sat down again. He was at the candy again. "Saman!" the women cried. He looked at them sweetly, clapped his hands, cocked his head, laughed, then grabbed an apple and took a grating bite, to his mother's and grandmother's delight. They cooed. He extended the apple to his mother's brother, said something his mother translated as "Eat, eat," but when the man moved closer, the boy pulled the apple away, behind his back. "This was a lie, the kind of lie your father always makes!" said his uncle. *"Dulu, dulu,"* crowed Saman, throwing the apple across the rug. He returned to the tray and resumed throwing candy around until his uncle ordered the tray to be taken away.

Aside from strategies for manipulating figures of authority, and judgmental criteria for deciding when commands can be ignored, children, like Saman in this case, learn by the oblique, inconsistent, even contradictory messages they receive how they ought to behave, how the world ought to be, what constitutes good and bad manners, right and wrong behavior. But they also learn that norms and virtues are not absolutes but are different in different contexts. They learn to choose from a menu of options, to calculate the options' risks and advantages. The faster and better they learn these skills, the more likely will they be called "smart" (*zereng*).

Well and Ill

Magical protection is routinized and scaled back because a toddler is considered less vulnerable than an infant; once in a while, wild rue will be burned to fumigate house and child against the evil eye. Until recently, amulets and some of the over fifty beads I have identified that were believed to be efficacious against various ailments of children commonly were fastened to a toddler's shirt. Any responsible adult will say "*mashallah*" when praising a child, to prevent the evil eye; will hold a hand over a child's head when it is drinking water at night from a water faucet outdoors so that no djenn will hit it; will not let it sit alone on a door sill in the evening because a djenn might linger there; will make sure somebody accompanies a toddler outside after dark as a precaution against djenn, who are said to try to lure the child away; and will watch out for little ones generally.

Physical protection of a toddler, especially one who is followed by a new sibling, largely is delegated to older children who will take the little one around, prevent it from putting dangerous things into its mouth, from falling, and from getting lost. Farokh, age eight, was sent to fetch a jug of buttermilk from his grandmother farther down in the village. He took his two-year-old sister, who had begged for it, with him. On the way home, full jug in one hand, sister on the other, he chanced upon a boy with whom he had had a fight. The boy, seizing the opportunity a loaded-down enemy presented, threw rocks at Farokh's back. Despite an almost overwhelming urge to let go of jug and sister to take on the challenger, he said later, Farokh ignored him, with difficulty and with revenge in his heart. He delivered jug and sister to his mother safely, turned on his heels and sped away like lightning to beat up the boy.

Many times Mahrokh has sent her twelve-year-old granddaughter over to her co-wife's room (which Mahrokh herself never visits—she is not on speaking terms with her husband and his second wife) to take care of the crying toddler who obviously was unattended. A neighbor carried a two-year-old boy home to his mother after a stampeding cow had knocked him down in the alley. Toddlers are forever kept from coming to grief in the streets by whoever is nearby. Despite the vigilance, toddlers are hurt often, most commonly by falling off a flight of stairs or a verandah. Railings or other toddler-proof safety features are unknown, despite great anxiety about young children coming to harm by falling from second-floor porches, and concerns about toddlers' movements. Young children "don't listen" when warned; they "don't watch where they are going"; they do not know danger when they see it, they have "no reasoning power" yet. They are very vulnerable and ought to be kept were they can be watched and restrained easily.

Toddlers still spend many hours indoors, close to mother, on carpeted floors, on her lap, on the cradle, unless it is occupied by a new baby; a mother was "rocking two cradles" all through one summer because her two-year-old did not want to give up his cradle. He was so cranky that she let him sleep on it and borrowed another one for the new infant. Outdoors, the little ones are encouraged to stay close by. They fall asleep on their mother's skirts while she is baking bread or on a caretaker's shoulders; they are walked here and there on somebody's arm. Most alleys and paths in and around the village are rocky and steep, and the toddlers are weak and used to being carried.

Susan, at two-and-one-half, wanted to ride on her mother's arm to a visit. Her mother argued that she was big enough to walk, and that the people in the street would mock her, would say, "Look, this baby!" Susan said, "You tell everybody Susan is sick, she has fever, her health broke down, then they'll say nothing." Susan, who rarely has to whine for what she wants, won the dispute and immediately put her head on her mother's shoulder, looking tired and "ill." Her mother took this as a big joke and told people about Susan's cleverness. Susan not only got her ride but compliments too.

Little boys are said to venture out alone more readily than little girls. They might be taken to the bathhouse by father, or to the gardens by older boys. After a boy is circumcised and has started school, he will bathe with the men, but the transition from being with women to being with men is gradual, and largely up to them.

Most young children in Deh Koh look unkempt and dirty. Fear of the evil eye has decreased markedly in Deh Koh over the past twenty years, but a grimy, "ugly" young child still is taken to be safer from the evil eye than is a clean, healthy-looking one. Mothers sometimes introduce their children with: "Look, this ugly, weak, little dirty one" to preempt any dangerous admiration. Mamalus blames the evil eye, among other things, for the fatal drowning accident of one of her sons at the age of three: "In the bathhouse was this woman with her own three-year-old. She said, 'How big and nice your little boy is—look at my skinny snotnose of a *tatalu* by comparison!' Her son was safe, of course, and mine was jinxed. A few days later he was dead." Especially little girls, whose hair is not cut at all or is left to grow longer than boys in any case, easily look "like a broom," strands of hair tousled, matted, and forever in their eyes. This theme is spun into mythology: Sister Moon was sweeping the house with her straw broom, and Sister Sun was kneading bread dough in the large, round dough-tray. They started to argue, then to fight. Furious Sister Moon stabbed the broom into her sister's face so that the straw was sticking out on all sides, and furious Sister Sun threw the tray at her sister's head so that it stuck to it. That's why Moon's halo is round and smooth while Sun's is bristly, like untidy hair.

There is no shame attached to one's young children being dirty and raggedy; until recently, there was no social difference either. Children of well-to-do, local upper-class families and those of paupers were indistinguishable in this regard. Our own two daughters, however, at that age stuck out everywhere because of their relatively large size and relative cleanliness, and regularly came home from visits with amulets against the evil eye pinned to their clothes by kind, protective neighbors. Children get the message that cleanliness is analogous to beauty and goodness while dirt, being soiled, is analogous to ugliness, to being bad, dirty-minded, and that each has its own advantages and disadvantages: there is safety in one's ugliness as well as a reason to feel ashamed; there is social approval and a good feeling in one's beauty but also reason to feel anxious. "I am clean and pretty, I am clean and pretty," a four-year-old girl chanted after her trip to the bathhouse; her aunt, who overheard her, smiled, and then admonished her sternly: "Say, *mashallah!*" This is the standard accompaniment to any praise, deemed necessary to ward off evil, an illness, for example, that might befall the praised object.

Toddlers have "colds, fever, diarrhea all the time," says Hurijan, the local specialist on children's health, speaking for all. Nastaran, at two, was described by her mother as "hot and feverish," as "without health, weak, with a bloated stomach, yellow face, bad odor from her mouth, eyes half-closed, no appetite," so frequently that her eldest brother described her as "half-dead always!" According to various physicians who have practiced in Deh Koh over the years, children suffer from avitaminoses, protein deficiencies, subnutrition, chronic internal parasitic infections including giardiasis and amoebiasis (in 1994, 100 percent of Deh Koh's children were infected, many with multiple intestinal infections), respiratory infections, eczema, cuts and bruises, bone fractures, eye diseases, toothaches. These conditions account for malnutrition and for feeling unwell much of the time. All drinking water in Deh Koh is polluted with parasites, according to administrative officials. Eating dirt is as much a part of children's expected behavior as is whining. Says a woman: "All my seven children ate dirt after they were weaned. My first son ate so much dirt that he was totally constipated. His intestines stiffened and dried. Local remedies didn't help. A large dose of castor oil killed him. He was three." She watched her second child, a girl, more closely, but could not prevent constipation either. Together with being clogged up, the child lost her speech for two days; the dirt had dried, stiffened, immobilized not only her guts but her tongue too, says the mother. A remedy suggested by a woman from Shiraz, consisting of crushed almonds, the yellow part of willow-tree bark, and two local herbs, made her well again.

With vitamin syrup dispensed at the clinic in the next village, and with a slightly more diversified diet and a larger food supply since about twenty years ago, geophagy has diminished somewhat but is so common still that it is taken to be just one of the bad habits children eventually will outgrow.

Measles, whooping cough, diphtheria, and scarlet fever were deadly infections until a generation ago. One couple lost five children within twenty-four hours to diphtheria in 1965; in 1976, the physician claimed to have saved more than sixty children in that year's bad whooping cough epidemic. "Diphtheria kills, measles make blind, chicken pox makes young," goes a proverb most people can recite even today. Rheumatic fever afflicts fewer children now than a generation ago, due to the liberal dispensation of antibiotics. In the tribal area outside Deh Koh, these diseases still are largely unchecked, according to health officials in the provincial capital. In Deh Koh, most children are immunized against childhood diseases now. The leading causes of toddler death today are accidents and respiratory and intestinal infections.

Asiye remembered: "My son had just learned to walk and talk when he got measles [soru]. He was burning with fever, lying on my skirt folds while I was baking bread. I had no choice: seven, eight people to feed every day. I cried, looking at him burning up next to me. Once in a while I put my ear to his chest to see if his heart was beating still. When it stopped, I let him lie there, next to me, until I was finished with the bread. Then I washed him and we buried him."

We were in Deh Koh when a neighbor took his first son, three years old, to the district town's doctor with diphtheria in 1976; there was no doctor in Deh Koh just then. The boy died while his father was waiting his turn in front of the doctor's office. So he shouldered him and walked back home, twenty miles, in the night, and buried him at dawn.

Today, a young child's death is an isolated, often dramatic, occurrence: Tahera, two years old, was shooed away by her mother, who was baking bread, ran after a rolling tire out into the street, and was killed by a truck instantly. Another two-year-old girl, a very weak, undernourished child who could not even walk yet because her mother had had "no milk" and after a fight had left her in the care of an harrassed mother-in-law, died of "nothing": "Suddenly, at night, her health broke down. No car was available, there was a lot of snow, we couldn't get to the doctor." (The clinic is about two miles away from the house.) "When we got around to taking her, she was dead," said the old woman defensively. To "let a girl die" has become an uncomfortable accusation in Deh Koh, and she wanted to emphasize that the child's death was not her family's fault but was "the will of God," she said.

The relative rarity of toddler death means that the dread of a young child's sudden death no longer colors feelings toward young children. "A mother can afford to get attached to her child much earlier now," says Mamalus. But young children's poor health causes much anxiety in parents, and obvious stress and misery in young children. Much whining and crying, and many a withdrawn, unsmiling face actually may reflect how unwell many young children feel much of the time. Expressions of their bodily discomfort become a cultural norm, an identifying feature of the toddler stage.

While infants are said to show not much individuality beyond differences in the amount and intensity of fussiness and crying, and differences in health and the rate of growth, toddlers exhibit many signs of their basic humoral disposition. A child who has to pee often, including wetting the bed, which is common, shows that its "temperament" (*tou, mejaz*) is cold; a tendency to rashes, to a flushed face, sores in the mouth, shortness of breath, eczema, swellings, and bloatedness are taken as signs of a warm disposition. As in adults, warm conditions are rarer and easier to deal with than cold ones: "Cold is cured with doctors, warm with a single pomegranate" goes a proverb. For young children suspected of a "cold"-related condition, two of the favorite foods of children, yogurt and buttermilk, will be curtailed, together with many fruits, such as apples, watermelons, grapes, and citrus fruits. In such cases, whining will get a child some of this "unhealthy" food, but in the context of disapproval. "He shouldn't eat apples with his cold," said a twelve-year-old girl about her three-year-old brother, "but he cried and cried . . ." By watchful stealth, the little boy then managed to squirrel away three more of the forbidden apples while I was visiting with his mother. Most children show signs of being *bitou, bein mejaz*, between the two dispositions, and thus always prone to dietary imbalances. This is circular reasoning: a sickly, weak child is said to be "*bitou*," because nothing becomes him or her; once identified as such, the recommended dietary restrictions are likely to weaken the child further. When three-year-old Alam was recovering slowly from a very long, debilitating upper respiratory infection—antibiotics "don't work well any more, and patients don't use them as instructed," says the physician—his mother took pains not to give him any "too strong" or "cold" food so as not to weaken his already weak condition more. He got no eggs, very little meat, no fruits, no buttermilk; he had thrown up sweetened, boiled milk, which is the only way fresh milk is served, showing thereby that milk did not become him either. The child subsisted mostly on white rice with a little shortening, bread, a little yogurt, a few dates, which were questioned by grandmother, and tea and sugar. Dosages of the drugs were halved because the full dose was deemed "too strong," and antibiotics were withheld because they were known to be "too warm."

From the children's point of view, what is done about an illness or a feeling of distress is of more emotional consequence than is the pain or disease itself. Thus, parents' interpretations of their children's nature and ailments, and parents' decisions about treatments, may change dramatically how the toddlers perceive their condition. A travel to a pilgrimage center where father fulfills a pledge for the child's health feels entirely different from a series of injections the child gets at the clinic; shots become less scary when one gets to keep the syringe; swallowing a local healer's herbal tea is worse than being fumigated with burning wild rue seeds; being fussed over has an entirely different quality from being ignored because crankiness is taken to be simply part of growing up. One young mother killed herself over her husband's repeated refusal to take their little girl to the hospital in town where the mother thought she ought to be treated for a persistent ailment. This left the little girl much more miserable and much worse off than before. Nilufar, age four, after having been tired and listless for many weeks, finally was diagnosed with anemia caused by favism. The alarmed parents discussed this so often that Nilufar started to identify herself with it: "Meh, meh, I have *favi*, you have nothing!" she bragged to her brother in a chant she made up. Her earlier, unnamed "weakness" had held no bragging potential for her. Amin, three, who had to see a doctor in town for a series of tests for chronic diarrhea, was so fascinated by the urban scene on Main Street on his first visit that he told his father to "go for a drive alone so that I can stay and have a good look at everything." The four visits to town became a special treat for him. And when I asked Keyvan, who had burned his foot badly when he was four, what he remembered about it six years later, he promptly said, "The many sweets I got."

Memories of toddlerhood are dim and vague in adults. Much more alive are elder siblings' memories of toddler brothers and sisters. Most of these stories deal with the little catastrophies of everyday life, with falling down, losing something, obstinacy, breaking things, and are interspersed with accounts of illnesses and the pesky crankiness that is the hallmark of this age.

Good and Proper

Some children are basically "good," easy to have, healthy, easy to train, obedient, reasonable, quiet—"*musalman*," good Muslims, as Mamalus sums them up—while others are the opposite, wild, unruly, troublemakers and troublesome, loud, full of mischief—*kafir* and *shei-tun*, heathen and devils, "bad" for Mamalus and others. A child's character and disposition are declared as due to good or bad luck, fortune, *shans*, especially if the misbehavior of one's own children is to be explained, and is declared a consequence of the moral quality of a father's semen, a mother's womb, and a mother's milk when the misery or misbehavior of the children of others is discussed. A child likely will be bad if the father is a thief; if the mother conceived while ritually unclean, such as before she had performed the ritual bath after menstruation, or—not mentioned often, but known—if she conceived while wearing clothes soiled with a baby's urine or excrements. In such cases, children are the cause, via mother's negligence or laziness, of other children's character deficiencies. Such parent-induced moral disposition cannot be changed substantially by educational means. However, if a child is doing well, is "good" and healthy, mother will take credit for it. Hejab said that her eight children were "good, strong, reasonable" (*fahmide, aqel*) because she was reasonable and vigilant: she watched over them so that djenn and the evil eye could not harm them as babies; she made sure that health problems were taken care of right away, that they learned early to work and to have respectful fear (*tars*) to keep them out of trouble. She also knew when to talk to them nicely and sweetly, when to scold, when to praise, when to punish. For her, these educational caretaker skills were just as important as the children's disposition in determining behavior, character, and health. When, a few years later, two of her sons got into trouble despite her care, Hejab blamed it on the bad influence of their schoolmates, but also asked herself whether it could be God's punishment (*muqafat*) of her or her husband's sins of which she was not aware. An annoyed neighbor saw the boys' misbehavior and disrespect as God's punishment of the boys' paternal grandfather, who for many years allegedly had mistreated his wife.

An as yet unreasonable toddler quickly may acquire bad habits such as drinking tea, for example, usually from older siblings, but this cannot be avoided: young children are prone to being fooled, to do things that are harmful to themselves or annoying to others, people say. Education efforts consist largely of supervision with the goal of keeping the children out of trouble until they are able to decide and reason for themselves. Until then, they have to be watched constantly, have to be directed, admonished, restrained. Toddlers have few toys. Mostly they play with whatever they find and manage to hold onto before somebody takes it away: sticks and rocks, containers, occasionally a doll, a plastic toy, tools, spoons, kitchen utensils, garbage. In consequence, they hear, "Let go of this, it is dirty, bad" many times a day. As a toddler's range of movement potentially is as wide open as its mobility allows it to negotiate space, and as most household activities take place on the floor, the child is tempted to grab, open, break, put in its mouth any object in use in the house; everything is on its own level and an invitation to handle.

Alia, age two, cut her hair with a pair of scissors she found unattended; two-and-one-half-year-old Behrokh, on wobbly legs, was chasing chickens across the verandah with a long knife in her hand; Daud, eighteen months, had his mouth full of tiny glass beads one day, from a box his sister had forgotten to squirrel away, and full of little pebbles from the courtyard another; Ervand, three, with speed and concentration shredded one of his sister's school books he had taken out of her school bag in an unobserved moment; Fati, two, liked to poke holes into the seams of cushions until feathers would fly; Ashkan, three, in an unwatched moment, and perfectly aware of what he was doing, joyfully upset a tea tray, teapot, glasses, sugar bowl and all, with his legs; while his mother was shooing chickens away from the tray of rice she was cleaning, her three-year-old son was wasting rice with both hands behind her back. Taking things away from young children is considered as much a necessary act of protection of the child as of self-defense. When our younger daughter, at three, took a broom and started to sweep the porch of our host's house as she had seen the women do, an old woman very quickly grabbed it from her: a toddler sweeping was the bad omen of an unexpected and inconvenient visitor. Unlike a local child, who would have protested loudly, our daughter, startled, hid behind me. (The interference was to no avail, though; an untimely visitor came anyway, confirming the omen for the old woman.) Two-year-old Ized had a small mirror wrestled away by her aunt: a little child may see a djenn in the mirror and fall sick, said the aunt. Ized cried. The effect of such interferences on children is plain: whenever a child reaches out it has to expect a frustration, which it can deal with by protest, cunning, speed, vigilance, perseverance, by sifting and discarding what adults say, by watching for opportunities.

Children are forever admonished to sit still and right (*dorost beshin*), not to do this or that (*nakon*), not be loud and wild (*sholuq nakon*), to let something be (*vellesh kon*). The child realizes that noncompliance more often than not is the only way to get what it wants or needs. It learns that it is sweet (*shirin*) to parents and elder siblings by being handled affectionately, touched, kissed, fed, carried, cooed over, by having things often done for it with joy; but most of a child's own initiatives and actions are likely disapproved of and foiled, and its space is invaded by the very people who cuddle and pamper it.

Nastaran, at two-and-one-half, dressed only in cotton pants, was lying in the shade of the porch on a very hot afternoon. She had taken off her top after she had spilled a glass of water on it—she cannot stand wet clothes, her sister, Elham, fifteen, explained to me, a frequent visitor at the house. Elham had brought her a dry shirt, but Nastaran did not want to put it on yet. She was playing with it. Elham was sitting next to her on an old rug, cooing at her, petting her. "Look, how soft she is," she said. "I like to touch her!" She was feeling her shoulders, rubbing her back. Nastaran squirmed, squealing, "Don't, let me be!" Elham paid no attention. She petted her arm: "So soft, so smooth," she said. Nastaran, squealing louder, shook her off. "And here is her smallpox scar!" Elham said. Nastaran turned around, whined, poked Elham's arm. "Go away!" she shouted, clearly irritated. Elham "bit" into her ribs. "I like (want) you so much, I will eat you!" she cooed, then nibbled her arm. Nastaran yelped, kicked her legs, and rolled away from her sister toward a pillar supporting the porch roof. Elham wanted to roll her back, but Nastaran hung onto the pillar, screaming. Elham, laughing, picked her up, yanked her loose from the pillar, and carried her inside, but Nastaran was screaming and kicking so much that Elham dropped her just inside the door. Nastaran screamed "Mother, mother," crouching in the corner behind the door, banging at it with her feet. Elham laughed again, and left. Nastaran opened the door suspiciously, came out again when she did not see Elham, whimpering still. When she saw only me, she stopped crying, sat down at the pillar and got interested again in the T-shirt her sister had dropped.

In this encounter Nastaran had learned, or was reminded, that people might irritate, inconvenience you even if they love ("want") you; that your feelings do not count much with big people; that screaming will show results; that you have to—and can—fight for your space.

As standing toddlers and sitting adults are on the same eye level, adults in this position seem eminently accessible to the youngsters: a mother's eyes can be held without even tilting a head; her face is within reach of hands, her lap is ready to step into, her back can be climbed, her ear can be spoken into, her face kissed. And just as easily, her veil and hair can be pulled, back hit, nose pinched, cheeks scratched, arms boxed, ears screamed into. But intimate accessibility of an adult diminishes in circles radiating outward from mothers and elder sisters and has to be replaced by formality and distance: "shyness," the proper attitude of young children toward people in authority positions, becomes the correct mode of interaction. Physical and verbal contact is to be initiated by the adult; the answering child's voice drops; displays of emotions and of wants recede behind a mask of serious blankness. By about the age of three, children have learned this mode of interaction; it is one of many proper, polite stances of a well-behaved, reasonable child.

13 · Boys and Girls

The care (safd, but also sahmat, troubles) said to be required to keep children well and to make them well-behaved is the same for boys and girls: "clothes, food, bath, admonition" is the string of requirements that came to the mind of whomever I asked. But gender interferes with the seemingly egalitarian program of care. A newborn right away is defined by its genitals as either a boy or a girl, and from then on is expected to differentiate in other aspects as well, as it grows up. These expectations are communicated to children early on; they become a self-fulfilling prophecy. For example, girls are said to develop better, to become "fat and strong" more easily than boys because they are kept from moving around, from roaming—they are house-people, as a mother of four daughters said, and this is to their advantage. Girls also are said to be smaller and weaker than boys by nature, and therefore to need less food or less "strong" food. The resulting sexual dimorphism is taken as proof of the assumptions.

Individual exceptions notwithstanding, girls are socialized and enculturated foremost into a style of life marked by subordination to males, and boys into one marked by domination over females. The ideology of male dominance in an authoritarian social hierarchy informs how both are made to look, to perform, to feel, and how they think of themselves.

Girls are made to look different from boys early in their lives by hairstyle, adornment such as earrings, necklaces, hair bands, and by dress. Although since about 1985 girls and boys both wear pants and tops, girls also may wear skirts and dresses or the traditional tribal costume of wide, colorful skirts and tunic; boys may not. At around three years of age, most girls want to wear headscarves, at least once in a while, maybe even a veil-wrap in public, in order to feel and demonstrate their girlhood. A boy may "run around naked" in public, occasionally quite literally so—Saed, about three, found his wet shirt and pants uncomfortable, took them off, and was stark naked (*lokht sirili*) for about an hour in the street, ignored or smiled at, before his mother caught him. Barat, almost four, strolled up the alley, long stick in hand, little penis peeking over the top of his very low-riding cotton pants, to nobody's concern. A girl, by contrast, no matter how young, has to be dressed always, meaning that her upper torso but especially her lower torso and legs have to be covered by untattered clothes. Huri's father had a fit when Huri, three, who had taken off her pants at home for some reason, briefly exposed her behind while she was roughhousing with her six-year-old brother in her dress. A man was praised as a very good neighbor when he brought a little girl home to her mother after her pants had ripped while she was climbing the steep bank of the channel in the alley, partly exposing her leg and thigh.

"Naked" for girls from the beginning means something different than for boys. Baby girls are cleaned surreptitiously if a male is present; as soon as a girl can sit she is admonished to keep her legs crossed and tucked under, to cover her feet, to sit still, much more emphatically than is a boy: extended legs and uncovered feet are "naked" for girls, their exposure is improper, *zesht*. In the bath, even toddlers will wear panties or a wrap if boys are present.

Lale, two, walked into the room where I was being entertained by her elder sister. She came from the bath, wrapped head to toe in a big towel. She sat down, demanded tea, but refused to extend a naked arm to get it. Instead, she asked her elder sister to feed her the lumps of sugar and to hold the saucer with tea—poured from the glass to cool it—to her mouth. Lale was "embarrassed" (*sharmonde*) because she was naked, her sister told me. To Lale she said in sing-song baby-talk, "Lale is naked, oi, shame on you!" and then kissed her cheek. Lale, happy person that she is, smiled, hugged the towel tighter, made sure not one toe was visible. Eventually, Lale hid in her mother's voluminous skirts though no man or boy was in the room, and had pants put on her. Now Lale was "dressed." She sat down again and drank the next glass of tea by herself, bare upper body and arms notwithstanding.

For Lale, "naked" obviously means an uncovered lower body and bare legs: a naked belly, bottom, and legs render all else "naked" and to be ashamed of. Later, at around five years of age, an uncovered head in public will make her feel "naked"; at eleven, she will feel exposed without a veil-wrap; and should she become an orthodox believer she will feel "naked" when her chin and eyebrows are visible. At two, Lale has defined essential nakedness for a girl, and has accepted as necessary the charge to keep her bottom a secret, to see it as the focus and source of embarrassment, and her feet as extensions of this delicate region. A girl's honor, she understands, is much more dependent on how carefully she covers herself than is a boy's on how well he is covered. Only a "crazy" girl will expose herself. Adults and children in Deh Koh take a somewhat retarded local woman's negligence of proper coverage as a sign of her abnormalcy. "She did like this," said a five-year-old boy, rolling up his pant leg and scratching his knee. "She is crazy."

Well-brought-up young girls are able to sit still for hours and may even fall asleep in a sitting position. Their brothers will fidget, run in and out much more frequently and without motherly comment. They are, after all, boys, for whom lack of manners is a defining attribute. City kids cannot sit still properly at all, they are "wild," and city girls are a lot less shy about their bodies than are girls in Deh Koh, people say—not necessarily because of a lack of honor and manners, but because of an expectable difference in the customs of different regions and of different lifestyles. While city manners now are catching on in the village, too, for local girls, relaxed behavior still brings shame.

The concept of shame is introduced early to both boys and girls, mostly in the context of soiling themselves, but is emphasized and used with consistency for girls of toddler age and above. Little girls who do any kind of wrong likely are told to be ashamed (*kejalat be-kesh*); boys who do wrong are given to understand that what they did was annoying, maybe was a sin (*gona*), that they have no manners, that they are "devils," that they might be cursed and driven away, but their wrongdoing rarely is linked to shame. Rather, it is ascribed to their nature as boys.

Praise and admiration, given sparsely and cautiously to both, is gender-coded: girls likely will hear that they are pretty (*malus, mangol*), clean-beautiful (*tamiz*) and reasonable (*aqel*), while boys more likely will hear that they are good (*khub*) and strong (*zereng*). Hugging, kissing, and affectionate touching by adults diminish rapidly for boys after about five years of age; for girls, such intimacy usually lasts longer, but almost exclusively with adult women. Mothers continue to help their daughters in the bath until adulthood, while both parents will encourage their sons after circumcision to go to the bath with their father or an elder brother. By then, touching by women or girls and gestures toward them will more likely be playfully or openly aggressive than caressing. Liberal signs of affection, people say, will make children *nazeli*, spoiled, boys more so than girls.

By the time they can run and talk, boys and girls clearly look different, behave differently, and identify themselves and other children with one or the other sex. "Girls have hair clasps and are with the women, boys have no hair and are anywhere," said a three-year-old whom I asked how she knew that an even younger toddler sitting with its mother was a girl. A boy of about four identified a toddler as a boy because he was "dark-skinned and skinny." Boys walk with a swagger, arms slightly extended from the shoulders; girls walk with smaller steps, arms close to the body, and slower. Boys move more readily than do girls, who forever are told to sit down, to sit properly. Girls talk with the high-pitched, soft voices they hear when others talk to them; boys talk louder. Boys' closely cropped hair is carefree, while girls' longer hair needs constant attention: it needs to be combed or braided or pushed out of the eyes or tucked under a scarf. Fumbling with their hair and scarves remains a lifelong activity for females of all ages past babyhood. "It is our national women's sport," said a high school student. "My little sister started to practice it already." After puberty, hair takes on an additional gender meaning: girls and women ought to be hairless except for sleek eyebrows and the hair on their heads to qualify as "clean and beautiful," and spend considerable effort on removing it from elsewhere, while adolescent boys may look "like bears" without embarrassment, said a sixteen-year-old girl.

A young child is taught that its identity as a boy or a girl is dependent on gender markers and behavior. A six-year-old girl pleaded with her mother for earrings she wanted very badly so that she would "look like a girl," she said. Our elder daughter, at five, wanted clarification from us about the consequences of her playing with the neighbors' four-year-old son and his slingshot: was it true that she would turn into a boy, as his mother had said? Mahmud, two, wanted to help his mother wash clothes. She quickly rinsed the suds off his arms and scolded him: "Do you want to turn into a girl?! Go away!" A three year-old-boy played with his big brother's chains, flagellating himself as he had seen his brother do during Moharram mourning displays. But when his five-year-old sister picked them up, her mother yelled at her: "Leave the chains alone or else you'll turn into a boy!" Hesitantly, but without protest, she put them down—it is not worth the risk, slight as it might be, her gesture seemed to say. Children hear a man who is unmarried, meek, easily overcome by emotions, engaged in unmanly activities, mockingly referred to as "sister." Although children of either sex rarely are empty-handed, what they hold onto is gendered: girls carry pieces of paper, string, rags, plastic bags, pails, things to transport other things with, "nothing," as they say, while boys are much more likely to carry toys like "cars," balls, or weapons such as rocks, sticks, or slingshots.

Just as important as looks and tools for the expression of gender identity are gestures, how things are handled, emotions expressed. For me it was uncanny to watch twenty-month-old Maleka, who cannot talk yet, rock her "baby" (a doll) in her lap, sitting cross-legged on the floor, one elbow propped on a knee, chin in hand, looking hot, tired, and bored as she has seen grown-up mothers sit and look; or to watch three-year-old Huri, wrapped in a veil, give a play-performance of an "old woman" (*pirezan, dalu*), dragging her feet, back bent, head bobbing, chanting, "I am old; old age is a bad pain; let me die," just as her old neighbor does. Such performances are rewarded by the audience with laughs, hugs and kisses, and good-natured ridicule. But girls rehearse these behaviors, postures, tones of voice, and appropriate affects alone, without audiences, too. My four-year-old neighbor was playing "baby," half hidden under the vines in her father's courtyard. Nobody else was in sight. I watched her from a window of my house. She was "nursing" a doll, lifting an imaginary breast out from under her shirt, guiding baby's mouth to the nipple, spreading the veil over the suckling infant, looking out into the middle distance, stretching a leg awkwardly so as not to dislodge the baby from her breast, then, soundlessly, she started to "talk" to an imaginary visitor, occasionally checking on the baby, readjusting its head, patting it on the back—a flawless performance of mothering.

At age two, most girls already have a large conceptual, if not verbal, vocabulary of how grown-up women conduct themselves around babies, how they work around the house, cook, bake bread, talk to other women. When I asked about differences in young boys' and young girls' play behaviors, Leila, a mother of seven, a teacher, and an avid observer of people, said that boys practice being boys, girls practice being women. Indeed, I have never seen a young boy in Deh Koh playfully rehearse fatherly behavior or men's work. Little boys do, however, work on the skills valued later in boys' playgroups, such as running after things or away from somebody, throwing rocks, shooting birds, driving cows or goats, stoning dogs, commanding others. Adults encourage them to be assertive, including vis-à-vis their own sisters, and they encourage little girls to yield to their brothers. For example, a young girl may be made to accept her brother's claim to something she would like to have, even to consent to having it taken away from her. When the four-year-old brother of two slightly older sisters tried to grab from them the pieces of gum I had dispensed among them equally, their mother told them to give in to his demand. "He is your dear brother," she said, and the two girls gave up their gum with hardly any resistance. A four-year-old girl, who cried after her six-year-old brother had snatched away a tin she had been using for "cooking," kindly and lovingly was told by her elder sister not to mind, to play something else instead; the elder sister made the hand-gesture of dismissal and contempt toward her brother, cursing him under her breath, but neither girl even tried to get the can back from him.

In such situations, young girls learn that deferring to men is an intrinsic part of being a girl and a woman, but also that women have misgivings about it, and they learn how to express those misgivings. They learn that it does not feel good to have to give up and give in, no matter how inevitable it is. They learn to react by scolding, cursing, gestures of protest and threat, passive resistance, refusal to speak, and other quiet avoidances. "My sister is mad (*ve qar*) at my brother," explained a five-year-old when her elder sister bolted out the door after her brother had entered. Whatever the reason, the five-year-old recognized the expression of displeasure with a sour relationship when she saw it in her sister, and thereby had a model for expressing misgivings of her own.

Boys' assertions of power do not always go unchallenged—far from it; fights between brothers and sisters are frequent and noisy, but boys meet little enough resistance and overcome it often enough to affirm their right to superiority over their sisters in these encounters. A boy of six, home briefly with high-laced boots he did not want to take off to enter the house, from the door shouted to his much older sister inside, "Bring me my sweater!" When she did not do it right away, he got louder and more insistent. After a few minutes of increasingly loud and aggressive demands on his part, the sister appeared in the doorway with the sweater, scolding and cursing him with colorful language, which he ignored. He grabbed the sweater and ran off. "He is a tyrant," she said bitterly.

Not all boys develop into tyrants. At times, children and adults express deep affection for a sibling of opposite sex, especially one close in age. As adults in difficult situations, women often identify one or another brother as their closest ally. However, the hierarchical relationship, which demands of sisters obedience to their brothers and of brothers responsibility toward their sisters, frequently leads to brothers' violence toward sisters, and to girls' tongue-lashing of an overly controlling, "crazy" brother, to bickering and angry withdrawal. Thus, many more girls are known for their sharp, long tongue than are boys, who easily dismiss all their sisters' angry talk as "just talk, nothing."

A condition that afflicts mostly female children and often stays with them into early adulthood is a seizure called *tasa*. A child may be said to "have been taken by *tasa* [*tasa bordesh*]" after a crisis or a trauma, often at a very early age. Meinir was about two when a neighbor girl sneaked up behind her and pinched her cheeks, whereupon Meinir fainted, says her mother. After that, whenever she had a scare, such as being yelled at, she would faint with open eyes and blue lips, trembling all over. A *tasa*-bead controlled the seizures while she was very young, until she lost it. Then a written amulet around her neck helped somewhat but did not cure her either. (Fifteen years and two children later, her condition was much improved.)

According to her mother, Maryam was just a year old when, after eating a double dose of "cold" food—a tomato and a boiled potato— she had her first spell of *tasa;* she screamed uncontrollably, stiffened, fainted. A very "warm" remedy—browned sugar candy—an amulet, and a *tasa* bead controlled further spells until they stopped on their own when she was about ten years old.

In 1992, three-year-old Peri fell off the verandah onto a cement floor one story below and had a mild concussion. She recovered from it, but since then, any fright, a loud noise, a sudden movement, may bring on fainting and uncontrollable trembling. Six months later her grandmother was asking around for a *tasa* bead because neither amulets nor the doctor had helped much. The doctor reportedly said that her condition was outside medicine proper and ought to be treated by a local healer.

Although young boys throw violent tantrums easily and often, rarely do they show signs of *tasa*. *Tasa* of little girls was and still is a frequent enough occurrence to call any fainting or signs of emotional exhaustion, such as after a tantrum, *tasa*. Over the years, several physicians in Iran, including a local physician in 1992, identified *tasa* behavior to me as hysteria, and as quite common in Iran generally. I am aware of the problematic of this diagnosis—hysteria is no longer recognized in the latest *Diagnostic and Statistical Manual of Mental Disorders*. Yet health workers in Iran claim that classic hysteria still exists in Iran. This discrepancy may pose a challenge to the cross-cultural validity of medical definitions, but for our purpose it is of no great import—the people in Deh Koh as well as medical doctors practicing in Iran work with a concept that comes very close to the old "hysteria," and this I need to take into account. For the doctors in the area, a hysteric seizure at age two suggests that young girls have precariously few emotional outlets for dealing with stress. For me, it suggests also that by age two girls have internalized all coping choices for "stress" available in their culture, including the "proper" or locally recognizable form of a hysteric gesture.

Tasa-incidents are said to be declining in Deh Koh recently. Hurijan, the local specialist on children's health, links this decline with a change in the way girls are treated: "Life is better for girls now," she said.

The fact that girls are encouraged to stay close to mother and home may work to their advantage as far as access to food is concerned; mother, the main source of food, can be tapped more frequently and easily by a child who is around its mother while she handles food than by one who comes home only occasionally, as boys do. This proximity does not imply, however, that girls necessarily will get better or, overall, more food than their brothers. Furthermore, by watching women feed others, girls learn their low place in the social hierarchy that determines food allocations. At weddings, for example, as on other occasions, adult male guests are served first, including their young sons, if they chose to come along instead of eating with their mothers. After the men have eaten, leftovers are rearranged in the kitchen, serving trays are refilled, if possible, and women guests, their young children, and older girls are served. Last, cooks and servers eat what is left over. They, however, had discretionary power over allocations all along.

Talking about the distribution of food by status, Aziz remembers what his grade school teacher had told about the time he was kept at the khan's fort by the khan to prevent him from teaching in Deh Koh. The khan's wife used two pots for dinner: one held soup made with meat and barley, the other held hot water. For the khan, she ladled out a serving of soup; then she added a ladle full of water to the remaining soup in the cooking pot. Next, guests were served soup, and more water was added. Then the secretary and scribe got soup, and more water went into the big pot. By the time the servants got served, the soup was so watery one could have taken a bath in the pot and come out clean. Aziz says that in some houses in Deh Koh, too, by the time women and children are served, the stew or soup cannot even remember the meat that was in it once.

At weddings, this pattern is subverted by two different interest groups. Young men of the host's family may usurp choice pieces of meat to roast on a spit and eat with early servings of rice or bread provided by obliging cooks, well hidden behind the big cooking pots. "Look at them!" Leila said with disgust at such an occasion, while trying to calm her hungry two-year-old, "My own uncle and my cousin's son—just about purring, stomach full, licking their chops like cats who have just swallowed the biggest mouse!" The other unscheduled but predictable, attack on kitchen resources at a feast comes from worn-down mothers battered by their hungry toddlers, who, by the time it finally is the women's turn to be served dinner, are cranky, crying, genuinely distressed with hunger. One or the other mother or elder sister who can muster the nerve, courage (*ri*, literally, face; begging food is disgraceful), will persuade the cooks to uncover their pots for a few early helpings of food. These sneaked meals will be long on rice and short on meat and stew. A few very well organized, compassionate hostesses prepare a simple dish made of rice, yogurt, and spices especially for children, to be served long before adults eat. However, there are few children who would not prefer meat stew over this rice-mush. By the time dinner is finally served to women, at about ten at night, most of the little ones are asleep in a corner or on mother's lap, hungry or not. The little boys at least had the choice to eat earlier with their fathers. Amin, six, got a piece of kebab from his uncle when he came upon the secret feast behind the giant cooking pots on his wanderings; his sister, age four, who had stayed with mother, as well she should, got none.

At a wedding feast, a two-year-old boy was sitting on the ground in front of a row of big trays the cooks had just filled with rice and meat, crying. "Mother, I am hungry, hungry," he kept repeating, but his mother, one of the helpers, ignored him. After a while he stopped whining and slowly sidled closer to a tray. Looking around to see if anybody was watching, he slid closer, looked around, moved closer yet, and stealthily and carefully, watching his surroundings all the time, moved his hand under the big flatbread covering the heap of rice and took out a handful of rice. "Don't!" cried his mother and pulled him away by his arm. He screamed. She let go of him, and he started the maneuver over again, managing to stuff two handfulls of rice into his mouth before his mother caught him again. She dragged him away, he kicked and screamed, she slapped his hand and his head. Next I saw him asleep on his mother's shoulder, and then curled up on a small pillow, a scarf put over him. His four-year-old sister did not even go near the trays. Her grandmother told her that it was "shameful" to whine for food or to steal food, no matter how hungry one was.

From toddler age on, boys are said to be easier and cheaper to raise than girls because their appearance and conduct is less consequential for their elders' reputation as responsible parents and less reflective of their parents' honor (*abru*) than is their sisters'. Already at a very young age boys may be "turned out in the morning like cows," as a male teacher said disapprovingly, to come home only to feed and sleep, while a girl is discouraged from leaving the house alone. In addition, a girl ought to have mastered household skills at least rudimentarily (in contrast to fully as in the preliterate, very-early-marriage Deh Koh of a generation ago), by age twelve, so as to be functional in her father's and her future husband's households. This means that a mother has to start training her daughters at an age when boys are under no pressure yet to learn anything at all.

Daughters hear that they are *sahmat*, troubles, even if they are sweet and good to have around the house. Boys and girls hear that boys are more of an asset, more valuable to their parents than are girls, who, after the expense and trouble of their proper upbringing, will be of use to some other family upon marriage. The relationship between the expense of raising a child and later benefit for parents is inverted for brothers and sisters. Although these sentiments may be expressed in many direct and indirect ways, often between brothers and sisters in a fight ("You are good for nothing—I can't wait until you are sold!"), girls do not seem overly put out or deeply troubled by it. They think that they are much more reasonable and much more of a help to their parents while they are children than are their brothers, that they are dearer: "Mother always cries when I leave for school after vacations, and she is very glad when *you* leave!" said a sister to her brother, and another one expressed the same idea this way: "You boys gave father his white hair, not we sisters." Yet, the double messages in how they are treated lets girls realize an ambiguity in their position as daughters and sisters. "My father and my brothers say they like me; they buy me clothes and feed me—why then did they not let me finish school?" a seventeen-year old girl said.

No rituals accompany the growing up of a girl until she gets married; until then, all transitions are taken in stride, including menarche, whose most obvious significance is a loss of ritual purity and the necessity of abstaining from prayer during menstruation, which is called "without prayer," *binamaz*, and is considered "dirty," often painful, and very private. In contrast, a young boy's growing up is punctuated by circumcision, a ritual that is celebrated within the family and not only is said to make him more of a Muslim than before but also to make him more "clean" than before.

A boy should be circumcised before he starts school so as to spare him potential embarrassment and ridicule from his schoolmates. Circumcision (*khatne*) is referred to euphemistically as "wedding": "Mahmud is going to have a wedding feast soon," a mother may say about, or to, her five-year-old son. This talk always carries the ambiguous notion of something great and to be proud of, yet also of something the boy ought not to be afraid of, which means that a scare is somehow implied. Mothers impart uneasiness about it. "I left the house when my eldest son got it done," a mother whispered to me from behind her hand, in front of a younger son, who heard her very well. "I heard him scream all the way over to my mother's house—I was so sorry for him that I cried." The boy did not let on what he thought of this.

Circumcision might be done by a barber (cheap) or else by a physician (more expensive), at home or at a doctor's office, in Deh Koh or in town. It is a men's affair—no women are present at a circumcision. Reportedly, neither mothers nor fathers discuss with the boy beforehand what is going to happen. I could not find out what, if anything, young boys may hear about it from older boys. In any case, they are said not to know what circumcision means until it happens, and to react with screaming and fighting, or else with terrified silence, depending on their temperament, when the operation starts. "Three men had to hold him down!" a grandmother said about her grandson, proud and sorry for him at the same time. Afterward, the boy is pampered by the women in the house: sweets, good food, visitors with gifts all make the point that the pain was a joyful occasion, the endurance was heroic, that now he somehow is "better," cleaner than before, and well along to manhood. When he is ready to leave the sickbed, his mother gives him a long wrap-skirt to wear instead of pants until the wound is healed. Boys wear this garment if not with pride then at least with complete ease—there is no shame attached to being circumcised or to drawing everybody's attention to one's penis, as a mother explained, chuckling. From now on, boys separate themselves further and further from their sisters as well as their mothers, and may try more boldly than before to get the women in the house "under their hand-fist," as is said. A fourteen-year-old boy who was angry at his elder sister because in his opinion she kept bossing him around and did not obey him at all, said, "Men"—and he counted himself as a man at this point—"men are *adam*, people, women are like sheep: they need to be told what to do, they are dumb, there are plenty of them." More and more likely a mother or elder sister now will say about the growing, circumcised boy, "My power [*zur*] doesn't reach him." This is a source of anger and frustration, *daq*, for women and girls, while their challenges to the boys' claimed superiority is a source of *daq* for boys.

14 · Talking To, Talking About

Young children until the age of around ten address each other mostly by their first names. When they refer to other children they may use the first name, first name plus "son/daughter of ———" ("Ali, Uncle Hasan's son"), or only "Aunt Maryam's son." Using these forms of address means children learn to relate to other children as particularly named individual playmates and as exponents of a certain family. Referring to a person whose name or proper kin relation a child does not know, the child may use the person's relationship to somebody the child knows for identification: "I saw Ali's sister."

In disputes, children reduce each other to "Boy!" (*kurr*) and "Girl!" (*duar*), as in "Let go of me, boy!" or "Get lost, girl!" just as children themselves are reduced to these categories by irate adults. A misbehaving child verbally is depersonalized and isolated from family relations.

Older boys and girls above ten or so years, who are close in age and not siblings, avoid addressing each other. For reference, they prefer to use descriptive terms like "Uncle Hasan's son." Girls do this more than boys. It is an expression of modesty not to use the personal name of a young, potentially marriageable male. Boys are more likely to continue calling girl relatives by their names. Children observe this pattern in use by their parents: mother is likely to address father, her husband, by his last name or as the father of his eldest child ("Ali's father, come here!"), but father more likely addresses her by her own name. A boy who is much older than a girl relative other than his sister, however, might not even know her name. For example, a young man, looking for a potential wife among his countless relatives in the village, asked his sister, "What about Uncle Mahmud's daughter? Is she good?"

"Which one—Goli or Simin?"

"I don't know . . . the taller one."

Girls of all ages know many more names of children than do boys; they are more interested in names of infants, and, being around women more than their brothers are, have more occasions to learn new children's names. Frequently they supply a name to a man who is at a loss for it. For example, an elderly man informed me: "Last year we married off my wife's sister's daughter."

"Which one? She has four."

"Ah . . . hum . . . well, the eldest."

"But she has been married for three years!"

"Then it's the next one . . . what's her name?" Before I could answer, a seven-year-old girl said the name.

Thus, as far as knowledge of people's names is concerned—knowledge important for conducting everyday affairs—boys and men are considered, and boys learn to consider themselves, as not quite responsible.

Adults, especially women, address children by first name or simply as "Boy" or "Girl," especially when conveying annoyance or urgency. Adults also address child relatives teknonymously: a mother's sister may call her niece *khale* (mothersister) or will answer a niece's call of *khale* with "What do you want, *khale*?" Father and child may be *bou*, father, to each other, grandmother and grandchild, *nana*, grandmother.

Generally, children are taught by example and admonition to use kinterms as polite terms of address and reference for any relative who is older than the child. "Older" is not defined rigidly by age but is modified by factors such as level of intimacy, spatial proximity, and social status of the older relative. For example, in family A a pair of young sisters (seven and nine years old) call and refer to their twenty- and twenty-three-year-old married sisters as *dada*, sister. The older sisters had left home soon after the two little ones were born, cogni-

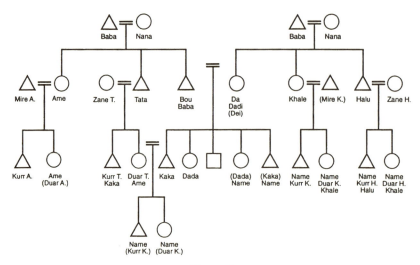

Figure 1

tively widening the age gap for them. In family B the eleven-year-old sister is on first-name basis with her twenty-two-year-old unmarried sister who is a student: their age gap has not been widened by social factors like marriage and different residence.

Children learn to use fourteen kinterms, paired by gender. With these and personal names they can label all people in the social field of *famil*, "family," a new, vague term meaning "close relatives," especially paternal ones, and *qoum khishi*, "relatives," especially patrilineal relatives. Figure 1 is a schema based on how people in Deh Koh, including children, describe their kinship terminology. Where terms of reference differ from address terms, they are put in parentheses. All terms are used by both sexes.

The Terms

Baba and *Nana* means father and mother of a parent, in all ascending generations. In multigenerational Deh Koh, a child usually grows up with several *babas* and even more *nanas*. Six-year-old Keyan has six living grandfathers and seven grandmothers in three generations above his parents. To keep them separate, *baba* and *nana* are followed by first name ("Baba Ali") or a non-kin title, such as *"Nana* Meshhedi" for a grandmother who has made the pilgrimage to Imam Reza's shrine in Meshhed.

Bou, or *baba*, means father. Only the biological father is labeled father. In case of a father's death and mother's remarriage a child will call the mother's second husband by the kin term appropriate for this man. In a levirate marriage, for example, the mother's new husband actually is the child's father's brother and will be addressed and referred to as such: "Fatherbrother-plus-name." If absolutely no kin relationship can be established, the child will not likely be living with the mother because children belong to their father's patrilineal group. In this case, the child will refer to mother's husband as just that ("Husband-of-Mother") or by a title (such as Meshhedi) or by the man's family name ("Kerimi" or "Mr. Kerimi").

Fatherhood itself is inalienably linked to siring; there is no such concept as social father in Deh Koh. For example, after Ali's father had died shortly after Ali's birth, his mother stayed in her dead husband's extended family for another year. When none of her husband's paternal male relatives married her, she moved back to her father, taking little Ali with her. Ali's paternal grandparents, however, took him away from her; their son's son belonged to *them,* not to her father. The child's father's brother brought him up. The boy calls him "Fatherbrother," and this man's wife, who in effect raised him, "Fatherbrother's wife."

In Deh Koh, more and more young children call their fathers *baba*, as city children do, instead of *bou*. Unlike *baba* for grandfather, *baba* for father is never used with the personal name or a title. This newly popular term for father no longer implies the unique, exclusive position of authority of *bou* but implies a relationship that is at once generationally further removed and more easygoing, the way grandfathers are perceived to be. Used for father, *baba* comes close to a term of endearment.

Da, dadi, or *mamani,* in address, or in reference, *dei,* means biological mother. A stepmother is addressed and referred to as "Father's wife" unless a kinterm is appropriate. Upon the death of his first wife, Goli's father married his first wife's daughter by a previous marriage to make sure little Goli would be well taken care of. Little Goli called her stepmother "Sister" or else "Father's wife," and referred to her as "my father's wife."

In a mellow state of mind a young child may call his or her mother *mamani* like city children and children on television do. The emotional hue changes from *mamani* (soft) to *da* (strong): Amin, age four, walking to his house with a message for his mother on his mind, started calling her, softly, long before she possibly could hear him. "*Mamani, Mamani,*" he chanted, rhythmically swinging his head from side to side. As this drew no response he switched to "*Dadijuni, Dadijuni,*" chanting still. Then, more urgently, head held rigid, he called her, "*Dadi, Dadi,*" and finally, loudly, head back, he yelled, "*Da, DA!*"

Young children are allowed to use kin terms somewhat idiosyncratically. A two-year-old girl was taken care of by the mother of her mother's father while her own mother was studying in the city. She called her caretaker, her great-grandmother, *Da*, and her own mother, *Mamani*.

Some first- or second-born children may, at least for a while, address their parents also with the parents' first names, as they hear grandparents and other relatives do.

Kaka means, in reference, father's son and mother's son. If one wants to express closeness to a patrilineal male relative, *kaka* may be used: "After all, we are all one family, he is my *kaka*." In address, *kaka* is used for an elder brother, often in the context of submission, such as in asking for a favor, to butter him up. "*Kakajun,*" a six-year-old boy said to his sixteen-year old brother, whom usually he called by his first name, "*Kakajun,* give me a little money." A ten-year-old sister, speaking of herself and her siblings, said about her fourteen-year-old eldest brother: "We call him *kaka* only when we like him." Fifteen-year-old Aida said about her elder brother: "How can I say *kaka* to this blasted son-of-a-dog! No, he is just Hasan, Hasan-the-moron!"

The first-born brother is built up as the potential family head. He tries to wield authority over his younger siblings, pulling rank as their *kaka*, as it were, which more often than not is resented by them, especially by his brothers. *Kaka* implies the postulate of cooperation, mutual support, and loyalty, and the realistic possibility of conflict over authority, inheritance, and economic issues among brothers. To his sisters, a *kaka* is a guardian who, along with their father, is fully responsible for their well-being as long as they reside at home, and partially responsible for their well-being after marriage. As such, *kaka* is a source of potential comfort and support as well as a source of potentially heavy-handed, autocratic authority.

No longer popular but remembered still is the use of *kaka* for fatherbrother's son. This use produces a psychological paradox if not a dilemma: for a woman, a fatherbrother's son theoretically is the preferred marriage partner; as *kaka*, terminologically on a level with her biological brother, he is in the incest category of brother. Although not much was ever made of this disturbing way of looking at father-brother-marriage in conversations with me, it nevertheless is one of the many inconsistencies children grow up with. In a love song, this dilemma is addressed explicitly: "I don't want to say *kaka* to you," a woman sings, "I want to say lover, [*yar*]."

As "black *kaka*," *kakase*, finally, the brother-term takes the negative meaning of black slave, synonymous in tales with disloyal man and molester of women.

Dada means, in reference, father's daughter and mother's daughter. In address, *dada* is used for an elder sister, followed by her first name: "*Dada* Fateme." Girls are identified to babies as *dada* even if there is no kin relationship at all. *Dada* connotes trust, warmth, liking, support. In the folktale "The Shah's Horse," a princess deceived by her maid laments: "*Dada*, what did you do to your *dada*? You tied your *dada*'s braids to a tree so that the lion would eat your *dada*." The strong emphasis on the betrayed sisterly relationship between women makes the maid's crime look more heinous yet.

An elder sister is a surrogate mother, taking care of her siblings and the house if need be at a young age. Traditionally, however, the skills and responsibilities an elder sister had to display and assume at times did not mature into a position of authority in her natal family because she moved out upon marriage, while still in her early teens. As long as they live relatively near each other, younger sisters keep close ties to their elder sisters, although visiting them means visiting a "stranger's house" (the sister's husband's house) and may become socially problematic once a girl reaches marriageable age.

Sisters are said to fight easily and to make peace easily. As daughters do not inherit property according to local custom and are not expected to manage property together, their disagreements, unlike those between brothers, are mild and not of much consequence, people say. Emotionally, *dada* is much more endearing than is *kaka*.

Dada and *kaka* connote respect for an elder sibling as well as supportive intimacy. Children learn early on that *dada* and *kaka*, nuisance that they might be at times, are their most important family because, unlike parents, they are likely to be around throughout one's life. A child without at least one brother and one sister is pitied because "it has nobody." This perceived need for a complete brother-sister set explains why two sons and two daughters is taken as the absolute minimum number of children a couple should have.

Tata means fatherbrother, brother of father's father, etc., and is followed by a personal name. The term is also used for an elder son of a fatherbrother if the age/status difference is to be emphasized. If fatherbrother is younger than oneself, first names will be used as long as both speakers are children. As adults, they might call each other *tata*. As *tata*, a man is a potential guardian for his brothers' children. As such, the term carries authority and respectful distance at the same time that it marks the person as belonging to the child's own family. A little boy of about seven mentioned an Ali. "What Ali?" his sister asked. *"Our Ali,"* he answered, referring to his fourteen-year-old fatherbrother. Had this Ali been related on the mother's side the little boy would not have identified him as "our Ali" but as "Ali, son of motherbrother Mahmud."

Ame means fathersister, sister of father's father, etc., and is followed by a personal name (fig. 2). The term is also used for an elder fathersister's daughter and for all women in ascending generations whom father or mother call *ame*. Little A hears mother and motherbrother's daughter address each other teknonymously as *ame*, fathersister, and thereby learns to call his or her motherbrother's daughter *ame*. Such misnomers are tolerated readily in young children. They might be redressed later or else stick for life.

Ame may be used for elder women to express politely an age or status difference. This may backfire, though: "What makes her think she can call me *ame*—she's barely older than I am! She makes me look like an old woman!" Parvin, eight, hears her mother complain. In such expositions, children learn manipulative uses of kin terms.

Halu in reference, *hal* in address, means motherbrother, brother of mother's mother, etc., and is followed by a personal name. It is used also for an elder son of a motherbrother if the age or status difference is to be emphasized. A *halu* is a close relative but does not belong to a child's *famil*. He does not have obligations toward the children who call him *halu*, but usually cultivates a friendly, easygoing relationship with them. For children, thus, motherbrother and fatherbrother are very different kinds of relatives.

Khale means mothersister, sister of mother's mother, etc. This is the

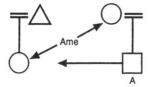

Figure 2

most versatile term of address for women; it may be used for any woman who is about one's own age and status. Little girls call each other *khale* in *khalebazi* (*khale*-play), in which two or more *khales* with their babies are visiting each other. In this "auntie-play" they imitate their own mothers' politely casual interactions with other women, and the display and caring for babies in the presence of others. For children, adult *khales* are women like their own mother: youngish and with children. A *khale* is nice, kind, feeds you. Indeed, mother's sisters might be more sympathetic to your wishes than are your own mother or elder sister, who are more likely to get irritated by demands. Asked where she was heading, three-year-old Nastaran said, "I want to go to *khale* Perirokh to eat rice and yogurt" (her favorite food). When Alia needed a quiet place to study for an examination, she stayed with two of her mother's sisters for a couple of weeks successively. Mother's sisters proverbially have a soft spot for each others' children. Children expect all *khales*, even fictive ones, to be kind to children.

Kurr or *korr* means boy. The term means son if suffixed with a possessive marker: *kurrom*, my son; *kurr* Ali, Ali's son. Used by itself as address ("*Kurr! Kurr-o!*") the term is likely to convey urgency or irritation. For example: "Ali, come"—no answer. "Ali, Ali, COME!"—no answer. "*Kurr-o*, are you deaf?!" Descriptive combinations such as son-of-fatherbrother (*kurr tata*) rarely are used as terms of address.

Duar means girl; suffixed with a possessive marker it means daughter. *Duar* is the female equivalent of *kurr*. Unlike *kurr*, however, children frequently use *duar* in the plural: "I'll go play with the girls"; or: "The girls in school said . . ." Girls are perceived as sitting, playing, working, traveling in bunches. Walking home from high school in the next hamlet, the tight group of girls looks "like a flock of black birds" to Mamalus. The male equivalent to the casual use of the term "girls" more likely is *bacceyal*, boy-children, than *kurral*, boys in the narrow sense. "You are a girl, you play with the girls (*duaral*); I'm a boy (*kurr*), I'll go play with the boy children (*bacceyal*) in the alley," a nine-year-old brother told his seven-year-old sister.

Merd means man, the life stage following *bacce-kurr* with age and upon marriage. As every man has a wife, *merd* implicitly connotes a married man. Children might—rarely—hear the term used in address or reference by a woman for her husband. *Zan o merd* (woman and man) means a married couple.

Mire means husband. It is used as term of reference for "husband of ———": *mire dadam* is my sister's husband. It is never used as a term of address.

Zan means woman or wife. For children, a *zan* is a woman who was or is somebody's wife. *Zan-e bou* is father's wife in address and reference, *zan-e tata* is fatherbrother's wife, etc. The transfer of a bride to her husband's house is called "to bring a *zan*." Jamal, six, chanted to himself about his brother, who is twenty-one, "Ali wants to get (buy) a *zan* but nobody'll give him a *duar*." For the anthropologist, *zan* is much more complicated than that, but the complications hardly ever concern children practically in a village where the sexual activity of women is tantamount to conjugality.

With these fourteen terms, a child is able to identify most people in Deh Koh in terms of somebody's own people (i.e., patrilineal relatives: *bou, tata, ame,* one's *kurr, duar*), mother's people (*da, halu, khale*), and affines: wife of ———, husband of ———. In reference, young children trace adults through playmates: *bou Ali* is Ali's father. They avoid direct address. Shahrom, three, entertained the neighborhood when he told a neighborwoman at the water faucet in front of his father's house, "You somebody's wife, you some boy's mother, turn on the water for me, I want a drink." If address is unavoidable, *Agha* (Sir) and *Khanom* (Madam) are the polite, and modern, terms to use.

Given the relatively small marriage pool in Deh Koh until recently, as well as endogamy (preferred fatherbrotherson/daughter marriage), levirate, and the shifting of generations due to great age differences between husband and wife, children not only have a great many kin ties in the village but also several ways to trace their ties to individual people. Unless a child has learned from parents or siblings how to categorize specific people, it may be at a loss in awkward situations. Soheila, who is sixteen, reported on a chance encounter with a distant male relative she had not seen or heard being talked about in years. Her mother was curious about how she addressed him. "I said nothing, nothing—I don't know what he is—some *tata* or *halu* or somebody's something . . ."

Deh Koh is a large village; most children have so many relatives that they will not likely ever come close enough to all of them to have to call them anything at all. Beyond the nuclear family and the spatially and genealogically closest sets of grandparents, that is, the *famil* in its narrowest sense, children interact with those relatives most who have close social ties with their parents. These relatives may include mother's brothers and sisters with whom the mother gets along especially well, or exclude one or more father's brothers with whom the father is not on good terms despite coresidence in the same compound; it may include a distant mother's cousin who happens to live nearby, and exclude a father's sister who has moved to the other end of the village upon marriage. See appendix for some examples of the application of naming principles.

With the spread of the national-urban culture into Deh Koh, nonkinship status titles and last names are displacing traditional forms of address. *Agha(ye)* (Mister, Sir), and *Khanom* (Ms., Madam; the term connotes social distance but not marital status). Either may be combined with a title like *Doktor* or *Mohandes* (engineer), and/or with the last name. *Khanom* may also be used followed by a woman's first name, but this urban practice is not yet common in Deh Koh. Even close relatives may become "Mr." or "Doctor" when a child operates in a national culture setting such as school. Amin, six, answers my question about who his teacher is with "Motherbrother Ali." He is corrected by his mother and his elder brother: "You have to say: 'Mr. Hoseini.'" Children who in school hear their teachers, that is, various uncles, aunts, wives and husbands of relatives, address each other as "Mr." and "Ms." carry these titles over into their home life. Uncles and aunts thereby come to be thought of as more distant now that they are "Mr. Hoseini" and "Ms. Kerimi." "*Doktor*" and "*Mohandes*" may be used as forms of address and reference by themselves. In the few families where a son has studied or is studying to be a doctor, his parents, especially his mother, and his younger siblings refer to him as "Doctor," and may even address him as such. But the two women doctors Deh Koh has produced so far still are addressed and referred to by their first names by their parents and siblings. Mothers use their sons' high status to build up the status of the family, people say, but not their daughters': daughters eventually will marry, and their title, status, and income will benefit the husband's family.

Traditional terms of address and reference are losing popularity as the social conditions they describe are changing. For example, while older women of the former local khan's family still are referred to and addressed by the traditional honorific title "*Bibi*" (e.g., *Bibi* Maryam), the younger women in the family no longer are. A teacher who has made the pilgrimage to Meshhed will be addressed and talked about as "Mr. Kerimi" rather than the traditional, old-fashioned, "Meshhedi Ahmed." Family names are displacing kinterms, first names, and the traditional honorific titles. For children, people become easier to classify, but thereby lose their significance as relatives and occupants of certain positions in the social hierarchy of the village.

Among themselves, children are liberal with derogatory terms and curses (*fosh*). These epithets allude to:

• Lack of brainpower: *kelu, divune,* crazy; *kamhush, biaql, nafahm,* dumb, brainless, moronic; *khar,* donkey.

• Dirt and pollution: *nekbat, kessafat,* dirty, filthy; *puside, faset,* rotten; *kon bout,* your father's butt; *mufu,* snotnose; *bugard,* stinker; *gikhar,* shit-eater; *tokhm harum, harumzade, bou sokhte* refer to the unlawful seed of the addressed's father; *sag,* dog, and *pedar sag, tokhm sag* liken the addressed's father to a dog, an animal considered so dirty and polluting that it cannot be touched.

• Deficiencies of character and upbringing: *tambal,* lazy; *bad jens,* of bad quality; *dozu,* thief; *durugu,* liar; *bitarbiat, biorze, lus,* lout, rude, unmannered klutz; and the most widely used, *fuzul,* bad, misbehaving.

• A woman's private parts and sexuality: *kussu,* vagina; *kula,* whore; combining such terms with "mother" enhances their curse-challenge: *kirrom men kus deit,* my penis in your mother's vagina. These and similar expressions are used mostly by boys.

Inventiveness in bad language and the command of a large derogatory vocabulary are valued among children, especially boys, never mind what the words mean. Ali, age six, who learns new bad words every day in school, said his mother, cursed his elder sister: "*Tokhm sag, dei kussu,*" (seed of a dog, vagina-mother).

"What is 'Seed of a dog? Vagina-mother'?" asked his mother.

"You know yourself! I am little, how am I supposed to know?"

Girls are more likely to curse and chew somebody out—a brother, sister, playmate—than are boys, who more readily turn to physical aggression. Boys treat their sisters' angry language as helpless gestures, either ignoring them or else responding with laughter or with blows.

Children rarely call adults names or curse them, except under their breath or from a safe distance. Adults, especially women, tongue-lash children readily, using strong language if irritated enough. The derogatory terms used most frequently by adults are *fuzul*, naughty, misbehaving, bad; *sheitun*, devil; and *pedar sukht*, son of a scoundrel. These terms contain a strong double message, however: a child, especially a boy, who is "a devil of a bad son of a scoundrel" is likely to be strong in body, health, and will. These attributes are valued highly— *sheitun* thus communicates an adult's anger yet also pride and approval. Through such language, children, especially boys, are rejected, threatened with death and perdition, and approved of simultaneously. If you are strong and watch out for yourself, the message goes, you will anger people, but never mind. Girls are called such names much less often than are their brothers. For them the double message is weak.

15 · Tongue

The earliest talking game is the animal-talk game. According to this game, which is extremely popular with toddlers, a sheep says, "meh," a donkey says, "ihooihoo," a sparrow says, "jigjig," a cat says, "myoo," a dog says, "habhab," a bee says, "bzzz." Directly and through tales, children are told that animals have their own language, which only very few, legendary people understand. This is a pity because animals around the house see much and hear much, are loyal to their masters even if they have reason to complain of mistreatment or hunger, and would help people if only they could communicate with them. Djenn, too, have their own language. Speech is a sign of being alive and of liveliness in all God's creatures. "To be quiet" is a sign of humbleness but also of a dim wit. Quiet children may be "good," modest, shy, but for a parent this is more worry than joy. The several words for people who talk little all belong to the category of people who are miserable (*bicare*) or poor (*faqir*). *Zounbaste*, tongue-tied, dumb, is a synonym for this condition in animals as well as in people.

Language must be practiced. A neighbor was greatly amused by a young rooster's first tries at crowing: "Just like my little daughter learning words!" he said. Children are encouraged to talk well, to learn polite phrases and when to use them. A polished young man in a neighboring village with a wife and children remembered the agony he went through as an eight-year-old when he was sent by his mother to invite us to dinner. "All the way I rehearsed the speech," he said. "I was so afraid I would forget the polite way of saying, 'Come to dinner'!" Mastery of elaborately polite speech (*ta'arof*) is valued as highly as is being quick and clever on other occasions. *Tatalu*, blabber-stutterer, for a two-year-old is a term of endearment; for a ten-year-old it is an insult. Making oneself understood in Luri is easy: Luri grammar has no gender markers or cases; a basic vocabulary consists of largely one- and two-syllable words; baby language replaces difficult sounds with easier ones, such as *l* for *r*; narrative speech contains patterns for repetitions and words to fill gaps in the flow, such as "came," "went," "said" ("I came, came, looked around, looked, said, said . . ."); mistakes young children make are considered sweet. Yet it is difficult for young children to talk in the presence of older children because competition for attention is fierce. By the age of around three, children who need to say several sentences, rather than just short ejaculations, tend to speak more rapidly than their facility allows, which makes them stutter, repeat words just for the sake of being able to keep talking, shout and whisper alternately, change speed of delivery greatly, and gulp air, with signs of great stress in breathing and body language. This pattern is intensified in school, where, at the slightest hesitation or mistake in the rapid recitation of learned lessons, other children will take over. In school, furthermore, Farsi has to be learned, and intelligence is measured by the ability to memorize great amounts of written text, verbatim. Luri is a nonwritten language; all books, all television shows are in Farsi. All children eventually are bilingual.

Verbal facility is taken as a sign of wit, of mental strength, and is much appreciated. After a woman's five-year-old daughter had vexed her so thoroughly that she cried, "If only I had miscarried you!" the girl cheerfully yelled, "Good for me that you didn't!" Her mother had to laugh about this despite her anger, and told the story around the neighborhood in the spirit of, "What is one to do with such a clever one?!" Children who say clever things are hugged and praised with laughter that, like most laughter, conveys a hint of embarrassment; there is a fine line between cleverness and cheekiness, between making fun of things and "having a sharp tongue (*zoun dare*)," which is disapproved of. Ahmed, after cleverly having told off an ill-mannered, cheeky girl who made indecent remarks on the phone, was gratified by his elders' amusement and by the retelling of his story to others, but he also was scolded for answering the phone at all, for talking to a very bad child, and for having acted improperly by letting his wits and tongue get the better of him. "Don't you start any telephone games yourself!" he was told (to no avail).

In riddle-games, children invent and practice similes and metaphors for ordinary things, the poetics of everyday life. Most of the nearly fifty riddles I recorded—a fraction of what children come up with spontaneously while playing—deal with familiar objects. For example, "A smooth, flat plain full of round rocks" is a bread cloth with balls of dough; "Four brothers tight in a container" is a walnut; "A snake's two heads come out from two holes" is the waistband in traditional women's skirts. One riddle refers to praying, one to aging ("First four feet, then two, then three, then eight"), and two to the sky: stars are likened to lentils in a lentil-rice dish, and the Milky Way is a trail of straw. As adults, people are greatly amused by ad hoc rhymes they (mostly men) make up about somebody's mishap, a funny embarrassment.

Children often chant, loudly or silently, to amuse or console themselves. Ministories, feelings, social commentaries are interspersed with nonsense words in singing rhymes children, mostly girls, make up while playing or working. The songs accompany them through their day as running commentaries on places, activities, and events that, within the peer group, model how to feel about things and how to judge situations. Hoda, ten, stepping smartly around her grandmother's house on a rain-soaked afternoon, chanted slogans like, "We have no soap, we have no suds, death to America!" Such political slogans are repeated and embellished by school children and their little siblings in "demonstration-play" (*rahpeimani bazi*). Marching up and down the alley in front of their house, Mimi, age four, shouted the two-step rhyme, "Death to communists, why do they say there is no God?" in pure Luri, which gave the grim political slogan a twist of unintended hilarity for the neighbors. In 1981, children sang, "Don't

cry, Shahbanu, the Shah wants to die, Carter wants to marry you."
But when an eleven-year-old boy sang a protest song he had learned
while visiting in Shiraz ("We don't want goat-beards, we want bread")
a fine line had been overstepped between private political jokes and
dangerous political protest, and he was shushed emphatically; he got
the message that in a tight community like Deh Koh, where "smoke
holes have ears," as children know very well, mimicking of a protest of
"the state" (*doulat*) might have grave consequences for the family, involving police, revolutionary guards, jail, and execution.

Five-year-old Behruz, absorbed with scratching lines on a wall
with a stone, chanted to himself, "I'll dig a big hole, a very big hole,
for you to fall in, I'll dig a deep hole . . ." He was venting his frustration over having been left behind by his playmates. Two girls, standing back-to-back, lifting each other up on their bent backs may chant,
while getting increasingly out of breath: "My tale has two tails, calf-
skin makes a good skin-bag, crickets say *qaqa*, sparrows say *titerimeti*,
lets go to Damcenar to eat pomegranates and to bring back elm
leaves." Damcenar is a village in the southern part of the tribal area
famous for its elm trees. Elm leaves were the traditional substitute for
shampoo. Both, elm leaves and pomegranates, were hard-to-obtain,
much appreciated items. "Two plates got the sky, the khans got the
land," and, "I went to the doctor, he gave me no medicine," our
daughters sang with their playmates twenty years ago, succinctly
glossing the local political as well as the national structure. "I am in
tatters, I am burned, I am boiled," four little girls loudly sang on a hot
day in 1994, describing the hardship of the day while perching on a
high wall like birds on a branch. "I am hungry, thirsty, tired, I am
hungry . . ." six-year-old Jamal was chanting softly on the way home
from a long day in the orchards, over and over again, a marching beat
to his steps. Whenever Susan, three-and-one-half, was approaching
her quarter riding in a car she sang, "We have allived, we have allived, I wish we hadn't allived," adapting a song she had heard at a
wedding to express her feelings about traveling. "Hello, hello [*allo*],
two women, hello, hello, bunch of boys, hello . . ." two little boys and
two girls of about six were addressing passers-by on the road from
the safe distance of a rooftop. They knew very well that this was
impolite, and reacted with giggles and flight when an adult looked
up to them.

In 1994, during lulls in the action at weddings, a tireless group of four- to twelve-year-old girls kept spirits high with songs they remembered from other weddings, adapted from tapes, or made up: "A veil full of green sequins; we got Maryam for nothing," very directly expresses a groom's family's glee over having had to pay only a small brideprice for the bride. When fervor slackened, the leader, a ten-year-old girl of admirable resources and energy, performed a shrill solo: "Clap, clap!" she sang, "Whoever isn't clapping hard will be married off next!" This always inspired the group to enthusiastic clapping. It was the most direct opinion I have heard voiced by a girl about marriage. The younger girls in the group thereby learned to link the fun of the wedding with apprehension and negative feelings toward marriage long before they knew what marriage really meant. When there is not enough wind for winnowing, children may clap their hands and sing: "Wind, come, I'll give you sugar, wind, come, I'll give you onions." This verse, a lie-for-a-good-cause, invites wind to come to Deh Koh, which in earlier times had the reputation of an onion-growing and sugar-eating, or well-off, village in an area where little agriculture was practiced.

A relational pattern toward father's relatives is learned in a rhyme to a bug (*kuku*, a brown, flat bug) in its tiny sand hill that is said to give a clue to an unborn child's sex: "*Kuku, kuku,* come up if it is a boy, go to your father's brother [i.e., get lost] if it is a girl." If the bug does not show, one may dig it up with a stick: a small, weak bug means that the yet unborn child will be a girl, a big, fat one that it will be a boy. Ants may be fed with breadcrumbs to a chant that contains a complex philosophy: "This is for the snakes and the ants. May they leave my bones alone in the other world." A seven-year-old girl explained to me that a buried corpse was in danger of being eaten by "worms and bugs and ants" in the grave so that nothing would be left of the body for the Day of Judgment. To her and her playmates, it was a disgusting image. A few years ago, if a group of little girls wanted a playmate to join them, they would sing a question-answer rhyme in front of her house: "Who is out, who isn't?"—"Maryam"—"How is she?"—"She is with child"—"Whose child?"—"The boar's child"—"What iron spit?"—"A long one, in her butt." She will come out right away, to avoid the embarrassment of the boar's child. When a girl gets stuck in a blackberry or rosehip hedge, she may sing out, "Thorns let me go, I'll marry you!" This is a clever false promise, a white lie, showing that a girl knows how to deploy her main asset long before she knows what marriage entails. "I'll marry you," or "I won't marry you" are frequent promises or threats in situations where a girl wants to gain an advantage. Like all lies and false promises, an idle promise of marriage can be voided by flicking the tongue left and right over one's lips, usually with averted head and behind a cupped hand.

Among the first words a child likely will learn, after *mama*, breast, *da*, mother, and *na*, no, is *dulu*, the child-language word for lie. Fourteen-month-old Ali used the word liberally and routinely whenever he was teased, threatened, or promised something to make him behave in a certain way. "Lie, lie," a two-year-old girl matter of factly countered her mother's promise of a sweet. Lies, children learn early, are the background to the give-and-take of everyday life. They learn that lies are bad in principle, marked as a sin in the Book of Deeds angels keep for everybody, but actually are often necessary. Some lies even are better than the truth: bad news, for example, ought to be given in small doses wrapped in lies lest the sad truth might harm the receiver. Children ought to be kept from harm by a lie, if necessary: "Get away from the rooftop, come quickly, I have a candy for you," a three-year-old girl told her baby brother, and was praised for it by her aunt. By extension, any advantage may be pressed with a lie, and one does well to doubt anybody's assertions. Children, especially girls, lace their speech with sworn assurances such as "This is true, by your soul, by your father's soul; I swear! By God!" at the most trivial occasions, and doubt each other's oaths just as routinely. A bright, smart (*bahush, zereng*) child will learn soon when to lie acceptably to advantage. This lying will not be approved of morally, but a simpleton who tells the truth to his or her own or others' disadvantage or embarrassment is scolded for being a fool. "I don't know what will become of him," the mother of a six-year-old boy told me worriedly in his presence, "he never says a lie, he gets upset if somebody tells him a lie, and he gets duped all the time!" (To this the boy reacted with a tantrum.) *Gul khordan*, to be deceived, and *gul zadan*, to deceive, are result and method of dissimulation and false promises. "The boys say there is a young donkey running around on the Hill—take me there so I can ride it!" a five-year-old boy requested of his elder sister. She suspected that the boys would proclaim him the young ass as soon as he was on the Hill but had a hard time convincing him. "He wants to be deceived," she said. He, in turn, accused her of deceiving him by inventing the "lie" about the boys mocking him because she did not want to accompany him. A nine-year-old girl was raiding the larder at home for goodies to take to "the girls" in school. Her mother disapproved of this in terms of deception: "The girls just deceive you," she said. Her daughter understood (and disregarded) her but I needed explanation: the girls in school would take the sweets but not reciprocate in kind or with loyalty despite their promises, the mother said. Believing others naively and not being able to see through such schemes made her daughter a simpleton, *sadelu*. The opposite is somebody who has a "long tongue," or "sweet speech," who "knows everything," that is, a child who knows how to use words and how to evaluate what others are saying. Such children are *zereng*, smart-strong, which is desirable.

There is no gender difference reported for gullibility or smartness in young children save for girl children learning to talk a little earlier than boys. According to gender philosophy, girls and women ought to be more gullible than boys and men, but in everyday affairs no such difference is expressed.

Six-year-old Olmas was smart at a game of "Whose House?" that he was playing with his four-year-old sister and three girl cousins, who were smart in a different way. He had to think of a real house and say the number of men, women, boys, and girls living there, and the others had to guess the house. Girls know households so well that boys do not stand a good chance of winning. Olmas cunningly tried to stay ahead by changing to a different house when one of the girls guessed right, but eventually they got suspicious: "Liar! Say the house!" they cried. "Liar yourself!" he said, "I don't know the house any more, but you didn't guess it anyway and so you lost."

At another "Whose House?" game that an eight-year-old girl initiated with her mother, she said: "Two men, two women, two boys, three girls who just cried a big pot full of tears," thereby informing her mother of a row in a neighbor's house. "I never know what to make of her talk," said her mother. "She is really smart."

A few children, especially girls between the age of about eight and the time they are married, are known as excessive liars (*durugu*). They often tell stories about themselves and others that are blatantly and obviously not true, and they frequently answer the most simple and inocuous questions wrongly or give contradictory answers in the same breath ("No, I mean yes, no, no, I mean, I swear, yes!") all without discernible purpose and to nobody's advantage. People give no explanation for this behavior other than that the children had "gotten accustomed" (*amukhte vabi*) to it. Hava went through such a phase when she was in high school. Once, in my presence, her mother sent her to deliver a package of sugar to her aunt's house and to ask the aunt something. The girl left, returned after about half an hour, which was later than the errand should have taken her, and then played an "I swear I did it, no, I lied, I didn't" game with her mother as long as I was there, reporting several different, contradictory answers to the question she had been supposed to ask. In the end the mother, who alternately scolded her, made her swear to tell the truth, pleaded with her, cursed her, and laughed at her tall stories, left to check it out herself. (Hava had delivered the package but probably had not asked the question. Her mother never found out.) This case and similar ones I have observed suggest that such children learn to use lies, fanciful stories, and other subversive verbal tactics to manipulate authority, to hide from adults' interferences and demands behind their unreliability, and in a few extreme cases to create and inhabit a world of their own. Their odd behavior may indicate that they feel stressed by a lack of social space, and may also indicate a lack of choices to deal with such feelings. This particular kind of elaborate lying thus is available to children as a common, familiar, even if disapproved-of, response to pressures, demands, and controls. Quite expectably, more girls than boys are "liars" of this sort; they are controlled much more tightly. As to Hava, her younger brother predicted that her future husband would beat the lying out of her.

Strictly speaking, all folk tales, most stories in books, most films, anything not demonstrably, literally right count as lies, but most of these are considered harmless lies. Nobody, people say, could be entertained for long without lies, tricks, and make-believe acts. According to the everyday ethics of talking, only lies that do harm are really bad. The fire-eater at the circus lied in an entertaining way; should a child try to imitate his trick and get hurt, then the fire-eater's act would have been a bad lie, a harmful deception. Children learn that the world is not a place where truth is easy to come by; this makes for insecurity but it also provides moral room to press one's advantages without being too concerned with the truth.

The most endearing and enduring "lies"—"Why should I listen to my mother's lies when I have the radio!" a young man said when his mother started to tell a folktale—that children likely hear are a group of tales that state nothing less than a basic philosophy of life in a form so simple that children have no trouble absorbing it. In these short tales, no escapist ideal world is created where goodness triumphs over evil, paupers turn rich, and beauty is goodness triumphant. Rather, these tales make plain statements about the workings of the real world, where everybody, humans and animals alike, acts true to form, predictably, schematically. The world of these tales is a place of hardship: food is scarce, meat beyond most people's means; all that exists—trees, animals, old women, even rocks—live by impinging, out of necessity, on the comfort of others. Dearth is a backdrop to a life in which generosity is foolish and should not be expected; goodness and a morally blameless life guarantee no reward in this world; the pious and simpletons come to grief and only have themselves to blame for it. The wise know this and act accordingly; they respect the natural, immutable, essential qualities of things and people. Wolves cannot be trusted with sheep; poor old women are necessarily stingy and cannot be held to their promises; deals are risky because anybody will lie if it is to his, her, or its advantage; foxes steal and deceive to get by because they are foxes; husbands beat their wives; people are gullible; bartering keeps things moving; the wise turn requests into bargaining chips; wisest is the "Clever Little Bird" who manages to trick others into working for it. Whoever ignores the facts of life will come to harm.

There are no "bad" characters in these stories. Nobody is judged on moral grounds. Hardships and pain emerge not as consequences of moral turpitude but as by-products of life, of every creature's given nature, which makes fox long for meat and snake want to bite, which makes rooster crow, duck muck up water, and mouse steal wheat. There is no point in blaming, only in knowing and in being a little faster and a little smarter than the good neighbor next door.

The two following tales are examples of this genre. The first was told by Hurijan Sayadi, one of the famous storytellers in Deh Koh, and the second by Bishah Kerimi, while she was working at her loom. Both tales are told by people in Deh Koh in different versions.

The Old Man and the Snake

Once an old man was riding home from his fields on his donkey. He arrived at a river. There was a rock in the middle of the river and on the rock was a big, black snake. "For the sake of God and your kindness," cried the snake, "save me, and I'll be your faithful servant forever." The man was a kind-hearted old man who took pity on the snake. "I will throw you my pipe-bag on a rope," he said. "Get into the bag and I'll pull you across."

"You are a fool," said his donkey.

"And you are an ass," said the old man, "shut up." He got the pipe-bag from the saddle, took the water pipe out, tied a rope onto the handle of the bag, and threw it to the snake. The snake crawled into the bag and the old man pulled it ashore. When the snake came out of the bag, it cried, "Yuck, yuck, what a stinky old bag you made me crawl into! I'll bite you!"

"But I was kind to you," said the old man. "Don't be ungrateful."

"In this world kindness is not rewarded. You are dumb if you don't know this," said the snake.

"I don't believe you," said the old man.

"All right," said the snake, "we will ask the cow."

They found a cow wandering around in the pasture. The snake asked, "Cow, what is the reward for kindness in this world?"

"I will tell you," said the cow. "As long as I gave my master a calf every year and a pail full of milk every day, he gave me straw to eat and a roof over my head. But now that I am old and skinny, he turned me out and wants to slaughter me. Thus is the reward for kindness in this world."

"You hear?" said the snake to the old man. "Now I'll bite you."

"I still don't believe you," said the old man.

"All right," said the snake, "we will ask the tree."

They turned to a tree standing all alone in the wilderness. The snake asked the tree: "Tree, we want to know how kindness is repaid in this world."

"I'll tell you," said the tree. "I have been standing here for many years, giving shade to man and beast alike. But the gnats climb up into my branches and eat my leaves, and the people chop down my branches with their axes. Thus is the reward for kindness in this world."

"Now I'll bite you," said the snake to the old man.

"I'll ask one more witness," said the old man. "Here is a fox hole; let us ask the fox."

"All right, one last try," said the snake. They called the fox. The fox came out of the hole and the snake asked him: "Tell this simpleton of an old man how kindness is rewarded in this world."

"That depends," said the fox. "Tell me about it."

"This black snake was stuck in the middle of the river," said the old man. "I pulled it ashore in my pipe-bag. But instead of being grateful, the snake wants to bite me."

"I don't believe a word," said the fox. "A big black snake is too clumsy to get into a narrow pipe-bag."

"You just watch," said the snake and crawled into the bag. The fox quickly grabbed the bag and pulled the strings tight and took a rock and hammered away on the bag until the snake was dead.

"You are an old fool," said the fox to the old man. "Don't you know that snakes bite?!"

And then the fox went home into the fox hole and the man rode home on his donkey.

The Rock and the Walnut

Once there were a rock and a walnut. The rock cracked the walnut's head.

Walnut said to the rock, "Why did you crack my head?"

Rock said, "Why does the grass choke me?"

Walnut said, "Grass, why do you choke the rock?"

Grass said, "Why does the sheep eat me?"

Walnut said, "Sheep, why do you eat the grass?"

Sheep said, "Why is the wolf after my tail?"

Walnut said, "Wolf, why are you after sheep's tail?"

Wolf said, "Why does the dog bark at me?"

Walnut said, "Dog, why do you bark at the wolf?"

Dog said, "Why does the Old Woman only feed me bread crumbs?"

Walnut said, "Old Woman, why do you feed the dog only bread crumbs?"

Old Woman said, "Why does the hen peck holes in my bread cloth?"

Walnut said, "Hen, why do you peck the Old Woman's bread cloth?"

Hen said, "I pecked and I will peck, and I'd peck her vagina too if I could."

At that Walnut decided to beware of the rock.

16 · The Logic of Children's Miseries

A child's persistent health problems, troublesome behavior patterns, or odd character dispositions beg explanations, especially when customary medical, religious, or educational interventions fail to provide a change for the better. The explanations do not necessarily ease the children's lives or solve their problems but they put them into a cognitive frame in which they make sense and thus can be handled. They are, in this sense, philosophical diagnoses, with all the purported benefits that naming of adverse conditions and postulating their ultimate causes creates.

Above all, caretakers have to know about the nature of children.

The Nature of Children

Young children are said to be without sin (*bigona*) because their reasoning power and knowledge of good and bad develop from zero, so to speak, and need instruction, good example, and pedagogical means to be developed fully by the time the child is a young adult. All a child's misdeeds and mishaps, from destructiveness to disasters, from harming itself or others to torturing animals and tormenting each other in fights and games, foremostly are attributed to intellectual immaturity. If sin is a potential variable in the cause of a child's misery, it must be the parents' or an ancestor's sin, not the child's, the argument goes.

The development of reasoning, intellect (*aql, hush*), which is said to start a few months after birth, on the one hand leads to the accumulation of knowledge with which much misery can be avoided, and on the other hand to the knowledge of good and bad, of criteria for moral judgement. While secular, practical knowledge is seen as the key to a successful, largely pain-free life (our own children are taken as an example for this link in Deh Koh), knowledge about ethics, and making morally right decisions, often is said to lead to misery in this world; healthy, vigorous, strong children are "devils," while "very good" children often are "poor, quiet, meek, weak." This contradiction between morality that is "good" but favors misery, and behavior that is "bad" but produces health and wealth, runs through Deh Koh philosophy on all levels.

The well-being of young children thus partly is a function of parents' knowledge and its wise applications: a mother who hustles medicines or baby formula at the health clinic, who disregards "old-fashioned" advice in childcare, if successful, is simultaneously approved and disapproved of as "strong, clever, impertinent," while one who is waiting for her husband's permission for spending money on the baby, who does not hustle and expose herself socially, and has a weak, sickly child, is approved/disapproved of as "a meek, good, obedient" woman.

.   .   .

A child's basic humoral disposition is a given around which a clever, alert mother applies knowledge and resources to keep the child in humoral balance. Considerable effort goes into dietary considerations even if economic constraints curtail their realization. Seen from the outside, these efforts often produce malnutrition, and thus misery, in children. But as all local health personnel, including Iranian medical doctors working in and near Deh Koh, so far have subscribed to the same model, including what to us look like extreme dietary prescriptions and restrictions, and as food resources are very limited anyway, in this case trial and error experimentation is all but impossible. When we and our children frequently violated humoral dietary common sense without any of the dire consequences people predicted, our status as Westerners was used as an explanation for our deviant reactions: local children surely would get sick eating like our children, said our neighbors. This reasoning allowed the people to keep their system beyond challenge.

.   .   .

Inheritance (*ers, räg*) is seen as responsible for some features in a child's well-being. Light hair, certain facial peculiarities that may make a child beautiful or ugly, a tendency to twin births, the (rare) evil eye, the (even rarer) gift to heal eczemas with one's spittle, are said to run in the "blood-line" (*räg*) on the father's, but also the mother's side, as does intelligence. A teacher, looking at his brood of exceptionally bright (*roushan*) youngsters, said, "It shows that they have an intelligent mother and an even more intelligent father who decided to marry her!" In the opinion of one of the local khans, the unruly (*fuzul*) character of his children, which got them into accidents and trouble frequently, is due to "the blood (*khun*), the blood-line of Lurs (*räg-e Lur*)." For him, as for townspeople outside the tribal area, Lur is tantamount to being wild (*vakhshi*) by nature. Birth defects are called *madarzad*, implying that they stem from the mother. A neighbor's children's unusually high aggression was said to be due to their mother's morally rotten (*kharab*) milk; this woman, an outsider from a family in a distant village infamous for violence, had been given to her husband's family in compensation for a homicide committed by one of her brothers. "Rotten family, rotten milk, rotten children," was the general verdict. Defects may also be said to be in father or mother's "soul" and thus also in their children. Likewise, asthma was in a local woman's "soul," she said, and in two of her six children. Governmental media propaganda warns of cousin marriage because the children of such unions might have severe birth defects such as brain damage. Retarded children in Deh Koh now summarily are said to be the result of too close a kinship relationship between their parents.

A man who marries a *seyed* woman, a woman from a family tracing its ancestry patrilineally to the Prophet Muhammad, has to be very careful not to inconvenience or trouble her lest his children will be damaged (*eibenak*) in some way; this explains to everybody, including the children themselves, why a particular *seyed* woman's children in a neighboring village all have serious health problems.

.   .   .

Children are vulnerable by nature. They get sick frequently, are fooled, suffer because of lack of knowledge, lack of strength, lack of judgment. They will outgrow some miseries inherent in their weaknesses as their bodies and minds grow. Children may be said to "make their own calamity" (*qassa*), by playing very roughly, running fast, stubbornly eating "wrong" food, doing things they are warned against. Mehri, four, fell off her father's porch twice within a few months, breaking first an arm, then a leg. Her mother called this *qassa* the child brought about herself by not heeding her mother. However, children are said to be especially prone to calamities that sometimes "hit" unpredictably and without provocation: a child falls and breaks a limb, is run over by a car, is injured one way or another, falls ill suddenly. When two-year-old Masume fell from the porch and dislocated a shoulder, her neighbor called it a *qassa*, and said that "God does not watch over Masume's mother and her children," thereby putting the frequent accidents and illnesses and the poverty in this family into a wider perspective of causes of hardships.

Calamities may announce themselves in dreams. In such cases, a special sacrifice (*raf-e qassa*) of food or money given to the poor can deflect or cancel the impending troubles. Huri, always one for watching dreams carefully, said: "Last night I dreamt that I was at a river filling a goatskin water-bag of the kind we used before we had the water pipeline. My baby was with me. Suddenly the water swelled as it does in an irrigation channel when one opens a major lock upstream. The flash flood pulled the water-bag out of my hands. I let go of it and grabbed the baby in the nick of time. In the morning I gave a sacrifice—and it worked! Nothing bad has happened to us, thanks be to God."

After a dream had announced a calamity, a man gave alms to deflect it. The next day, while he was out making firewood with his young son, he suddenly felt the urge to call his son away from where he was standing, a moment before a boulder crashed down from the cliff to hit the exact spot where the boy had been. When a lamb got lost a day or so later, the man knew it to be the substitute for his son.

Graveyard stories are told as further proof of the efficacy of *raf-e qassa*. This one was told by a grandmother in the presence of several children, who demanded further explanations regarding dead people's whereabouts after the story was finished: "A man returning home from a journey slept near a graveyard. At night he heard a woman ask another woman for a bread board because she needed to bake bread for her sister's child, who would join the dead tomorrow. Her sister would wash her husband's dusty clothes at the river and her child would fall into the river and join the dead aunt. The man understood that he and his wife were being talked about. At home, his wife insisted so vehemently on washing his clothes that in the end he had to give in, but with the command that she give six kilograms of wheat as a *raf-e qassa*. She did so, and came home with the baby hale and well. That night he went back to the cemetery and heard the woman cry because her sister's child had not joined her after all."

The circularity of the argument with its built-in infallibility is not the point here; children hear such stories and see mothers give alms with dream-motivation frequently. By example, belief and concomitant action become choices for the management of adverse human affairs.

. . .

As their mother's and father's offspring, and as members of their father's patrilineal group, children may have to pay for an ancestor's sins with their grief: retribution (*muqafat*) is any "dis-ease" (*nourahat*) that may be seen as God's punishment for a misdeed that the child's father (or mother, to a lesser degree) or an ancestor up to seven generations back might have committed. The term is slightly accusatory, said either behind people's backs or by a distraught and contrite parent: "I don't know why my child is so sick—maybe it is a retribution," Hoda says about her son's lame leg. "Maybe I or his father have sinned, although I am not aware of a sin."

A stern and upright old woman with a long memory sees the death of her neighbor's baby as a retribution, a punishment for the neighbor's purported immodest friendliness with a strange man that the old woman claims to have witnessed years ago. The mother herself says, "I don't know what God wants of me that he makes this child suffer." Everybody else labeled the baby's illness and death a *qassa*, an unprovoked calamity.

The children of the second wife of a man in the village all are "deaf, dumb, or crazy," and this is generally proclaimed a retribution, a punishment of the father for having taken a second wife over the objection of his first wife, and for treating his first wife badly. No blame is laid on the second wife; she had no say in her marriage. The fact that two other polygynous men in the vicinity have ailing children strengthened the opinion in Deh Koh that taking a second wife is a sin. A popular understanding of Qoranic pronouncements on the legality of polygyny among women in Deh Koh is that a man has to treat his wives and children completely equally; as this is patently impossible, the taking of a second wife is a sin, punishable as are all sins.

The logic in punishing a parent by harming his or her child is accepted fully in Deh Koh, with few exceptions. It is seen as a visible sign of God's justice, heavy on revenge as it is. "No, no, this has to be; it is good so—where would the world be without it?!" Perijan explained to me. Her loss of a young child in an accident is labeled a calamity, not a retribution, by all, including herself. "Why children?" I asked, "Why not let the sinner himself break a leg?"

"This happens too, but a man suffers more when he sees his child suffer than when he breaks a leg." Retribution by harming a sinner's child is seen completely from the adult's point of view, from a level of power and authority way above the child's. Children are treated philosophically and theologically as their parents', especially their father's, assets, and thus as moral bargaining chips in their elders' dealings.

Leila, a mother of seven children, is one of the few who takes the children's point of view and disputes the didactic wisdom of harming children as retribution for a parent's sins: "It is not the fault of the child that a father or mother committed a sin," she argued. "If the purpose of retribution is to demonstrate God's justice, then the father who committed a crime should be punished right away, and for all to see so that all will be afraid to sin. If the retribution strikes years later, and not even himself, people only will say, 'Poor child has to pay for the father's crimes.' This is of no use."

This is Leila's model of the beneficial example of retribution: "A man in a small town on the other side of Snow Mountain was stingy. He hid a piece of meat in the refrigerator when a beggar came to his house, and sent the beggar away empty-handed. When the man opened the refrigerator, the meat had turned into a hide. The man was so moved that he put the hide around his shoulders and set out to walk the land, giving testimony. I have seen him myself." The four children who listened to the story were impressed and asked for details.

Mamalus, too, illustrated direct retribution with great satisfaction, in her case for unkindness toward children: "When I was little, we had nothing, nothing. The poorest of the poor in a poor village. My father was cutting hay way up behind the village. In the morning my mother gave me a small hide-sack with some acornbread-buttermilk-mush to take up to him. And I had to take my little brother along too. He could hardly walk yet. So we toddled along, skin-sack on my hip, little boy on my hand, pull, drag, push, up, up, up. We did not know where exactly our father was up there, either. So I said to the kid, 'Way up there I can see branch huts—let's go up there and ask.' It was hot, noon, sun beating down on us, thirst, hunger, we were half-dead when we came to the first hut. It was my motherbrother's daughter, milking her sheep and goats. They were well off. We two children, dry and tired, asked about father. 'Farther up,' she said, 'over there,' milking, milking, swish, swish into her pot, not even looking at us. We were starved. But she had nothing for us, not one crumb of bread, not one drop of buttermilk, nothing for two half-seared, tired little children. We left. Little brother was crying. We walked and climbed and stumbled along. I half carried, half dragged him, crying myself. It was late afternoon when we found our father. We were no longer quite alive, not quite dead either. That was one against Bibi.

"Not long afterward there was a wedding feast in the family. We all went to watch the dancing, hand clapping, singing. I and my little brother went too. I had never seen rice and meat stew in my life, ever. Bibi was the cook. She sat at a big pot with meat stew—the smell! An old woman was helping her. She saw us two little scrawny kids with big eyes and big empty stomachs, and she said to Bibi, 'Here, ladle a little out into the bowl for these two.' Bibi said, 'No, it is hardly enough for all the guests anyway—am I a cook for children?! Go away, get lost,' she told us, her fathersister's children!

"But not long after that a scorpion stung her and she died slowly, slowly, and with great pain. That was God's retribution for her stinginess and lack of compassion."

Old widow Zeynab, who is uncommonly interested in theology, objects to the misfortune-as-punishment argument on other grounds: "Only God knows," she says. "It is easy for us to say: 'this or that trouble is a punishment, it serves the scoundrel right.' But what about an innocent newborn with an earache? What about a sheep with a broken leg, bleating with pain? No, no—to call somebody else's pain a punishment for sins is a sin. God simply sends pain and suffering along with everything else—we don't know why."

There is no remedy for pain from retribution; if the doctor relieves one pain, another will befall the victim.

Beyond miseries children suffer because of natural, inherent inclinations or qualities, some children have more, and some less, luck or fortune, *shans*, which will make them suffer very little or very much. Some are identified as obviously *kamshans*, lacking good fortune, almost from the beginning: hit by a djenn or by the evil eye, neglected by an incapable mother, prone to accidents, ugly, unreasonable, dumb, poor, without relatives who might help, married early—none of it the child's fault or the parents', but owing to a constellation of adverse circumstances, bad timing, and missed opportunities beyond anybody's control. Mina, deaf in one ear, with a disfiguring twitch in her face and a withered arm, is *kamshans*—nobody can find fault with her or her elders' life, nobody suggests retribution. A baby girl slowly dying of hunger because her mother has no milk and because she is a girl, is *kamshans*; for that matter, every girl is *kamshans* because she is not a boy. Danesh, a boy of seven suffering from cirrhosis of the liver, is *kamshans*, especially so as none of the doctors' efforts seem to help. Fati was *kamshans* when she was little because her mother got pregnant again when Fati was only two months old—she is by far the smallest of her many siblings because of it, she says. All children in Deh Koh are *kamshans* because of the contaminated water that gives them diarrhea and abdominal pains, and because Deh Koh is a village, which in the eyes of many villagers is tantamount to lacking facilities for staying healthy and for advancement, and implies lots of flies annoying children and spreading disease, lots of dirt, ignorance, illness.

A few unfortunate children are mistreated by their mother or father. Mostly, either "troubled" (*nourahat*) mothers or aggressive, irascible (*tondrou*) fathers are seen as agents of their children's suffering, be it through neglect or excessive punishment. Either behavior is seen as deplorable, as not right, as sinful by others, is often denied by the parents themselves, and is remedied rarely. Older children can flee or hide at signs of imminent violence at home, but young children are terrified victims without recourse, unless adult relatives intervene. In a fit of rage over a series of misbehaviors and disobediences by one of his older sons, who wisely had fled wrath, a father started to vent his fury on his four-year-old son who had irritated him by bawling with fright. "I'll kill all of you!" the man yelled, swinging a huge club, chasing the screaming little boy across the courtyard. The man's mother in the next courtyard, troubled witless, she said later, started to wail loudly, as if somebody had died. This brought neighbor-relatives to the scene who calmed down the man. The little boy hid behind his crying mother. He wet his bed and had nightmares for several nights afterward, said his mother. The father was very contrite by evening, but this was neither his first nor last rage. "He has a lot on his mind," said his wife by way of explanation. The neighbors found his behavior "shameful" because it had caused a public nuisance.

A young woman has borne three children in four years. She is nineteen, has no relatives in Deh Koh, and does not get along well with her in-laws either. Frequently, the children scream in the house, behind closed doors: she is beating them, poking them, pinching them, pricking them with needles, her neighbors say—the marks on the children are obvious. Complaints to her husband result in his beating her up, "and then she is even meaner to her children than before," says her unhappy mother-in-law.

A seventeen-year-old girl who is "small, weak, sickly" by her own account blames the fights between her father and mother and between her grandfather and grandmother for her bad health: "I am a runty kid [karre korpe]," she says, "because scared children don't grow [rosht kardan], and I was scared every day. Just my bad luck."

There is a fine line between pedagogical violence, which is approved of, demanded even, and excessive, sinful violence. A father beat his son and his brother's son, both six, with a long switch because they had played hooky from school. The whole neighborhood heard the children scream. When the man came out of his courtyard, his other brother's seven-year-old daughter told him that there had been no school. "Not so," said a passer-by, a teacher, "there was school, but you weren't there either." Whereupon, without any further inquiries, she got her uncle's switch, too. Although the neighbors pitied the children, the consensus was that they had needed to be taught a lesson.

Ill fortune overrides parental routine efforts to keep a child well, but pledges, nasr, to a saint may bring superhuman intervention; God may be persuaded to pity a suffering child, to "keep it in his eye." Sometimes children are said to be saved from harm in accidents by their guardian angels. But one cannot count on benevolent superhuman interference. It can only be used as a post-hoc explanation for escape from danger. Such escape is frequent, though, people say, a sure sign that God and the saints more likely have pity on innocent children than on adults who all bear heavy burdens of sins. It is pointless to ask why God is "looking" or "not looking," though: it is his pleasure (meil). No matter how hard it might be, a good Muslim has to say, "Thanks be to God," (shukr khoda). Together with such words, with admonitions and stories, children learn the concepts that define their nature and explain their pains. "*Shuuk, shuuk,* thanks," said three-year-old Susan, examining her unharmed hands after having fallen off the swing. "Was this a *qassa*?" I asked.

"No," said her eight-year-old sister, "she was just stupid."

17 · A Bird Flies Off into a Tree

Two cold nights before Ali died, his mother heard a strange bird calling, loudly, close by, in a tree. She was troubled by it—hoot, hoot, jig, jig, jig . . . She got up and took a glowing log out of the fireplace. Sparks flew when she placed it near the walnut tree in the yard for the bird to warm itself in case it was cold, maybe. Later, in her sleep, a woman in black was passing her in an alley, wordlessly. Huri was scared. In the morning she changed her dark green, sad, old-woman headscarf for a white one to dispel the gloom. She meant to give alms to the poor, a bowl of rice, a stack of folded flatbreads, just to be on the safe side of fate, but then forgot about it as the day's worries chased her hither and yon: seven children, a sick husband, a cow, chickens . . . no alms.

He fell off the cliff above the gardens the next midmorning, breaking to pieces on the rocks. He was eight.

He would be alive today, had I given alms. His death was a qassa—*the woman in black had announced it to me. Maybe I could have averted it, directed it to myself, to the cow . . . I keep thinking . . .*

His younger brother had been with him. "Ali, Ali," he had yelled into the nothingness. He ran through the snow, down the gentler slope on the other side, sobbing with fear. After he had found some men down in a garden pruning apple trees and had delivered his fears, garbled, breathless, chokingly, he fainted. He was six years old then.

The day before he died, his mother was in the bath with him. She was looking at him: tall and healthy, bigger and broader than his elder brother, stronger than most boys his age, she thought. She told him that her arms were aching, he should wash himself, he was a big boy now.

Maybe I brought his death about myself, admiring him; maybe it was my own evil eye, my salt-eye. Praise is so very dangerous, even silent praise.

"He was leaning forward, holding onto a bush. 'Look at the crooked tree,' he said to me behind his back. Suddenly he was gone, like a bird, gone." This was all little Ahmed could tell, then.

The rocks were wet, icy. Slippery mud everywhere. He may have slipped with his worn-down canvas shoes. Or else the rock itself took him—a man had fallen to his death there before, years ago. "Blood-rock," they call it. But then maybe it wasn't that either. Maybe God just wanted it this way.

From that day on Ahmed was different: quiet, withdrawn, easy to cry, didn't want to go to school, didn't want to stay home, summer and winter out somewhere, sleeping in a branch hut in the gardens in good weather, or in the schoolhouse with boys from other villages who go to school here and have nowhere else to stay. When he was home, he did what he was asked to do, little chores, but hardly spoke. He got very angry whenever he met his mother or sister in the village. "You belong at home!" he would shout. He said he wouldn't let his sister go to school any more unless she kept out of sight in the back alleys. He was strange, distant, restless.

I know I have a heathen djenn-twin. She killed my first son in the cradle: one day he suddenly cried, and cried, without reason, flapping and flailing his little arms like a bird, and then he died. Like a bird—this gave the djenn away. Maybe Ali's own djenn-twin had pushed him off the cliff—a reasonable boy like he doesn't simply fall, holding on to a bush. A jealous djenn-twin . . . one can do nothing against them.

Unlike some of her other children, he had been a big, healthy baby. She had taken all precautions she could think of: a *mohre bacce*, beads, amulets; kept him from places where people gathered for fear he would be hit by the evil eye, even missed her favorite brother's wedding. From neighbor women near and far who were nursing baby girls she begged milk: girl's mother-milk is the best food a boy can have. He was doing well. All the troubles, all the care . . .

His teachers, too, were worried about Ahmed. They liked him, everybody liked him, but his mind was wandering, he was failing in school. People said it was probably because of his father's illness. But it was really because his nerves were shattered when his brother died.

When misfortunes announce themselves in dreams, they can be averted by alms: instead of a child, a goat may be hurt. Instead of death, a broken leg . . . Once, during the war, I had seen airplanes in my sleep, bombing the village while I was praying. Blood was spouting from the palms of my hands. First thing in the morning I took a bowl of lentils to poor old widow Sakine. Her blessing is powerful. In the evening I was missing a chicken . . . only a chicken! It works, praise be to God. A misfortune comes for no other reason than that it is its time to come. Only God knows why it killed my favorite son.

Ahmed was seen in the fields, in the mountains, the gardens, here and there. While nobody complained about him, nobody approved of his loafing either. He grew up a thin, pale, quiet boy. Nobody but the other boys he hung out with could make much sense of him.

A dead child goes to heaven without being questioned by the Angel of Death. It is without sin. The souls of dead children become birds sitting in a tree in paradise, eating heavenly fruits, singing. This is written somewhere. But how can a mother forget? One day she scolds him for a rowdy, cuffs his ears, feeds him, keeps the flies off his sleeping face, and the next day he is gone.

Children's graves have no markers so as not to remind parents of their child's death. A dead child is troubled by its parents' mourning. Whenever somebody sheds tears at a child's grave, the child has to get up and stand on its feet until the person leaves. This is written in the books too, people say.

I cried and cried. People said I was ungrateful (nashokri), that another misfortune would befall us if I didn't stop. But I couldn't help it. Then I saw him in my sleep. He was scooping grayish-brown, smelly water out of a stream with his cupped hands to drink. "Dear," I said, "my soul, my life, why are you drinking dirty water?" He said, without even looking at me, "Your tears are flowing into my water like heavy rain, muddying it up." I stopped crying, but my heart was broken.

They talked to Ahmed, pleaded with him, his mother, father, elder brother, his uncles. He got angry, cried, got angrier still. His people spent a lot of money on prayer-amulets. They made promises to saints; they gave alms for years, to no avail. But slowly, slowly, he got a little more reasonable, stayed home a little more, seemed less driven, more interested in his books. It took years until he was himself again.

It is a sin to mourn for a dead child. I don't even look at his grave any more. This is his photograph, but his face isn't very clear . . .

Now Ahmed is a teacher with a fiancée. He can chant the Qoran like no other. He talks a blue streak, tells the funniest jokes. He makes everybody laugh and cry with his music, his songs, his poems, with the stories he writes. He remembers: "We were cutting poles for something. Ali stood with his back to the steep slope and pulled hard on a branch he had cut into. Suddenly the branch snapped off, he lost his balance, started to slide in the frozen mud, slid, faster and faster, toppled over, and was gone.

"It was very hard for me."

18 · Alphabet Philosophy

Children in Deh Koh learn much of their culture, of who they are, what is expected of them, what they can expect of others, of life and the beyond, in short little stories such as those that follow. Of the great many I have heard over the years, I chose only those that were told to children or in their presence, or else are about children. The storytellers' names follow the titles. Where the name is omitted, the story's politically or socially sensitive message makes anonymity advisable.

Neither the messages nor the concepts in which they are transmitted require explanations.

The format I have chosen is modeled after a rhetorical skill mullahs command: the ability to provide a sermon, a legend, a short instruction spontaneously on any letter of the alphabet in response to a query or a challenge. To avoid confusion I use the English alphabet instead of the Persian one. I ask indulgence for omitting the X, and for using local terms for Y and Z.

· · ·

Adam and Eve (Keomars Azizi, an old man)
One day the prophets in paradise wanted to make a person out of earth. But the ground didn't want to part with any soil and shook itself. This was an earthquake. Only when the prophets promised the earth that the person eventually would become earth-dirt again did it keep still. The prophets made Adam and Eve. As soon as the two

people were finished, they sneezed, and while they expelled air God's soul took the air's place in Adam and Eve's bodies.

.   .   .

Bee (Reza Pakbaz, a middle aged man)
The bees went before God to make a deal. "We'll make four *man* of honey every year for the hungry people who are after our honey always," they said, "but those we sting will die." God thought about it, and then turned it around: bees don't have to work hard—a little bit of honey is enough; but when one stings a human, the bee will die.

.   .   .

Co-wife (Sarigol Pakbaz, a young woman)
There was a man in a village down at the river—he is in jail now—who had a wife. He went to Isfahan to work. There he married another woman. When he brought her home his first wife cast a spell (people know such things down there) so that the man didn't want his second wife anymore. He killed her, put her into a pit and heaped rocks over her. But the people got wise, and now he is in jail. Although not all co-wives are like this, most are trouble for each other.

.   .   .

Djenn (Heydar Nikeqbal, an old man)
Some twenty years ago a camp group was on migration to the summer pastures. In the evening a girl went to fetch water but did not return. After a whole day of useless searching her people moved on. Next year the group camped at the same place. A man left the camp to hunt. He shot a bear next to a cave. A half-naked woman ran from the cave wailing, threw herself on the dead bear—it was the lost girl. She had a baby. The hunter brought her to the camp. She told her people that a strong hand had grabbed her as she was bending over the spring, and carried her away a year ago. Her people killed her and her djenn-child too. It wasn't the girl's fault, but what else could her people have done with her?

.   .   .

Evil (Nezakat Bandarzadeh, a middle-aged woman)
Evil came into the world like this: Sheitun (Satan) was a prophet who lived with all the other prophets in paradise. When Adam and Eve were made, they sat down in a house. All the prophets came and bowed before them, all except Sheitun, who did not want to greet them. The other prophets complained to God. God advised them to build a low door so that Sheitun would have to bow his head while entering. They did so, but when Sheitun went to see Adam and Eve the next time, he turned around, so that his behind was entering first, and he bowed to the outside. This was worse than no greeting at all! The prophets complained again. This time God punished Sheitun: he made him ugly and confined him to a deep pit. Sheitun moaned and groaned. He begged and whined and pestered God until God got tired of it and allowed Sheitun to live in Adam and Eve's bellies. There he sits still, in every one of Adam and Eve's children and children's children, and tries to talk the person into doing evil.

.   .   .

Fool (The stories of Mullah Nasr-ed-din (Nasrein, locally), the fool, prankster, and wise man, are as popular in Deh Koh as elsewhere in Iran, and considered very funny by children and adults. Several people told me this one.)
Mulla Nasrein was up in a tree sawing the branch off on which he was sitting. A man walked by. He said, "You'll fall!" Mulla Nasrein fell. He said, "How did you know? You must be God's brother! Now tell me when I'll die." The man said, "If you fart once while you climb the hill over there, your soul will come up to your knees; at the second fart it'll come up to your chest; at the third your soul will leave you through your mouth and you will be dead." A few days later Mulla Nasrein had to cross the hill, and it happened just as God's brother had predicted. Strangers passing by carried him away for dead. At the river they were at a loss as to the ford. Mulla Nasrein said, "While I was still alive we always crossed the river over there."

.   .   .

God Provides (Nosrat Kerimi, a middle-aged woman)
After my husband died, I had no money, not one little coin. I lay awake at night, worrying about how I would feed my children. The next morning a little boy stood at my door with a handful of bills—

his father had sent him, it was a vow (*nasr*). And another time, when my last penny was spent, I was rummaging in my cabinet and found a whole bag of twenty-toman bills—and to this day I don't know whether my husband had hid the money there or whether God had put it there for me to find. For those who have faith, God provides.

.   .   .

Heaven and Hell (Hurijan Seyadi, an old woman)
Dead children go to heaven, they are innocent, they don't know things. Some men go to heaven, some go to hell. Most women go to hell: they talk badly about others, they don't take care of their children properly, they bitch, they don't obey their husbands, they fight with each other. They'll go to hell . . . maybe. We don't really know; nobody has actually come back from THERE. People read about it in books, have dreams. Books lie, people lie, dreams lie . . . But then again, maybe not.

.   .   .

Ingenuity (Mahmud Ghafari, a middle-aged man)
A sparrow found a fluff of fleece in an abandoned campsite, brought it to a woman, and said, "Card, card; if you can't card fleece, I'll do it myself." The woman carded it. Sparrow flew with the strand of wool to another woman, and said, "Spin, spin; if you can't spin, I will." She spun. Sparrow took the ball of yarn to another woman, said, "Block it, block it; if you can't block yarn, I'll do it." She blocked it. Sparrow took it to a weaver and said, "Weave, weave; if you can't weave, I can." She wove. Sparrow took the fabric to a woman, said, "Sew, sew; if you won't sew, I will." She sewed a wheat bag. Sparrow took the bag to a threshing place and said to the men there, "Fill, fill; if you don't, I will." They filled the bag with wheat. Sparrow flew to a woman with it, said, "Sew it shut, sew it shut; if you won't, I will." She sewed. Now sparrow sat down on top of the full bag, ruffled his feathers, craned his neck and said, "Not even the Shah's wife can do better than I did!"

.   .   .

Jinxed (An elderly woman)
Three days after my cousin had delivered her seventh daughter, she went outside and stood under the trees for a little while. Suddenly

she shivered . . . From that moment on, once or twice a week she used foul language, bit and hit people, threw rocks—she was jinxed by a djenn (*mazerati*). The doctor sent her to the psychiatric hospital in Shiraz for electroshocks. Then her people took her to Meshhed and to the Jewish amulet writers in Shiraz. Over the years she got much better, but since then her body is weak and full of aches.

.   .   .

Kismet (Gordaferin Boir Ahmedi Fard, a young woman)
A *seyed*, a descendant of the Prophet Muhammad, predicted of a newborn boy that a wolf would eat him on his wedding night. When the boy was about to get married, he built a special house for the bridal chamber: it was built of big rocks, had no window, no smoke hole, a spiked fence around it, one heavy door guarded by riflemen. Twelve hunters patrolled the countryside around the house to make sure no wolf could come close. The groom brought his bride into the house. As they were about to sit down on their bed the bride turned into a wolf and ate him. This is kismet!

.   .   .

Lie (Heydar Rokhforus, a young man)
The Lur say: "When I don't say a lie for a whole day I get a stomachache." Of course they think everybody else is lying, too. When the first radios appeared, my uncle bought one. When he turned it on, a voice said, "Here is Tehran." My uncle got mad and yelled, "Your very first word already is a lie!"

.   .   .

Modesty (Zahra Daghestani, a young woman)
One day a blind man came to visit the Prophet. The Prophet's daughter, Fateme, got up and left the room. After the blind man was gone, the Prophet said, "Why did you leave? He is blind!" Fateme said, "Yes, but I am not blind." This is true modesty, and not the veilgames our girls play!

.   .   .

Nails (Zeynab Seyadi, an elderly woman, to two of her grandchildren)
Whenever you cut your nails, make sure you pick them up and put them somewhere safe, in the crack in a wall, under a rock, some-

where out of sight, because: on the Day of Judgment the donkey *Dojal* will walk the land and shit dates—plonk, plonk, plonk. People will run after him to pick up the dates but he will lead them straight to hell. The nails, however, will turn into trees blocking the way for those who had saved them carefully instead of scattering them. These will be the people who will go to heaven. Make sure you will be among them!

.   .   .

Old Age (Zahra Azizi, 9, is singing merrily, sitting on a swing:)

> "Mother, oh mother, the troubles of this life!
> "Mother, oh mother, my body is like water,
> This world is full to the brim with troubles.
> Mother, oh mother, I belong here no longer,
> Old age has killed me . . ."

She has learned this song from her grandmother, who sings such lines often, swaying to and fro in the sun on her porch.

.   .   .

Passion (A young woman)
A woman has more passion (*eshq*) than a man. But in a woman it is in the sole of her feet; there it is stamped on and weakened with every step a woman takes. This is just as well because otherwise a woman would "do it" with everybody! A man's *eshq* is in his head where his reason (*aql*) can control it. But passion is strong—it is a bad pain for a man.

.   .   .

Qom (A middle-aged man)
A man complained to God about the bad condition Iran is in. God listened for a while, then said, "Iran's affairs are in my hands no longer. Khomeini is in charge." The man went to Qom to see Khomeini. Khomeini, however, sent him on to the Imam Reza in Meshhed. But when the man arrived at the Imam's shrine, the Imam was not in his grave. "He went to Qom," people said. The man returned to Qom, found him at the door to the shrine of his sister, Masume, with a big club in one hand and a machine gun in the other. The man

said his complaints. Imam Reza said, "Instead of complaining, every man should guard his sister with a club and a gun as I am doing. Go home and guard your sister, and Iran will be well again."

.   .   .

Rainbow (Zamangol Sadeghi, a young woman, to her four-year-old son)
See where the rainbow touches the earth? Never go after it! Whoever reaches a rainbow will turn into the opposite: a boy into a girl and a girl into a boy, for sure.

.   .   .

Smallpox (Zeynab Seyadi, a middle-aged woman)
On their flight from Mecca, the Prophet's daughter, Fateme, ordered her maid to cook rice. One kernel of rice fell to the ground when the maid poured it through the sieve. Somebody stepped on the kernel. Fateme saw this and became very angry. As a punishment for the maid's negligence, she made smallpox. The maid was the first one to have her face marked by pocks in the shape of cooked rice kernels. But then the doctors came . . .

.   .   .

Turtle (Mehri Seyadi, an old woman)
A woman was baking bread. She was all alone, had nobody to help her. Her baby was lying next to her. The baby soiled itself. To help the mother, who couldn't very well have left the dough and the fire to wash the child, God sent her a fine silk scarf to wipe the child clean with. But the woman thought, what a pity to waste such a fine scarf, and hid it under her skirt. She took a freshly rolled, soft flat-bread to clean the child with instead. God became very angry. As a punishment, he put the griddle on her back, the bread board on her belly, the dough roller in the back as a tail—she was a turtle now.

What happened to the child? Well, his father took another, better wife, who took good care of the baby . . . for sure, maybe.

.   .   .

Uncanny (Shahzade Pakbaz, a middle-aged woman)
Thursday evening food ought to be given to the poor. This is important for the dead. Once a man from Deh Koh was traveling with a

caravan through the tribal area. On Thursday night, they camped near a graveyard. When all but the Deh Koh man were asleep, a girl came out of a grave, went to another grave and said, "Give me some bread—my people haven't given me anything today, they are on the migration. They'll be here tomorrow, and then I'll repay you." She got a bread-roll and stepped down into her grave again. The man was badly frightened but so curious that he and a few others stayed the next day to see what would happen. Indeed, a tribal group came and pitched tents there. The people slaughtered a sheep, gave the man from Deh Koh and his people a big piece of meat. That night the girl came out of her grave with a piece of meat in her hand, went to the other grave, and handed the meat down inside.

This is how we know about what the dead people need, even if such encounters are uncanny and dangerous.

.   .   .

Visitor (Shukrullah Hoquqi, an elderly man)
Once a stingy rich man was eating dinner. His son cried from the door, "A visitor is coming." The man threw a rag over the dinner tray and crawled under a pile of fleece in a corner. "Tell the visitor nobody is home," he said to the boy. So the boy shouted, "Nobody is home!" But the visitor was the prophet Isa (Jesus), who could see everything. He said to the pile of fleece in the corner: "Up, up," and the hidden man turned into a sheep and ran away.

.   .   .

Women (Shahrbanu Pakbaz, a middle-aged woman)
In the beginning of the world, men had a period every month, women didn't. The men complained to God about the bother. God saw their point. He gave the period to the women. Now the animals say this about it: "Am I glad not to be a dog," says the boar. "Am I glad not to be a person who menstruates," says the dog.

.   .   .

Yaqi (repulsion felt for a husband; a young woman)
One of the women in Deh Koh, people say, was a weak, sickly little girl. Her people promised her to a *seyed*, a patrilineal descendant of the Prophet Muhammad, without a brideprice, as a vow, if she would live. Soon after, he came for her. But she loathed him, she was *yaqi*,

did not want him at all. She ran away from him, hid in the gardens, in the barn, at home. Her mother and sister lied to him when he came after her: "We haven't seen her," they said. But then they beat her and scolded her for running away from him. Whatever they did to her, however, she refused to go back to him for three more years. Very young brides often are *yaqi* . . .

· · ·

Zesht (obscene, ugly; Einullah Muzafari, an old man)
Drinking alcohol is *zesht* because it leads to ugly, outrageous, sinful, bad, *zesht* behavior. A woman in Shiraz had a brother, a young fellow who once got drunk at a friend's house and started a brawl. This was *zesht* enough. His sister said, "If you have to drink at all, do it at home where people can't see you." Next time he got drunk at home and raped his sister. When he was sober again, she told him, and cried. He was so troubled and ashamed that he slit his stomach with a knife and died. After nine months the sister delivered a son. For three years she hid him, but then was afraid of being found out, and so she put him on a donkey and sent the donkey out into the wilderness. Several years later, a young stranger came to the village. He married her. Eventually he told her his story—it was her son! This is how a bottle of wine can lead to a long string of *zesht* acts!

19 · "Just a Fine Kids Feeling"

—text on a little boy's T-shirt in 1994, the summer the government expressed concern over the many English slogans on clothes.

Fear and Fondness

"Threat in the eye, warmth in the heart," our grandmother-neighbor summed up the right parental attitude toward children in Deh Koh. Without *tars*, threats, fear, proper respect due to elders, to anybody in a higher position of authority than oneself, the society would crumble, people say. It is a quality ordained by God to make ordered life possible, and ought to be instilled in children early. This is a father's duty. A father's threats better be taken seriously; a mother's can be ignored. "Just wait till I tell your father!" mothers may say, using father's authority to bolster their own. "He or she 'has a father'" means the person had learned to behave well and to walk among people with dignity. But without *delsuz*, fondness, empathy, warm feelings in the heart for one's offspring, children will suffer, will not grow well in body or intellect. The secret of educational success lies in the proper balance: too much fear and punishment will make young children unbecomingly quiet, shy, fearful, weak, small, tearful, and dumb, and at a later age sneaky, uncooperative, and generally unsuccessful in life. A seven-year-old boy lost his speech for several weeks at the frightening sight of two armed soldiers at his house. Girls especially may become *puhu*, slow, withdrawn, unable to work if beaten, scolded, or frightened too much; boys even might run away or become *vellou*, unmanageable loafers and troublemakers. One very young bride was sick for several years after her wedding night—she had been frightened out of her wits by her husband, who had "used a lot of force," said her aunt; too much fear makes anybody sick in mind and body, but especially youngsters. Overindulgence, on the other hand, unrestrained fondness, too much giving in to children's demands, too much cuddling, too much overt affection spoils children, people say, makes them rotten, impertinent, without manners, crazy, troublesome, the more so the older they get: "The older, the shittier," goes a saying. The adjective used for such children, *nazeli*, spoiled from too much affectionate lenience, implies criticism of the doting parent and identifies lack of discipline (*tarbiat*) as the cause of a child's annoying behavior.

After a fight between her father and two of his sons, the eighteen-year-old eldest sister of six siblings berated her parents, under her breath but very emphatically, for having spoiled all their younger children and thereby having produced worthless troublemakers. "As if you wouldn't know better!" she said.

A woman ascribed the erratic, irascible conduct of one of her little nephews, the last born in his family, to his lack of discipline. "His mind has suffered," she explained. "His reason does not function well, he is crazy. I can tell by how he does not mind anybody, not his mother, not his brothers, not even his father."

In boys, the bad outcome will be more dramatic than in girls: spoiled boys might end up as thieves in jail, unable to care for aging parents or a wife, unsuccessful in their enterprises, *vellou* forever. Spoiled girls do not know how to work; they talk back, pick fights, but are expected to straighten out eventually under the increasing pressure of demands on them and under their husbands' disciplinary measures. "She is not afraid of my father and not afraid of me—just wait until she gets married!" said a frustrated brother about his younger sister. "Spoiled" with all its variants is a verdict levied on others, not on oneself. It is used freely among siblings: heavy-handed elder brothers may be called "crazy" by their sisters and younger brothers; temperamental sisters may be called "shameless" by an elder brother or sister; uncooperative playmates will call each other "stupid"; youngsters hear from all siblings that they are "spoiled" as likely as that they are sweet and dear. About themselves, children usually express satisfaction: "I am good—my mother is bad!" said a sulking five-year-old girl who just had been spanked and called naughty by her mother. "I am very good and pretty," a seven-year-old boy shouted at his elder sister, who had been pestering him to wash his face; "You are old and ugly!"

A rich vocabulary for good and bad character qualities and for potential causes, especially of bad ones, provides children with concepts expressing the philosophy of character formation. "Good and bad" (*khub va bad*) constitute the essential ethical matrix: clean and beautiful are good, dirty and ugly are bad; quiet and demure are good, loud and aggressive are bad; food and hospitality are good, hunger and miserliness are bad; politeness and obedience are good, rudeness and disobedience are bad; right is good, not-right is bad. A "good" young child is rewarded by cooing, by terms of endearment, by caresses, by tempered praise, by eye contact, which otherwise and generally are rare. A "bad" child, especially after the toddler age, is shooed away, yelled at, cursed, hit. But "good" and "bad" frequently are contextualized and might shift within seconds. Many categories of children's behaviors are ambivalent: "strong," for example, is both good and bad, as is "quiet," depending on the judge and the occasion. From the inconsistency with which adults relate to them, children learn the variable ranges of "good" and "bad" together with how to manipulate the authority that defines them.

Hurijan, a mother and grandmother of firm principles and great experience, had this example: A family in the village has the reputation of being tough and rough, economically successful but morally rotten (*fased, puside*). Hurijan once came upon one of the boys in this family as he was stealing a bunch of beets from a field. She said, "Shame on you for stealing! What will your father say when you bring home stolen beets?!" The boy said, "He'll say, 'Well done, we'll eat good beets today.'" Knowing the father, Hurijan believed the boy. "From old-woman-me he learned that stealing is bad, and from his father, that stealing beets is good," she said. "The boy will call himself a thief but will not be troubled by it." In other words, by the time he was six or seven, the boy had both moral contexts for stealing internalized and used them to his advantage.

"Respect makes children mind their manners," said a father whom I had asked to explain *tars*. "When my father called me or gave me an order when I was a boy, the only possible answer was, 'Yes!' Anything else would have brought a blow. This is *tars*." Fathers today still insist on being answered properly and loudly when they call a child (or sister or wife), but the prompt, affirmative reaction no longer can be taken for granted. A woman teacher elaborated on the link between respect and good habits and manners (*raftar*, conduct): "When children are young, they need to be told what to do and how to do it because they don't know; to obey, they need *tars*. Later, their manners will have become a habit; good manners and good habits will make a good person, bad manners and bad habits will make a bad person." The little boy who stole beets with impunity will grow into the habit of thievery without qualms; the man who respected his father grew up into a respectable man.

People say that respect is in decline today. An order to a son likely will be challenged; children talk back to their parents; a girl refuses a suitor her parents approve; a boy is lazy despite requests, admonitions, and blows. Teachers' slaps and other punishments in school, administered to instill respect and good study habits, now are said to make children recalcitrant rather than respectful, if they have any effect at all. For some of the older people, these changes are signs of the impending end of the world; children take them as signs that times are changing for the better, except when their own younger siblings' mischiefs and disobedience annoy them. "I'll show you *tars*!" a seventeen-year-old brother screamed, drumming his fists on the back of his younger brother, who earlier had subverted an order to help irrigate an orchard by quietly slipping away from his post at the channel. "She has no *tars* whatsoever," said an angry mother about her daughter's many failing grades in school, thereby explaining her daughter's unwillingness to study.

Good manners, good habits are morally good, but they do not come naturally; they have to be learned. Bad habits come more easily, people say, but it is not clear why that is so. "The devil never sleeps," is one explanation, but it is not given often. It makes more sense in Deh Koh to say, *"amukhte vabi"* and *"adat gero"* that is, s/he got accustomed to something, for describing the mechanism for acquiring habits and skills, preferences and dislikes. It is used to explain a toddler's craving tea and sugar, excessive whining, tantrums, attachment to a toy or to a routine; for an older child's wetting the bed, stealing, lying, being *vellou*, becoming addicted to tobacco or worse drugs.

A mother explained that, because he was weaned early, her son had "gotten accustomed to" falling asleep consoling himself with his hand on her breast; a year later he still refused to go to bed without her. "If only I could send my breast with him to bed!" she sighed.

A preschool-age girl's destructive way of leafing through books, ripping page after page, she "got accustomed to" so firmly that nothing could be done about it, said her ten-year-old sister.

In the company of children with bad habits, a child likely will learn bad habits, parents explain; in the company of understanding (*aqel*), good people, a child will learn good habits, will become understanding and responsible. Girls are said to be less likely "bad" and troublesome than their brothers because they are wise sooner than boys by nature but also because they are at home around adults much more and thus sheltered from the corrupting influences of the street.

A fifteen-year-old boy who was chewed out in very strong language by his mother, elder sister, and another relative for his laziness (*tambali*), countered their criticism by saying, "You yourselves are wild, uncultured [*vakhshi*, a term used, for example, for wild animals]; so why should I be better?"

A girl of high school age, discussing a family whose members fought a lot, where "everybody was beating up everybody else," said that the children were bullies in school too and could not be expected to be different—they had learned this at home.

Leila, a teacher who is very much attuned to the difficulties of setting good examples for children to emulate, has this story: Once a mother came before the Prophet with her child, who was ill from eating too many dates yet continued to eat them. The mother asked the Prophet to order the child to stop eating dates because the child did not listen to her. The Prophet said, "Not today; come again tomorrow." The next day, the Prophet forbade the child to eat any more dates. The mother said, "And why didn't you say this yesterday?" "Because yesterday I was eating dates myself," he said. Leila remembered this story while she and some other women were discussing a fourteen-year-old boy in the neighborhood who smoked cigarettes despite his elder brother's objections and punishments. The elder brother was a chain smoker—to Leila this disqualified him from giving nonsmoking orders to his brother.

The more naïve, simple, trusting (*sade*) a child is, the easier it can be seduced by others into bad behavior. For this kind of persuasion, the word deception (*gul zadan, gul khordan*) is used. "His comrades [*hombazi, rafiq*] deceived him," explained the mother of a boy who was in trouble with the law. However, left to their own devices of moral and intellectual development, nothing good is expected from children either. Deprived of human relations and guidance, children are said to grow up without refinement, boorish, like wild animals. It is a parental duty and the goal of parental pedagogy to mold children into responsible and skilled adults. Karima, supported by her brother, objected to a suitor on these grounds: he walks with his head tucked between his shoulders; he sniffles; his clothes are always rumpled; he does not know polite speech; he drops food from his spoon when he eats; he mispronounces words; he has no taste in gifts; he only wants to sit behind his father's fireplace, like a dimwit; he is boorish (*vakhshi*); he slouches. His people did not teach him how to talk, how to behave, and now it is too late to teach him.

Once habits are instilled in a child, they will stay; it is very hard to unlearn habits, good or bad.

Polite and Proper

Good conduct (*raftar*) consists of morally good behavior from cleanliness to prudent honesty, and of manners guided by respect and propriety. Of these, etiquette and polite speech informed by understanding of everybody's place in this world and of propriety and ethics, are the most important in everyday encounters. This kind of behavior is entailed in the term *ta'rof*, polite etiquette involving status, generosity, honor (*abru*) displayed by giving honor (*ehteram*) where it is due or advisable.

"Didn't you make *ta'rof*?!" a ten-year-old girl was scolded by her mother, who had missed a visitor. Yes, she had, said the girl. "I said, 'Please come in, sit down, my mother will come right away,' but Aunt Huri did not stay, no matter what I said." By her mother's dissatisfaction, the girl got the point that her skills of polite persuasion had not been strong enough or else the woman would have stayed.

Two male high school students, friends (*rafiq*, mate, comrade; the Farsi term for friend, *dust*, rarely is used in Deh Koh) since toddlerhood, who always walked home together to a crossroad near our house, inevitably parted with a slight bow to one another, and the simultaneous formulaic invitation to come to the other's house, which just as inevitably was declined with another polite formula of regret. This routine of expressing mutual honor never varied.

Telephone conversations even between young girls start and end with strings of polite speech, repeated questions about the other's well-being, assurances of being happy to be of service to the other, to comply with any wish, to be the other's sacrifice. "If I didn't do this," a ten-year-old explained to me, "my cousin would either think I am mad at her or else that I have no manners." Boys start to use and elaborate the politeness routines a little later than girls.

When some chickens and an ill-defined border between two neighboring relatives led to resentment in the women in one of the houses, a discussion arose there as to how to log a complaint with enough *ta'rof* to make the point without giving offense. The women concluded that it was impossible. In the end, they sent a six-year-old boy with the rehearsed order to say, "Aunt Goli, your chickens are eating our herbs. Please watch your chickens better and build the wall higher. Thank you. Good bye." Only a young child would be forgiven such direct speech, the boy's mother said. Aunt Goli later told me that it was wrong to make use of a child in this way instead of teaching him proper, polite speech, but she also had to laugh about him. "Children's cheekiness comes in handy sometimes!" she said. The little boy knew very well what was going on, had listened to his people's deliberations, which explained the full range of implications of his speech, and compared them with his aunt's reaction. Judging from his swagger and the glee with which he told his story at home, he felt very important and successful.

At a wedding, the bride, who had a salaried job, gave the children of one of her poorer relatives money for the barber who was publicly shaving the groom. "She wants her own relatives to make better *ta'rof* than the groom's relatives," commented her grandmother in front of the children, expressing to them very directly the link between politeness and contestations of status between families.

Another little boy of about six, practicing *ta'rof* by mistake, caused the loss of several pounds of expensive sugar. His mother had sent him to his grandmother with a sugar cone, saying something to the effect that unlike herself, grandmother had time to spare for cutting it up. The boy came back empty-handed; "I made *ta'rof*," he said. "She kept it." It was clear to him as to everybody else that it would have been utterly humiliating, a loss of face and *abru*, the very worst opposite of politeness and good manners, to reclaim the sugar. The little boy learned by his own mistake about the politics of politeness.

A girl of thirteen, who liked to visit one of her uncles' house and to make herself useful to his somewhat overbearing wife, was ordered by her mother not to go there any more after a falling-out between the elders of the two families. "Don't go there, don't make any more *ta'rof* there! You are not their servant, you are taking away our honor!"

Although nobody in Deh Koh claims that good form, *ta'rof*, necessarily makes a good person, or denies that it may mask a bad character, most anybody will agree that good form goes a long way toward making social contacts smooth, to avoid ruffled feathers, to keep the peace. *Ta'rof* subsumes the formulas for expressing politeness, for offering generosity and good will, for professing humility and esteem, for honoring status differences. Even if it is not sincere—and *ta'rof* implies a dose of flattering and conceit—it is considered indispensible for staying clear of overt hostilities in everyday encounters. People say that aggression and ill-temper among members of a household, between close relatives, within the family, often go hand-in-hand with the lack of *ta'rof* among intimates.

"Why do you always scream if you want something from my brothers?" a seventeen-year-old girl questioned her mother's manners. "If you would make a polite request [*khahesh*], if you would use a nice (soft) voice, if you made a little *ta'rof*, they would help you more."

Knowing that they do not measure up to the demands of the complicated patterns of politeness makes children feel insecure and inadequate easily. A boy of about nine loudly protested a requested errand that would have taken him to an important relative's house. "No, I won't go there! I don't know what to say, I don't know *ta'rof!*" he yelled. Yet, by observing countless habituated performances of etiquette, by their own and others' trials and errors, most children eventually learn how to behave politely when the need arises. Over the years, I have seen most of the aggressive boys turn into polite men; nagging, whiny toddlers turn into pleasant, properly shy fourteen-year-olds in the company of adults; loud, demanding youngsters who beat up on their siblings and yell at their mothers be quiet, observant, and unassuming guests in other peoples' houses; wild boys who terrorize their peers make willing, competent, and polite servants at a wedding; insolent, big-mouthed little girls grow up to be sweet-tongued, soft-spoken young women.

The total range of potential—if not unconditionally approved-of—behavior children learn includes the extremes of physical violence toward intimates of lower position in the age/sex hierarchies and of impeccable courtesy toward outsiders of equal or higher social standing. An eight-year-old boy, trading little odds and ends to other children in the street, who had just angrily wrangled an unpaid cookie out of a toddler's hand, offered his passing uncle the cookie with a flourish; crybaby Minoo never failed to give me a proper welcome, no matter how loudly she was wailing; a young man with a toilet-can on the way to his outhouse felt such an urge to be polite to my husband that he heartily invited him along; a brother and a sister engaged in a loud quarrel both instantly switched to flawless *ta'rof* when a woman relative turned into the alley to their house.

The ability to shift quickly between direct, informal, impulsive modes of relating and formal, restrained ones has an emotional price. The many variables involved in making appropriate choices at the spur of the moment seem to produce considerable stress in older children, especially in boys. Boys from an early age, and especially after circumcision, find themselves deferred to by women, given precedence over their sisters, and thus pushed into a higher position not only than their sisters but older women, too. At the same time they are cramped by demands of courtesy and respect toward adults and outsiders, by demands of responsibility toward those they outrank, by demands of obedience to other men, and by demands of competition among themselves. Boys often seem nervous, excessively fidgety, moving fingers, toes, arms almost involuntarily, scratching themselves constantly, touching the pants over their private parts, cracking their knuckles over and over again, startled at the slightest provocation, preoccupied with their appearance, self-conscious, suspicious, and ill at ease in company, even that of their own peers. Girls express uneasiness by picking incessantly at hair, clothes, pillows, lint on a rug, the scarf, if they do not withdraw altogether in their veil-wraps or else busy themselves erratically with somebody's baby, with chores, with whispering or giggling among themselves. However, they seem to be much more relaxed in the company of their peers than do their brothers in the company of theirs.

In both boys and girls, an abnormal (by local judgement) condition called *vasvasi*, fussiness, pedantic concerns, at best, and, at worst, what we would call compulsive behaviors focused on cleanliness and order, may develop at an early age.

A first-grader became so concerned with the preservation of the pristine condition of his pencils and books that he insisted on two schoolbags and two sets of all school stuff, one to be kept in school, the other at home. His parents were concerned about this but complied with his demands.

A girl developed a tic in her face when she was about eight, her elder sister says, a "bad habit" for which she was scolded and punished, but to no avail. A cousin of the girl blamed a lack of consideration at home, the "coldness" of her father and mother. "They punished and troubled her too much," she said.

A young woman with a compulsion for washing her hands claimed to have developed the habit when she was a child, "for no good reason," she said before speculating that, as the eldest girl in the family, she had to do the family wash at such an early age that maybe this led to her preoccupation with cleanliness.

A mother complained that her youngest son was driving her and his sisters to distraction with incessant demands for keeping his clothes spotless. "Ten times a day he changes his shirt and pants!" she said.

A first-grade teacher was worried about a boy in his class who seemed overly concerned with getting everything right. "If I say, 'Copy what is on the board,' he asks: 'On one page? Every other line? Write on the back of the page too? With a pencil? How fast?'" The teacher thought the boy was "becoming *vasvasi.*"

Such cases are seen as exceptions, though. Most youngsters seem to adapt to what we would see as conflicting demands of assertion and politeness without impairment of function, and life in the village is the better for their social skills. Despite the discontent, misgivings, serious disagreements, and resentments among relatives and neighbors that must be expected among people who live close together in a confined space such as Deh Koh, public life in the village is remarkably calm on the surface, and serious crime is very rare. For this, people credit good sense, good manners, and a strong sense of honor expressed in conduct befitting humans and Muslims.

Honor and Face

Honor, *abru,* is derived from the word "eyebrow," and thus is linked to "face," to one's skills in facing others with a straight face. This kind of honor is a quality everybody has, including children, people say. It can be increased and decreased by one's own deeds but also by the actions of those with whom one is associated. "You have taken away my honor!" is an accusation children hear who have conducted themselves reproachably in public. A girl who has much *abru* stays at home, casts her eyes down in public, never looks at a man, especially not a stranger and not in public, works hard in her father's house, does not talk back, is impeccably but not flashily dressed, walks with short, light steps, is not seen laughing, hardly ever smiling—she is "heavy" (*sangin*), in contrast to "light" (*saboq*). Loss of *abru* brings embarrassment and shame (*kejalat, sharm*). Embarrassment is a state that girls are admonished to be in so frequently, a feeling they express so readily, that a young man said about his sister that she should better be called "Ms. Embarrassment Shame" than by her real name.

A fifteen-year-old boy missed his ride to town because he could not find a plastic bag opaque enough to spare him the embarrassment of revealing the clothes he wanted to take along on the trip. Another boy of about that age, in an emergency, consented to take home bread from the bakery, but only with a "chic" bag in which to hide the bread—carrying home bread, a task of "little kids," was "too embarrassing" for him, he said.

The ever-present danger of losing honor is used as a means of domination especially by brothers over their siblings, and by sons over their mothers. "Don't laugh! You take away my honor!" an eight-year-old boy screamed at his thirteen-year-old sister on grounds that laughing is considered morally reprehensible, especially for women and girls. *Abru* is at stake when a girl over the age of around ten is walking in the streets alone—her own honor and thereby her family's and especially her brothers' honor. "If I see you again in the street without your coat, I'll beat you up with the biggest stick I can find! You have no *abru*, ha, and so you have to take mine too?!" a sixteen-year-old boy shouted at his eleven-year-old sister. "Wear a big black scarf, wear a big black scarf," a second-grader firmly demanded of his mother, "you take away our honor if your hair shows!" Likewise, an angry mother evoked her and her husband's honor when she tried to forbid her son, a high school student, to hang out with the son of a man who was on bad terms with the father: "You are taking away your father's honor if you are seen with this son-of-a-dog in the sweet shop laughing—buying him soda pop too, of all things, with your father's money!" When I asked a small group of children playing "Wedding" who was the bride, the girl so identified got very angry and hit the speaker furiously, crying, "Don't say this, don't, you are taking away my honor!" "Bride" carries the implication of embarrassment for a girl, especially a very young one.

The death of a ten-year-old boy in a village some ten miles away led to negotiations of honor: Behruz, a member of a very honor-conscious kin group in Deh Koh, had killed the boy with his car as the boy was walking with his mother along the busy road. The boy was the son of a very poor man from outside the tribal area. Behruz's people decided that they would offer the father of the boy a hundred thousand Toman (four hundred dollars, about the equivalent of three monthly teacher's salaries in 1994). This seemed commensurate to Behruz's standing in the community, to his family's honor. The poor man who lost his son, it was hoped, in turn would live up to his honor as a pauper and a stranger with little to recommend him, and "pardon" the accident and Behruz without pressing charges.

Although the danger of losing honor is seen as much greater than the likelihood of gaining honor, occasionally such an increase does happen, for example when somebody acknowledges a child's achievement in school or praises some other competence or politeness, or when a high school student is accepted in a prestigious field at the university, or a daughter gets a very advantageous proposal of marriage. Such occasions, however, carry the danger of undue pride, of gloating. *"Fitu,"* one who *"makes fis"* or who *"makes masmasi,"* is a derogatory epithet for showing off, or simply for presenting one's advantages with emphasis. An old neighbor woman explained it this way: a rooster who is very *shik* (chic), with a high comb and a long tail, and who crows a lot, who fights with every other rooster he can find, who runs after the hens—such a rooster is *fitu*, he is drunk *(mas)* with himself, and a nuisance for others.

Little Maryam, strutting into her grandmother's house without taking off her brand new shoes, was mocked: "Are you maybe showing off? Shame on you!" But grandmother smiled at Maryam, and also said, "Nice, beautiful, may they bring you good fortune, God willing," giving Maryam the whole ethical context of feeling good about new shoes, about bragging, about beauty, about God's hand in all, and about the impropriety of walking indoors with shoes. Accordingly, Maryam smiled, squirmed, tucked in her head, fidgeted, and put out her foot in front of her grandmother simultaneously.

Ahmed, seventeen, self-consciously sporting a small moustache, was commented on by his elder sister: "Look, how he shows off, without manners *[bitarbiat]*, cheeky *[porru]*, crazy *[kelu]*, rotten *[fased]*, ugly, ugly *[zesht]*!" This tirade gave him an alternative evaluation of his looks and behavior, even if it did not motivate him to change it. He laughed, but uneasily so.

Showing off belongs to "bad" behavior and easily brings the accusation of being full of pride *(taqabor)*, which is a sin, or at least of being *porru*, cheeky, impertinent, which is an aggravation for others.

Ri, face, is a metaphor for courage. Most children are *kamri*, they lack courage, guts, in dealing with people of authority. *Kamri* makes young children run away or giggle or hide or stutter when confronted with figures of authority, or refuse to accept a piece of chewing gum from me. Such shyness is accepted as fitting for an as yet ignorant, and by definition inferior, child, especially a girl; it is a sign of humbleness, a good indicator for proper manners later as the maturing child will learn propriety by example, counsel, and punishment. Children are taught to be shy indirectly. I have never heard a child being admonished to be shy except in the moral sense of shameful em-barrassment, *kejalat, sharm,* for a misdeed, but adults accompany a youngster's shyness behavior with signs of approval, and counter it with the vigorous demand not to be bashful, to speak up, to take the chewing gum, to drink the offered tea, to come in and sit down. The wider context of bashfulness is authority; children show proper hu-mility and deference to adults by being silent, passive, invisible even to a fault. They are rewarded for waiting for their elders' order to act, for playing coy, being hard to persuade, for resisting being elevated from the lowest position into the position of guest, of recipient of favors.

When a seven-year-old boy whose teacher had been visiting his house told me that he did not know what the teacher had said, his mother explained: "My son is a devil at home but very shy with others. He hid in the kitchen during his teacher's visit." Her tone was reproachful but her hand was stroking the little boy's head while she said it. He had behaved properly, if a little more on the shy side than had been necessary, her gesture said.

In the tale "The Seven Brothers," a little girl finds her lost brothers living alone, without a woman to keep house for them. "Shy," she hides from them, and works in the house secretly during their ab-sence, making them wonder about the situation. Her shyness routine is described at length in the tale. It is broken only when her youngest brother catches her one day while she is cooking. Although her brothers scold her for being so overly bashful, the prominence of her behavior in the tale leaves no doubt that she had behaved correctly as far as the storyteller and the audience are concerned.

"*Lim ni bellam teish,* I don't have the courage to go to her," said a three-year-old girl when her mother tried to persuade her to sit next to the girl's aunt across the room at a wedding party. Too young to pronounce the *r*-sound correctly, she nevertheless handled the con-cept of "face" with sophistication. "What, are you maybe *kamri?*" her mother asked her. "No." she answered. "Only the many people here took away my courage."

Especially for girls of all ages, *kamri basi porru,* shyness is better than audacity, people say. Girls are forever admonished to stay within a field of behavior that is marked by shyness, silence, embarrassment, hiding (behind the veil-wrap, in her father's house, in a room away from visitors) in the presence of anybody not very familiar.

Once I came upon three sisters between eight and fourteen years of age crammed behind a half-open door to a room where their eldest sister's proposal of marriage was being discussed. The sister whose future was at stake had "fled" altogether, out of embarrassment, they whispered. I found her in the back of the house under the open window of the room with the visitors, listening intently. All four girls were properly *kamri* by hiding from the important visitors, the mother later said; a marriage conference was no place for girls. Primed already for shyness, the younger sisters learned from their elder sister's example how to turn up the shyness behavior a notch vis-à-vis a suitor, without necessarily missing out on information.

At another occasion, entering a house by a back door I chanced upon a brother and sister in their early teens, glued to a window under which, outside, two aunts were discussing some scandalous happenings in the family. Later, their mother scolded them: "Be ashamed!" she said. "Why?" said the girl. "The aunts did not see us!" This attitude was not quite proper morally—mother and daughter giggled about the answer uneasily—but it showed that the children were no simpletons (*sadelu, setul*), which the mother thought was good.

Easily, an excess of shyness and propriety can result in simple-mindedness, in a paucity of the kind of wit and skills that one needs to survive or at least to make life easier. God-pleasing as humility and simplicity may be, no parent wants a child to be the butt of others' jokes or to be called simple, or poor (*faqir*), or dumb-mute (*zounbaste*), or an ass (*khar*) by others.

The exact opposite of shyness, of having little courage, is having so much as to be cheeky (*porru*), insolent. It means to speak out, to demand, to disobey, to disregard higher authority, to overstep one's place. A toddler picking father's pocket or wasting candy is called "cheeky," as are a girl who tells her scolding mother to mind her own business, a boy showing off his new clothes, or a girl haggling over a price with a shopkeeper. On principle, insolence is disapproved of, it is "bad." It shows lack of manners. Yet, the success of insolence often vindicates the offense it gives: money in the fist, a mouth full of candy, getting mother off one's back, furtive admiring glances at the new pants, a good price for the book, make cheekiness worth the criticism. Just like adults, children who are cheeky get ahead of others in life, people say. To please people and to please God is not always to one's immediate advantage. The best of two worlds is had by those who learn to be audacious in effect and humble in appearance.

By the age of three or four, children have incorporated this knowledge into their choices of behaviors: they are alternately shy and cheeky as they see fit. A few years later, what we call dissimulation has become a permanent part of the children's structure of morality, and their modes of behavior are habituated.

Sins and Merits

Although people say that bad behavior of children under the age of reason (about nine for girls, twelve for boys) most likely is not sinful—there is not unanimous consent on this in Deh Koh—children learn early on about sin (*gona*) and its place in theology and in everyday life.

In a folktale a little girl is persuaded by a woman's empty promise of a doll to kill her own mother. Subsequently, and quite expectedly, the girl comes to grief because she no longer has a mother to take care of her. The woman who deceived her, however, comes to grief as punishment for the grave sin of having caused the girl's mother's death. Children who hear the tale learn that morally the death had been the woman's fault; the girl had had no powers of reason yet and therefore was *bigona*, without sin.

Theoretically, children hear, any disobedience of God is a sin that will be punished either in this world or in the next. Practically, sin is mainly evoked by adults in the context of harming others. Children are told that it is a sin to throw rocks at animals for no good reason (there are good reasons such as control or fear); to trouble others (*asiat kardan*); to make a young child cry by taking something from it or by playing very roughly; to fail to console a crying baby or toddler; to mock handicapped people. "However much I said, 'Don't, it is a sin,' the boys did not listen and made fun of Ahmed the Cripple," complained a four-year-old girl about bad boys in the street. It is a sin to hurt people, especially those much younger, much lower, or much superior in status than oneself. A father who beats up a misbehaving child is doing his duty; a father who hurts his child badly by doing so commits a sin. An adolescent brother who hits his sister to keep her from embarrassing him is doing his duty; if he hits his toddler-sibling for no good reason, he commits a sin.

Several years ago, the mother of a thirteen-year-old boy tried to kill herself after her son had thrown rocks at her when she accused him of having stolen money from her, and cursed and insulted (*fosh dad*) his father ("I'll choke you with my penis in your throat!"). The son's behavior had been so outrageously wrong and disrespectful, and the mother had felt so humiliated and so powerless to stop him from troubling everybody, that she saw suicide as the only way out of the problem for herself. "I didn't have another way out," she said. "Maybe what I did was a sin, but what my son did was a very big sin for sure."

When a fourteen-year-old boy proudly announced to his playmates that he had beaten up another boy in revenge, his mother, who overheard him, called him names for being without manners (*bitarbiat*), naughty (*fuzul*); but when the same boy hit his three-year-old sister after she had broken his ruler, the mother said, "Don't, it is sinful."

Children are not expected to be motivated to do good or to be deterred from doing harm by the "sin" label. It is expected, however, that by the repeated labeling of their and others' actions as correct or as sinful, they learn what is right and wrong, so that, once their reason has developed enough for them to make mature decisions, they will be able to judge wisely and to act responsibly. An eight-year-old boy who misbehaves and disobeys is only "naughty" (*fuzul*); a fifteen-year-old acting this way would be called *vellou*, a moral lightweight; at twenty years of age, he would be called rotten, dirty, and crazy, and be the despair of the dishonored family.

When I objected to a thirteen-year old boy's relentless shooting and stoning of chickens, his mother readily agreed that he was doing wrong. "You tell him it is a sin," she said to me. "Maybe he doesn't know that; he doesn't listen to me."

The opposite of sin is religious merit, *savab*, but this concept is much less popular among children, or with adults who address children, than is "sin"; the small meritorious services children can render fall within the frame of reasonable requests from adults, which children have to honor anyway. There is no religious merit in everyday obedience.

A neighbor woman frequently ordered her young granddaughters to take care of a crying little grandniece, either adding, "It has religious merit," which implied that the service the girls rendered was beyond their ordinary duties, or else, "It is sinful to let the child cry," which implied a duty shirked. Sometimes the old woman said both in one breath. Although it was not clear whether grandmother was talking about her own sins and religious merits or those of her granddaughters, who actually consoled the youngster, the girls could not but learn from grandmother's talk that caring and not caring for somebody else's unhappy young child fall into the frame of sins versus religious merits.

Threats of God's purported punishment of sins—misfortunes in this world, dreadful sufferings in the next—leave children cold. They hear an irate mother or sibling curse them, "May God punish you," but this is taken as an empty threat. The long list of usual sins of adults, sins against people, like theft and gossip, and sins against God, such as not paying religious taxes, not fasting, or not praying, hardly apply to children. Young children harm an animal or lie or steal something out of ignorance, not sinful malice. Rather, parents commit a sin if they fail to teach their children right and wrong or how to pray or if they fail to provide a good example by fasting or by giving alms. Lately, the task of religious education has been largely taken out of parents' hands, people say, with the strong emphasis on religious studies in schools. But most children keep what they learn in school about religion separate from the moral principles that inform their lives. School-knowledge is straightforward and complex, to be known verbatim when tested. The good and the right, as defined at home and in the street, are simple yet ambiguous. Here, the emphasis is on conduct; the gravest sins are said to be sins against people: stealing, speaking ill of others, lying, neglecting one's duties, miserliness, disrespect. Sins against God, they learn, such as neglecting prayer and the fast, He will pardon in his generosity as long as one has not sinned against people.

An old man had this story to tell: A man set out on the obligatory pilgrimage to Mecca, an expensive and time-consuming enterprise. After a few hours on the road with his fellow travelers, he met a beggar-child. He was so overcome with pity that he gave the child all his travel money and returned home. After a few weeks, the other men in his party came back from Mecca and acted as if he had been with them; they said that they had eaten and slept together, they had made the circumambulations, and had performed all the other required rituals in Mecca together. It became clear that before God the man's act of kindness to a child had been equivalent to the pilgrimage.

Rituals children observe at home mostly revolve around protection, often of themselves: amulets, beads, fumigations against diseases and other, unspecified, dangers; blood-sacrifices of a rooster, a lamb, to ward off dangers or to fulfill a pledge to a saint; pilgrimages to shrines of efficacious descendants of the Prophet all fall into a cognitive frame of dangers women know how to ward off by enlisting or manipulating some extra-human power that is much closer than is God.

To children, God comes across as a powerful, good, and just khan or shah, but so remote as to incite little curiosity, except about his omniscience and omnipresence.

"God made every person?" four-year-old Nastaran asked her mother, just to make sure. "Yes," mother said, "everybody: you and me and grandmother and Khanom, and father and everybody."

"He also made the people who are dead? And each baby?"

"Yes."

Nastaran paused. "God is a very busy man," she concluded.

An extremely quick and bright three-year-old boy once had a similar problem. "God really sees everything?" he inquired of his mother. "Yes," she said.

"Everything you do and I do and my sister does, and—"

"Yes," said his mother.

"Then he sees me also in the outhouse?" Mother suppressed laughter. "Yes," she said.

"So God is sitting on the roof of the outhouse watching me poop? Why would he want to do that?"

Although not well described and not much talked about, God and the saints, certain descendants of the Prophet Muhammad, are evoked frequently by adults and by children as they imitate their elders. "By God!" gives emphasis to even small assertions; "With Ali!" accompanies exertions, even minimal ones like getting up; "[Day of] Judgement!" expresses feeling overwhelmed by bad news or a hardship. "God willing," "Praise be to God," "Go with God," are routine speech patterns children hear many times a day. "Oh Saint Fateme!" is a standard supplication. "Who was Saint Fateme?" I once asked a six-year-old girl who had just evoked her. "A very good woman," she said, and promptly was ridiculed by her elder brother for being ignorant and a heathen.

Hell and paradise are not talked about much either. The impact of the promised sufferings and pleasures is subverted in De' standard afterthought to discussions about the afterlife: "v̇v̇ nobody as yet has come back to tell us about it," people say an̆ children hear. Death, or better, the dead, concern children more. Dead people are buried with great commotion in the graveyard, and women visit the graveyard every Thursday evening to cry and wail there, but dead people also are said to be in heaven. "I don't see no heaven," said a four-year-old boy, gazing around him. "I only see the sky." His mother got him to accept, with reservations on his side, that paradise must be behind the stars and the clouds, somewhere far away. A dark, tight grave, and worms eating a stinking, squishy body, however, touched him. "It frightens me (*zahlama ibere*)!" he said, hitting his mother's arm to make her stop describing her own such fears after a funeral. "I'll go to heaven because I am good, and my brother will be buried in the graveyard because he is bad," was a five-year-old girl's understanding of death, worms, and paradise.

When a bulldozer unearthed skulls and bones in the old graveyard, two siblings asked their seventeen-year-old brother, who was working at the site, what happened to the scrambled dead people at the Day of Judgement—what if a head was missing, or a leg? "God will give them a new one," said the brother, but the young ones were as little convinced as was he.

Whispered stories of strange happenings involving djenn and dead people emerging from their graves make the cemetery a place of some interest, but do not seem to cause much anxiety in children. I asked a preschool girl who fervently wished she could read like her elder brother, what she thought the light that customarily is put on a new grave might mean. "The dead person wants to read at night," she said.

Feelings

There is no special word for feeling used in Deh Koh, no way to inquire after one's emotions. "How are you [*ceturi*]?" or "How is your health [*ahvalet*]?" will bring a noncommittal, formulaic answer from a child. A more pointed question, such as, "Are you well [*khubi-i*]?" might be answered with "Yes," for example, or with "No, I am very hot," or, "No, my brother gave me trouble." Most feelings that children express spontaneously in the course of a day relate to the body: I am hungry, tired, sleepy, hot, cold; it hurts; it itches. The vocabulary for emotions is small, consisting of words with broad fans of meaning: "I am well, happy, at ease [*khoshhal, rahat*], or troubled, unhappy, sad [*narahat, badbakht*]; I like [*khoshom ia*]; I want, I long to have or do [*dellom ikha*]; I am scared [*sahlom ra*]; I am enraged [*deq va dellom ra*]; I am bashful [*rim ni*]." For describing somebody else's state of mind, adults and children use a few additional, more specific, terms. These words roughly refer to what we call angry (which is linked to a weakness of nerves), anxious, stubborn, angry withdrawal, sudden outburst of violent rage, depression, showing off, shyness, passion, haughtiness, and pride. A few more are described indirectly. All are inferred from how children behave.

"Leila is happy [*khoshhal*, in pleasant disposition, good health] today," Leila's six-year-old brother said when I inquired after his little sister. "She sings all the time and doesn't cry at all."

A three-year-old could tell that her mother liked the new baby because mother called the baby "*Jun*, my soul, my life," because she kissed the baby, and because she gave it her breast. The mother in turn could tell that the three-year-old liked the baby by her kisses, by "not giving the baby any trouble [*asiat*]," and by rocking the cradle willingly.

Women in our neighborhood diagnosed "severe fright" in a girl of about fourteen by circumstances and her behavior: when she was about eight, the girl had found her mother dead, hanging by a rope in the barn, and since then was extremely quiet, did not play, did not go to school, and did not develop physically.

After the electricity went out on a dark, rainy day, a five-year-old girl was walking up and down the verandah, cheerfully singing, over and over again, "Other than killing myself, I don't know what to do." Her elder brother and the mother interpreted it as boredom: "Time is very long for her today."

A young boy who had lost a fight when his playmate fled home cried, slapped his head with both hands, stomped his feet, and shouted obscenities. "He is mad because he wasn't quick enough for his enemy," his elder brother explained what I would have called frustration.

Already toddlers command a patterned vocabulary of facial expressions, gestures, and utterances that can be read by those around them easily as to feelings. Only in a few cases did I disagree with interpretations. For example, what I saw as expressions of discontent and of restlessness due to fatigue in very young children tended to be labeled summarily as naughtiness or as sickness. One group of habits, however, I cannot read at all without recourse to loaded terms pertaining to psychology and thus lying outside the frame of reference I have set myself in this book: the readiness to hurt oneself out of frustration or anger, to turn aggression toward oneself, especially in women. Worked-up children may bang their heads on the floor, slap their heads with both hands, or pinch their arms or legs. To underscore a point of deep discontent, a young woman burned her arm with a hot iron spit, in front of several children; drinking agricultural poisons now is the preferred mode of suicide attempts for women. "I'll kill myself!" girls shout when they are vexed or angered. By the age of four or five girls will have been pinched often, playfully as well as for punishment, with pain and anger reactions I would see as appropriate. They will have seen women pinch themselves demonstratively to underscore an empassioned claim to having been wronged by somebody. But girls sometimes pinch each other in the arm or on the hand seemingly for no reason and without a pain reaction at all; one of two young sisters, who for quite a while were crowded into each other and their mother in one hot place on the rug at a party, pinched the other's arm, hard and long. The pinched girl did not flinch. When she had her arm to herself again, she looked at the welt at length, expressionless still, and then ignored it. Girls might even demand to be pinched: "I'll do your errand only if you pinch me," said a ten-year-old girl to her mother, extending her arm to her. The mother ignored her and repeated the request. The girl slapped her mother's arm slightly and hopped away. "No, I won't do it," she cried. "You didn't pinch me."

Purported feelings of contentedness and well-being in a child are not detailed but simply referred to as "s/he is well, *khub*, is of good health, *khoshhal*," or put into a moral context: "You are reasonable, good-natured today." Children who like each other may say, "I get pleasure" (*khoshom ia*) from being with the other; playmates are *hombazi*, those who play together, or *rafiq*, mates; they are an good terms with each other. The Farsi concept of *dust*, friendship based on liking, is not used in Dch Koh; "friend" in our modern sense, which implies keeping company and exchanging support and loyalty based on liking instead of on kin relations, is an alien concept.

The older children get, the more they are expected to control their emotions. Thus, I did not find out what three sisters between eleven and fifteen years of age thought or felt while their father was complaining to me that their forty-year-old mother, who was sitting with us making bitter remarks, objected to his intention to take a second wife although she was "old." All three girls kept their heads down and picked at lint on the rug. Later, after the father had gone, one of them quietly said, "He is crazy."

Children are said to laugh and cry easily; content and discontent, "sunshine and rain," are close together. This is taken as a sign that reason, which in adults controls emotions, is weak. In girls, reason is not expected to become as strong as in boys, ever; women are more emotional—or less rational—than men. It is good so, some pious people say and all children learn in school, because a mother's weak resolve and uncontrolled empathy, her "warm heart" will benefit her children. It is, however, also a mark of inferiority, easily ridiculed. "Crybaby, crybaby [girvaru]," a six-year-old boy mocked his mother, who was crying while she busied herself at the water basin in the courtyard. He even threw a little pebble at her, playfully, to underscore his contempt. A boy of about seventeen explained, after a fight at home that he said his mother had lost, that his mother was at home "crying like a child," that "all girls and women cry easily, for nothing. They are weak."

Crying as such is considered "good" because it cleanses the soul. "When my parents fight at home we children always cry," said a twelve-year-old girl. "Otherwise we would die of fright." Sadness has no negative moral connotation. Crying over somebody else's pain or loss even has merits. Laughter, however, although it "comes by itself" and cannot be helped, is said to open the person up to the influence of the devil. Laughing is taken as a sign of moral lightness, especially in a girl or woman. It is categorized as eib, a shortcoming one ought to be ashamed of. "They laughed together," is a metaphor for indecent behavior between a man and a woman. Yet women very readily link laughter with feeling good, with the opposite of hardship, sadness, and anxiety, and with happy memories of childhood. Children say that laughter is "good," or "good in the belly." People even say that parents ought to laugh with their children, that without fun (shukhi) and laughter a child will not grow well. A party without at least some laughter, however restrained, is "dull." Wit is highly valued as a social asset in Deh Koh. Thus, Islamicist interpretations of laughter as potentially evil and traditional local morality support each other, yet oppose individual experience. This creates one of the paradoxes of life for adults and children in Deh Koh: laughter is good and necessary but bad too. The paradox of laughter provides the basis for harsh judgment of others' behavior, as well as for the challenge to others' harsh judgment of one's own.

Commands to stop laughing, like other commands to stop extroverted, emotionally ostentatious behavior, are located in the context of the assertion of power between siblings, between children and adults, between older and younger children, and between males and females. The lower a person's rank, the more likely such a command will be received. Girls, therefore, hear it the most frequently. When a group of four girls around the age of ten distracted their aunt, who was talking to me and another woman, she produced this string of commands: "Don't make a ruckus, girls, run, run, go away, go play, don't make such noise, shut up, don't laugh, DON'T!, let go of the teapot, leave me alone, don't laugh, get lost, be quiet." The girls were not much bothered by this, but even if such commands are heeded rarely, they put laughing in a judgmental context in which the urge to laugh at an unguarded, inappropriate occasion, especially in the company of other children, becomes another potential source of embarrassment. Nevertheless, despite moral reservations and the politics of laughter, with the exception of the severely sick, depressed, or zealously pious, all people, and certainly older children, find a lot around them funny.

If laughter is morally somewhat suspect on principle, laughing and crying easily, for "no good reason," in older children and adults, especially males, shows emotional and mental instability, crazyness (*kelu*).

A sixteen-year-old girl usually called her fifteen-year-old brother, who grinned and laughed often when etiquette would have required him to be earnest and composed, "Crazy-Ali." To me, his grinning and chuckling, together with his body language, revealed embarrassment and tension. To her, it revealed a disordered mind, the result of too much indulgence by his parents.

Commenting on photographs I took of children, people called laughing children "ugly" (*zesht*), especially if the mouth was open, and selected as "beautiful" (*malus*) serious, bland faces with averted eyes. One of the most popular posters in Iran features a pretty child

of undetermined sex with a very sad face and a big, shiny tear rolling
down the cheek. It is considered "very beautiful."

20 · Tantrum

Twelve-year-old Goli and her mother are squatting behind their
breadboards, rolling fist-sized balls of wheat flour dough into thin,
round flatbreads with long, perfectly straight, smooth wooden roller-
sticks. Fateme, eight, is stoking the fire under the iron griddle on
which the breads are baked, and turning the flatbreads on the griddle
with a flat iron spit. They are working on their breezy porch and I am
watching them. Tak-tak, tak-tak—the rhythmic sound of wooden
stick on wooden board carries through the neighborhood. Daud, at
six the youngest in the family, was lured home by it. He sits on the
floor between the bakers, behind the dozen rows of dough balls on
the bread-rug between the bakers, and watches the dough being
stretched on the board by the steady, controlled movements of the
rollers under his mother's and sister's hands. For a few minutes he
takes it all in, the smell of flour, hot dough, smoke, until the temptation to grab a ball is too great. Dough firmly in a grimy fist, he dives
behind Goli, who ignores him. His mother cries, "Don't do this, boy!"
and threatens him with the long roller-stick. He ignores her. Between
his hands and on the floor, half on Goli's skirt, half on the packed
dirt, he tries to squeeze and stretch the dough into a thick, little,
round flatbread. It rips, he tries again, and again. The dough now is
black with dirt, a hard lump. "Look at him, the dirty hands! Filthy
thief," his mother says. He drops the useless dough and grabs another ball, quick as lightning. Mother is on her feet in an instant.
Stepping over Goli she swings her stick. "Go away, get lost," she
shouts. He screams, jumps back a few steps, grabs the next best thing,
a shoe, and throws it at her with great force. It lands on Fateme's
head. Fateme lets go of the spit with which she had been poking
embers and turning breads, leans into Goli, starts to whine, but looks
at me and loses the courage to let herself go in front of a visitor.
Mother pushes the screaming Daud against the wall, stick held high,

an arrested gesture of empty threat, cursing him: "May a djenn hit you, black death, ill-mannered son-of-a-dog, I'll kill you . . .!" Fateme sees her chance, gets up, takes the roller out of her mother's raised hand, sits down at mother's board and starts to roll out a bread. Daud meanwhile, yelling louder yet, has thrown himself on the floor, his back against the wall, and is hitting his mother in full fury with a log of firewood, without letting go of the dough in the other hand. The log gets tangled in the soft fabric of her wide, long skirt. "Leave him alone, he is just a boy," Maryam shouts from her verandah across the courtyard. Daud's mother backs off, cursing still, but running out of steam. He is lying face down on the floor, pounding the dirt with the log, scratching up dirt and throwing it on his head, howling. Fingers spread against him in a gesture of contemptuous dismissal, she returns to her board—Fateme's bread is not round and smooth but five-cornered and bumpy—and nudges Fateme over. "Be quiet," Goli yells at her brother, slightly hitting him on the back with her roller. He turns around, eyes half closed to slits, teeth bared, rolls behind her, kicks his feet hard against her back in a barrage of blows. "Pussy, pussy," he hisses, drumming on her. "Boy, leave me alone," she cries. His mother laughs. "Devil, devil," she says, shaking her head and smiling. His fury dies with this exercise, though. He sits up. Leaning against Goli, now he squeezes and pats his dough into another small bread, puts it on the rim of the griddle, but it burns. Disgusted, he throws it on the breadrug and takes another look at the dozen or so remaining dough balls, but Fateme lifts her hot iron spit and Goli pokes her roller into his ribs. "Leave them alone, hear me? I'll beat you up; Take a baked bread and get lost, clear out!" they say. He sharply kicks Fateme's back and runs downstairs, two wide steps at a time.

21 · Play

Terms and Cognitive Context

Play (*bazi*) in Deh Koh is contrasted with work (*kar*), including school, and with resting, taking it easy (*esterahat kardan; neshastan*, to sit). Play is placed outside the range of normal, responsible, adult activities of working and resting. It implies idleness, which, in turn, for adults and adolescents easily implies laziness. Play fits children rather than adults, except in its metaphorical meaning of flirting, love-play, sex. A groom and bride may "play" in the bridal chamber; men are promised never-ending "play" with the paradisical virgins in heaven. Obscene nuisance phone calls by older children, illicit note-passing between boys and girls in school, boys and young men harrassing girls in the streets (which is much more a problem in the cities than it is in Deh Koh) are called passion-play (*eshq bazi*). "*Eshq-bazi-e bacce!* Children's passion play, childish prank!" a woman said dismissively when her sister told her of an annoyance call early in the morning— "Forgive me for having peeled you from your husband's arms," a high-pitched voice had said before the line went dead.

Ordinary men and women in Deh Koh say they have no time to play; they are busy with making a living. The traditional women's round-dance is called "play" (*varbazi*), as is the men's stick dance (*tarkebazi*), a rhythmic display of skillful aggression and dodging; both are confined to the extraordinary time of wedding parties. Chess (*shatranj*), backgammon (*takhtebazi*), fancy horseback riding (*asb bazi*) were "play" mostly of men of the chiefs' families in Deh Koh in the past. Outlawed in the early years of the Islamic Republic together with dancing, chess and backgammon are not popular in Deh Koh now that board games are allowed again, either. The only playful activity women remember having engaged in casually in the past was swinging on a rope swing (*hilu khardan*), but this was not called play. Men sometimes played organized games that now are known as boys' games. Rifle shots in the air or at leaves in a tree at weddings are, mockingly, referred to as "play" of young men who want to show off. *Futbal bazi* (soccer), volleyball, and martial arts are recent boys' pastimes, not men's; are labeled exercise and sport, which places them in an urban, "modern" lifestyle; and likely interfere with parental demands for a son's help with chores. "Instead of helping his father irrigate the vineyard, he is out playing soccer! At his age!" said the mother of a seventeen-year-old boy.

Traditional musical instruments were used by hereditary musicians only, and new instruments like electronic keyboards and the recorder are only now making their debut among young men in Deh Koh. The verb "to play" is not used for making music, though.

For children, play is analogous to adults' work. Just as adults are legitimately busy with work, children are legitimately busy with play. Refusing his mother's request for help, a four-year-old boy said, "I can't do it, I have work to do, I have to go play." Much of little girls' traditional play is imitation of their mothers' work: making mud-bread, collecting grass, making fire, washing, spinning on a stick-spindle, babysitting. In these activities the shift from play to work is gradual. Boys' play activities do not as obviously hone male adult work skills.

"Play" implies a use of time and energy only young children can indulge in freely—boys more and longer than girls. It is said that as a child's reason develops, the urge to play will diminish. This change is supposed to happen sooner in girls than in boys, and this expectation informs socialization. "Instead of playing with little kids—which you should be ashamed of anyway—you ought to stay home, study, wash, help me around the house. You are old enough to work!" a mother told her eleven-year-old daughter who had come home with a ripped skirt from climbing trees with her much younger cousins. Her twelve-year-old brother, however, still was sent away frequently to "play." Using play as indicator of maturity, boys stay in the child stage longer than girls. For both boys and girls, staying in the play-mode longer than expected by this theory brings disapproval and is a source of shame.

Players

From late toddler age onward, children increasingly are encouraged to play with same-sex, similiar-age playmates. Some people claim that in the past sex segregation for children was stricter even than it is today, although others say the opposite. I cannot decide whose history is correct. However, given the wide affective and conceptual differences in boys' and girls' games, traditional as well as contemporary ones, large mixed playgroups must have had a hard time agreeing on what to play. Within the household and among close relatives and neighbors, little boys and girls may play together without reprimand. Usually, however, such mixed groups consist of one or two little boys and their sisters and female cousins; rarely will one little girl play in a group of boys: girls "don't like it," boys "don't want them," and adults disapprove of it.

Nastaran, age three, was brought home from somewhere by her

brother, five, much later than seemed reasonable to mother. Said Nas-taran: "There was a bulldozer on the road, and Amin stopped to watch it with a lot of other boys. However often I said, 'We have to go, let's go,' he did not listen to me." All her mother, aunt, and elder sister responded to was that Nastaran had stood in the road with a bunch of boys. "Weren't you embarrassed [*sharmonde*]?" asked her mother. Everybody giggled, including Nastaran; everybody hugged, touched, petted her. "Yes," she said. Had she not already known that a girl's place is not among boys in the street and that embarrassment is the proper feeling in such a situation, she would have learned it right then and there, and in the nicest possible way.

The lone boy in a group of girls very likely will try to exert leadership, even if he is not the oldest—usually with success. Indeed, the opportunity to be a leader may be a strong incentive to play with girls for a boy too young, shy, or weak to have much to say in his boy–peer group. Often when Behruz, five, was tired or hurt playing with his boy mates he would search for his younger sister and three girl cousins (who were four, six, and eight years old) to get them to play games like "Snake" with him: holding on to each others' shoulders, they formed a line, with him in the lead, always. He ran as fast as he could and in as winding a pattern as space and speed allowed, pulling the girls along to trip them up or break the chain. All the while he was yelling "like mad," said an elder sister, while the girls were quiet or giggling. He never got tired of this game.

When more boys gather around such a group, the boys inevitably will break off from the girl group and do their own thing.

If girls get tired of the boy playmate's bossiness, they fade away or become quietly disruptive, or they send him away, with a lie if need be. Expulsion from a girl group often brings tears and aggression. At one such occasion, when Mina had said, "Go home, put your mother's butt into a sack, then come back," and skipped with her sisters, her four-year-old boy cousin went home crying and consoled himself with painting his toenails red with his big sister's nail polish, which she never used, and with putting a string of plastic beads around his neck. "You look like a girl," his mother teased him. "I am better than a girl!" he screamed. At another exclusion, a four-year-old boy yelled from afar, "Mother, bring me a stick, quick, quick, I must beat up the girls!"

After Kemal had started school, his mother said that he became so

bossy with his next-younger sister, who had been his favorite playmate, that his sister no longer wanted him around. His interaction
with her became an exercise in dominance: he ordered her around,
cursed her—"Sit over here, I said, you deaf ass!"—took things from
her, yelled at her. Over the two months I observed them he played
with her less and less and stayed out with the boys longer and longer.

Occasionally a group of girls wants a boy to join them for a particular purpose: Zeynab, eight, took her five-year-old boy cousin with
her and her girlfriends to the big willow trees above the village to
have a "man" to play the role of bridegroom in "Playing Wedding."
Mostly he had to sit on a rock while the four girls were dancing and
singing wedding songs. But when an argument broke out between
Zeynab and his sister, Zeynab, the leader of this group as of any other
she is part of, sent both away with strong language: "Who needs such
an ugly bridegroom anyway!" she said, among other things.

Adults do not play much with the very young and only rarely play
with older children. "Go play" (*borro bazi kon*) is an order and encouragement to go elsewhere, to leave an adult alone. Boys are sent away
to play more often than girls, who are more likely to be admonished
to "sit down" or to "do some work" if they seem idle or get on an
adult's nerves. Girls after the age of about seven face a conflict: if they
stay close to home, as they are encouraged to do, they find themselves burdened with chores that curtail playtime; to escape demands,
they had better leave, join playmates in a garden or in another courtyard, but this becomes less and less proper the older they become.

Adults talk fondly about how they played as children: "We had
nothing to eat, nothing to put on our naked bodies, nothing by day
and nothing by night, no toys either, but did we ever play!" remembers Mamalus about being a little girl in Deh Koh in the 1930s. "Play"
to her and most adults I talked to quintessentially marked childhood,
the child stage, and put it beyond rich and poor or any other quali-
fiers of life.

Eight- to twelve-year old girls like to play with young children,
especially little girls, people say. Learning how to take care of babies
and play merge easily: Lale, not quite two, played the baby for her
two cousins, who were seven and nine, at her grandmother's house.
She cried and whimpered with hunger and rubbed her eyes as instructed; coached by the older girls she knew by then how babyhood
ought to be expressed. The girls in turn let her drink milk at the

breast, rocked her to sleep, pretend-fed her dirt-pilaf cooked in a broken plastic bowl, braided her hair into tiny braids, until Lale was tired of it and left, saying, "Go look for something else to play with." "Go play with your dolls!" scolded a mother when her one-year-old daughter loudly protested the incessant hugs and tugs and commands and teases with which the neighbor's three girls entertained her, or better, entertained themselves. Rivalry between two girls may be expressed in terms of whom a baby "likes more to play with." Parvin, nine, was carrying her little cousin around the courtyard, cooing to her, after she had a falling-out with the baby's elder sister. "Look," she told me, "the baby wants to play only with me, and not with her sister!" Knowing how to keep a baby quiet and satisfied is a sign of competence, of a "good" woman, Parvin knew.

Children, especially girls, often play by themselves, even when they are with others. Each may have a separate activity, loosely connected to the others', such as a different "fireplace" for "cooking," a different "house," a different "field." Mina and her two sisters were cooking on three separate fireplaces for about ten minutes without saying anything, seemingly oblivious to each other, but within the framework of playing "Wedding Party": they were cooks for many guests. Meanwhile, a few feet away, two-and-one-half-year-old Susan was putting little rocks into a circle of around two feet diameter. When I asked what the circle was going to be, she said, "Nothing." But when it was finished she wanted the others to look at it anyway, clearly proud of her solitary achievement.

Lale's father remembers how he and his playmates used to build "mills" of sticks along the irrigation channels. Each boy built his own. With their voices they imitated the whirring and swishing sounds of rushing water that drove the waterwheels in the old wheat mills, and then argued about whose mill was the loudest.

Four little girls and a little boy crowded a small space at a pile of sand near a new house under construction, squatting next to each other. Each formed little mounds of sand, calling them "House, Man, Woman, . . ." seemingly talking to him- or herself; no one needed the others for the task at hand, no one seemed to pay attention to what the others were doing or saying, but obviously it was important that they all did it together.

A new toy, an interesting thing, an activity of special appeal, however, will prompt children to try their hands at it simultaneously, jostling each other for a better grip, competing for the decision as to what to do and how to do it. This interaction makes for hasty, jerky movements that likely will damage the object, is frustrating for most players, and often ends to nobody's satisfaction. It does, however, establish leaders and rewards speedy, aggressive action.

Even young children have, by our understanding, extraordinary capacities to sit still and do absolutely nothing for long periods of time at certain occasions, such as being guests in somebody else's house. They will sit on their mother's lap or arm and just watch people or stare unfocused into space, slowly falling asleep amidst any amount of noise and hubbub. Such behavior is valued as "polite, understanding, proper." Especially girls will sit still, feet tucked under, not saying a word, in a circle of adults. They get admonished to "sit properly" as soon as they can sit, and watch their elder sisters sit this way. At a dinner party, five sisters between the ages of three and fourteen, lined up next to each other along a wall, with identical veil-wraps that covered all but half their faces and a hand, sat still for two full hours. The four older ones hardly moved and did not speak either, except to the little one, who was a little restless. Their only brother, meanwhile, was sitting with his father, fidgeting and moving a good deal more.

During the long wait for the groom at her elder sister's wedding, two-and-one-half-year-old Effat was lounging, leaning, lying, sitting on her sister's lap, while both gave an appropriate performance of sadly departing sisters although in this case the sister-bride was moving only a few houses away. For almost five hours the little girl stayed glued to her sister's lap until she finally fell asleep and was carried away by her mother.

It is hard to learn what these children, unsmiling, unfocused, quiet as they choose to be at those occasions, feel and think. In the two examples above, the girls behaved as if they were on stage, performing particular roles expected of them under the social circumstances. In a sense, they were playing. Effat, like others, had quite a repertoire of appropriate behaviors she could display by the age of three. But at many other occasions, the context of performance is absent. Sometimes I could guess that a child was playing a silent game. Nastaran, at three, played by herself "all the time," said her mother. Her play often was obvious even when it was silent. Sitting on her mother's lap on the porch next to a reed screen while her mother was talking to another woman, Nastaran, comfortable but slightly bored, was moving a finger along the reeds, murmuring, "One, two, three, five, nine, ten, six, twenty-two, twenty . . ." She had learned to count from an elder brother. She tapped the reeds over and over again, with one finger, then another, touching every reed, then every other reed, with great patience, for nearly an hour. Just about every day for a while when she was four, hugging a dilapidated doll to her bosom under a veil-wrap, she retreated into a quiet corner in her house or in the courtyard, talking to the doll, her "baby," about things that moved her. For example, at one such sitting she described an imaginary trip she was about to take the baby on, waiting for the baby's replies, in silence, to which she then in turn reacted with a giggle, with a kiss, with an answer. As "mother," she, like other little girls, talked like her own mother and moved like a grown, tired woman, rehearsing, as it were, the "tired-woman-with-a-baby" script.

During a boring stretch of a long afternoon, Lale, age two, was sitting in the shade of her courtyard with outstretched legs, watching the toes on her left foot chase those on the right foot sideways, and then the right toes chase the left ones. Her mouth was moving silently. She kept this up for nearly one-half hour, slapping one or the other foot occasionally for "being bad."

Hoda, eight, was holding a "loudspeaker," a cardboard tube, to her mouth, silently walking around her courtyard with measured steps, rolling her eyes occasionally. After a while she tried out loud what, apparently, she had rehearsed in her mind: "Brothers and sisters who you hear me, be advised to go to the mosque . . ." she chanted through the tube, imitating the revolutionary guards' stilted language for calling people to some official function.

Mitra, seven, on the porch, mirror-shard in one hand, was watching herself comb her short hair, moving her head to some inner rhythm and throwing her arms around once in a while, for some twenty minutes, oblivious to her sisters' and cousins' departure to play elsewhere. She was absorbed in an internal dialogue, but what about remained a mystery. Similarly unaccounted for are the thoughts of an about five-year-old boy who, hunched in a corner behind women and girls lined up along the walls of a room at a wedding feast, watched the party, seemingly half bored and half fascinated, for more than an hour in total silence.

Ali, five, like boys generally, was less self-sufficient: finding himself sitting on the porch next to his busy mother, staring at birds in the poplar tree and drumming a beat on the rug with his fingers, he soon got bored enough to leave. A few minutes later, while jumping across an elastic band he had strung between two poles, he was shouting and grunting loudly, but when this went unnoticed he left to round up spectators. (He jumped like a born athlete, all muscles and instinct, seemingly effortlessly high up, and landing in a soft, springy crouch, tirelessly so, "Like a flea," said his mother.)

Observing closely what goes on around them easily becomes a diversion in itself for young children, substituting for a game. Girls often simply watch; some five or six regularly congregated in the alley in the late afternoon, sitting in a tight bunch on the big rock at the corner of my neighbor's house, a little sibling on one or the other's lap, quietly watching boys play tag loudly and fiercely. Sitting there, murmuring to each other or handling a restless toddler, the spectacle of the wild boys in front of their eyes, counts as "play" for them. "What did you do down in the alley?" a mother asked of her daughter, one of the spectators on the rock. "Nothing," she replied, "just playing."

Through their skills in watching and listening, girls' intelligence capacity is unparalleled in Deh Koh. Girls likely are the first to know of new babies, new marriage matches, fights, travels. In school they have access to domestic news through their schoolmates, at home through eavesdropping, in other houses through delivering messages, running errands, or visiting. Whenever I visited Nuri while her eight-year-old daughter was at home, the girl would place herself right outside the door to the good room where her mother and I were talking; she could hear all we said, she could watch television in the hall, observe the kitchen, answer her mother's occasional questions, and have a good view of the courtyard through the open door, all while either playing (jacks, for example) or doing homework. Although such nosiness might be ridiculed at times by adults, especially those who are being watched, the frequent demand for the girls' knowledge validates this type of information-gathering for them.

By age eight, a girl's access to boys largely is confined to her brothers who, if older, are likely to annoy her with their demands, ridicule, or violence, and, if younger, are likely to be her wards, irritating her with whining and challenges to her authority, girls claim. At that age, a girl no longer is the sweet little sister she might have been earlier but a "servant," as one brother said, like all other women in the house. All girls eventually ought to obey their brothers just as they ought to obey their fathers, yet they do it grudgingly: they fight, they try to dodge demands, they protest. "My brothers and I fought all the time," remembers a woman, which is not as things ought to be but as one expects them to be. When she was around thirteen, Soheila refused to play with her toddler brother or to take care of him; he "stinks," she said, using a metaphor for disgust; she did not even want to touch him and looked away when he was naked because of her aversion to seeing his "foot" (*pa;* in this case, penis), she said. Nine-year-old Fateme was lugging her two-year-old brother around nearly everywhere when she was not in school so that her mother could work on the loom with which she supported the family. Fateme took care of him ably but rarely played with him; he was a chore, not a playmate.

From around the age of about six, a girl's closest, most reliable playmates likely are her sisters and female cousins who live in the same compound or else close by. A few years later, after neighbor girl cousins have married out or moved away in the course of the likely split-up of compounds, two or three sisters who are close in age will emerge as the most stable group, but by then play will have grown into work-cooperation and other support activities.

Likewise, for boys of about eight, access to girls for playing is limited to sisters and female cousins who live close by. Interaction with them will be marked by challenging authority claims of elder sisters, by escaping demands and wrath, mocking ridiculing, hitting, and by cuddling, teasing, protecting babies and toddlers in the family. Relationships between brothers and between male cousins, however, likely will be marked by competition that easily may swing to hostility, and their playing, such as it is, as adults may reflect these interactional patterns. Boys are much more likely than girls to play in large groups, and to play games with set rules and a lot of noise and commotion. A game even may end in fighting and rock-throwing.

If a boy and a girl between the ages of eight and twelve who are not siblings are together in a room, such as, for example, while a girl is on an errand in a relative's house where a boy is present, the girl is expected to be torn between embarrassment and curiosity, even an urge to show off, although this is not quite proper. Likely she will exhibit a kind of exaggerated shyness and covert flirtation with quick glances in the boy's direction. The boy, especially if older than the girl, is a potential suitor, and girls know this, even may threaten each other playfully with suitor possibilities. The display of coyness and embarrassment jokingly is called "shame/shyness game" or "playing ashamed, playing shy" (*kejalat bazi, sharm bazi*). No rigid norms exist for quantifying such behavior, but if done too readily, too obviously, it easily may bring accusations of being fresh, importunate (*porru*), flighty (*lus*), a moral lightweight (*saboq*). Haleh, a coy beauty at age eleven, watched all boys and men with great concentration whenever she thought herself to be unobserved, ready to start a self-conscious, shy/coy game at a mere glance from a man. Her mother was getting pointed advice from women relatives for managing this inappropriate behavior of a nearly mature (*dorosht*) girl. Had Haleh an elder brother, was the neighborhood's opinion, he would have seen to it by now that she behaved less conspicuously.

The most elaborate shyness game performance I have seen was by an eight-year-old girl visiting her aunt and sitting opposite her twelve-year-old male cousin who was listening to his mother explain something to me, another visitor. The girl was fumbling with her veil-wrap constantly, attempting to cover all but her eyes, which darted back and forth between me and him, lingering on him just enough longer to show where her fascination focused. Several times, when offered tea, she refused vehemently, eyes darting to her cousin; finally she drank a glass, hiding completely under her veil-wrap, peering out from under it just once to check if the boy was watching. I do not think she heard a single word of our conversation. Throughout her performance, the boy seemed disinterested in her but I could not see his eyes.

Until adulthood, boys and girls are expected to "play shy" when offered a gift or food, sweets, or tea as a guest in somebody else's house. It is good manners to avoid eye contact, to avert the face, and to refuse offers several times—not too persistently, though, or else one might be called "without courage" (*kamri*) or "timid" (*sharmelu*), and this is not good, although much better than being called brash, saucy, and without manners. The ideal behavior is narrowly placed between the two extremes—to be on the safe side for their gender, girls more likely will chose the "shy" path, while boys will try to avoid situations testing their social skills or else will choose the more assertive way.

Playthings

Despite a gaudy-colored assortment of cheap plastic wares in stores, toys are scarce in Deh Koh. One reason is that there is not much of a tradition of playing with toys other than a few homemade ones and therefore they are considered an unnecessary expense by most of the financially strapped parents, and another is that they break all too easily. A class difference is emerging in toys: some children of educated, middle-class parents recently have started to demand television games with some success, provided in the name of education. Gender differences become more pronounced now too, with toy guns, airplanes, cars, and balls coveted possessions for boys, and dolls for girls. Small plastic toys are expected as gifts from a close relative returning from the city, or are won by extra-long, extra-insistent whining from parents. They are shown off or hidden, and in any case soon lost, stolen, or broken.

Children are known and expected to be destructive and to break, lose, or wreck everything they get their hands on in no time. *Kharabkari*, to wreak havoc, to destroy, is part of their devil-image, a natural attribute of the child-stage. Things fall apart not so much because children want to know how something works or moves, but because they want to find out how something comes off or caves in or stops moving. All things are grabbed, flung, swung, pressed, thrown with full force, and not many toys or other objects survive such treatment. "Every time you come I have a new destruction machine [*mashin kharabkari*] in the house!" one of my woman friends described the situation to me in 1992. Indeed, over the years I had watched one or another of her six children destroy handbags and books, two television sets and innumerable watches, tapes, radios, and toys.

Until a child has developed its reason (*aql*) between eight and twelve years of age if a girl, after twelve years if a boy, it will break things "as surely as a fox will steal chickens," as a father said, unless one is vigilant and on the defensive. After Jamal, age six, had created a crisis in his house by destroying his eldest sister's tape recorder, his frustrated mother told me of a man who, after years of pledges and pilgrimages and expensive consultations with physicians to get his wife pregnant, finally got a son. A few years later, tired of tight supervision and scolding to minimize damages, he said, "And to think at what costs I have bought myself this 'Boy-don't-do-that!' [*kurr-na-*

kon]." "Kaputt, gone, broken, stolen, lost," a seven-year-o.
chanting over and over again while he tried to put a dilapidate͜
tic car back into service.

The most durable, cheap, replaceable, and accessible playthings in
Deh Koh are mouth and voice, fingers and toes, rocks, sticks, water,
mud, and found objects, from discarded tin cans and bottles for playing cooking to empty ballpoint pens for blow-shooting mudballs, tiny
rocks, grains, or mung beans; from pilfered string for cat's cradle and
stringing up bugs to used hypodermic needles for squirting water—
garbage is everywhere and holds many possibilities.

A garbage plaything and dirt led to a dispute about religion, witnessed by several children: because of a shortage of irrigation water
and other reasons, the irrigation channels flowing down through the
village are now very filthy by local standards, and clogged with garbage that the slow, muddy, smelly water cannot transport through the
large village fast enough anymore. In the tangle of twigs and rags and
plastic bags under the bridge to a house, a small, red ball was caught.
A little boy saw it, wanted it, and was about to climb down the lit-
tered bank, fear in his every move. A young local woman, an outspoken mother of four young children, stopped and told him to let the
ball be because it was so dirty that he would get sick playing with it.
A woman across the street, a well-known Party of God (*hezbollah*)
supporter took issue with her. "How can you, a woman with years of
schooling, say such nonsense?" she asked, rhetorically. "You have
read the *rizala* that expressively says that all flowing water is lawful,
halal! You are misinforming this young child!"

"I am not talking about lawful or unlawful, I am talking about
clean and dirty, about germs, about worms, about getting sick," said
the young woman. "This water is filthy because nobody cleans the
channels."

"This talk of yours is so senseless and uninformed you should be
ashamed of yourself! And to tell such godless lies to a child!" The
older woman gathered her veil resolutely, reached down into the
channel, fished out the ball, jerked it around in the stagnant puddle a
few times, handed it to the little boy, demonstratively, and moved on.
Later, the young woman told the story to her sister-in-law, who has
the gift of seeing something funny everywhere. "Yes," she said, "all
some of these so-called religious people care about is how to go to the
toilet in a God-pleasing way and how to drink water, and how to—

well—how to go in and out, and if you sweat doing it, to have a bath, but do they say the father and mother should bathe their sweaty children every day!?" Her thirteen-year-old daughter kept a studied blank face; the two little ones wanted to know who the boy was and what the ball looked like. All of them, on account of a little red ball, had been exposed to a lesson on hygiene; to criticism of village government; to opinions regarding the relative merits of religious and secular definitions of cleanliness; and, if they had the receptor for it, to a description of sexual habits.

Things are used to play with as they are found, with little modification. The only elaboration in toy-making for boys are slingshots made of wood or metal rods, string and rubber, to shoot birds with and, at times, anything else that moves.

The quest for good rubber got Ali, age eleven, into big trouble and prompted his elder brother, sixteen, to articulate his educational philosophy for his grandmother and me. The elder brother had gotten a bike a few years earlier, after a year of intense pleading, whining, and promises to be good and study hard. Although it was not holding up well in the steep, rocky, narrow alleys leading nowhere he wanted to be, and although he did not take care of it, he regarded it as his prized possession. One dark day he noticed that one of the inner tubes was missing. Ali had pulled it out of the tire, cut it into pieces exactly right for a slingshot, and had partly hoarded, partly sold the pieces. His elder brother vented his anger: "Ruin! Kaput! Destruction! And father does not say anything! I am speechless! He never says anything—all his young children are growing up rotten, rotten to the core, without manners, like wild animals. But I showed Ali! I beat him up, and he ran away, and when he shows up again I'll beat him up some more. Ruining my bike, an expensive bike, too! And what for? To play with little boys! Mother and father spoiled the brat from his first day, they ruined his character because they let him get away with everything. They should have beaten him up a thousand times . . . Now it is too late, but I'll do my best . . . It is my duty to put fear into him because my father does not do it. Just let him come home . . .!"

Girls make dolls of sticks clothed with scraps of fabric; they name them Mother, Father, Baby, Lady, Bride. Recently, plastic dolls, *arusak*, have become available in stores, but for playing "House" outdoors, simple stick-people are preferred; they are truer to the scale of the small houses and fireplaces, and handy everywhere. The Farsi word for doll, *arusak*, never was used for these figures. Occasionally, an older girl or a woman will make a *leili* or *bibi* or *arus* (a dollie, lady, or bride), an elaborate, stick-based doll of about twelve inches with a painted face surrounded by real hair, decked out in fancy traditional women's costume, and with moveable arms for "dancing," but these figures are not as much played with by little girls as admired. They are local female beauty incarnate. "Now that all my sons have left, I made myself a *leili* to keep me company!" a woman said, only half jokingly. She let her daughter's little girl hold it and look at it, but did not permit it out of the house. "It would be dead as soon as it was over the sill!" she predicted.

Ad hoc playthings are as casually found as discarded. Play spaces are created as fast as they disappear again. Lale, three, made a make-believe fireplace, a small semicircle of mud, into which she placed little sticks very carefully; then she made the movement for striking a match, blew the imaginary fire into a blaze, shielded her eyes from the imaginary smoke, waited until it had burned down a little, placed a pot (a plastic lid) containing a few pebbles on the embers, cooked the scrambled eggs and fed them to her baby, a tattered plastic doll on her lap, and then, very carefully again, poured water from a can she had fetched from the outhouse especially for this purpose all over the fireplace to dampen the fire. The whole game had lasted about a half-hour, and after it was over, nothing at all remained of the elaborate stage except a muddy, broken plastic lid in the dirt.

Fati, age four, had begged some dough from her mother's sister, who was baking bread on her verandah. She made little round balls, miniature versions of her aunt's larger dough balls, and, with a stick picked off the ground in the courtyard tried to roll the dough flat on the edge of her indulgent aunt's breadboard. When this did not work out well, Fati gathered her dough balls, placed them in a corner of the verandah together with her dough roller, "for later," as she said, and left. About an hour later, a heavy foot had crushed the stick, and the chickens had eaten the dough balls.

The variants for playing "House" are so schematized that children, especially little girls, can without any effort tell by arrangements of the most neutral-looking things at a recently abandoned play site what had been going on even if they had not been present. The remaining dough crumbs and crushed wood in the corner of the porch told a six-year-old girl that somebody, most likely her little cousin Fati, she correctly said, had been visiting while mother had been baking bread. On a spongy tree trunk, an assemblage of small objects signified to me that girls had been playing here very recently, most probably "House"; four-year-old Nastaran, who had not been near the play group, identified a feather and a wilting rosebud stuck into the surface as "for beauty"; a brushy weed of the kind women bind into brooms as a broom; a tuft of fleece to her was a rug; a heap of match-sized sticks in a corner was a pile of firewood; three pebbles laid in a triangle was the fireplace, swept clean; a piece of broken glass with water was a pot; various bigger rocks and sticks probably were people, she said; a button with a smooth round stick next to it she easily identified as a bread board and roller; a fragment of a comb was a comb; only a wad of paper and a small pile of dirt at the edge of the uneven surface she could not account for. A girl of about nine, seeing a few smooth pebbles on the ground outside the door, yelled for her sister: "Mehri, you'll lose your rocks!" she warned her. To me she explained: "Mehri always plays jacks, and she always loses her rocks. She doesn't take care of things." She assumed correctly that I would know that well-balanced, smooth rocks of a certain size and weight are cherished for playing jacks.

Until the midsixties, wheels were not in use in Deh Koh (other than as tires on cars); neither was pottery, save for the ceramic teapot. Little balls were made of rags but used only for very few boys' games. Even now, wheel-based playthings are rare: Hamid, age nine, was threatened with death and perdition by his cousin after he had dismantled his cousin's bike to use the wheel for playing "driving a wheel" (propelling a wheel with a stick as fast as one can run) with other boys in the alley. Girls do not use wheel-based playthings at all, just as they do not ride bicycles or learn to drive a car later, and neither do they keep weapons ready. They are more likely to carry containers with them, a can, a bag, a pitcher, a scarf-bundle, or paper or string—rarely are boys or girls seen empty-handed, but what they carry likely marks their gender from a very early age.

Just about all of a boy's playthings are potential weapons. After he had lost an argument with his father on pain of threats of a beating, Jamal, seven, locked himself into a storage shed. About an hour later, he cautiously emerged, five sticks in one hand, a fistful of rocks in the other, a solid piece of firewood clutched to his chest, watching out for the enemy, he said. For several more hours he kept the weapons near him, threatening anybody coming too close for comfort. Likewise, a man, after he had lost an argument with his son of about six by the boy's limber flight, kept two long switches next to him while he was sitting outside the door repairing a tool, "to be ready for the scoundrel," as he explained.

Things are not expected to stay with a child for long, either by children themselves or by adults. Things to which a child gets attached enough to really want to preserve them have to be hidden from others. "I don't have the toy cars anymore," a five-year-old boy lied to his cousin, who wanted to see them. Abed, eight, kept moving his cache of valuables from one hiding place to another in the house, "like a cat moving her kittens," his mother said, to foil his younger siblings. Seventeen-year-old Muhammad hid a box of tapes on top of a pile of household goods to keep them safe from his sisters; sympathetic adults such as a grandmother may be pressed into providing a safe space for a new toy, some beads, a fancy pen, a shiny hairpin, money. The general feeling among children is that on the one hand nothing is safe anywhere from anybody, and that on the other hand the risk of punishment and wrath often is worth "stealing" (*dozi kardan*) other children's unguarded things. "If you take your new crayons to school, everybody will steal them from you!" a mother warned her second-grader. "And if I leave them here my little brother will break them!" he answered.

Quite generally, toys and possessions a child uses and shows to others are reduced to the level of least complexity in a short time. Accusations of stealing and lying, of taking things away, of losing and destroying them, are commonplace in interactions among children in regard to playthings. Just as common are refutations of such accusations, often in the form of counter-accusations ("You are lying! You are too dumb to take care of things; thief yourself!"); oaths of innocence ("By Saint Ali, by your soul, I have not seen your gun . . ."); or general refutations ("You lost it yourself! It was broken from the beginning . . ."). The vernacular vocabulary of interpersonal ethics regarding things and ownership is fully in place and is practiced daily by the age of less than four years.

22 · Games

Between 1971 and 1994 I have documented close to sixty games in Deh Koh as I observed them being played or as they were described to me. Some of these games are described in a book of games from around the northern administrative center of the tribal province to which Deh Koh belongs,* while others seem to be unique to Deh Koh. People in Deh Koh claim that they played more games in the past than children play today. They ascribe this change to school activities and the introduction of sports and television. Most of the organized games played by boys were also played by men occasionally until about the 1960s.

Sixteen of the games are predominantly girls' games; the rest are played mostly by boys. An analysis of the games suggests gender-specific themes that script different interactional patterns for boys and girls, and that boys and girls are socialized into very different social realities by the games they play.

Girls have fewer organized games with set rules than have boys. They tend to play alone more likely than do boys: swinging, cat's cradle, jacks, hopscotch. "Baby" with a doll, although more fun if played in company, can be played alone as well. Spinning on a small, crude toy spindle, baking bread on a flat stone with mud-dough, and building a fire with little sticks are activities for only two hands; the more hands there are the more likely they will meddle with one's task, yet, again, company to talk to is welcome. For boys, the equivalent to such solitary games is practicing with the slingshot or throwing rocks at a target. If company is present, however, more likely than not the boys will make a competition out of the shooting or throwing. Boys building "mills" along the irrigation channel tried to establish whose mill was the loudest. When girls play in groups, the groups are small: two or three may play jacks; a small group may play rhythmical games such as *hoshtela*, a stationary dance performed at weddings; two may play a lift-me-up game that consists of two girls of comparable height standing back-to-back with elbows linked, lifting each

*Fareydun Amirian, *Bazihaye Mahali Ostane Kohgiluye va Boir Ahmad* [Local games of the Province Kohgilu-e and Boir Ahmad] (Yasuj: Publications for the Contemporary World, 1991).

other alternately to the rhythm of a chant until they are tired; or three or four girls may play "House" or "Fort," "Auntie" or "Child-Child," with sticks, stones, weeds, and found objects serving as people and household goods arranged in circular or rectangular roomlike spaces outlined by stones. Twelve of the sixteen girls' games are verbal; they contain a considerable amount of patterned talk, chants, rhymes. An extreme example of this category would be "Don't laugh" games (*bazi makhandu*), which sometimes also are played by boys. They consist of a question or a demand to say a particular word, followed by a rhyme to this word that abuses or ridicules the partner. The images manipulated in these games are food, sexual organs, and excrements. For example, A asks, "What did I see behind the fort?" B answers, "Mung beans [*mashak*]." A rhymes this word with, "Your mother's vagina is full of ash [*ashak*]." In the game "Say" (*begu*), A demands of B, "Say 'One'." B says, "One." A rhymes this with, "May you explode." Or, "Say, 'pestle'" is rhymed with "I'll pee in it, you pound it." Some of these rhymes are well-known; many more are created while children play. In these games, children learn by example to see humor in the combination of words for everyday, emotionally neutral objects with violent death and scatological and sexual images, and to laugh about insulting others verbally. A rich body of immodest, bawdy, *zesht* language is placed in the context of play, beyond reprimand. The "Say" game, however, occasionally leads to hurt feelings, even blows. Children practice such language also in curses, but there it is placed in the context of direct aggression.

Other examples of girls' verbal games are secret languages, or one in which several little girls sit in a circle on the floor chanting a rhyme, shaking their outstretched feet together at a certain point in a gesture that in other contexts would be regarded as obscene.

In girls' games involving more than two players, the dominant mode of interaction is cooperation or at least equal participation, without "it" or leader, losing or winning, and with constant talking. One girl pushes a swing for another, then switches position; two or three sit around a "pot" to be stirred; a "house" is constructed by the combined efforts of several girls. An exception is a game for which girls beg enough flour from their elders to bake a flour-water bread in the hot ashes of a fire in the gardens. The dough contains one pebble—whoever finds it in her share of the bread will be punished by the others. A young woman remembers that at one such game when she was about seven, she was so terrified of the punishment that she hid the pebble in her mouth and almost choked on it.

Leadership is not built into girls' games. It emerges when one or another girl's suggestions for games or her attempts to motivate others are frequently successful in the group, like, for example, the request to play house there instead of here or to chant this rhyme instead of that. Exceptions are games that allow a girl to assume a female position of authority, such as Mother, or Cook at a wedding, or Teacher or Nurse in the modern context of playing "School" or playing "Doctor." In these contexts, girls act out complex scripts of skills and tasks, body language, speech patterns, and manipulative tactics such as praises, but also false promises of rewards, empty threats, lies, emphatic assurances such as "I'll give you a sweet, by my soul!" There are no equivalent acting games for boys, save playing "Car" or playing with toy guns. These games, however, do not let the boys practice skills actually relevant for driving a car or shooting.

In contrast to the girls' games, most boys' games are played in larger groups, and half of them operate with an "it" and a leader, called head (*sar*), khan, or shah. Whenever a leader is the focus of a game, all players except the "it" are dependent on the leader and subordinate to him. These players have no power, do not cooperate with each other, and relate to the leader in star-shape. Often they are handicapped in some way, confined in a circle, for example, tethered to a stake, or covered by a rug, and the leader has to defend them against the attacks of an enemy (*doshman*). In these cases, the action is between the leader and the enemy, with the other players passively at the mercy of the skills and fighting spirit of their leader. In some games, a leader has to defend one person against the attacks of many enemies, but the hierarchical and adversarial relationships are the same. In these games, furthermore, even the leader cannot win: the process of the game is a slow losing as the chief's men are taken out by the enemy, and the game has come to an end when the enemy has "killed" all the chief's men.

In one game, the leader chooses an aggressor to hit the players who in turn defend themselves as best they can within the boundaries of a defined space, until the leader, who stayed out of the fights, orders the aggressor to stop. The sixteen-year-old who explained the game to me jokingly remarked that it resembled the traditional chief and his rifleman, a hand-picked, loyal executor of the chief's orders, and the villagers who were subject to the chiefs' arbitrary demands and violence. This and similar games were interpreted as a playful dramatization of the traditional chief-peasant relationship that structured social life in Deh Koh until about 1965. The game in which the leader has to protect his people against enemy attack mirrors another aspect of the traditional chief-peasant relationship, that of the chief's duty to protect his people against raids and attacks by outsiders. Such raids and fights were common enough in the area before the area's pacification after 1965. Two games label the leader a shepherd, the players sheep, and the enemy a wolf, thus furnishing a metaphor for the hierarchical and authoritarian relationships among men. The same authoritarian, hierarchical theme is expressed in the setting of a "shah" who orders his vizier to investigate the complaints of a leader of a tribal camp about a theft. The thief is identified, and the vizier administers a punishment. The punishment is the high point of this game, as of many others.

In only four games do groups of boys fight each other without a leader, or else one boy defends himself against many enemies.

In these games, the players do not cooperate, neither amongst themselves nor with the leader. If they act at all, they do so as individuals in their own interest. At best, the individuals' acts may add up to benefit the whole group. For example, the members of two opposing groups throw rocks at each other's "fort," a low wall of stones. Each hit is recorded. The more skillful the members of a group are, the more points their group will score. Neither defense nor cooperation are possible.

The only games boys play involving cooperation can also be played by girls, such as guessing games. But here, too, the relationship between the players and the questioner is star-shaped, and the guessers do not interact with one another. One game that seemingly rests on cooperation has players forming a chain by clutching one another's hands and the leader(s) trying to break the chain by pulling hard. The weaklings who break the chain are punished. This cooperation among three people, literally holding on to one another as long as possible, is motivated by self-interest. This game, like so many others, determines losers, not a winner.

In games that are not based on a group-leader structure, the mode of interaction among the players is one of competition: the goal is to run faster, jump higher, shoot more accurately, throw farther, act more quickly, aim better, outwit the others. Unlike in games for girls, there are very few boys' games in which two or more boys are supposed to derive pleasure solely from playing together: playing "truck" together with others is "better" than playing it alone; pushing a wheelbarrow-car and being driven in one rest on the mutual trust of reciprocity. Having to push somebody in a wheelbarrow may, however, also be a punishment for a loser. A young boy may play "House" or "Wedding" with a group of girls in the girls' noncompetitive play mode, but this is the exception rather than the rule.

Winning for its own sake, without a reward or without the right to administer punishment to a loser, hardly is seen as a worthwhile goal of playing a game. Most commonly, the goals are material gain, such as winning the partners' tokens or pebble-marbles, to remain anonymous and unpunished, to avoid being "it," to be able to mete out punishment, and to gain a position of leadership, of power over others. Punishment or fear of punishment is more of a motivation for action than is the prospect of a reward. Punishment always is either physical, such as being whipped or being swung by arms and legs against another swung loser or against a wall so that rump is banging against rump very hard or against the even harder wall, or consists of an act of subordination, such as carrying the leader on one's back over a distance, or letting a chief walk over one's body. Carrying somebody on one's back is sign and symbol for subordination; a high-ranking person will be offered, or may demand, to be carried across a river; djenn are said to mount their victims; servants have to carry heavy loads, as do cows and donkeys.

Boys and girls get different messages about the way people relate: girls learn to appreciate cooperation and to derive pleasure from being together and talking together, even if it is not always a clear give-and-take. Girls and women frequently talk in simultaneous monologues; they can talk and listen at the same time. "Winning" is to be with others rather than to be different from others. Boys, on the other hand, in their games re-create the traditional authoritarian political hierarchy, stress anonymous individualism, keep a low profile in their dependency on a center of power and authority, dodge violence and act aggressively themselves when possible, and are noisy and openly competitive. They practice skills fit for hunting and war, rather than for agriculture and husbandry, which were traditional economic activities of men. Even where a farming theme is elaborated into a game, such as in rather wet and high-spirited mock fights over water rights at irrigation channels in the gardens, the mode of interaction is violent.

Modern games for boys, such as volleyball and soccer, were introduced by teachers about twenty years ago. These games have become very popular for older boys, displacing the more traditional games involving "chiefs" and "wolfs." Boys play them with vigor, often acting out misgivings between different groups of boys from different neighborhoods or kingroups, and, reportedly, often ending games in fights. It is "much easier," a fourteen-year-old boy told me, to "beat up on some enemies" while playing soccer than to do it in any other context. Games played in school in physical education, even if not based on aggression, likely work with the notion of authoritarian relationships and individualism. For example, in one such school game for second-graders, the players form two lines facing each other, with a line of pebbles between the lines, corresponding in number to the number of boys in each line. The teacher assigns each boy a number, starting with "1" in each line. When the teacher calls a number, the identified boys run toward the pebbles. The first one to arrive there grabs the pebble and brings it back to his line. Then the teacher calls another number, and so on, until all the pebbles have been claimed. The group with most pebbles has won.

Boys say that playing together for a common goal does not come easy. But this does not mean that the boys do not grasp the concept of cooperation or are unable to play as a team, just as their competitive games do not prevent them from forming cooperative enterprises with other men later. It does imply, however, that the trend to violence, competition, and forming authoritarian relationships needs to be modified, balanced with other notions and social skills to produce a village that, despite its large size, has few public, serious outbreaks of violence among men, and that these skills are not readily practiced in games.

In contrast to boys, older girls above the age of about twelve have very few game options. In school, ball games occasionally are played as part of physical education. At home, skills and behaviors practiced in games become applied to real work. In groups, older girls do not play as much as talk "nobody knows what about," as a mother of three unmarried teenaged girls said. "Play" is discouraged; traditionally, normally, as it should be if things were right in the opinion of a great many adults, older girls should not be girls at all but married women, occupied with adult tasks they played at as girls.

23 · Stick Dance

The Game

Needed are: two male players; two poles, about five feet long; rhythmic oboe-and-drum music playing variations of the "stick dance" motif; spectators.

Surrounded by spectators, the two players skip around in a circle, one behind the other, holding their respective sticks over the head with both hands, then behind the back, or twirling and swinging them fancifully to the beat of the music. As the beat accelerates, the men stop circling and face each other, hopping more or less in place with small steps anywhere inside the circle. One man, the defender, plants his pole vertically in front of himself as a shield against the other man, who tries, after several mock attacks, to hit his legs. If he is successful, women trill, and attacker and attacked switch roles, or another player takes one or the other's place.

This stick dance (*tarkebazi*) was the most popular dance game for young and old men in the area before the revolution. Outlawed for more than a decade, it is making a comeback now that governmental sanctions against music and festivities are easing somewhat. It is the main attraction at wedding parties, played in courtyards for all to see, accompanied by taped music. Little boys imitate the movements and practice the dance with each other throughout the long afternoons at weddings, cheered on by women's trills, and occasionally later too, at home and in the alleys.

The Little Children

After having watched men dance around and hit each other for hours during three days of his uncle's wedding, four-and-one-half-year-old Amin gets his elder sister, Zahra, eight, to play *tarkebazi* with him. Although playing it with a girl is not quite as it should be, and without the beat of the drum the rhythm is hard to coordinate, especially when one player has long legs and the other short ones, both are engrossed in the game. Amin does not lose much time twirling his stick and shaking his legs in the show-off rounds, even gets impatient when Zahra embellishes her movements—he wants to hit. "Tak"— his stick on hers; they change places—"tak." Amin hits again—"tak," with full force. The stick breaks, which is more fun yet. Another stick is found—"tak"—"tak." Neither of the children even makes an attempt to hit the other's legs; their goal for playing is to produce as loud a "tak" noise as possible. About fifteen minutes later, Zahra is tired of the short, rather monotonous routine, and Amin starts a whining performance to get her to play more. He throws his stick after her when she runs away.

The next day he practices the game with two little boys; in less than no time all three want to "hit," which leads to a free-for-all and ends in a chase.

The Big Boys

Amin's grandmother enlightens me about the drama Amin—and I—had missed watching the stick dancers at his uncle's wedding.

A few days earlier, a small party of men and older "boys," unmarried young men, from the groom's family had gone to the orchards to pick fruits for the wedding feast. There, in high good spirits, they had bantered and made fun of getting married. Unfortunately, one of the young men had taken offense. One word led to another, sides were taken, old grievances resurrected. By the end of the day, some of the "boys" were not on speaking terms with one another. Efforts by a grandfather and an elder uncle to mend fences and soothe wounded pride were partially successful by the time of the wedding. But at the stick dance, the younger members of the two main parties sought each other out as partners, revenge in their hearts, determined to hit to hurt. After a protracted display of stick skills, Ahmed hit his cousin Behruz on the shin with such force that a thick welt appeared under the pants; Behruz, jumping with pain, whacked Ahmed on the thigh when Ahmed defended his shins too skillfully; Ahmed almost went down with pain. Ahmed's brother took his place, hitting Behruz on his other leg; one of Behruz's allies shouldered the limping Behruz aside and went after Ahmed's surrogate with a vengeance. By then the women had all but stopped ululating. "Oi, *bacce, bacce,* boys, boys!" an aunt cried. After the second try Behruz's substitute smacked Ahmed's ally over the fingers that held the defense stick. Now they were stalking each other in earnest, bent on doing harm, women nervously shouting at them to stop, when a level-headed older man stepped in, wrestling the stick from one of the two fighters with some difficulty, and diffusing the impending fight with the measured steps of a practiced dancer. The other fighter gave up his place, too. Ahmed had a bloody thigh, Behruz bloody shins. But, somehow, the proxy fight had settled the matter. No further hostilities ensued.

Amin's eldest brother, fifteen, who had kept out of the altercations and is "too shy," he says, to play the stick dance "in front of all the women!" summed it up: "A boy's game has many possibilities," he said. "*Tarkebazi* is a good game."

24 · Children's Hour

The television is on in the hall/family room. Hoda, age eleven, has pulled up a chair. It is the only occasion she will sit on a chair at home. Jamal, four, comes running from the bathroom when he hears the familiar noise. Wriggling and stuffing himself inside his pants, he hops around between his sister and the screen. Hoda pushes him aside with her legs. Jamal slaps her leg, but then rolls a big cushion over from the wall, lies down on the rug on his belly in front of Hoda, arms on the cushion, jeans forgotten around his thighs. I am sitting on the rug leaning against the wall, children and television within my field of vision.

On the flickering screen—the reception is not so good since Jamal pulled out the antenna in a fit, Hoda explained—we are in somebody's living room. A boy of about twelve and a girl of about nine (Saed and Zahra, we soon learn) are sitting on a rug on the floor, bent over books on a short-legged, small table. Saed is facing us. His shirt looks clean, his dark hair is neat. His sister, whom we see in profile, is wearing a yellow, loose dress with long sleeves, and a big scarf pulled well down over her forehead.

The children are working quietly.

The telephone rings. Zahra gets up, grabs the phone, and with a tiny little-girl voice says, "What can I do for you [befarmait]?—Daddy, it is you?" Listening, she gets excited, says, "Movies!' and "Yes, yes . . ."

Saed jumps up, runs to the door in the background, but mother, in the regulation head-garment (maqne) required of female government employees and of girls in school and a long, gray, formless garment with long sleeves, stops him. It turns out she has been checking his homework. "Where are you going?" she asks with a mean face. "To the movies, with daddy," Saed says defiantly. Mother is all disapproval. "No, you are not going—not with so many mistakes in your work!" She leaves, finality in her step.

The children look disappointed. Heads and shoulders drooping, they slink back to their books. They read and write for a while. While Saed is thinking hard, he absentmindedly is drumming on the table with his pencil. Zahra, off screen, screeches at him to stop. He drums louder. Now she starts drumming too. He drums, both drum. Mother enters, scolding them. The children stop. She takes her veil and an-

"Homework," says Jamal. "Look, what a funny table they have. Who are they?" Hoda ignores him. She is chewing gum.

"They have a telephone. We have one too." He gets up, tripping over his jeans, takes the phone off the hook. "Hello, Daddy, *befarmait*," he squeaks in falsetto. "Be quiet, leave the phone alone," Hoda says and kicks her legs towards him. Jamal slaps her leg but plunks down on the cushion again. He turns around to face her: "They want to go to the movies! But they won't, for sure . . ." Hoda is blowing a bubble. "SHUT UP," she yells, glueing her lips with the gum.

"Look, she won't let them go!"

"Is she a teacher, Hoda? Is this a teacher?" Wordlessly, Hoda pokes him with her foot. "She'll spank him, for sure," says Jamal, slapping the cushion.

Hoda is drumming a staccato on the seat of the chair with both hands. Jamal pounds the floor in front of him. "Stop it," says Hoda. Jamal stops, starts again. Hoda ignores him. She is drumming silently now.

"Where is she going, Hoda, where?" Hoda is blowing an-

ounces a short visit to the neighbor. The children are working quietly.

Saed sees something running across the floor. Both children are after it, looking under the cabinet, under chairs, behind the door. There is quite a racket. Mother comes in, scolding them. The children stop their search, slink back to their table.

Father appears in the door, dressed in the customary suit without a tie. Amidst greetings the children run to the cabinet for their coats but mother stops them. "They did not study right," she tells father. "No movies for them." Now father makes a speech about the importance of studying. The children listen dejectedly, heads down, shoulders sagging. Mother and father look at their children, and their faces soften. Saed says, "Can we go if we promise to study after the movie?"

"No," says mother, "then it is time for bed." More disappointment. Father has an idea: "Do your homework right now, do it fast and well, and we will catch the six o'clock show." The children race to their books. All are relieved and happy; even mother smiles a little.

The doorbell rings: visitors . . . Father and mother greet them warmly: "Come in, come in, you are welcome, how are you? . . ."

other bubble. "To her mother," she says. "Lie," says Jamal, "There is no grandmother. She is lying."

"What was this?" asks Jamal, "What, WHAT?" "A mouse, for sure," says Hoda. Jamal starts to sing, moving his head left and right: "There was a mouse, there was an ant . . ." "Shut up," says Hoda. "They have furniture too," says Jamal.

"They didn't catch it, either," says Jamal, laughing, and shaking his head vigorously.

"Like Farokh," Jamal says. "Lazybums never does his homework either." Hoda is swinging her legs, peeling gum from her lips.

"They won't spank them, anyway. No spank-spank, nothing." Jamal slaps the floor with both hands.

"Lie! He just says this to get to the movies."

"Lie. He is just saying it so they'll do their work. Lie, lie . . ."

The children pull faces of disap-
pointment and disgust.

"Who are they? Why are they
coming?"

"Just visitors," says Hoda,
"no movie."

Jamal rolls onto his back and
laughs, slapping his forehead.
"NO MOVIE, nothing! It was a
lie—Don't they have television?
We have television . . . !"

Postscript

Jamal knows dashed hopes and frustrated initiatives so well that
he can predict failures, can suggest coping strategies, and can infer
motivations for children on a television show. The frustration motif
frequently propels plots not only on television but also in children's
books, which are available in school and in some homes. Children
understand what television children and book characters feel even if
dress, gadgets, and lifestyle are urban. On this theme and on a cognitive level the worlds of urban and rural children overlap.

Of the thirty children's books I analyzed, which exclude books of
explicitly religious content, *Yo-Yo the Little Yellow Cat** best represents
the life-is-full-of-frustrations genre. In thirty short poems, each illustrated with four-panel cartoon-style drawings, the author tells of a
cat's thirty adventures. Yo-Yo, dressed in a bow tie, walks upright and
acts human; he is a boy, Jamal and his sisters said. Two-thirds of the
episodes end in frustration: Yo-Yo receives a soccer ball, which he
kicks through a window inadvertently; he tries to rob a bird's nest
perched on the roof but and falls into a rain barrel; he waits for the
cuckoo to fly out of a cuckoo clock but is whacked on the head
instead; he sits on a big egg, hoping for a chicken, but hatches a
crocodile. (Of Yo-Yo's ten successes, six involve dodging work or de-
fending his sleep and rest, which are two other popular motifs.) Although the environment and several key objects depicted in the book
are strange for Deh Koh children—the cuckoo clock, a rowboat, a
birthday cake—the ever-present likelihood of things going wrong is
the same in Deh Koh. The children with whom I read the book, however, did not dwell on the easily predictable mishaps; they wanted to

*A. Tabilesku, *Yo-yo, gorbe-ye zard kucilu* (n.p.: Sahand Press, 1991).

know what happened after the cat's failures, how he solved his problems, how he got punished—surely his father would beat him for the smashed window!—or escaped punishment. In effect, they explored different scripts for the consequences of familiar mishaps that they were prepared to accept as unavoidable.

25 · Playing Teacher, Playing Nurse

Sima, a third grader, got her little preschool sister to play "School" with her at home. Sima is the teacher, Salma the student. Sima, loosely wrapped in her mother's veil-wrap, is leaning against the wall, facing her class. On a rickety folding table next to her lie an open book, some pencils, and Sima's mother's handbag, which her mother uses when she has to go to town. All the women teachers in school have handbags. Salma is standing in front of a chair at the far end of the "good" room, where I am being entertained, a room with a big rug, and unusually furnished with two rarely-used chairs and the small table that now serves as the teacher's desk. Salma is reciting a poem about pomegranate seeds that are like rubies. She learned this and many others from her elder siblings, who in turn learned it in school or from books. Head back and body rigid, she starts out slowly, making slicing motions with her right hand as she falls into the rhyming words, but gets stuck soon. "Come out here," says Sima, shifting her weight to her other leg in a tired gesture of sore feet and tried patience.

Salma walks up to her, turns around to face the class (her empty chair, that is), and starts again, words tumbling out fast this time, as if she had to compete with a classroom full of children who might take over the recitation at her slightest stumble or hesitation: "A hundred rubies sit row after row well-mannered next to each other each one opaque of beautiful color with, with, with . . ." Salma is breathless and out of steam. She swallows hard, fingers her dress nervously, looks around at her teacher, stuttering. Sima, who seemingly had been lost in her own thoughts, head propped into a hand while Salma was talking, shouts, without looking up, "A white heart—"

"—in its chest a white heart in its chest . . . the rubies tight together under a soft cover, cover, red and beautiful its name is pomegranate, ememem, pomegranate—it is tart and sweet and juicy." Salma ends abruptly and runs back to her chair. Sima gathers the folds of the veil-wrap in her left hand and pulls the top down over her forehead. This movement occurs every few moments. "Very good, excellent," she says with a studied lack of enthusiasm, rummaging in the handbag on the table with her free hand. Salma slouches in her chair, legs dangling. "Sit properly!" Sima says without looking at her. "We will do math next." She tucks the folds of the veil-wrap under her left arm, takes the pencils, holds them up in her left hand with stretched fingers, as if she had to worry about long fingernails. Leaning against the table now, she addresses the corner of the living room: "I have three pencils. If I take one away—how many remain in my hand?"

"Two," Salma shouts at the top of her lungs, as if she had to compete with thirty other children.

"The correct answer is: 'Three minus one is two,'" says Sima to the ceiling, boredom in every syllable. "Salma, come out here." Salma jumps out of her chair. "Say, 'Three minus one is two.'" Salma, slowly, rhythmically, shouts, "Three manus—no, manis, no, minus one is two!"

"Very well, good job," says Sima, indifferently and to the lightbulb overhead. "You can sit down again. We will do dictation next. Salma, have you done your homework?"

Salma giggles. "Yes," she says. She jerks a smudged and raggedy notebook from the schoolbag next to her chair, and finds a pencil and a big eraser. Salma is dictating from her book. "Write, 'Father.' Are you done? Write, 'Wind, *bad*'—no, this is an error; erase this, write, 'Water, *ab*'—have you written 'Water'?" Salma is erasing furiously. The paper rips. Sima is gazing into a faraway distance. "Write, 'Father gave me wind—' no, error, write, 'water—father gave me water.'" Salma has found another page and is writing slowly, pressing the pencil into the paper hard. She erases her scribbles again. Slowly, Sima ambles over to her. "Show me your work!" she says. Salma is rustling paper, turning pages fast and jerkily. "You have not done your homework!" Sima shouts down to her.

"Yes, I have," says Salma. "Look, look—"

"No, you are a liar; you will get a bad grade, your father will spank you, you will not get to second grade, you are lazy, you have no brains."

"No brains yourself!" says Salma, throwing notebook and pencil on the floor. "You can't even dictate. Now you write, I dictate, it is my turn now, listen . . .!"

                    .   .   .

The next episode has two locations: the health clinic, and a court-yard. Zahra's aunt told me what had happened at the clinic, a place I know well, including the nurse, whose performances I had watched at similar occasions; Zahra's imitation and interpretation of the nurse I saw from my porch across the courtyard.

Zahra, ten, has accompanied her aunt and the aunt's three-year-old boy to the health clinic in the next village. The little cousin had a throat infection. The Pakistani doctor had given a prescription; the prescription had been filled at the dispensary. By midafternoon, Zahra, her aunt, and the little boy are tired. They stand before the nurse's station, ready for the injection. Zahra is impressed by the nurse, a young city woman with arched eyebrows and a faint hint of red on her lips, and a gray regulation head cover that hides all but a tiny lock of hair. She sits behind her desk, knitting, a big glass with tea at her side on a chair hidden behind the desk—Zahra sees it any-way, and the sugar cubes too. The nurse neither looks at them nor stops knitting as the aunt extends her hand with the ampoule. Even-tually, she jerks her head to the right. "Go to the next room," she says, into her knitting. The three walk along the cold, tiled corridor to the next door. It stands open but nobody is in the bare room. Aunt and children wait a while, then march back to the nurse. The aunt, in deferential tone and polite words, asks for help: the ampoule is ready, it would take the esteemed madam nurse only a minute . . . The nurse looks up briefly and in the mellow tones of Tehrani Farsi says, "No, I can't give an injection to a male child. Only a man can do it. Go back and wait." They leave, they wait. Nobody shows up. After another while, they go back to the nurse. Couldn't maybe, as an exception, the nurse give the shot after all? The boy is only three . . . Absolutely not; a male is a male; orders are orders, for everybody. The nurse yawns, tucks her stray lock half back under the head cover, takes a sip of tea. Another woman comes with an ampoule for a whimpering little girl.

Nurse puts her knitting aside with a sour face. Deftly, compu
and with great diffidence she injects the drug into the girl's arm wiu.
out even leaving her chair. Mother and little girl leave. Nurse picks
up her knitting again and sighs. Now the aunt starts to complain—
politely still, but complaining nevertheless. "We have been here for a
long time, the boy is ill, we—" The nurse interrupts her. "Madam,
you make me tired!" she says, piqued. But she puts her yarn aside
and gets up, protest in every move. "One gets tired of complaints!"
she says, to no one in particular. Shoulders drooping she slowly shuffles into a back room. After a short while, she reappears with a man
in a white coat. He is a public health care worker who keeps the
records at the clinic. He jokes that he has never properly learned to
give injections. He hurts the boy. The boy screams, the aunt blows her
top. The nurse, eyebrows arched high, flutes, "Oh Madam has a tem-
per!" yet manages to give the air of total boredom.

Zahra has not said a word but has taken it all in.

At home she plays "Clinic" with her cousin. Zahra is the nurse,
dressed in her big brother's white shirt atop her own clothes, and the
head cover she has to wear to school. Carefully, she teases a strand of
hair out and lets it dangle above her left eye. She gets a chair from
somewhere, a glass of tea, a ball of yarn, a crochet hook. Parvin, the
patient, can be herself; she only has to sit on the rim of the water
basin in the courtyard, waiting for a "needle." She is a prop for
Zahra, who sits on the chair, surveying the set. "You have to whine a
little," she tells Parvin. Parvin whimpers. Zahra wrinkles her nose,
pouts, picks up the yarn, and then, in an instant, transforms herself
and the scene: Zahra, who usually is fast, loud, and wild, who climbs
poles and trees, walks with a straight back, suddenly slumps. Her
tight body is lazy and tired, her shoulders sag, her legs go limp, her
face is a mask of boredom. Eyebrows arched high, she fumbles with
her scarf, turns ever so slowly to look at Parvin, nasally complains
about whiney children, about the draft that makes her bones ache;
she sips from the tea glass surreptitiously, tells Parvin to stop whining
because her head aches, "knits" a little, complains about the work,
about the backward village, about Parvin's dirty sweater, in musical,
drawn-out Farsi learned from television. She slurps more tea, turning
her back to Parvin, hides the glass under the chair with a quick, fluid
motion, pulls her scarf forward, then gets up languidly, shuffles to
Parvin's side. "All these dirty little children make me tired," she de-

clares loudly, before she pokes her crochet needle into Parvin's arm. Parvin, startled, gives a loud yelp and hits Zahra hard on the back. "You are not supposed to do this!" Zahra shouts, herself again. "You are supposed to cry!"

26 · The Devil and the Telephone

Deh Koh got electricity in 1975 and telephone cables in 1990. Children like to use the telephone for any reason, legitimate and not so legitimate. In the minds of most adults, the telephone has become a toy for children—an expensive toy. Indeed, quite a bit of children's *fuzuli*, naughtiness, now involves the telephone.

The following scene took place in a kitchen where I was a guest, sitting on a worn rug drinking tea and watching my hostess cut up a sugar cone.

Wide-eyed, head between his shoulders, fingers splayed, six-year-old Ahmed runs from the phone in the hall back to the kitchen, plants himself in front of his mother and her sugar cone and stutters, "The tel-telephone rang. I got-got it. I s-said, 'hello,' I said. It said no-nothing. I said, 'Hei, you, who are you?' It whispered, 'I'm the devil.' I was scared. I said, 'What? Who? What?' 'I'm the devil,' it said, very softly. Now-now I was very sca-scared, I put the telephone down very fast. Mother! The devil, it said!" Ahmed almost jumps onto the cloth on which his mother is heaping little sugar pieces. We all laugh. He looks at us, then laughs too, but his eyes are almost squinted shut and his shoulders are tight. His rigid fingers are rubbing against each other fast. "I'm the devil, the phone said, ha, ha!" he cries, jumping up and down, playing up to our joke. His mother explains that this was not the devil but a bad, naughty child, very ill-mannered. "Have a drink of water," she tells him, "to shake off the scare."

The phone rings again. Mehri, ten, picks it up. "Hello—hello!—HELLO!—Hell-o brat-o, fool-o!" she shouts disgustedly, and slams the receiver down so hard that the phone falls off its little table. "Nobody said anything, just whistled," she reports. "The devil!" Ahmed shouts, stuffing sugar cubes into his pant pockets. "No, for sure it's a boy who wants to hear Lida's voice," says Mehri and instantly is whacked over the head by her big sister. "Crazy, foul-mouthed idiot," Lida cries, "keep your mouth shut!"

The phone again. Ahmed beats Mehri to it. "Hello, brat-o, fool-o," he yells into the receiver, "you broom-scraggly bogeyman [*sarparparuk*], I'm a devil too, hoooii!" He slams down the receiver and swaggers through the hall basking in the suppressed laughter from the kitchen. But this time it had been an aunt, his mother's favorite sister, now a joke richer.

"So, I am a broom-headed monster," she said to him next time she saw him. Ahmed, mortified, kicked his mother to rid himself of his embarrassment and hid from the aunt for a week.

. . .

Ahmed had another memorable encounter with a child-devil playing a popular game with the telephone. He is reporting to his big brother Ali, nineteen: "The telephone rang. I said, 'Hello.' A girl said—[here Ahmed goes into a squeaky whisper]—'Is this Ali?' I said, 'What do you want?' She said, 'I want to marry Ali,' and then she did like this into the phone: 'Smack, smack, smack,' and I said, 'Do your homework instead, you brat.'" Ahmed was both scolded for his brashness and admired for his presence of mind, and got the message that he had made a great joke.

. . .

A few weeks later Ahmed and Lida, seventeen, gave me the opportunity to watch yet another play-use of the telephone while I was waiting for their mother.

A small circus will give performances in the schoolyard of the village down the road today and tomorrow. Ahmed wants to go today. He wants to go very badly, but as nobody at home has the time or the inclination to take him he decides to join his cousin Mitra, a good friend of Lida who earlier had said she was going with her sisters. Ahmed is pestering Lida to phone Mitra right now and to tell her to take him along. Lida does not want to ask such a favor—she considers it cheeky and disgraceful. But Ahmed does not accept her refusal nor her promise to take him tomorrow. He is adamant, loud, and not to be diverted. Whining and pleading turn to screaming when Lida, impatient and fed up, hits him. He throws himself down, bangs his head on the floor and howls even louder, holding his head because the banging hurt. The result is encouraging, though. "All right, you son-of-a-dog, I'll phone her," Lida hisses. Ahmed stops the racket instantly, goes to the phone with her, watching her every move. Lida dials, says, "Hello, Mitra, is this you? Here is Lida. How are you, how is your mother, how is—I am sorry, I hope it isn't too bad—thank you, we are all well—thank you, my cold is much better—yes—yes," Lida laughs. "No, it is about the circus—yes, of course, Ahmed wants to go—" more laughter. "Never mind, no, really, it is all right, we will go tomorrow—thank you—yes, no problem—thank you, good bye—yes, I'll tell her—good bye." Ahmed is standing in front of her, scrutinizing her face, frowning in deep mistrust. "Well," Lida says, "they planned to go but they have a big bag of garbage they want to burn behind their house, and this will take them all afternoon." Ahmed is listening, body rigid, brows furrowed, doubt and disappointment around his mouth, but he does not challenge her. Instead, he turns on his heels to find his mother and another way to get to the circus. Lida giggles behind her hand and winks at me. She had faked the phone conversation so well that not only I, a simpleton in such matters, but also the perpetually suspicious Ahmed had been fooled.

"It is easy to lie on the telephone," said the mother a little later, when Lida told her the story. "Sometimes this comes in handy," said Lida.

· · ·

After his house got a telephone, Ahmed found out that he could rile his elder sister, Lida, very gratifyingly with the telephone. Lida keeps in touch with her girl cousins over the phone rather than by visiting them because she and the other girls hesitate to go out. She has many phone calls. When the phone rings while Ahmed is in the house, he will try to be there first. If somebody asks for Lida, he shouts into the receiver, "Who? Who?" pretending not to understand. Or he yells, "Who? Mina?—Sima?—Ziba?—Who?" until the caller gives up or Lida has wrestled the receiver from him. Or else he says, "Lida you want? No Lida here! Get lost!" Or, "I am Lida, what do you want?" Or "Which Lida? We have too many of them!" He has learned this from his elder brother, whom Lida calls the devil of all devils. But while she can only tongue-lash her elder brother, who finds this funny, Ahmed gets scuffed and whacked if she is quick enough to grab him. Her annoyance is well worth the occasional pain for Ahmed. He does not dare to play such jokes on his three big brothers, though, out of healthy and respectful fear (*tars*), they say, a respect no woman in the house commands.

27 · Traders

For several summers Rahmat was the neighborhood boys' envy and inspiration. His father (little land, few skills, many children) had sat the seven-year-old on a little wooden stool in their doorway, next to a battered aluminum tray on which cookies, candies, and gum were laid out neatly in rows, for penny sales, piece by piece. Rahmat was the most tireless, diligent, watchful, and friendly street vendor I have ever met. He also was successful: according to his mother he turned two hundred Toman worth of goods into twelve hundred Toman for his father during his summer vacation—the profit of countless small, slow deals, day after day.

One of the boys inspired by him was Farokh, nine years old, wild, bright, fast, and unruly, and Rahmat's playmate and neighbor. Farokh kept Rahmat jealous company for many long hours in the alley. When Farokh's father denied him start-up capital ("It is all right for Rahmat to sell things in the street, but you want to be a doctor or an engineer, right? If you have free time, study!"), and his mother refused to lobby for him ("You'll get sick from the dust, the dirt. You'll get even wilder than you are already . . ."), he decided to get rich on his own. In the middle of the hot, long summer he broke his bank, a bottle that held all the money he had ever wheedled from his parents, found here and there, gotten as gifts from his generous mother's brother, penny by penny: 140 Toman, a plastic bag full of change and small bills. He took it down to his grandfather's store and bought stuff with it: small cartons with cookies, sticks of chewing gum, a hair baret, combs, balloons, whistles, a toothbrush, odds and ends. In a shaded, dead corner of the alley across from his father's house, a wobbly, dusty, upside-down cardboard box served as a table on which the goodies were displayed. He sat behind his stall on a rock, ready for business. His father let him be. "He'll get tired of it soon," he predicted. The neighborhood children gathered around. Most of his customers were young children. They brought five Rial for a cookie, a Toman for a stick of chewing gum. Business was slow. Combs and toothbrushes were of little interest to his customers. When Aunt Janperi was walking by he called out to her, "Aunt Janperi, buy a comb to straighten out your braids!"

"I am bald, what do I want a comb for?" she answered. News of this exchange made it to Farokh's people in no time, to the great amusement of the whole house. His uncle he tried to talk into buying some cigarettes: "If you smoke, I have cigarettes for you; if you don't, it's time you started, you are old enough!" In the afternoon, he moved with the shade to the other side. Over the hours he learned not only to watch out for customers but also for thieves: he lost a whole box of pink cookies to a kid with quick fingers without noticing the black deed. Now he stored his reserves under the box. In the evening he had grossed fifty-five Toman.

The next morning, he sold two batteries, a ballpoint pen he had pinched from his elder brother's cache of school supplies, and some cookies, when his grandmother walked by. "Grandmother," he cried, "you need a spool of thread to sew your ripped skirt—look at that hole!"

"To lick is better than to wash, to knot is better than to sew!" she quoted the proverb of untidy women. "Boy, who cares about a ripped seam—I want tomatoes."

"I don't have any tomatoes but I have money. How much do you need? Twenty Toman?"

"Dear me, no, what would I want with a donkey's load of tomatoes? Give me five Toman."

"Very well, here you go, God bless you." His grandmother took the money, bought her tomatoes, and at home was full of praise for her grandson's understanding and good manners.

The encounter with his grandmother had left Farokh feeling important and encouraged. "Grandmother didn't have any money," he told his elder sister a little later, "I helped her out." But his sister was less impressed with his generosity than annoyed with the matches she saw on his counter. "Here they are!" she shouted. "You thief, I have been looking for them everywhere at home!" He lost the matches. But later, he scored at least a very good laugh when he enlightened a young man about little round pills he had for sale: "Vitamin pills! They are good for young and old, alive and dead, healthy and ill. You need many!"

Little kids were his most reliable but also most irritating customers. They would come up to him with a small coin in a tight fist, wanting things that cost much more, and were in no mood to listen to arithmetic or to accept a "No." They were tiresome. At noon, when the sun was heating up dust and pebbles in the alley, he stuffed all his things back into the bag and called it quits for the day, with fifteen more Toman.

When he reopened business again, he had replenished the cookies from his grandfather's store, bought three little plastic cars, and added a handful of hard, wrapped candy from a bowl for guests that temporarily and by mistake had not been under lock and key at home. At his grandfather's store, he had asked an uncle why he was buying cigarettes from grandfather instead of from him. This became his grandfather's favorite story for days.

Soon after he had taken his seat on the rock behind his box, a young neighbor woman with her two-year-old son came up to him. The baby had been wearing his mother down, whining for candy in their doorway. He selected a yellow plastic car, a piece of hard candy, and a big round double cookie filled with yellow cream. Farokh figured a price of four Toman for all, but the woman gave him only two. Farokh was courteous and reasonable at first. "This here costs fifteen Rial, this costs five Rial, this costs twenty Rial," he said. But she did not want to hear explanations. "Two Toman are enough," she said. Now Farokh wanted to take back the car. The toddler yelled. His mother said, "Let him be, I'll give you the money later." Farokh took this promise for the little it was worth. "Four Toman, four Toman!" he shouted, as the woman pushed her kid back toward their house. Torn between leaving his store unattended and going after his money, Farokh hesitated a moment, but the big, yellow, unpaid cookie in the toddler's hand close to disappearing behind a door tipped the balance. "The cookie!" he yelled, lunging forward to bar their way. The toddler screamed, pulled his hand away squeezing the cookie tightly—it would crumble any second. At the last moment, Farokh had an inspiration. He put his hand into the breast pocket of his shirt, took it out in a fist, said, "Look what I have here . . ." The toddler, unconvinced, very much on his guard but curious too, looked at the fist, easing the grip around the cookie. In a flash, Farokh had pulled it out of his fingers and was running back to his store. The toddler looked after him with a sour face, but his mother said, "It doesn't matter, I'll buy you another one tomorrow," and pulled him inside. Back on display, the cookie looked a little worse for wear. Two cigarettes were gone. Annoyed, Farokh yelled at his audience to beat it. He whisked dust off his display and arranged his wares. But without the children around him, Farokh got bored. He stuffed his things back into the bag, cookies, balloons, cigarettes, cars, combs, and all, and took it to his grandmother's house for safekeeping until he would be back from playing soccer. There, his six-year-old sister found the bag a little later, rummaged through it and took a red comb and a pack of cookies. In the afternoon, Farokh beat her up for this theft "with hands and feet," as he said with emphasis.

By then, however, he had lost a good deal of his money while playing soccer—the coins must have fallen out of the various pockets he had stored them in, he said. And after he lost the rest of his cookies because he could not withstand the temptation to eat them, his career as a street vendor came to a quiet end.

·   ·   ·

Nine years later Farokh, by now a student short on cash, decided to raise money by selling two big boxes of peaches, which he had harvested from his father's orchard with the help of his younger brothers, and over his mother's objection (she wanted to dry the peaches for winter). The enterprise was a qualified success. Says Farokh: "I thought of everything: I sent this brother to buy a bag of plastic bags. I sent that brother to borrow a pair of scales, and I even thought of the weights (four rocks). I paid my brothers to help me to carry the boxes down to the bus station at five in the morning. The bus was full, didn't want to take me with my load. Our neighbor's pick-up truck took me, for good money. I was in the cab in front, and four, five guys and the peaches were in the back. I swear, they ate five kilos of peaches each on the ride to town, but at least I got there in time for morning rush on Main Street.

"But now the embarrassment started: everybody who ever knew me was walking by and greeted me: 'Doctor Kerimi,' they said, 'Good morning!'—of course they all know that I am a student, and wanted to have their fun: what business does a 'Doctor Kerimi' have selling peaches on Main Street! I was so embarrassed that I found myself a boy to do the selling for me while I just hung out around him. He told everybody a different price and ate five kilos himself. People have no money, it is true. Men would buy only one or two pieces when I asked sixty Toman per kilo, which was cheap compared to what the grocery stores charge. In the afternoon, we were down to three kilos for one hundred Toman. And ever so many peaches went to lousy, raggedy little beggar kids I felt sorry for. By midafternoon I was sold out—now I had to pay the boy. Then I had to pay the bus fare. Then I paid another boy fifty Toman to carry the empty crates home from the bus in Deh Koh. I didn't have the guts to do it myself, make a fool of myself again with a white shirt and shiny black shoes and two wooden crates on my shoulder! But the blasted kid took the boxes to his own house, and now nobody has the nerve to go there and claim them.

"I made 4000 Toman on 140 kilo. I don't know why I didn't get more, though—"

"You'll never make it as a trader," said his mother. "Selling peaches at the height of the season to people who have no money, and paying for every move; all these expenses, and losing the boxes too! 140 by 50 kilo, let's say, is 7000 Toman, minus 100 for the bus, minus 100 for the kid, minus . . ."

This bookkeeping reminded his father of an old uncle who lost all he had in his house to a thief many years ago. The uncle added up the loss: "A wheat bag, 30 Toman; a straw bag, 20 Toman; a salt bag, 5 Toman; a copper pot, 40 Toman . . ." His wife got furious just like Farokh's mother did. "Why do you make it all so cheap?" she cried. "You have to say, 'A wheat bag, 100 Toman; a straw bag, 100 Toman; 400 Toman for the copper pot'"—as if this made a difference to their loss!

And then he remembered the story about what it takes to be a truly smart businessman, in contrast to Farokh: A wise shah once said: "Our city is very dirty because we have too many dogs; we have so many dogs because we have too many cats; we have so many cats because we have too many mice. If we get rid of the mice we'll get rid of the cats and dogs, and then our city will be clean." He put a reward on dead mice to entice people to catch them. The people brought lots of mice but the mouse population didn't go down—

an even smarter businessman was breeding mice in his courtyard. "That's what it takes to be a successful businessman! Farokh better stick to teaching," he said.

28 · Bugs on a String

People in Deh Koh regard wild animals (*junevar*) as dangerous, to be avoided, even killed, or else as game (*shikal*) to be hunted and eaten, and present them as such to children. The wolf and the bear, for example, are considered a threat for people and livestock, of no use other than as scares for children. Animals people keep around the house, such as *heiyun,* sheep and goats, *ga,* cow, *morgh,* poultry, are of great use but dirty (*kassif*), potentially even dangerous, such as a sharp dog, a cat that may be a djenn in disguise, a carrier of germs (*mikrub*). The dog is *haram,* ritually unlawful, polluting, and not to be touched at all. "Dog" and "donkey" are used as abusive terms. In polite speech, these words are avoided or else a disclaimer or apology accompanies them. Where people live in close proximity with barn animals, such as in a summer camp or in a house atop a barn, they do it out of necessity, not choice. A "modern," comfortable, clean house has no animals around.

Barn animals are seen as livelihood but also as wards, as God's creatures that are dependent on people's care. To let a cow go hungry, to kill an animal, indeed any of God's creatures, even a bug or an ant, is considered a sin. Children hear admonitions to this effect and occasionally hear hunters and butchers discussed in terms of this morality. They also hear a farmer dismiss complaints about mice or bugs damaging a crop with, "These animals have to eat too—God made them." To kill a cat deliberately is said to bring years of misfortune. A sixteen-year-old boy who shot most of the members of a large flock of birds that were hunting a neighbor's bees was lauded and was told that it was sinful simultaneously. He described his feat as "mostly good," he said, because he thereby saved his uncle's income from the sale of honey. The help he gave his uncle amply compensated for the sin of killing a flock of birds. Pity (*delsuz*) enters the discourse on animals mostly with women. "Her heart always burns for the cat," a four-year-old boy commented about his mother's occasional offer of leftovers to a begging cat outside, an act he found funny and fascinating. Compassion for animals and empathy with them is a female attribute. Boys and girls both are socialized into the possibility of compassion with animals by observing their older female relatives, but both also learn that it is more fitting for a woman to express it than it is for a man. When a neighbor woman reported on her sadness about an unwanted puppy its owner had buried alive in the orchard— for to kill it outrightly would have been a sin, he had said—her two daughters, ages nine and fourteen, were almost moved to tears and said how much they commiserated with the young dog and with its mother, while their seven-year-old brother, after a few moments of reflection, shrugged his shoulders. "Look at the girls!" he said.

Children in Deh Koh grow up surrounded by animals and with these conflicting attitudes toward them. No matter how fascinating and obviously enjoyable a chicken, a lamb, or a cat may be for a youngster, no term exists for a friendly relationship with an animal. The sight of a kitten following our daughter around because she fed and petted it prompted our neighbors to call the kitten her *rafiq*, mate, with raised eyebrows. Fifteen years later, one of the neighbor women still remembered this unusual relationship with misgiving and blamed it for the persistent visits of a cat that recently had started to slink around the houses regularly: our daughter had accustomed cats to the courtyard fifteen years ago, she said. She made it very clear to the children around her that this was inappropriate and unwelcome.

The idea of keeping pets for company is astonishing, revolting, or hilarious for people in Deh Koh. In government propaganda, with which people in Deh Koh agree in this case, pet cemeteries and money spent on food for dogs in the United States are much-cited signs of moral depravity of Westerners, who put the welfare of mere cats and dogs above the welfare of other, hungry, people. "In America, fathers love their dogs more than their children," a fifteen-year-old girl told me earnestly. The absence of pets in Deh Koh thus makes local people better people than Westerners in their eyes. A few cases of older children being fond of a particular cat, or a young shepherd favoring a dog, or children wanting to pet a lamb, are known in every house but are not elaborated into patterns, and ignored as "childish." Minoo, eight, was unconsolable after her uncle inadvertently squished her pet kitten in the barn door. "Ah, children!" said her grandmother, irritated by the ruckus. "Cry for a cat!" It was a strange story in the neighborhood.

Children are said to like to play with animals, but this play, like so many others, is mostly rough and destructive, seemingly void of empathy. Children do not know any better, people say, but this assumption informs what children are taught. From their first encounters with animals, children are encouraged to hit them, yell at them, shoo them, and/or be afraid of them. The many sounds people use to direct animals, such as *kesh, cekh,* or *gulu* for shooing away chickens, a dog, or a cat respectively, are among the first ones children learn. The joy expressed over seeing a chicken, a sheep, a cow, lambs, thus is linked strongly to aggression and dominance. This reaction is considered expectable, normal child behavior. When he was a baby, Amin laughed with joy at animal pictures and animal sounds, at the sight of a cow or a goat. At barely two years of age, he would stand in the half-open barn door, vigorously shaking a stick into the dark inside while steadying himself at the door post, yelling, "Don't come out, sheep! Stay in, sheep! I'll beat you!" Facial expression, body language, and voice left no doubt that he felt in control over four sheep twice his size. For Amin, as for most other boys, no matter how young, threatening yells were on the tip of the tongue, sticks and rocks always close at hand in encounters with animals.

Fear of animals easily prompts aggression, which just as easily may turn to playful gestures of dominance.

Three boys between eight and ten years of age, who were pushing a heavy wheelbarrow, hesitated to pass a house where a skinny dog with a broken leg had found a shady spot to sleep, half hidden behind a stack of wood leaning against the mud wall. The boys, who obviously were afraid of the dog, after a short indecision pelted him with rocks, ducking behind the wheelbarrow. When the animal finally hobbled away into the doorway, the pelting increased while the boys ran after him, yelling and laughing. When I asked them why they had stoned the dog they said, "Because we were afraid [*sahl imana bord,* it had taken our ease of mind]," and, "Because the dog is dirty and *haram* [polluting, religiously unlawful, synonymous with disgusting in this context]." Fear of harm and provocation of disgust by "filth" are concepts children hear from the time they are babies.

Similarly, two girls of about six stared, paralyzed with fear, at a cat crouching under a shrub about three yards away. After a minute or so, they slowly sidled along the path, eyes fixed on the cat. Before they turned to run, one girl picked up a stick and threw it back. After a few hasty steps, both stopped and, giggling and laughing and obviously having fun, they threw rocks at the bush until the cat disappeared. When I asked them why they had stoned the cat, they said, "Nothing—the cat is bad." Bad children are to be punished, they know—why not a cat?

The link between aggression/control and play in dealing with animals becomes even stronger when fear of animals is diminishing as children get older. Ali, seven, once threatened a young bird that, instead of sitting in the nest he had made for it with grass and paper, had flown into the vine-arbor. "Stay there until I get my sling, hear me?!" he shouted. "I have to kill you!"

If no adults interfere decisively—scolding or pleading alone rarely are enough—goats, sheep, and cows returning home from pasture likely will be teased or pelted with sticks and stones or chased or mounted or have tails pulled by one or another boy along the way, for the fun of it. Chickens are scared, cats chased, dogs stoned, sparrows shot; kittens, bugs, young birds are handled, "played with," until dead.

Children are informed by adults and older girls that mistreating animals is sinful (*gona dare*), that one ought to have pity and compassion (*delsuz*) with all God's creatures, but nobody expects children to heed such admonitions, and rarely is the mistreatment stopped: eventually children will become reasonable anyway and will outgrow this along with other misbehaviors. "Ei, children!" a mother shrugged when her five-year-old son, unimpressed by her "sinful" verdict of decapitating birds, tried to persuade his fourteen-year-old cousin to shoot him another bird with his slingshot so he could cut off its head. (Why? "Beause I want to," he said.)

A seven-year-old girl demanded that her mother tie a string around a young sparrow's legs, which she did, all the while telling her that playing with birds this way was sinful. To "play with a bird," the bird is whirled on the string in a circle to make it spread it's wings, until it is dead. This is a favorite pastime in late spring and early summer.

Only if his or her property is endangered will an adult likely get serious about God's creatures. Furious, a man whacked his grandson off his donkey after the eleven-year-old, riding backwards, had raced the frantic animal through the alley by drumming a barrage of blows on the donkey's behind. "This will stop you laughing, you ass!" the grandfather cried. A little later he was laughing about it himself, though—the sight had been very funny to him, too. "We did it too when we were boys," he said.

Children, especially boys, respond to the simultaneous disapproval and tolerance of their playful-destructive treatment of animals by ignoring most admonitions and commands and by taking calculated risks; mother's talk of sin and compassion "is only good for yourself," a nine-year-old informed his mother at such an occasion, when he was stringing two big black beetles on twine, to swing around for the whirring noise the bugs made. The only effective way to stop children is by violence and threat of violence; grandmother's curses and adept hurling of a log promptly convinced her eleven-year-old grandson to let be the chicken he had been about to catch to "play with."

Like many other young children, the little boy who wanted to kill the uncooperative, disobedient bird ("It won't listen!" he complained) was fond of animals and interested in them. He never missed milking time; he asked questions about the handling of sheep and goats, about cats and mice and birds; he even remonstrated with "bad" boys stealing kittens from their cat-mothers out of nearly inaccessible hiding places if he was not trying to catch one himself. But for a young child, especially a boy child, the few patterns of attitudes toward animals, and the few available choices for interacting with them, are based on fear-agression and the urge to control, and are located within a rough-play context. Explained and justified by the purported intellectual and moral immaturity of children, children learn to act out destructive impulses toward animals much like toward other things, with impunity. They learn that such behavior is sinful and bad in a moral sense, but that this link may be of consequence only for adults. From adults, however, they learn by observation that the economic necessity of domination of all creatures for one's own benefit easily overrides moral considerations.

29 · Stories Children Hear

"People talk and children listen with long ears," a neighbor said when he explained how children get to be well-informed about goings-on in the village. As people summarize, embellish, and comment on daily happenings to each other, children not only get to know what happens but also learn how to tell the stories and how to evaluate what people say and do. Morality, ethics, humor, and manners are compacted in tidy bits of information. In Deh Koh, "Listen . . .!" is the preamble to a philosophical pronouncement; presented in the vernacular language, it is easily accessible to even very young children. Often, children even are the main subject in a story. I selected three as examples for the range of topics, style of delivery, and emotional tone children are exposed to.

Mamalus, on Sending Children on Errands

Mamalus is talking to me in the presence of her twelve-year-old daughter, Banu, and two younger children. She thinks of this story after having accused all girls of today, and especially Banu, of being excessively, yet laudably, *kamri*, shy.

"This morning I saw my cousin Hadi drive his old cow down through the village, he as skinny as she, and I said to Banu here, I said, 'He's going to slaughter his old bony beast.' Because, you see, I know that cow, she was old when I was Banu's age, by my soul, and he just bought a new one in Deh Rud a few days ago, and has straw and hay for only one cow, barely, anyway. It wasn't hard to figure out what he was going to do with a skinny ol' cow on a rope of a midmorning in early fall, poor thing. 'Well,' I said, 'Banu, you go down and get the cow stomach, and I'll teach you how to make sausage.' But Banu, shy as she is and well should be, put up a fuss: 'I'm not going, go yourself.' I was pissed at her and cursed her, but she still didn't go.

"So, after a while of cussing and fussing I went after cousin Hadi myself, and a good thing it turned out to be. Sure enough he had butchered the cow and was selling the tough leather 'n' hides and strings 'n' bones for meat, in my grandfather's old store, the blind hole, dark as the inside of a cow's guts, and so wobbly and leaky it's just about ready to cave in over your head with the next earthquake rumble.

"Well, I step over the sill and I say into the dark—I can't see my hand in front of my eyes, just in from the bright sunlight—'How are you, Uncle Hadi?' I say, and that his good cow was of service to him beyond her death, even if it was a sin to kill her, poor God's creature, and whatever else one says to a cousin who has just slaughtered his grandmother-cow, and did he have the stomach still? 'Yes,' he says, pointing somewhere backwards with his bloody knife. By now my eyes can make out some shapes in the blackness, a pail in the far corner. As I was eyeing it, not seeing it all that clearly, you understand, it looked as if it were moving, by Banu's soul here, just a-jittering and a-rocking to and fro like there was a little earthquake right under the pail, while all else was steady and moving in its own God-pleasing way. I squinted. It moved. 'Mamalus,' I told myself, 'there is no such thing as a pail rocking all by itself, and you better look at something else.' So I look at Hadi again, and at old Nuri for whom Hadi is weighing a piece of cow and who is haggling over the price. Then I glance at the pail again, and it's still jittering—huh! And I think either my eyes are going crazy on me or it's something unwholesome-like. But now Hadi is done with old Nuri. He turns to the corner and gets something out of the darn pail and wraps it into a piece of plastic, and takes my good money. I grab the little package and walk out into bright-glare sunshine. Out in the light I lift a corner of the plastic wrapping, and by the soul of my son and the soul of my father and of Banu here and of your own daughters—that cow stomach was about to walk right out of my hands, it had so many moving parts all over. It was a twitching and tittering mess of red worms. I yelped—'huh, huh,' I cried, and just about fell over backwards into Hadi's dark hole again, holding on tight to that cow-piece trying to crawl away from me.

"'Hadi-brother!' I cried, 'in all my living days I've never seen a stomach run away without the cow, by my soul! I can't use this for a sausage, I couldn't get it home without putting it on a rope! You nail it onto the floor and—with due respect—eat it yourself!'

"And the son of a bitch, poor guy, stood there scratching his head and said he hadn't put the worms into the cow, nor had the worms asked his permission, and it wasn't his doing that cows had worms. But in the end, what could he do, the wretch, but give me my money back to get rid of me and my tongue, and shut the stomach into the pail again. Am I glad I don't know what he did with it in the end! And am I glad I didn't make lazybum Banu here go shopping for me today!"

Huri, on How Children Suffer under Troubles at Home

Huri is talking to me in the presence of three of her own children and two nieces, all under ten years of age. She is illustrating the concept of *qar*, of not being on speaking terms with somebody, in this case, she with her husband.

"The father of these children here is easily riled. He boils over like a pot of milk on a hot fire. The black eyes and arms and back I have had over the years! Just ask my son here . . . The troubles, the tears . . .

"When I ran away from him last, a year ago, it was all about children. This my youngest son here was three months old, rosy, clean, healthy. I walked to the next village with him for the mourning of my mothersister's son who had died in an accident, barely sixteen. His mother was in bad shape—I stayed with her through the afternoon to keep her from crying, from dying of grief. It was an act of charity— we all are good Muslims, aren't we! When I got home at dusk, my children's father stood on the porch with a log of firewood. He yelled at me: 'The children are hungry, I didn't give you permission to stay out day and night, you are shameless, no food is in the house . . .!' He ranted and cursed and beat the wood over my head and my back. I almost dropped the baby. The children cried; everybody was afraid of him. I put the baby down, didn't say a word, got bread and buttermilk and walnuts and onions out, made tea. He left. The children ate. I bedded the baby down, and then I left for my father's house. I just couldn't take it any more. My heart was bleeding for the children— but they are *his* children, *his* responsibility.

"I stayed away for six months. In the end, I went back because of the children. The baby almost died—he is weak and thin yet. These others were dirty and hungry. I came back because of them—what is a mother to do?"

A Man, on Possible Reasons for a Child's Bad Behavior

I heard this story several times, from different people, in different contexts, and with two different moral conclusions. This version came up when the speaker, his wife, and I were discussing the alleged misbehaviors and troubles of several children in the former khans' families. Two of the couple's children were listening.

"In the case of the old khan's children it is bad semen, bad blood, bad milk, and bad example that makes them insolent and naughty [*fuzul*]. Bad heritage makes them a pain for their own people and for everybody else. Their parents had done bad things in the past, it is in their blood. And then they see and hear worse from them and from their relatives, more bad talk, more bad behavior. They learn it.

"Take Hamid, for example—I was there when he told the story, and proudly too: he and his brother were traveling from someplace across the river to here in their pickup truck. The road is bad, not many people live there, it is a lonely woods and wasteland. In the middle of nowhere, they saw a herd of sheep grazing among the bushes, heading toward the road. A shepherd was with them, a kid from one of the small tribal summer settlements or tent camps in the area. Hamid, a grown man with a wife and half a dozen children, mind you, stopped the car under a tree and waited until the herd had crossed the road. And while the kid was up ahead, and sheep and car and people were in a cloud of dust, he and his pal grabbed one of the last sheep, and another one, threw them on the truck, and drove off. At home they were big heroes. They slapped their thighs and laughed. What a good joke! What bravery! They killed the sheep and roasted them, may their bellies burst, and had a big feast. They told their children how clever and fast and strong they had been, that this was something to be proud of, that this was what made a Lur a Lur! Stealing sheep! Like in the old days, when this was a sign of strength. But now—did they think of the poor kid who would be in trouble in the evening for having lost two sheep? Did they feel pity for the people who would spend hours looking for the lost sheep? Did they think of the souls of their own children when they fed them stolen meat? No—they want their children to be strong [*zereng*] . . ."

The other version, identical as to what happened allegedly, puts an entirely different spin on the significance. It takes the thiefs' point of view: the strong take risks; pious talk is for the weak. Children get to know both versions and both moral arguments. The ambiguity facilitates manipulation of ethical principles and provides room for rationalizing one's actions in moral space.

30 · Beauty, School, and Men's Desires

Comments from Within

A boy's good looks are not described in detail; they do not much matter. Even "ugly, crooked runts," Soheila, seventeen, said, will be given a wife. Girls talk about boys' looks among themselves, for no one else to hear, but this is of no consequence at all: girls do not select their own marriage partners.

"Pretty, clean, red-and-white, healthy" (*malus, tamiz, sorkh o sefid, bazhes*), are the most frequently used adjectives describing female beauty directly; many analogies describe it indirectly. Girls say you are beautiful: if your skin is light, but not sickly pale—stay out of the sun, if you can—and without freckles—don't you have a cream against freckles, Khanom?; if your hair is full, heavy and shiny; if your face is like the moon, round but not fleshy, with high cheekbones that do not stick out; if your eyes are big and dark, set not too close to your nose, and framed in black; eyelashes long, eyebrows black, smooth and arched high, like the tattoos of some of the older women; if the nose is straight, not too big, not too small, not crooked; teeth are even and white; mouth is not too big, lips red, but not painted; neck is slim; body is tall but not skinny, rather on the voluptuous side, but not fat either; ankles are firm and slim. Bearing should be straight but not cocky; stride purposeful but not hasty, steps measured. The eyes should be kept down, especially in public, and the mouth closed. A girl who is overly meek, shy, pale, effacing, may be called "saltless," looking the way rice tastes without salt. If she is pretty and uses her good looks, she may be called "salty," and this, too, is objectionable. A girl with a dark-skinned face is called "black," or "burned-and-black," and is considered ugly. Cosmetics such as mascara, make-up, and lipstick can make any girl pretty, but other than occasional mascara nobody in Deh Koh uses cosmetics except women from the city and, nowadays, brides on wedding days. To be beautiful is good, it makes life better for the pretty girl and for those who look at her, but it does not guarantee an easy life. For one thing, it may make the girl proud and others jealous. In a friendly circle of close relatives, a father complained bitterly about his troubles with his two sons. "You say this only because you are old and begrudge them their youth and strength," said his cousin. The father had to laugh. Indeed, maybe it is like that, he said: "Years ago, I was once in the camp of the khan. All the old, fat, ugly women in the camp were sitting there on their thick rugs. A young, beautiful, tall, healthy woman walked by in front of them with a firm stride and head held high, breasts like oranges under her shirt. The old women got jealous: "Get lost," they shouted, "produce yourself for your husband, not for us!"

The father of three very bright, beautiful little girls whom he sees in his dreams at the university, as doctors for sure, thought of this story when I asked him what might keep them from higher education: "In the old days of the khans, Yusufkhan was after every woman he laid eyes on, married or virgin, young or very young or not so young—only the old, toothless bags of bones were safe from him. He strutted around like this—chest out, head high, eyes everywhere, left-right, front-back. And when he saw something in skirts with moonlight skin or big black doe eyes or eyebrows like the antlers of a ram or a tattoo on a wrist, on a heel—well, her father or husband wouldn't have a moment's peace until Yusufkhan, may God punish him, had her. One of his servants had a wife so ugly, so dark of skin and squinty of eye, so crooked and wrinkled and skinny it hurt your eyes to look at her. One day Yusufkhan saw her. He shuddered. He said to his servant: 'How can you stand living with such an ugly woman? It takes an effort to look at her!' Said the servant, 'Nothing against the effort it took me to find a wife I can keep for myself!'"

To which a neighbor woman, a mother of three school-age daughters, added by way of supporting testimony: "The only thing we were truly afraid of as little girls was the khans. If one saw them riding up from their village through the fields, Yusufkhan and his brothers and their riflemen, she would yell, 'The khans are coming,' and we would shriek and run, one faster than the other. We hid in the barns, behind woodpiles, on roofs, in the gardens. I was sitting in a tree once, alone, for hours, not daring to come down because the girls had forgotten to tell me that Yusufkhan had left. He hadn't even been near our house, but still we knew bad things could happen when the khans were around. People said they stole girls, the black death be upon them . . ."

. . .

Two women teachers, themselves mothers of daughters, and the mother of two daughters who had been married before finishing high school, speak for many others: with the girls in high school it is like this now: every day they walk through the village to school, they walk the length of the village back. Yusufkhan is a blind old cripple now, but a hundred other hungry wolves' eyes are on them. No matter how many yards of black stuff they wrap around themselves, some young man or another with lecherous eyes sees the tip of a nose or the sole of a shoe and, overcome with desire (*eshq*) on the spot, wants her. Men's desire prevents a girl from finishing school. Men's desire stands between her and a life of her own. The girls are dragged out of school, one after the other . . . It is their fate . . . Only the ugly ones stay.

. . .

Farhad, a young man of twenty-one, said, "This is my third year at the university. It is time for me to look for a wife—but where? The beautiful girls are gone by ninth grade while they are illiterate children, have no interests, no knowledge. What would I want with an eighth-grader?! My women classmates at the university are either married or, well, they may be good students and good Muslims, but they surely aren't beautiful at all. They are either very short or very long, or dumpy, or skinny, or have pimples, or they have very dark skin, bushy eyebrows, glasses on a big nose; and they are old, at least as old as I am. They also have tongues as sharp as swords, my friends say; I myself haven't talked to a single one, for propriety's sake. Where can I find a beautiful wife I can talk to and who will make life comfortable for me?"

A mother of three teenaged boys counts unfulfilled passion, *eshq*, among potential causes for diseases of the soul of young men, together with "too much studying, hardships of life, and thinking disquieting thoughts."

. . .

Peri, who is sixteen and in tenth grade, is allegedly a sender and receiver of occasional illicit notes to and from boys, and is not very particular about *hejab*, modest dress, either—one of the "bad girls" in school. "We girls have to be very careful on the way to school, "she says. "I never walk alone. The school principal tells us to keep the veil and the headscarf tightly wrapped so that nothing shows, no hand, no hair, for our own protection. It is a bother because the veil-wrap always wants to slip off. 'Don't ever laugh or smile,' she says, 'don't turn around, don't stop, keep your eyes down.' She is right. The boys drive by in a car, on a motorbike, watching us in their back-view mirrors and out of the corners of their eyes. They hide in the dark shops and stare at us as we walk by. They send little boys to thrust a slip of paper at you—a letter from a guy without manners and decency, and next thing you know you are in deep trouble with the principal because somebody snitched on you. And if your brothers hear about it they'll beat you up. And who wants to cope with a dirty-eyed suitor when you are in tenth grade? The less people see of you, the safer you are."

Since Soheila graduated from high school two years earlier, she is studying at home for the university entrance examination. She has walked the main road of the village only once. "I don't want to be seen by dirty-minded guys," she explained, "and not by their mothers either, who are on the lookout for wives for them . . ."

In the fall of 1994, the school administration ordered that even girls in middle school had to wear a veil-wrap in addition to the obligatory dark pants, tunic, and headscarf, "for their own protection," as a teacher said.

When school is out in the afternoon girls walk in bunches, wrapped tightly in their black veils. "Look at the flock of black crows flying home," Mamalus said. Farokh, seventeen, likes to be there with his friends, strolling up and down, watching them flutter by.

·   ·   ·

Some school statistics for Deh Koh are given in Table 3.

A senior female middle-school teacher said, in 1980, that only girls who are not spoken for go on to high school. Their fiancés' families want their future daughters-in-law to have some education but also to be kept out of potential harm's way by being watched at home and taught housekeeping. "It is much better now," a woman teacher told me in 1993, but two of her students disagreed: "People don't let us be," they said.

Table 3
School Enrollment of Girls
in Three Grades in Deh Koh

Year	First Grade	Eighth Grade	Eleventh Grade
1980–81	63	6	9
1982–83	50	32	9
1994–95	78	62	40

Note: Eighth grade is the last grade in middle school; eleventh grade is the last grade in high school.

.   .   .

In 1981, a well-regarded white-beard in Deh Koh said that a girl should quit school after fifth grade and prepare for her God-ordained fate and purpose: to run a household for her husband, to serve him and their children—a great responsibility, this—competently, quietly, with a soft voice and agreeable manners. He spoke for the great majority.

By 1992, he had changed his view somewhat; times had changed, he said. It should be left to the future husband and his family to decide how much schooling a girl should have. His own daughters-in-law, in any case, had just enough learning to be able to help their children with homework. Again, he spoke for many a concerned mother-in-law and father-in-law.

.   .   .

If the streets are dangerous for girls with educational ambitions, classrooms are not entirely safe either, not even in the sex-segregated schools of the Islamic Republic. All unmarried, male high school teachers (for there are not enough women teachers in certain fields) are on the lookout for potential wives among women students, people say, and they can back it up with examples. These young men are looking sharply from under their piously lowered eyelids for the prettiest, smartest girl with the best Muslim bearing, the one who keeps her eyes glued to the books, who does not look at the teacher at all, never is caught with frivolous tap-tap-heeled shoes and sheer pan-

der the obligatory pants, but is clad in black from head to
single hair showing; the one who does not giggle, let alone
one who prays and fasts, and never writes notes to a boy.

Male revolutionary guards and state employees are admonished by
their leaders to marry young so that they can keep their minds on
their jobs and will not be tempted and distracted by every girl they
see. It is very wrong to let unmarried young men teach in a girls'
school or send desire-crazed young men to work among the people,
said Huri, a mother of several sons and one daughter. One of her
sons, a revolutionary guard, married for this reason when he was
seventeen.

This strategy does not always work, though. Married or unmarried, men are full of hot desires, Huri herself says, and often these
desires are ugly and dangerous. She told this story in the presence of
her fifteen-year-old daughter and a younger niece: "A teacher in the
next village, married and with a houseful of children, fell for one of
his girl students in fifth grade; she was eleven or twelve, and very
small. His desire had overpowered his reason, had made him crazy;
he wanted her so badly that he couldn't eat or sleep or teach. He
asked her father for her. The girl didn't want him—she hid in a corner and cried and cried and didn't go to school any longer. Her family refused to give her to him—a second wife! And she so young! But
he threatened to kill any man who ever would ask for her, and kill
her brothers too . . . In the end he didn't leave them a choice, they
had to say yes—and the girl hung herself by a rope that very day."

"He is a heathen," said Huri's niece.

"It was her people's fault," said Huri. "They should have tried
delsehi [black heart–magic] on her: put the fat of a wild boar on her
clothes to make her distasteful to him. Some co-wives are said to do
this to each other. It works."

"It is a sin to do this," said Huri's daughter. "And suicide is a sin
too." Huri's daughter and niece saw no way out of the dilemma. It
seemed nobody had a choice that would not have been a sin. "This is
fate!" said Huri.

.   .   .

Here is what happened to Mahin and Turan and Rudabe (and
Maryam and Golzar and Simin and Mahperi and Homa and Afsar
and . . .):

Mahin. Mr. Ahmadi, from a village to the west of Deh Koh, was a high school teacher in Deh Koh. Mahin was one of his best students in tenth grade. He had a wife and children back home and was very pious and correct. He also had a friend, an unmarried revolutionary guard with the carefully tended black beard of a reliable supporter of the regime, who asked him to look for a wife for him: a religious girl, a good girl, and beautiful. Mr. Ahmadi said that Mahin was the best on all counts. The young man's family came for her from afar. Her father, father's brother, her mother's brother, and all the cousins said no, he is a stranger, Mahin would have to move far away, and anyway, Mahin should finish high school and train as a teacher. But the suitor's people did not let go, they sent a white-beard (*rish safid*), and then a sheikh, a descendant of the Prophet, and they said that it was a sin to refuse one's daughter to good, God-fearing people, that it was a damnable form of pride. When none of her people's arguments worked, it was taken as a sign that it was her fate to marry him. Seven years later, she had five children, lived in poverty because her husband had had one misfortune after the other; not a good fate (*qesmat*), people say.

Turan. In high school, she was the best student in science, the best in the whole province. Her father was very proud of her. He had great hopes for her: university, a good job, a good life in the city, study abroad. Without letting her or anybody else know, he denied several suitors who asked him for her and discreetly discouraged several more potential suitors, for the sake of her future. Her science teacher, a young unmarried man from the city, befriended the family. He visited a few times. Predictably, people started to talk: he wants Turan, they said; no wonder she has good grades. Turan, her father, and the young man became so troubled that Turan's father asked him not to visit anymore. Turan graduated from the university at the cost of several spurned suitors who now are cold toward her father, but for the father it is a price well worth the success.

Rudabe. A suitor, one of her cousins, a teacher, came for her when she was in ninth grade. She was a good student, wanted to finish high school, and he promised that he not only would let her graduate but would allow her to become a teacher, too, and would pay all her expenses. His parents, who have two unmarried daughters and a daughter-in-law at home who help with housework, and therefore did not need her help, supported him—it was a good investment because

Rudabe would get a salary eventually. The arrangement worked to everybody's great satisfaction. Rudabe's cousin and classmate says that Rudabe has the nicest clothes of all the girls, and jewelry too, an appreciative fiancé now and a salaried job in the future—the best of all possible worlds. She has good fortune.

For most young women, the path of marriage will be somewhere between these extremes. The extremes, though, as best- and worst-case scenarios, provide the categories and the patterned expectations girls likely use to think about marriage.

. . .

Comments from Outside

What It Takes for a Girl to Stay in School

The relative rank of a suitor's and the young woman's families may be used to tip the balance of power. The lower a girl's family's rank compared to that of her suitor, the harder it will be for the girl's family to first set and then enforce any conditions of marriage. The higher is the status of the young woman's family compared to her suitor's, the easier, relatively speaking, it will be to deny a proposal, to make a suitor wait, or to stipulate completion of schooling. However, if a suitor elicits the help of a highly respected go-between he can shame even a higher-ranking family into a deal.

"They don't let a girl get anywhere," is a popular complaint in Deh Koh. "They" encompasses young men, their immediate families, and their supporters, whose concentrated efforts only the rare father of a girl can resist. It stands for "the people," as well as for a reasonable, if lamentable, expectation all girls have.

The degree of backing a young woman gets from her father and male close relatives, especially brothers, for her intention to finish school is crucial for her chance to do so. If they back her up, a suitor has to agree to their conditions or else leave. If the suitor is a close relative or a brother's friend or anybody with whom the father or brothers want to stay on good terms, the young woman has no support; she will be "given" or "sold" without any stipulations for the suitor. Mahin, for example, was "sold," her mother says, by two of her brothers, who were Party of God supporters (*hezbollahi*), poor and on the fringe of the more successful, career-oriented youth in the village. They cast their lot with one of their fellow *hezbollahi* although he was a stranger and economically marginal, because he had political aspirations and would, it was hoped, help them in time. (He did.) Mahin's parents were against the match, and for Mahin's education, but were silenced by their teenaged sons. Their daughter became a victim of her brothers' aspirations. This is one kind of "fate" that makes a girl a bride against her will. It is a familiar story.

Turan's two brothers, who saw themselves as educated and progressive types, kept out of their sister's suitors' wooings. Their encouragement for her to study hard for the university entrance examination, however, pointed to another danger: "If she isn't accepted in the university we'll sell her to some old fogey," they said, half jokingly. And after she was done with her studies and still not married, they said, "You are as old as a grandmother now—who'll want you?" Thus, Turan's brothers had laid out the available, unattractive options for her at each turn. But Turan, although annoyed to no end with her brothers, could live with being an old maid, she said; not getting married at all was much less of a terrible fate for a woman with a job in 1994 than it had been even only a few years earlier. Financial independence through a good job opens a new way of thinking about marriage.

The insistence and perseverance of the suitor in the end may overcome all the resistance of a girl's family. There comes a point where all discouragement tricks have been played, including asking an outrageously high bride price, the last "no" has been spoken, all arguments have been spent to discourage a less-than-hoped-for suitor. If he insists still and brings more and more people who talk in his favor, his tenacity is a sure sign that he is a girl's fate. "They did not leave us a choice," the mother of a girl married out of high school said about such a situation. "They" here again refers to the suitor as well as to his supporters, and also to the model of behavior and expectations all four parties, the suitor, his allies, the girl, and her parents, followed in their decisions.

"A club makes a shepherd, fate makes a bride," a proverb goes.

The numbers of suitors and how public their wooing is may influence a marriage decision. Each denial hurts a young man's honor (*abru*). Each spurned suitor becomes a potential adversary of the girl's family. After the third or fourth widely known suitor, or after much discussion of a proposal, a father or a young woman who says "no" yet again risks being reprimanded by their own relatives for being unreasonable and haughty. Such refusal is an embarrassment both for the young woman and her people and for the young man and his people. In a place on the other side of Snow Mountain, a young fellow who was denied his brother's wife's sister on grounds that her father did not want both his daughters married in the same family and far away, even killed himself. A girl's first suitor in Deh Koh darkly threatened the same when she refused him, backed by her mother and her elder brother, on the ground that she did not want a local man because all men in Deh Koh were bad. Another girl's most suitable suitor—most suitable in the eyes of her relatives—when denied by her father on grounds of too close a blood relationship, came home next with a wife from the city, peeved. It took years until the two families were reconciled.

With every rejected suitor, a girl's people are more likely criticized for doing wrong by the young man and by their own daughter: every girl wants a husband and children, suffers under her own unfulfilled desires, even if she cries "no, no" at the prospect of marriage—all girls do, people say; and a girl does not know who and what is good for her. She is easily deceived, she should not have much of a say. Mamalus said, "The end of the world is near when girls give their opinion and fight for their wishes." If a girl stays unmarried too long she will be unhappy, and this, finally, will be her parents' fault.

How long the marriage contract can be postponed may make the difference between finishing school and dropping out. Once the marriage contract (*aqd*) is written and signed, the girl is, people say, "sold." Now it is nearly impossible for her parents to stipulate, or even much influence, what happens to her schooling. It is an often-repeated complaint that promises of continuing studies after marriage are broken as soon as the contract ceremony is over. Parents who try to keep their engaged daughter in school therefore find themselves in a delicate tug-of-war with the fiancé's family: the girl's family wants to stretch the engagement time; the impatient suitor's family wants to shorten it. Every chance they get, a relative's death, somebody's illness, a little dispute over an item in the contract, the girl's family will use to postpone the contract ceremony and then the wedding. There is more or less mild animosity between quite a few families over the alleged delaying tactics of a betrothed girl's family.

If a girl does not want to study or flunks out of school, her formal education is over. Among students, second-chance tests to make up a failed subject in school are very common. A neighbor woman counted thirteen such tests among her four school-age children in 1994. Children also may repeat a class, but a girl is less likely to repeat a class than is a boy. Moreover, girls have much less study time at home than do their brothers. Boys who find unrest or demands on them at home unacceptable can disappear for days in the gardens, or may study in orchards, in quiet streets; girls cannot leave, for reasons of propriety. At best, they may hide in a quiet corner, a storage room or at a grandfather's house for a few hours, but very likely followed by rebukes for "never helping out" at home. Most girls learn early on, and are constantly reminded, that housework ought to come before all else. Schoolwork constitutes a line of duties, set ways of spending time and fulfilling circumscribed expectations and obligations in addition to familiar routines at home.

The eldest daughter in a poor family with seven children and a sickly mother finished high school at twenty; she had to repeat three classes, each time because she had to take over full-time housekeeping when her ailing mother had yet another child. Asked about further education, she just shrugged. "My parents won't even let me marry," she said, "with all the work I have to do at home."

Soheila, seventeen, and her brother Farhad, fifteen, were reading under the vines in a corner of their courtyard. Their grandmother was coming down the hill, shouting from afar, "Soheila, Soheila, what did you cook for dinner? Soheila dear, give me some water—Soheila, do you hear me?!" Farhad nudged his sister with his foot: "Get up, lazybum," he said.

Hasan, fourteen, and his sister Puran, sixteen, were studying for a test the next day, while we and some other people were dinner guests in their house. Hasan showed up only for dinner, while Puran was helping in the kitchen for almost two hours before dinner and was washing dishes afterward.

No one I asked could think of a case where a sister was requested to do the same or less work at home than her brothers. Housework is women's work. Best off are girls who do not have any brothers, girls said in the context of discussing demands on them: at least they don't have to be their brothers' servants. There is no set way, no pattern for a girl to demand time and space for schoolwork, not yet anyway. In each family, the children negotiated their needs and juggled their various duties according to how able and willing elders and siblings were to lighten their domestic duties. Girls undoubtedly had a harder time of it, collectively and individually, and expected this as normal, the way things are. The lower in the birth order a girl stands in the family and the higher the female:male ratio is, the more time a girl has to herself. However, the more older siblings and doting adults she has around her, the greater is the danger that she will be proclaimed "spoiled" and "lazy," and therefore not studying hard either. The same is true for younger brothers too.

Although parents hope that their daughter will have an easy life in her mother-in-laws' house, they insist that their son's wife ought to be subservient. This contradictory expectation has taken on a new twist in the age of education: one's own daughter or sister ought to be allowed, even encouraged, to get an education that may lead to an income that not only will increase her financial well-being but also her value, and with it, it is expected, the likelihood that she will not have to be at everybody's beck and call in her future husband's house. But the son's wife, who actually might be the daughter's classmate, ought to be the traditional helpmate of her mother-in-law, well versed in all housekeeping skills, and inferior enough in education to her husband that she will not get notions of insubordination.

Sara was married recently to a young man whose sister is two years older than Sara, and in twelfth grade. Sara, alone in a room with me for a few minutes, complained, politely but with passion: "My father did not let me go to high school; neither did my husband. I was a good student and liked to study; but my husband's people said they wanted a good wife, not a scholar. I had to quit after seventh grade. I envy my sister-in-law: her brother made me, his wife, leave school, but not her, his sister."

Life after High School

In 1994 young women talked about the possibility that the current intensive government propaganda for birth control and small families eventually would make it more feasible for women to work outside the house. Conditions would also make it more necessary for women to earn money. Young women know that in the continually worsening economic situation in the Islamic Republic, even a small family finds it increasingly difficult to live on the income of one wage-earner, not to speak of maintaining or reaching a middle-class standard of living. More young men and their elders now say they do not mind a wife/ daughter-in-law with a salaried job, even if her job might curtail domestic service. Money a bride brings in the form of a salary is persuasive and silences many a stubborn mother-in-law who would prefer her son's future wife to stay at home after fifth grade. In 1994, every girl in my neighborhood was commenting on the dizzying case of a pair of local young physicians who, every month, together allegedly raked in the equivalent of some eight monthly salaries of a teacher with fifteen years of service. The most common answer girls in grade school and middle school give to the question of aspirations for the future is: "Doctor. Doctors make the most money." Although this aspiration is unrealistic for most of the students, even so-called "lesser" jobs hold attractions now.

A local woman teacher got married and had two children while she attended teacher training college. She lost a year with a difficult pregnancy but finished eventually, and then supported her own family as well as some destitute relatives because her husband was sickly and made little money. Her case is mentioned often and positively by teenage girls discussing their future in the frame of economically hard times. "If she did not have a job the whole family would be hungry," a tenth-grader said.

A young woman who graduates from high school but finds no job and no place for further training will be "sitting in her father's house," as people say, working alongside the other women, disgruntled, maybe, but still "without a worry," until she gets married or is accepted into some training program. And although this may take years (Maryam made it into a secondary education teacher training program after her fourth try, four years after she graduated from high school; one of her cousins was accepted into medical school at her third try), she is provided for by her father, usually without reprimands: a high school diploma does not qualify a woman for any job in the village, and thus no girl with a high school diploma is expected to find work as her brother would be. As to the prospect of studying, the track record of women who made it into the university is not very inspiring; so far, in Deh Koh only four have succeeded in being accepted into medical, dental or engineering school; two more are in nursing programs, a few more in accounting, midwifery, and teaching. For village women high school graduates, this list exhausts the choices. But compared to twenty years ago, the few successes are seen as a dramatic improvement nevertheless.

Some university education for women is deemed necessary by the Islamic government because of the need for women in professions like teaching or medicine to serve female clients in the sex-segregated society. In order to open university education to men and women from lower classes and hinterland communities, a quota system was created for the allotment of a percentage of university slots to candidates from villages and to women. This percentage changes every year. The assignment of university places is administered centrally in Tehran. To qualify for these few placement opportunities, a girl has to have the highest scores in her quota category and be known as ideologically sound and as a good Muslim and regime supporter. Competition is fierce. The few successes in Deh Koh, however, are enough to keep young women thinking of this possibility, and to motivate them to work hard towards this goal. The first local woman who graduated from medical school is the daughter of an illiterate peasant. She had "good luck," said her girl relatives.

Two generations ago, a girl had no choice but to get married, and at a very young age at that: "The earlier she is fed to the wolves, the better," Mamalus remembered people saying then. Over the last decade, the new category of "old maid" (*duar pir*), an unmarried girl over twenty, has been created, and thereby a new identity for young women has become thinkable. As more young men marry outsiders, defer marriage for economic reasons, or leave Deh Koh altogether, more local girls remain unspoken-for into their twenties, especially if they are from a poor family or if they are considered "ugly" or simply do not have supportive relatives who sing their praises and act as matchmakers. They become "old girls," running their mothers' households yet "sitting with their hands in their laps," as a grandmother of two such girls said, confined to their fathers' courtyards because they are afraid of causing comment when seen out in the streets. For the barest necessities they are dependent on father and brothers, for whom they are a financial burden and a slight embarrassment. They are identified and identify themselves by what they have not—a husband and children, a house "of their own." This is considered a pityable state. Of eight such young women I know well, two take psychoactive drugs regularly for "nervous disorders," they say; two are habitual inventors of sensational stories and are called "liars" by others; one complains loudly and bitterly about her life, thus shaming her family; one developed a washing compulsion. "Being unmarried is not good for young women," said a physician in 1994. No subculture has developed for "old maids" in Deh Koh that would define these young women by attributes and activities that are unique to their life situations. Their sisters and cousins and former playmates are married, leaving them behind, as it were, without close companions. Since her cousin and neighbor got married, nineteen-year-old unmarried Ziba only rarely talks to her on the phone and sees her even less often; before, the cousins had seen each other daily and talked on the phone several times a day. Marriage had moved the cousin into a category of status to which a proper, unmarried young woman relative has little access. The attempt of a woman teacher from the outside to organize a mountaineering group for young women and to provide instruction in martial arts in 1993 got off to a very shaky start because it attracted a few older girls from poor families whose participation was more a deterrent than a trend-setter for others. Ziba, who complained of isolation after her cousin and other former companions had moved away, nevertheless rejected these groups as improper for girls of good social background like herself. A couple of unmarried young women learned to sew, a few more attempted to learn to weave rugs, with varying success. Neither skill affords them economic independence.

Most recently, however, several unmarried professional women from the outside—mostly teachers working in and around Deh Koh—and the few women university students from Deh Koh have introduced the notion that unmarried women can exist alone without embarrassment and without being a burden for fathers or brothers as long as they have jobs based on higher education. With the increasing likelihood of becoming an "old maid," the example of these "girl-employees" (*dokhtar karmand*) changes the frame in which young women with educational aspirations place themselves, even if, realistically, in the near future only very few will have the opportunity and the spirit, the *aql* as one of them said, to live lives independent of parents or brothers.

Two urban women medical students in the city, both in their early twenties, unmarried and unspoken-for, told me that they saw themselves primarily as physicians, not as women—marriage was secondary. So far, none of their suitors had seemed to be willing or prepared to accept them as professionals and equal partners, they said, and therefore they had rejected them. "In a year, instead of saying 'old maid,' people will say, 'Madam Doktor.' Who will care whether I am married or not then?" They also were quick to point out that most of their married women colleagues were harrassed (*ajes*, put upon, and *nourahat*, troubled), tired and overworked, and had to rely on the chancy help of reluctant mothers-in-law or some other relatives with housework and childcare. Zahra, an unmarried student from Deh Koh and their neighbor in the dormitory, listened to her urban friends' discussions of their philosophy of life, asked them for advice in the matter of suitors, and observed other unmarried women conduct their own lives. Should her "fate" be to stay unmarried she would not mind at all, she told me. She said this not just to me but also to her sisters and cousins back home. This declaration of the unimportance of the issue of marriage, or even the intention not to get married, is quite different from the protestations all young girls used to make about marriage as a gesture of modesty. The traditional girls' general refusal of marriage and men demonstrated their chastity and naïveté in sexual matters as well as their attachment to their natal family; nobody took it seriously. The new spirit of refusal entails a script for financial independence, even bread-winning capacities for others, living away from the natal family, and finding something to do outside the domestic sphere of action that until now was accepted as natural for women. It is a subversive spirit. Given the code of morality to which these young women subscribe, sexuality has to be denied and refused. The girls do not even want to talk about this matter. "It is unimportant," they say. "Passion is much more important for men than for women anyway."

In Deh Koh, young women like Zahra, few in number as they are, nevertheless furnish models for feeling differently about being a young unmarried woman in Deh Koh. These feelings entail a rejection of village traditions and village men, of a family-based existence. They fit urban, "free" (*azad*) life better. Yet, as "village girls" (*dokhtar dehati*), no matter how well-educated they might be, their chances to be accepted socially in the cities, and of finding a well-educated, acceptable husband there, are expected to be small. Zahra and two of her student-cousins in Deh Koh summed it up: "Men in Deh Koh want a servant, not a wife in the modern sense. They do not want to deal reasonably with a wife who has a job. They are louts. And city men won't marry a woman from a village." In any case, the new aspirations are at odds with the actual, slim possibilities for job training and for the increasingly competitive and prohibitively expensive opportunities to receive the kind of education that makes an independent life possible. However, "nobody can turn back in time," said Mamalus, the feisty, wise old woman. "Now girls say 'No' to suitors if they don't like them, even if it means they won't get married. Their fathers and brothers have to be very strong."

31 · Amene et Al.

The Story

A musical favorite with the wedding crowds in Deh Koh in 1994 was a mating song so heated it was hard to say if it was not maybe a parody of the whole genre, as one bride's sister said. Soheila and Farokh, both in their teens, working the tape deck as disc jockeys, she for the women, he for the men, with a very limited choice of tapes at three weddings of close relatives, played "Amene" ad nauseam. "It's like eating too many sweets," said Soheila's cousin. The singer, a famous performer living, the two disc jockeys assured me, in Los Angeles, is a man with a dark, heavy voice. He is dragging Amene into the bridal chamber by the powers of his trembling vocal chords alone, Soheila said.

She culled the text for me from between long strings of "A-me-neees":

"Amene, Amene"—he moans the name whenever he has half a breath left—Amene, your eyes are my wine-flask, Amene.

"Oh Amene, your aversion is my worry and pain." Sighs, grunts. "Amene—Your rejection has burned my soul, Amene, but you are in my heart still, Amene." Sobs, moans.

"Amene, oh Amene, my heart beats for you, Amene, don't scorn me or my heart will break.

"Your beauty, Amene, has stolen my mind, Amene. Amene, your name is on my tongue always." ("Ha, so we have noticed!" said Soheila.)

"Amene, I'll even take care of your mother, Amene, Amene." Here, instruments carry the pouting Amene away.

"Why would he want to take care of Amene's mother?" I asked, ever the innocent.

"He is so besotted with Amene that he wants to thank her mother for having raised her, fed her . . ."

"Maybe Amene has no brothers, no father, no nobody," said Farokh. "They all died of heartache when they heard him sing."

"No kidding," said Soheila. "I am glad my name isn't Amene. The guys are making fun of the name now. This morning when I heard my aunt call her own little Amene, 'Amene!, Amene!' I had to laugh."

"How do they make fun?" I asked. Soheila squeezed her shoulders up toward her head, tried to speak but had her mouth too full of giggles. Farokh burst into song: "Amene, Amene, your pee is oil for my lantern," he groaned. "Amene, Amene, your braids are stuffing for my pillow . . ."

"Your soapy bathwater is my yogurt and buttermilk," elder sister Hakime fluted from somewhere.

"Your—eh—breasts are volleyballs in my hand," Farokh was in falsetto now, bellydancing.

Soheila, clapping her hands to Amene's rhythm, was swaying. "Amene, Amene, your lips are my chewing gum . . ."

"Amene, your panties are in my bed . . ."

"Filth, dirty-minded . . .!" elder sister shouted but there was no stopping now. The next verse moved down Amene's anatomy to somewhere below her midriff. I thought I could make out some interesting words in the screeching but nobody was bold or able enough to repeat them for me later. "Filth, dirt, all men are dirty!" elder sister shouted. Little Jamal had joined the party, drawn by the magnet of hilarity. He liked the couplet with the chewing gum: "Your lips are my chewing-bubble-gum," he yodeled, hopping and clapping. "Your big nose is my bubble-gum . . ."

"Yecch, YECCH!"

Amene was finished.

At the next wedding, Soheila said, she would push this song:

> "The night is full of stars; flutter your eyes at me.
> I want to dance with you. You set my soul afire.

I want to be with you—your looks incite my desire.
I am singing from evening to morning."

This song is full of passion too, but the object of desire is nameless.

Context 1

Such pop songs are imported from the city, sung in Farsi. They are pilfered from videos and tapes that are smuggled in great numbers from abroad, especially from Los Angeles, the hub of international Persian popular music. For many years, this music together with most other, including traditional Lur music, was outlawed in the Islamic Republic as corrupting the hearts and minds of people. The view of life disseminated in the Islamic Republic by all arts, such as they were, suggested that life in this world is painful, a constant struggle against evil, sin, enemies, injustice, and imperialism, that death is a gateway to a place of leisure, to a lush garden where pure women provide pure sex, where pain, impotence, and death are unknown. In Deh Koh as elsewhere, no "noise" at all was made at weddings for years. Drums, oboe, singing voices were silent. Since the end of the Iran-Iraq war, people say, the official ban on music has been enforced less strictly, although it is repeated year after year at the beginning of the wedding season in midsummer. Now, cheap tapes are available everywhere. Traditional Lur songs—with single-minded and rather explicit lyrics, but with a wide range of imagery and metaphors, and no name-fetishism—coexist with pop music. "Amene" in particular was forbidden for a long time, the young people say, until a mullah reportedly pointed out that Amene was the Prophet's mother's name and the song was honoring her, in a way. Now it is tolerated, wine-flask and all.

Context 2

Between 1965 and 1994, I recorded close to one thousand traditional folk songs in Deh Koh, including those sung by women, or by men and women alternatingly at weddings for entertainment and for dancing. Some six hundred verses sing of desire and other relationships between men and women.

The lyrics are straightforward, simple commentaries on the world of the senses, realistic and down-to-earth, with miniature paintings' attention to setting and detail. In an essentially pleasant landscape of mountains, cool springs, meadows with sheep and game, people are placed between youth and old age, friend and foe, wealth and poverty, joy and pain, life and death, linked by passion for women, hunting, and fighting, which defines the speakers as men. In these passions joy and pain, life and death, merge. The essence of being alive is defined as the youthful dare of one's mortality; those who cannot or will not face the challenge, that is, the old, the poor, and the timid, are dismissed as inconsequential, as standing in the way.

> Scraggly-bearded, toothless old man,
> You can't kiss her anyway; let me have her!
> Did you see the old man's hand on the girl's navel?
> Babbling old man, get up from the girl's side!
> Rifles have ten shots, mine has only one.
> People don't give me a wife because I am poor.

The passions for women, hunting, and fighting, full of danger, pleasure, and pain, constantly intersect: the beauty of young women ("flowers" in the lyrics) arouse sublime pleasure but also may entail severe pain, derangement, even death, just as hunting and fighting do.

> I put my hand into the butter sack to take out butter.
> A snake bit my hand and I writhe with pain . . .
> She swings her hips on purpose to make the boy die.

Metaphors and similes are quite clear on this connection: a young woman's moon-face, antler-eyebrows, doe-eyes, blood/snow-skin, laughing lips, white teeth, slim neck, slender body, firm breasts, swinging hips, white ankles, may make a man sick, blind, restless, may fell him as if hit by a bullet, may destroy his sanity and his liver. In only six verses is beauty beneficial; it brings a man back to life. Young women are like game to be hunted, like birds to be trapped. Their paths may be blocked, their possessions, such as lips or the "butter" between their breasts, may be raided. An unmarried young man is called a hungry wolf.

> Last night on the mountain pass I ran into her.
> I raided her lips and stole her breasts.

Yet, spoiling for a fight with a potent rifle, for the playful conquest of a beautiful young woman, surrounded by flower-dotted mountain meadows, clear brooks, makes for the thrill of a life worth singing about.

No equivalent admiration and enthusiasm is expressed in the songs for the beauty of boys and men. A man's charms, rather, according to the songs, lie more in what he has and does than in his looks, although dark skin and old age are singled out as repulsive: skilled hunters are praised, as are brave fighters, wealthy and esteemed leaders.

Curiously, none of the objects of male desire in the poems ever cry "wolf." They do bemoan the absence of a lover, or his poverty, but not his close and intense admiration of their bodily charms from eyes to ankles. No protests accompany a girl's implied willingness to disappear behind a tent with a young man in amorous condition ("drunk"), to wink at him, even visit him clandestinely. Such interactions between young people of the opposite sex in songs is in as stark a contrast to both postulated and actual behavior in Deh Koh as is Amene's suitor's wooing. "That's what men *want*, ha!" said a bride's mother, identifying the love songs as the wishful thinking they probably are. However, the people who compose, sing, and hear these songs with obvious pleasure are in touch with their feelings, even if they have to create a romantic dream world to express them.

The world of this poetry is a heroic dream world of young men. Only about 20 percent of all verses deal with the world of women. This is the more remarkable as women sing these songs more often than men. Without the slightest hesitation they wish, in first-person narrative, "three things from God: a horse, a rifle, and a brown-eyed girl" and the like. Young women's desires are acknowledged, although nobody goes so far as to call a girl a hungry wolf, but a young woman cannot express those desires as freely and as sensuously as can a young man. Her desires have to be channeled into life as a bride. For her, courtship is tagged as fraught with anxieties; marriage can go wrong easily. The only unequivocally satisfactory relationships for a young woman, according to the verses, are with a mother or a sister. With a young daughter, a woman is likely to feel pity, with a son, pride mixed with annoyance.

By the time young women sing these songs or play the tapes, they have internalized many messages about passion and about their place in the game of desire (passion-play, *eshq-bazi*); the messages in the songs are nothing new for them: men stalk young women, the more likely so the more beautiful they are, and go crazy over them. Girls find safety in numbers and by hiding at home, behind relatives. The verb "to hide" is actually used in this context. Men's attention, other than the proper attention of a fiancé, is annoying. But then again: "Where would we women be if men didn't want us?" said a singer when I discussed traditional song lyrics with her and some other singers. Girls' and young women's attractions for men are their strongest asset, girls learn. With them, the temperamental Amene had her man dancing on an emotional string, and every expensive bride affirms this truth.

Context 3

The traditional folk songs and the new pop songs can be used to dance to, but in different ways. The traditional tribal dance is danced in a circle by women, preferably outside. With small, dignified forward-backward-sideways steps, women and girls of all ages move in a circle, rhythmically swinging scarves in both hands, and ever so slightly swinging their hips. The wide skirts of the traditional costume amplify the most delicate moves. Different rhythms and melodies require different steps and arm-movements. For the purpose of dancing, instrumental music is much preferred over singing. In the past, men could join the circle, jumping around and swinging scarves vigorously and with abandon.

The new dances that accompany pop songs are danced by women alone. Men are not even allowed as spectators. They are modifications of belly-dancing: women dance solo or in pairs, gyrating shoulders, hips, arms, and hands. This dancing was introduced by city people. In Deh Koh only some bold outsiders or certain older widows who like to play the buffoon dance this way. Girls, especially those of marriageable age, "don't have the 'face' (*ri*)," the courage, to dance; they are "shy" (*kamri*), properly embarrassed, ashamed of such public display. After the strict enforcement of the moratorium on all dancing in

Deh Koh during the past fifteen years, recently at some wedding parties women started to form small dance circles again, as allowed by
the indoor space to which all dancing now is confined. Boys crowd
outside around the windows to steal a look, until somebody inside
pulls a curtain. Girls only dance the traditional dances in the company of older, close women relatives, to taped music, trying to learn
the steps from their mothers and aunts, who had been accomplished
dancers by age five. There is quite a generation gap in the ability to
dance.

Traditional dancers ought to be dressed in festive tribal costume,
several very wide colorful skirts worn on top of each other, a preferably glittery tunic-like shirt, and a large scarf of sheer fabric, covered
with sequins. It requires dozens of yards of expensive fabric, thus
putting a heavy strain on anybody's budget. Girls, who have to dress
in uniform-like dark pants-tunic-coat outfits in school, rarely own a
tribal costume at all. Hoda, eleven, in pants, short skirt, and sweater,
hunted in several houses for pieces of a costume, at least a "decent"
scarf, so she could join a late-evening dance circle at her cousin's
wedding, but then urged the blue-golden scarf an aunt had lent her
onto her mother because Hoda was "ashamed" of her mother's "ugly,
poor" tribal dress. She and two other girls watched the pretty dancers
from a corner of the room, clapping and hopping gently in place.

32 · Lions Worried

I do not know of a boy who did not finish high school or who inter-
rupted his studies because he got married. Rather, in some cases,
prior to a young man's departure for studies or training in a city his
parents may try to find him a local wife, if for no other reason than to
make sure he will not take a wife in a city and stay there. A local wife
ties a young man to Deh Koh, boys learn listening to their elders.

Boys who drop out of school do so because they do not study; they
do not study because they are *tambal*, lazy, or *vellou*, flighty, loafing,
irresponsible, in an aberrant state of mind. They hang out with
equally useless boys, roaming the wilderness like restless lions, as the

sister of one such boy said, or aimlessly, lazily moving here and there in search of entertainment; they not only do not listen to their parents but talk back to them with foul language; they sleep late, wear fancy clothes, play soccer while their fathers are toiling; they smoke, disappear for days or weeks in town so that the father or an uncle or a brother has to go after them; they joke and laugh for no good reason—one can hear them in the gardens of a mellow evening. It is like an affliction, like a disease, or maybe like being drunk, people say.

A mother said about her nineteen-year-old son: "He was *vellou* for some five years. In winter, instead of going to school, he and his dirty friends stole firewood, tea, sugar, lugged it up through the snow to an overhanging rock high above the gardens. They built a snow wall to keep out the wind. They sat in the shelter around their stolen fire and had a blast of a good time smoking, slurping tea, and looking at naked women in a magazine." (The smoking was betrayed by a package in his shirt pocket and by his smell; the glossies his sister found by chance.) "What else the boys were doing in their hideout is anybody's guess—they aren't telling."

A neighbor described the *vellou* son of a very poor man in Deh Koh: "He flunked fifth grade at age thirteen but wanted to go to middle school anyway. The clerk in school said, 'I'll sign you up if you bring me seven hundred Toman.' The boy said, 'Why would I want to go to school if I had seven hundred Toman? I'd buy cigarettes and have a good time!' When his father asks him to help irrigate a field he says, 'Why did you sow it?' If his mother asks him to get heating oil from the storage drum he says, 'Why should I get smelly hands? You want to cook, you get it yourself.' He is home only to eat and to sleep, his troubled mother says."

Mohsen's story is well known in the village: he became *vellou* when he was a lad of ten and is *vellou* still at seventeen. When he was nine, he disappeared from home; together with another boy he walked up to the pass on Snow Mountain, where he ran into his mother's brother, who didn't believe him when he said he was to meet his mother on her return from a pilgrimage. The uncle loaded the boys onto his truck and brought them back to the village. There, Mohsen hid in the gardens all night, watching his family look for him with lanterns, too frightened of the dark to run away, too afraid to go home and face the sure thrashing.

A few years later, when he was about fifteen, he and his equally useless pal started to steal chickens to roast in somebody's orchard. His buddy flunked out of school, but Mohsen, a very bright and observant young man, is still getting passing grades although he plays hooky whenever he feels like it. Nothing seems to help: not the police (an irate neighbor denounced him for trying to steal a bike), not good words from his uncles, not beatings and punishments meted out by his father and brothers, not his mother's sorrow and tears . . .

A government employee tried to cure his *vellou* son by giving him a wife. This did not help. The young school dropout continued to steal money, to have fun in the city, to loaf. His wife left him after only a few months and went back to her father, with her embarrassed in-laws' consent, and pitied by all.

Vellou is like an affliction, people say, a state one hopefully grows out of, eventually. It has its roots in an underdeveloped rationality, *aql*, a condition peculiar to boys, caused or at least aggravated by the lack of fear, respect, *tars*, which in former times was instilled in boys at an early age by a father's firm hand, by the demands of hard physical work and obedience, and through timely and vigorous punishment of disobedience and laziness. Times have changed, though, older people say: *vellou* is a sign of our times, of parents' lenience toward their children, of a general lack of *tars*, the wholesome fear without which social ties eventually will break down. The young people agree that times have changed, but they draw a different conclusion: "You just don't understand anything," a recovering *vellou* boy of eighteen told his grandfather. "If you want the old times back, then give me your television set and your radio, and sit in the dark!"

Parents have to have patience and many firm and kind words in dealing with a *vellou* son. A boy at home, no matter how vexing, still is better than a son who leaves altogether. Many young men have left ("fled") over the years. Some surface months or years later, others are never heard of again. Why they leave or left—"to flee" has a long tradition for young men in Iran—is one or another variation on a simple story: they are disgruntled, they had a fight with father, with a brother, they cannot stand life at home anymore.

One such young man, after finishing his military service in 1986, came home to get married and settle down. Within days he got into a fight with his mother over her choice of a wife, left in a rage, and has not been heard from since. "He was angry," his mother explains. "Angry boys run away, they don't know any better." She sees him in her sleep, she says: he is all right.

A father said that in 1970 he beat up one of his sons because of his bad grades in school. Next morning he sent the son to town to buy motor oil for the mill. The lad, who was about sixteen, left with the money for the oil, never to return. "I should have known," said the father twenty years later.

A boy was so troubled and shamed by rumors of his father's alleged adultery that he disappeared for two years when he was seventeen, said his aunt. Not only for the unhappy boy but also for his aunt, his flight was a reasonable, if unfortunate, course of action.

In 1960, Mamalus' youngest brother was working with her husband in a port city. He was "a mere child," fourteen maybe. Already unhappy about the reign of terror of the khans and about oppressive poverty at home, he flew into a rage when his sister's husband ordered him to wash their clothes, and left. Thirty years later, he came back for a visit, unannounced, with a wife and four children, telling a long tale of ups and downs as a kid in the street who made good in the end.

Amene's youngest brother had run off after a fight with his elder brother when he was eighteen. Four years later, he wrote letters from abroad. His family was sad and upset about his flight, but nobody really was surprised.

For most boys who stay in Deh Koh and are more or less *aqel*, reasonable, rather than *vellou*, life is not easy either. "Jobless graduate" (*diplom bikari*) describes the large and growing group of young men—in Deh Koh the term is used for men only—who graduated from high school but cannot find a job or a place in an institution of higher education. While women high school graduates are "sitting at home awaiting their fate," as Masume said—Masume who, however, does not get to sit much but is working hard running her mother's household for her—male "jobless graduates" are in an even more awkward position. According to the villagers, they tend to value themselves as too educated and refined for menial jobs such as farming, brick-making, or construction. Most of their parents agree; the boys ought to aspire to white-collar status, the middle-class life of the cities. On them rest their parents' hopes for an easier life. Widow Huri went so far as to take care of her small vineyard herself so as not to instill the idea of farming as an occupation in her high school–

educated sons. Although this was "going too far" in the eyes of her neighbors at the time, the eventual success of her sons proved her right, they say now. If such a young man does work with his hands he makes sure his effort is valued as an exception: Ebrahim, two years out of high school, filled in for his seriously ill father at the apple harvest for a few days so that his father would not lose his job as a picker. As soon as his father could work again, Ebrahim donned a clean shirt and walked around with a book under his arm, his usual attire.

Irej worked off and on at odd jobs in harvesting and construction during his second jobless graduate summer to earn money for the fancy clothes his father could not buy him, and to have some fun money, as he said, for his planned visit to the city while waiting for the next round of university entrance examinations. He was truly upset by his "poor clothes," which mocked his achievement in school and his status as a potential university student, he said.

In an English textbook used in high school in 1993 was an essay about this topic; our country, it said, has too many young educated people who do not want to work with their hands. Our country needs fewer such people and more who do not mind getting their hands dirty. Maybe higher education should not be a goal for all.

Boys who drop out of school, however, do not have many attractive choices: unskilled manual labor is hard, underpaid, and not reliably available; white-collar jobs are not available unless one has at least a high school diploma; learning a trade is difficult unless one has help from relatives; capital for investment in a business is scarce; low-level government jobs pay very small salaries; farming provides a livelihood for fewer and fewer people. Considerable pressure is put on young men to finish high school, and to do well in school, by parents of all socioeconomic backgrounds.

Rarely does a young male student feel the kind of pressure to get married before he finished his studies that his sisters may feel. His problems, rather, are to find a suitable wife, to persuade his parents to help him find one, and to get her for him (literally, "to make a wife ready"), and to raise the enormous funds necessary to meet the expenses. A man's marriage expenses include gifts of clothes, food, small appliances, etc. to the future fiancée's family, marking the acceptance of his proposal of marriage, and gifts at visits to the fiancée's house. Not only the fiancée but also her father, mother, brothers, sisters, and other relatives ought to get gifts of clothing and/or jewelry occasionally. From the time of betrothal, and certainly after the marriage contract is signed, the groom and his family also have to pay the bride's room and board to the bride's parents and have to pay any other expenses the bride might incur, such as clothes, tuition, school expenses, doctor's fees, and travels.

The signing of the marriage contract, which in the past had taken place while the wedding was going on, since about 1985 has been elaborated into a celebration of its own, rivaling the wedding feast. This custom, imported from the city, is deplored deeply by a groom's family, but then supported, even insisted on, when the same family's daughter is getting married.

What formerly was the bride price, a sum of money with which the bride's father bought the essential furnishings for the young couple's household, since about 1985 has been turned into the custom of the "list": the bride's family submits a list of demands for household goods which the groom and his family have to buy. Depending on the economic circumstances of the two families involved, such a list may include the bare necessities of bedding and cookware or else may include the demand of a house, furniture, refrigerator, television, and washing machine. At the wedding, these items are displayed.

The groom has to pay for the wedding feast at both houses, his father's and his fiancée's father's. He has to pay for the bride's white, Western-style wedding dress and for her elaborate make-up at a beauty shop, a process Soheila calls "putting plaster on the bride," which she claims renders a bride unrecognizable even to her own mother. In 1994, this alone cost the equivalent of a teacher's monthly salary. At the wedding, the bride expects gifts of gold, such as bangles and a set of matching necklace, earrings, and ring.

"For the next five years my salary will go toward paying off the marriage-debts," a new young husband said. "And this does not take into account what my father paid and provided." While "getting a wife" always was a relatively great expense for the groom and his family, now, with the changes in lifestyle and high inflation, the expenses have become prohibitive.

Farokh, a university student, confided in me: "I really want a wife soon—my desires interfere with my sleep, my studies. But when I say, 'Father, what about so-and-so's daughter, I like her,' he gets mad at me: 'First you amount to something, stand on your own feet instead of eating my bread, and then we'll talk about a wife for you,' he says. He doesn't understand how unhappy I am, how lonely. Several of my classmates are married. Why can't I have a wife?"

This is the story his father likes to tell at this occasion: "When my fatherbrother's son wanted a wife his father said, 'Here is a rifle, go bring meat.' The boy went hunting, one, two, three days—he brought back a mountain goat and a couple of partridges. 'Now give me a wife,' he said. His father shook his head. He gave him one Toman and said, 'Go make a hundred Toman out of this one, then you'll be ready for a wife.' My cousin left home, bought some tin stuff, sold it upriver, bought butterfat for it, sold it in town, got clothes, sold it here and there, bought, sold . . . And when he had made a hundred Toman, he came back home and his father gave him a wife."

Farokh is sick of this story.

Young men like Farokh know that getting married means shouldering the responsibility of supporting a family. In traditional agricultural times until a generation ago, when sons shared work and life with their fathers and, for a time at least, with their brothers, this duty was relatively easy to fulfill. Now that more and more young men's livelihood depends on income from a job or a business, the responsibility of support of a wife and children weighs heavily on their own shoulders. "I don't know how I ever will be able to get married," a young policeman said. "I don't even have enough money to keep just myself alive." And another young man, a government employee, after discussing the high costs of living, pointed to his friends, all in their late twenties, and said, "We all will get old as 'boys'." If a father or elder brother cannot help out, getting a wife will be a protracted process. For a student, without his father's financial help, marriage, even betrothal, will have to be deferred until the young man has graduated and found a job.

The annual university qualification examination (*konkur*) is a national trauma; in 1994, more than a million young people competed for fewer than 130,000 openings in the so-called state universities, which are tuition free, and in the new tuition-based so-called free universities. Every year in early fall, after the placement lists are published, there is so much crying and moaning by the disappointed young people in the air that one feels like crying, too, said a mother of four aspiring university students.

Irej got into a university after his third try, but not into the lucrative field he wanted to study. "I'll be twenty-seven by the time I will be done, God willing, and then will have such big debts and such a small salary that it will take me ten more years before I can think of getting married, unless my brothers help me." For young men, passion-filled as they are said to be, the modern deferral of marriage for reasons of prolonged education necessary to make it economically later is a hardship, a bitter price to pay for progress. In addition to the responsibilities that go with marriage, young men today likely will have to help with the costs of the education and the procuring of a wife for their younger brothers, and with the education for their unmarried sisters.

At her second try, Parvane, at twenty, was accepted into a regional so-called free college in the nursing program. Her father and brothers took loans to pay the sharply increasing tuition for the next four years. Given the low salaries for nurses, Parvane calculated for me that it would take her the total anticipated salaries of four years of working as a nurse if she had to pay back the tuition loan. "They are crazy," said her grandmother. "All that money for a daughter! When the only one to benefit will be her husband! They should have let a fiancé pay for her schooling." This would have been very welcome, Parvane's brother agreed, but no one showed up who was willing to invest in the "Parvane Bank."

"I have four younger brothers and sisters, and they all are good students in school," said an eighteen-year-old first-year university student gloomily. "My father will not be able to pay for them as he does for me. It will be up to me to get them through the university." Just as Parvane's elder brothers took responsibility for their younger sister's education, so this student already is programming himself into the mode of the elder brother's financial responsibilities for his siblings.

For young men with a high school diploma and a few connections, some jobs are available in banking and administration, especially for active regime supporters, but most of the jobs pay too little to support a family. Failing placement at a university year after year, the young men are thus caught between the economic hardships of their father's farming or small business existence or of underpaid blue- or white-collar workers and the increasingly faint hope of getting accepted at a university. One sees them in the streets everywhere: well-groomed young men with carefully pressed shirts, black pleated trousers, shiny black shoes, serious faces, and nothing much to do.

Said a heart specialist in a city in 1992, "Never before have I seen so many young men with heart problems, strokes, signs of severe stress, nervous heart conditions." And a physician in the district town said in 1994, "The mental health of young people, especially of young men, is very bad. Many young men are on drugs, legally or illegally so. They see no future. Many cannot even get married because they have no money, no job, no land."

In Deh Koh, people say, the youngsters are relatively well off—at least their families support them. No one goes hungry, everybody gets a wife eventually, no matter how hard it may be for the parents. But worries are high among parents, too. No father or mother wants to be remembered by this mourning song: "My life's work isn't done—neither have I given away my daughter nor have I provided a wife for my son."

33 · Teen Wisdom

The following lists contain items discussed in the previous chapters and others that came up when I asked young men and women about their lives and while I listened in to their conversations.

What Girls Know

Women have smaller brains than men. Therefore they can't study as well, and only a few are able to become physicians, for example, or scientists.

Girls' reason (aql) develops faster than that of boys. This explains why girls study harder and get better grades, why they are more responsible and not vellou, and also why they can do a lot of housework and study at the same time, if need be.

It is hard to find time to study at home, especially if you have a lot of younger siblings.

Most high school girls are just biding time until marriage. Only a few are serious students.

Men are after girls, it is their nature. Beware, especially if you are pretty and from a good family.

It is dangerous to be beautiful, unless you want to marry young.

It is a great burden to be ugly; nobody will want you, not even your own parents, and not your teachers either. You will get bad grades in school and no suitors.

All girls say: "I won't marry, ever!" But then they all do. It is their destiny. It is their duty. And it is embarrassing not to get married when all one's sisters and cousins and schoolmates are married.

Once you are married, forget studying.

Yet: many women university students are married. They are from cities. Things are different for women in cities.

Some women in the cities refuse to marry. How ever do they manage?

Parents are likely to sell you, sooner or later, no matter what they say to you and no matter what you say.

Beware of your elder brothers' friends. One of them might want you, and your brother won't say no to him.

If you are well-educated you find village men boorish, but no city man will marry you, a village girl.

Most of your playmates will be married by age sixteen and stay young, while the girls in high school are getting old.

If you find a job and have a husband and children, you are going to kill yourself working, working, day and night.

If you are educated and have a job, men will want to marry you for your salary.

Girls who allow boys to look at them and look back at them and write notes are bad but they have fun, too.

Their fun, though, isn't worth people's talk; once a girl has a certain reputation no good man will want to marry her.

A bad girl ruins her family's honor; especially brothers are sticklers for this kind of honor, no matter how *vellou* they are themselves.

Girls think of work and school and home and what people say. Boys think of girls.

It feels good to sit around with other women and talk, to be at a wedding feast, to go on a picnic with others, to wear nice clothes, to be in the bath, to listen to music, to visit relatives, to travel, to drink tea, to laugh about jokes, not having to work, to be praised by a teacher.

It does not feel good to be sad, to have a lot of work, to be alone, to have others talk bad about you behind your back.

Keep hoping that, God willing, what you want actually will be your fate.

If things don't work out at all, you can always kill yourself.

What Boys Know

Men have superior mental powers; intellect guides emotions. Girls are driven by emotions, are weak, and therefore ought to obey. That they don't obey shows that they are intellectually inferior. That few of them get high school diplomas shows that they are intellectually weaker than boys.

Women are in the world to take care of men and their children. Some women also are capable of doing good work and bringing a salary.

Educated, salaried women are sloppy housekeepers, and not obedient. They talk back and fight.

Boys long for girls. This is natural. Boys are easily excited. Girls who long for boys are bad. Girls who make boys excited are bad. Boys can go crazy with passion.

Rich men can afford more than one wife, but the wives likely will quarrel.

Boys move everywhere. Girls stay at home or move in groups. This is a pity, except if they are your own sisters.

A boy has to watch over his sisters because they are weak and prone to be foolish around boys. If they are stubborn you have to beat sense into them.

Sisters sometimes gang up on you, and you might end up washing your own shirts and socks.

Boys are thinking of girls much—always! Nobody knows what girls think about.

A man has to take care of his family. This makes him the boss of the house.

Fathers and elder brothers call the tune at home. They fight with you often.

Your father and brothers likely will keep you from getting married when you want a wife, but eventually they will help you.

Studying is hard work, and getting good grades in school is nearly impossible, but only if you study can you get a good job and a beauti-ful wife.

It is useless to study. Only businessmen make money. Why study? Villagers are poor. If you want to become rich, go elsewhere.

City girls probably are better and more beautiful than village girls, but they are demanding and don't want to live in a village.

It feels good to have money in your pocket, to loaf, to travel to the city, to talk to other boys and men, to listen to music on tapes, to watch American videos, to learn karate, to hunt, to smoke, to watch girls, to walk around the village in good clothes with books under your arm, to play soccer, to have a fiancée, to be invited to dinner parties, to "play" at weddings.

It does not feel good to have no money, to have others laugh at you or make fun of you because your pants are torn or your shoes are down at the heels; if your father is mad at you; to be angry at some-body; to have to study hard.

If things don't work out you can always leave Deh Koh.

Appendix

Glossary

Appendix

NAMING PRINCIPLES

Here are some examples of the application of naming principles.

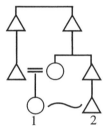

Figure 3

Number 1 is engaged to 2. She is his fathersister's daughter and also his father(father)brother(son)'s daughter. Same-sex intergenerational links often are telescoped. For her, he is both an elder fatherbrother's son, i.e., a *tata* or *kaka*, and an elder motherbrother's son, a *halu*. By not addressing him or referring to him at all she avoids a decision. He calls her by name, refers to her by name or as fatherbrother's daughter, emphasizing the patrilineal connection.

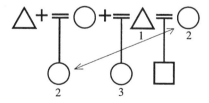

Figure 4

Number 3's father's wife is also her sister; 1 and 2's children are her siblings but also her sister's children. Number 3 refers to them as her siblings:

303

their relationship to 3's father overrides the relationship to her sister. They are *his* children.

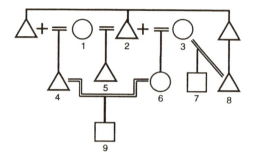

Figure 5

Number 1's first husband died. In a levirate marriage she became a second wife to her dead husband's brother (2). When he died, his first wife (3) married his brother's son (in a variant levirate marriage). Numbers 4 and 6 contracted a fatherbrotherson/daughter marriage. For 5, this means that his brother got married to his sister. For 6, 8 is both her mother's husband and her fatherbrother (she calls him fatherbrother, *tata*); further, for 6, the children grouped under 7 are siblings as well as fatherbrother's children (she calls them brother and sister). The children of 4 and 6, (9) may call 7 either fatherbrother's children or mothersister and motherbrother; etc.

Factors like spatial distance, actual contact, and age/status difference determine the choice of terms. The children grouped under 7, for example, call those grouped under 9 by their first names without a second thought because they are much younger.

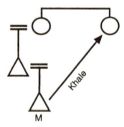

Figure 6

As children learn to apply the term to particular individuals by imitating their parents and siblings, the lineality-principle gets lost sometimes. Seven-year-old M calls his father's mother's sister *khale* like his father does. If questioned, he explains that she is his father's *khale*, not his own, but he calls her *khale*, mothersister, anyway.

Glossary

The terms given here are spelled and defined according to local usage.

abru: honor, good reputation.

aghlu: baby, very young infant.

bacce: child, especially male child.

bad: bad, the opposite of good.

bismillah: "In the name of God."

da'a: amulet containing a written prayer; a healing or protective ritual involving prayers or powerful words.

del: heart, solar plexus, seat of compassion and other emotions.

djenn: invisible beings inhabiting a parallel world and capable of interfering in the affairs of this one.

dorosht: mature in body; used especially for girls to connote their readiness for marriage.

duar: girl, daughter.

fuzul: misbehaving, naughty, disobedient.

girvaru: crybaby, whiner.

gol: flower, rose; metaphor for women; popular part of female names.

halal: religiously lawful.

haram: religiously unlawful, polluting.

hezbollah: member of the "Party of God;" a religiously committed and politically engaged person.

jun: soul, life; also a term of endearment.

kejalat, khejalat: shyness, shame.

kafir: unbeliever, heathen; a bad person.

kelu: crazy.

khanom: the most commonly used term of address for adult women, regardless of marital state. Also a female name.

khub: good, the opposite of bad.

kurr: boy, son.

mama: breast; midwife.

man: a unit of weight; used for grain, it equals about thirteen pounds.

mashallah: "What God wills."

mohre bacce: small rock or pebble, said to be extremely harmful to unborn and young children.

naf: navel, umbilical cord.

nafas: breath.

nana: grandmother on father's or mother's side.

nasr: pledge, promise to a saint, made usually with a plea for help in a difficulty.

nourahat: ill at ease, troubled, in pain.

peri: fairy; popular in female names.

pishraft: progress, development; a goal of formal education.

polu (kardan): having closely spaced births, getting pregnant easily.

qassa: calamity.

qesmat: fate, kismet.

rafiq: mate, such as playmate or classmate.

ri: face, courage; related to *kamri,* shy, and *porru,* cheeky, insolent.

Rial: the basic currency unit in Iran; ten Rial equal one *Toman.*

rizala: religious treatise; explicit written rules for ritual and ethical behavior.

rouhat: at ease, comfortable; the opposite of *nourahat,* troubled.

ruh: soul.

salam: "Peace," said as a greeting.

seyed: patrilineal descendant of the Prophet Muhammad.

shans: fortune, in the sense of good or bad fortune.

sheitun: Satan, the devil, or devils; an epithet for unruly, wild boys.

sirmei: a black paste made of soot and grease, used to line babies' and women's eyes for beauty and protection.

takhte: short for *takhte bacce;* traditional wooden cradle.

ta'rof: highly patterned, mostly verbal polite behavior.

tars: fear, shock, but also respect. A primary means of socializing children.

tasa: a seizure gripping mostly young children and girls.

tatalu: child's blabber, baby-talk; stutterer.

vasvasi: obsessive-compulsive behavior in children and adults.

yaqi: loathing and rejection of a husband by his wife.

vellou: state of prolonged disobedience and irresponsible behavior in boys and young men.

zereng: strong, clever, assertive.

zesht: improper, obscene, ugly.